ANTICHRIST
2016-2019

MYSTERY BABYLON, BARACK OBAMA
& THE ISLAMIC CALIPHATE

ISBN: 1501025392
ISBN-13: 978-1501025396

ANTICHRIST 2016-2019 emphasizes events in the middle of the author's timeline for the final seven years. His previous book, End Times and 2019, emphasizes events at the end of the seven years.

Scripture is from the New American Standard Bible unless otherwise noted.

ANTICHRIST
2016-2019

MYSTERY BABYLON, BARACK OBAMA & THE ISLAMIC CALIPHATE

CONTENTS

FOREWORD

In the Book of Revelation, John told us we need wisdom to understand. The prophet Daniel – the wisest man in Babylon – could not understand his own visions. He needed the Archangel Gabriel to help explain things to him. You may wonder, as one author has asked: "If a renowned prophet, sage, and dream interpreter like Daniel couldn't interpret his own visions of the future, why should I trust some preacher who says he's got it all figured out?"[1]

I'm not asking you to trust me – and I'm far from being a preacher. I am asking you to consider the evidence I've put together. If you read the facts, you will at least understand my conclusions, even if you disagree.

Most Bible prophecy books are written by pastors who have had a strong faith in Jesus for at least thirty years. I can't offer you a book from that perspective. My beliefs were evolving as I wrote this, and my book reflects two perspectives. Thirty years ago, I would have laughed at these topics. I was spiritually immature and had no faith in God. He certainly wasn't doing his job as I saw fit. Many good Christians tried to convince me otherwise, but I didn't see any logic in their beliefs. All I could hear was: "God made a horribly flawed creation on purpose, just so he could fix it later and prove a point by magically impregnating a virgin and arriving here as his own son. The son had to be killed, but because he is his own father he can rise from the grave like a zombie. He loves us all very much, but he won't use his omnipotence to end disease or war. In his plan to end suffering, I just need to believe in him – only then can he remove the evil that got into souls 6,000 years ago when a woman was made from a rib and was convinced by a talking snake to eat from a magic tree. Because that is the source of all the problems in God's perfect creation." Seriously?

Now – if you're a Christian – why would you want to read a book on Bible prophecy written by a young man with such an offensively atheist view of Christianity? You probably wouldn't want to read what he had to say – and he wouldn't have been able to write this book. But I'm not a young man anymore, and my lack of respect for the Bible has been replaced with insight. My views have taken a 180 degree turn. The chapters ahead will explain why not having a Christian beginning was crucial to my more recent conclusions. I would never have researched so many topics which, at first glance, seem to have nothing in common with the Bible. I would never have had the same journey or done the research necessary to write this book if I had been raised as a Christian.

As a young man, I had won some math and science awards and had a few scholarships to help pay for college. My dorm building was set aside for the students with the highest SAT scores, and I was pretty full of myself when I got there. I liked logic and lacked empathy. One night I saw a young woman I knew in the quiet study room reading her Bible. I could have just walked by, but my contempt for religion was too strong. "You don't actually believe that crap, do you?" She looked up and glared at me silently. Many months later, I was at a party when several new arrivals came in. She stopped in the doorway. Music was playing; college students were talking and drinking. She hunched down about a foot, pointed at me, and screamed at the top of her lungs: "ANTICHRIST! ANTICHRIST!"

I thought she was nuts. But in a broad sense, she was spot on. I was, in biblical terms, a denier of Christ – and therefore against Christ. As 1 John 2:22 says: "Who is the liar but the one who denies that Jesus is the Christ? This is the antichrist, the one who denies the Father and the Son." But such a definition has little to do with the focus of this book; for the Bible also tells us there is one particular incarnation of evil who is THE Antichrist – and I believe the Bible gives us keys to unlock all the information we need to know WHEN he comes, WHERE he comes from, and WHO he is.

I started my journey as a doubtful agnostic treating the Bible with the same scrutiny as any other historical, mythological, or scientific "proof." But my book has been completed from a biblical perspective (specifically from the NASB version of the Bible, unless noted otherwise.) I would hope that no one will dismiss entire categories of evidence because they assume that the Bible and everything else are mutually exclusive. I find them mutually supportive. Perhaps you identify with the atheist Ayn Rand when she wrote: "The truth is not for all men but only for those who seek it." Perhaps the words of Daniel 12:9-10 mean more to you: "these words are concealed and sealed up until the end time... but those who have insight will understand." Whether you consider yourself a skeptical atheist, a logical thinker, or a faithful believer – I wrote this book to provide you with my thoughts on the evidence, and let you decide what to make of my conclusions. Only you can decide what you think of Christ – and the Antichrist.

"Concerning that day and the hour no one **hath** known." Matthew 24:36 (Young's **Literal** Translation)

"For **nothing** is hidden that will not become evident, nor anything secret that will not be known." Luke 8:17

"These words are concealed and sealed up **until the end time**." Daniel 12:9

"**If you do not wake up**, I will come like a thief, and you will not know at what hour I will come." Revelation 3:3

"But **you**, brethren, **are not in darkness**, that the day would overtake you like a thief." 1 Thessalonians 5:4

INTRODUCTION

Most people have at least a vague idea of what has been predicted to happen at the end of the world. In the Bible, the prophet Daniel tells us that at the start of the final seven years a powerful politician enforces a covenant of peace between the Jews and their enemies. After three and a half years this leader - revered by millions as a political and economic savior in a time of crisis - reveals himself as the Antichrist when he simultaneously breaks the covenant with the Jews and demands our worship at a new Temple in Jerusalem. The next 3.5 years are the worst years in human history, full of economic collapse, famine, dictatorship, persecution, plagues, and wars. Most of humanity dies before Christ returns to destroy the Antichrist, end the world as we know it, and bring God's faithful followers to salvation.

But few people agree on **when** these events happen. Anyone who has read End Times and 2019 knows that my main focus on prophecy is on the timing. Is it even possible to organize all the prophetic clues in the Bible and deduce a timeline of events? I believe it is. "End-time prophecy is scattered throughout the Old and New Testaments like a giant puzzle. We are told [in Isaiah 28:10] that to understand we must add precept to precept and line upon line."[2] We are told to study, be awake, watch for signs, and understand. Proverbs 25:2 says "It is the glory of kings to search out a matter." As Douglas Krieger explains in Signs in the Heavens and on the Earth: God "likes secrets and treasure hunts.... He likes human beings fashioned in His image to hunt out these secrets and find the hidden treasures."[3]

The problem, up until the threshold of the end times, is that some of the crucial information is withheld from us. In Daniel 12:4 the Archangel Gabriel tells "Daniel, conceal these words and seal up the book until the end of time; many will go back and forth, and knowledge will increase." Until the end times, when such knowledge will be increased, some Bible prophecy is sealed – restricted. I believe that it only became possible to calculate a prophetic timeline as we drew close to the final years.

But millions of people believe that we can't know – or aren't ever supposed to know – when future events are going to occur. Many American Christians read Matthew 24:36, in which their English-language Bible tells them "no one knows the hour or the day" and they assume that we can never know future dates. But the original Greek verb οἶδεν ("oiden") in Matthew 24:36

1

Not in my [crossed out] + Greek Bible; + my other 3 sources say it is present tense!

is **past tense**; Young's Literal Translation reads "no one hath known" – and the correct modern translation is "no one has known" or "no one knows yet." No one – not even Jesus Christ – knew then, in 33 A.D. As Philippians 2:7 tells us, He "emptied Himself, taking the form of a bond-servant, and being made in the likeness of men." To better experience humanity, He chose not to access His divine knowledge – but only during the Incarnation.

Haven't we all said: "I don't know," only to find out the answer later? If we had asked a scientist 200 years ago why uranium is radioactive, he may have said "No one knows." That doesn't mean we don't know today. But readers of English Bibles looking at Matthew 24:36 read a statement about not knowing something in the past, and forever misinterpret it to mean that we can never know – when the Bible specifically tells us that all will be revealed. As John Walvoord (author, theologian and 34-year president of Dallas Theological Seminary) has written: "Because of imperfect translations, some important truth is hidden to the one who reads only the English text of the Bible."[4] I have found that to be an understatement.

└ True!

In English, Mark 6:3 asks: "Is not this the carpenter, the son of Mary?" I never heard anyone question that Jesus was a carpenter – until I discussed Him with Israelis and Palestinians, who said: "Look around (we were in Nazareth) – do you see a lot of trees? Everything in Israel is built out of stone." Where I live, wood is plentiful. Pennsylvania even means "Penn's Woods." We build wooden homes. Not in Israel. In the original Greek text of the Bible Jesus is referred to as a "tekton" (τεκτων) which means "builder" or "craftsman" – more likely a stonemason[5] than a carpenter. Like the "no one knows" in Matthew 24:36 – is the carpenter idea another false assumption Americans have gotten stuck with because of poor translation?

Again – not according to my sources

Did Jesus ever use wood or carpentry metaphors in his parables or sermons? He repeatedly uses stone metaphors – He changes Simon's name to Peter (stone is "petra" in Greek) and says to him in Matthew 16:18 "you are Peter, and upon this rock I will build My church." Jesus Himself is referred to as a stone, such as "a living stone which has been rejected," (1 Peter 2:4) or "the stone which the builders rejected, this became the chief corner stone," (Matthew 21:42) or "I am laying in Zion a stone, a tested stone, a costly cornerstone for the foundation" (Isaiah 28:16) or the "top stone" (capstone) in Zechariah 4:7. In Nazareth, they politely suggest that they portray Jesus as a carpenter because that is what American tourists expect – but that in the Middle East He has always been viewed as a stonemason.

 , agreed

We too often assume we understand something without investigating. Whether Jesus cut wood or stone doesn't affect much. But misunderstanding Matthew 24:36 and assuming we can never know the timing of future events in advance does matter. Of course the main point of the verse, in full context, was to emphasize that when Christ returns for us it is like a groom coming for his bride. This had already been explained in Matthew 22:2 "The kingdom of heaven may be compared to a king who gave a wedding feast for his son." In ancient Israel, when a couple decided to marry, the groom would pay the bride price to her father, then leave to build at least one new room at his father's house, where the couple would live after the groom's father felt the construction was complete. Only the groom's father could decide the new home was ready and no one else could plan a wedding date before he approved. So when the apostles asked Jesus when He would come back (to claim us, His bride) He replied: "of that day and hour no one knows, not even the angels of heaven, nor the Son, but the Father alone." He was making an important comparison to a groom returning for a bride. *True - that is part of it*

God has always known the date of the heavenly wedding. And eventually, the groom and the bride and other guests must know the date as well; it is a crucial part of the invitation. In Isaiah 45:19 God suggests: "I have not spoken in secret." Daniel 2:28 says "there is a God in heaven who reveals mysteries… what will take place in the latter days." A correct translation of Matthew 24:36 suggests that we simply don't know yet. And many passages suggest that we will know someday: Luke 8:17 says "For nothing is hidden that will not become evident, nor anything secret that will not be known and come to light." So when Acts 17:31 tells us "He has fixed a day in which He will judge the world," we will eventually know the date.

If it were true that we will never know such things – that would invalidate Bible prophecy, especially the Book of Revelation. "The very word, 'Revelation' (Apokalupsis) of Revelation 1:1 signifies a 'disclosure' of something previously unknown, hidden, or beclouded."[6] All will be revealed. When will the timing be right to fully reveal the identity of the Antichrist and all the other details of end times prophecy? Not until the second half of the final seven years. In Daniel 12:4 the archangel Gabriel explained the meaning of Daniel's visions to him, but told him to "conceal these words and seal up the book until the end of time." Sometimes, as Paul explained in 2 Corinthians 12:4, a prophet is allowed to have a special understanding of the future, but then "is not permitted to speak."

We were not meant to know all the details in the days of Daniel – or

Matthew - but all is revealed before the end, and I think the evidence shows that we are already in the first half of Daniel's 70th week: "a seven-year period that will become more and more intense as we get closer to Christ's second coming."[7] It must seem very convenient that I come up with dates in our very near future. But based on scripture, the only time anyone could correctly deduce the time of the end is right before the end! You may wonder – what makes my interpretation uniquely correct when so many other date-setters have failed? Most of them based their dates on nothing. Soon you will see the mass of evidence I have put together – then you can judge for yourself if it is impressive enough to take my timeline seriously.

Most Christians were also taught that when Jesus returns "He will come like a thief in the night." This is another misunderstanding based on Revelation 3:3, which tells us to pay attention: "If you do not wake up, I will come like a thief, and you will not know at what hour I will come." But as Mark Biltz explains: "Many people tell me they thought Messiah is supposed to come as a thief in the night. They are correct, but we have to read in context to whom *True* He comes as a thief in the night."[8]   This is conditional – not knowing is only for those who do not wake up. If we do pay attention – if we are "awake" to the clues we are given – then we can know – as suggested in 1 Thessalonians 5:4 "But you, brethren, are not in darkness, that the day would overtake you like a thief." Faithful servants are awake to the truth and aware of the clues.

The comparison to a "thief in the night" was a reference to the Jewish Temple's high priest and the Temple guards, and how they would be perceived by a Temple priest only if that priest neglected his duties and fell asleep at his post. The Hebrew people believed that the fire of the altar in their Temple was a heavenly fire brought down by God, and that this special flame could never be replaced if their eternal flame went out. So it was very important for Temple priests to keep watch. If they fell asleep while guarding the Temple, looters could steal gold and silver – or far worse – the sacred fire of the altar could burn out. So the high priest and other Temple guards made their rounds to repeatedly check on the priest on duty overnight. If they found him sleeping, they would set his robe on fire. The shame of a burned robe, coupled with the fear of being burned, generally kept the priests awake on their watch. To a priest who was awake, the coming of the High Priest was friendly and expected as scheduled. But if the priest was asleep, his master's arrival would be terrifying.

The lesson for the weary priest on night watch was "Don't fall asleep when you should be watching. If you are awake and watching, then the high priest will arrive as a friend at the hour you expect him. If you are neglecting your duty to God and are asleep, then you will be burned." Remember Hebrews 9:11 "when Christ appeared as a high priest" and Hebrews 10:21 "and since we have a great priest over the house of God…" Jesus is our High Priest of God's Temple! The lesson for Christians today is: Think about what the Bible says and be awake to its clues; then when the highest priest of all comes back, it will be exactly when you expected Him, and you will be ready, and He will come as a friend. If you choose to neglect what the Bible says and be mentally asleep, He will come as a thief in the night.

We are told it is "noble" to think, examine, and investigate scripture like the Bereans in Acts 17:11. Isaiah 45:11 tells us that God wants us to understand the future: "Thus says the Lord, the Holy One of Israel, and his Maker: 'Ask Me about the things to come.'" We are given many warnings and clues in the Bible, not to confuse us, but to help us understand as 1 Corinthians 10:11 says: "they were written for our instruction, upon whom the ends of the ages have come." Romans 13:11 warns us "Do this, knowing the time…"

Obviously I believe that we can know the time and that as good servants we are expected to know the time. I think there are clues that reveal such answers and that "seek, and ye shall find" applies. Which brings us to what I have sought and found. Just how do I think we can figure out when such world-changing events are going to happen?

Astronomical references are a crucial key. For many people the word "astronomy" sounds like something from the occult that has nothing to do with the Bible. But the exact opposite is true – astronomical knowledge is central to telling time on "God's clock" (the night sky) and understanding the timing of Bible prophecy! Astrology, not astronomy, is the problem subject.

Astrology is a superstition centered on the belief that the positions of astronomical bodies like the sun, moon, and planets at the moment of a person's birth affect their personality and their fate for the rest of their life. Astrology also teaches that the positions of such heavenly bodies today influences people's fate on a day to day basis, and that it affects people differently depending on where and when they were born. Astrology leads people to follow the predictions in their horoscopes as if being a Leo or a Capricorn or any other birth sign truly affects them for life. Such people think a trained astrologer who analyzes their birth chart of the heavens and compares it to the arrangement of heavenly bodies later can predict their future. Astrology is a warped perversion of the science of astronomy.

David Montaigne

Astronomy is the scientific study of celestial objects like the sun, moon, planets, and stars. Its only goal is a better understanding of the universe. Astronomy does not teach that the positions of these heavenly bodies have any influence on our personalities, our fate, or our daily activities. Obviously the orbits of the Moon around the Earth and the Earth around the Sun do affect things like tides, temperatures, seasons, weather, and agriculture. But astronomers do not claim to be able to make predictions as if planets and their positions in the sky affect people or cause historical events.

Yet the heavenly bodies we see in the sky must be relevant to future events because the Bible repeatedly tells us how important they are in this regard. The opening words of the Bible in Genesis 1:1 are "In the beginning God created the heavens." We are soon told in Genesis 1:14 "Let there be **lights in the expanse of the heavens**... and **let them be for signs**."

Only astronomers knew when Jesus was born. The three "magi" (Persian **astronomers**) calculated the birth of Jesus in advance through their knowledge of astronomy and prophecy. In Matthew 2:7 King Herod "called the magi and determined from them **the exact time** the star appeared." Seeing the "star" they expected merely confirmed their expectation – it was the **exact astronomical timing** that was crucial to determining the birth of the Messiah. (The process I believe they used for determining the future date of His birth from astronomical clues – centuries ahead of time – is described at length in End Times and 2019.) As Douglas Krieger says in Signs in the Heavens and on the Earth, "astronomy... and biblical chronology have a much deeper cosmic collaboration"[9] than most people want to understand.

As Joseph Seiss wrote in Gospel in the Stars, God "meant that they should be used to signify something beyond and additional to what they evidence and express in their nature... some special teaching different from what is naturally deducable from them."[10] Chuck Missler says "The Hebrew 'Mazzaroth' [zodiac] has nothing to do with astrology. Rather, it is a tool that uses the stars to tell a story.... a very important story."[11] I suggest that certain arrangements of astronomical bodies are indicators of future events – just like arrangements of letters and numbers are indicators on road signs.

A sign that says "Atlanta – 23 miles" doesn't make Atlanta manifest into being 23 miles later – the sign merely makes sure we are aware that Atlanta is in front of us and that in another 23 miles we will reach it. The same goes for astronomical signs. Arrangements of planets aren't causing events; but if prophets had visions of future events, and they saw the night sky during the vision, they might have described what they saw as a way to time-stamp that moment as if they had seen a clock or a calendar.

We need to realize that when our sky matches a unique and detailed description of the sky from a prophetic vision, we should expect the prophetic event to occur at that point in time. The night sky is like a giant clock – the clock God uses. We simply need to be aware of His clock, and be willing to try to tell time on it, instead of ignoring it as so many confusing and meaningless points of light. Genesis tells us it is worthy of study.

If someone from thousands of years ago could watch me make popcorn and look at the digital timer on my microwave as it counts down the seconds, he would have no idea what is happening unless I explain it to him. If possible, I would clarify that the tiny lines of light are signs we use to communicate the progress in a countdown to an event – that at a predetermined moment in the near future I know we will have buttery popcorn, and that this is clearly indicated by the changing patterns of lights. But it is only clear to someone who knows what the lights represent and how to read them. It could sound like superstitious nonsense to our ancient friend because he has not yet been taught how to read the changing lights. Before his first experiences with microwave popcorn he could be very suspicious of my explanation.

But the night sky is very similar to the example above. It was created on a much grander scale, and anyone who understands it can use the cosmic clock over much larger time frames. But not everyone was a magi, a royal astronomer, or a high priest of the Temple. In ancient times, one had to be initiated into understanding the mysteries by one of the priests, and many Bible descriptions are veiled in an "attempt to confuse the uninitiated."[12] The basic "mystery" is that the Bible is full of prophecy, and that many detailed descriptions of the sky are the key to prophetic timing. Those astronomical descriptions were put in place as clues – as signs – just as the opening page of the Bible tells us.

Daniel 12:9-10 explains that some knowledge is "concealed and sealed up until the end time... but those who have insight will understand." I believe this means that as Judgment Day approaches, more details will be revealed to us – partially through events, and also through our own scientific advances, which allow greater insight and understanding of biblical information. Even a few decades ago, we lacked the computer capabilities to accurately calculate where all astronomical bodies appear at any point in time. But in

2014 I can use astronomical software like Stellarium and see what the sky looks like from any vantage point at any time – past, present, or **future**.

I can read the Bible for a description of future skies in the end times, and use Stellarium to see when the sky matches the biblical description. I can teach myself to read the lights in the sky that are part of God's clock. Using all the available biblical clues isn't astrology or occult superstition; it is following the instructions of Genesis 1:14: to "let them be for signs."

Our ancient ancestors have foretold horrific prophecies of destruction, but they also gave us many clues to the timing of these end times events, warning us with astronomical descriptions of future skies. They knew that future astronomers could use their clues (in combination with other purely verbal prophetic warnings) to help calculate the dates of events in prophecy through the position of the sun, moon, and planets. Analyzing these clues is like any other forensic science.

"Forensic science is the scientific method of gathering and examining information about the past. This is especially important in law enforcement where forensics is done in relation to criminal or civil law, but forensics are also carried out in other fields, such as astronomy, archaeology, biology and geology to investigate ancient times."[13] I am most interested in "forensic astronomy" – gathering and analyzing astronomical information.

Quite recently an astronomer has used similar techniques to establish the date when certain artwork was created, and his example helps clarify my methods. Using forensic astronomy, and details like the relative position of the sun in the painting, Texas State astronomer and Physics Professor Donald Olson recently determined that Monet's "The Cliff, Etretat, Sunset" was painted on Feb. 5, 1883 at exactly 4:53 PM. After considering local topography on the Normandy coast, Monet's comments on local tides and weather conditions, and astronomical software with data on the exact path of the sun – Olson and his team were able to pin down the creation of the French impressionist's painting to within one minute of accuracy.[14]

This is not the first time Professor Olson has dated artwork using forensic astronomy. Over a decade earlier he used the same techniques on a different painting: "Using astronomical calculations and good old deductive reasoning, celestial sleuths provide the answer to a puzzle art historians have been trying to solve for years: the exact moment depicted in Vincent van Gogh's painting Moonrise. The answer: 9:08 p.m. local mean time on July 13,

1889."[15]   Olson's new book: <u>Celestial Sleuth: Using Astronomy to Solve Mysteries in Art, History and Literature</u> has many additional examples in which astronomical details, descriptions, and images have been the crucial clues needed to calculate times and dates of historical events.

Depictions of the sky in paintings, the alignments of monuments, and other astronomical clues can help us answer questions across centuries, even millennia – because with astronomy we are using God's clock and calendar. When researching the relatively recent past, Professor Olson uses the term "forensic astronomy" to describe the process of relying on astronomical clues to help solve historical mysteries.   Archeoastronomy is the science of applying astronomical clues to ancient history.   Dr. Clive Ruggles is the Professor of Archaeoastronomy in the School of Archaeology and Ancient History at the University of Leicester.   He considers archeoastronomy not only the study of ancient astronomy and the alignment of monuments to ancient skies, but also "the study of beliefs and practices relating to the sky in the past, especially in prehistory."[16]   I have been very interested in the ancient "practice" of prophets describing future skies while they describe prophetic visions of future events.

While Professor Olson has used astronomical clues to calculate the unknown timing of many events in the <u>past</u>, I have applied similar techniques to prophecies in the Bible and other ancient books and monuments, analyzing written clues and astronomical descriptions of <u>future</u> skies to calculate a timeline for our world's final seven years.   I cannot overemphasize the importance of the Bible's heavenly signs – these astronomical clues provide the solid foundation on which an accurate timeline of future events can be based.   If I am correct, the second half of Daniel's Seventieth Week - sometimes referred to as the seven year tribulation – can be pinpointed very accurately by applying forensic astronomy to biblical clues.   In many cases, astronomers from other ancient cultures such as Egypt, India, and Mexico describe similar signs and further confirm the biblical timeline.

There is some truth in the ancient maxim "as above, so below."   When an event of great importance – worthy of repeated mention in the Bible – occurs on Earth, we can expect a certain type of corresponding sign in the heavens. One such great event is the day in which the Antichrist will be revealed at the Temple in Jerusalem in the middle of the final seven years.

In the course of any studies involving the Bible and astronomy one cannot help but notice many comparisons between Jesus and the Sun.   Christ walks on water, as the sun can appear to do when rising or setting over the ocean. He turns water into wine at Cana, a process which normally requires grape plants and photosynthesis – the energy of sunlight. Psalm 84:11 very clearly says "the Lord God is a sun." Malachi 4:2 describes Jesus as "The Sun of Righteousness." In John 8:12 Jesus says "I am the light of the world." Matthew 17:2 tells us "His face shone like the sun." Christianity moved the Jewish Sabbath forward one day to worship Christ on the same day they had already been worshiping the Sun - on Sun-day.

Christ's opposite is associated with the planet Venus, the Morning Star. Satan was also referred to as the morning star. Isaiah 14:12: reads "How you have fallen from heaven, O star of the morning, son of the dawn!" (NASB) or "How art thou fallen from heaven, O Lucifer, son of the morning!" (King James) "This is the only mention of Lucifer by name in the Bible. He is clearly described as Venus, the morning star."[17] Since no other astronomical body has such an association with the embodiment of evil, I assume that Venus is the logical astronomical representation of the Antichrist.

In an alignment of the Earth, Sun, and Venus - Venus is on the opposite (anti-) side of the Sun (Christ) and we have an astronomical representation of the Anti-Christ. So it did not surprise me at all when I realized that, despite the low odds (1 in 4,261) of Venus being occulted by the Sun on any particular day - or the even lower odds (1 in 15,563,302) of that happening on a 6/6/6 date – the sixth day of the sixth month of a year ending in six – this happens next on the very date I had already calculated (in my last book, based on details in Daniel and Revelation) to be the day when the Antichrist will enter the Temple in Jerusalem to proclaim himself to be God. "Coincidences" like this help confirm my timeline of end times events, and there are many more coincidences and signs pointing to this exact date.

Skeptics can overlook a lot of coincidences, even with extreme odds. I talk to some skeptics who don't believe the Bible has a true message, and I talk to others who don't believe it is possible to deduce any new conclusions from such an old book. I would hope that readers are curious to understand the patterns and clues I have noticed in the Bible. But I know many people will look at my book not as if I analyzed the Bible and found any real pattern of clues, but as if I stared at a Rorschach inkblot test for too long, intent on finding a pattern whether anything meaningful is really there or not.

The coming of the Antichrist is not the Bible's easiest message to accept. Even devout Christians who take the entire Bible literally often have difficulty with the topic. Many Christians don't even think the Jews will ever build another Temple in Jerusalem. Muslims have been allowed to control the Temple Mount even after the Israeli recapture of East Jerusalem in 1967, in order to help maintain peace. As Ezekiel 44:8 says "you have not kept charge of My holy things yourselves, but you have set foreigners to keep charge of My sanctuary."

Most Christians assume the Muslims will never allow the construction of a Temple on or near their Dome of the Rock Mosque. They assume there is no need for a Temple anymore – based on the main idea of Christianity as described in Hebrews 10:17 "there is forgiveness of these things, there is no longer any offering for sin." "Who in their right mind," they may ask, "is going to build a Temple and start sacrificing animals to seek God's forgiveness? No one is going to do that in the 21st century." But Judaism is based on worship at a Temple. Bible prophecy tells us the Antichrist will be revealed from a rebuilt Temple in Jerusalem. Believing that a Temple will be rebuilt is hard for some. Believing that a man will be indwelt by Satan and lead the world into the great tribulation is even more difficult. It raises a lot of unpleasant questions. Where does the Antichrist first come to power? Who will it be? How soon could this happen?

Biblical evidence points to a few key conclusions on these topics. Daniel tells us the Antichrist will make his big move when he is revealed to the world at the Temple in Jerusalem. The Antichrist has many titles and names in the Bible, but the name that is used most often is the "King of Babylon." The Bible warns us that in the end times there will be a place it calls "Mystery: Babylon" – and that this land will play an important role in end times events. One upcoming chapter in this book is devoted to evidence which I believe indicates that the great city of Mystery Babylon is New York, and that the empire of Mystery Babylon is America. One man will be President of the United States, in charge of the right empire at the right time, and he fits the Bible's numerous personal descriptions of the Antichrist.

I dislike almost all politicians, including the last few presidents. I am not suggesting that Barack Obama could be the Antichrist because of his race or religion or politics. But I am suggesting that he will be in the right office at the right moment in history, and that we must consider the possibility that he will prove to be the Antichrist in 2016. As one blogger commenting on "America as Mystery Babylon" once worded it: "the spirit of Lucifer will eventually have indwelt a certain current or future President of the United States of America."[18] I believe I am living in the nation that will soon prove to be the evil end times empire the Bible refers to as Mystery Babylon. And I believe that the current President of the United States fits the detailed descriptions of the Antichrist; though he may not even realize it yet himself.

As most of my potential audience for this book will probably be Americans around 2015, it may seem like the lowest form of sensationalism to state that the central events of the end times focus on the United States and its current president in 2016. How convenient, right? Skeptics might also say "The Bible doesn't even mention America!" I suggest that it is very unlikely that the Bible makes absolutely no mention of a nation that was the greatest friend of Israel and the strongest economic, military, and spiritual force for good the world has ever known. I suggest it is much more likely that America is mentioned often – but in a context we don't like and with a name we had not recognized – because America has changed. I will present a lot of evidence for my ideas; you can decide what you think.

You may also be wondering how I went from being a blasphemous and God-hating young man to taking Bible prophecy seriously enough to apply any scientific methods to cracking its codes. I discovered something I couldn't ignore. A pattern of prophetic fulfillment. I had always been interested in the idea of prophecy, and eventually I stumbled on one that had very accurately come to pass. Then a second one. Then a third. And a fourth. I wasn't a Bible-thumper twisting words to make things from ancient scriptures fit modern events to justify my religious beliefs. I was shocked and dumbfounded to discover that Bible prophecies have been coming to pass – and not in vague, debatable ways one could argue for or against. Concrete, quantitative, fulfilment based on math I could respect.

In End Times and 2019, the first chapter is "Successful Bible Prophecies that lead us to Modern Times." One quick excerpt from the Book of Daniel will do here. In coded terms, Daniel describes the achievements and aftermath of Alexander the Great so well that many scholars cannot accept that the descriptions were actually written by Daniel in the 6th century B.C. Daniel 8:1-12 describes the Greek conquest of Persia and the division of Alexander's empire among his four generals. He suggests that Jerusalem and the Holy Temple will suffer foreign rule under one of these four Greek kingdoms, and verse 13 asks "how long" the suffering under foreign rule will last. Daniel 8:14 concludes: "For 2,300 evenings and mornings; then the holy place will be properly restored."

Passover is an "evening and morning" holiday, and it comes by once a year -

every solar year of 365.24 days. I think Daniel used this phrase of "evenings and mornings" so that no one would assume he meant 2300 "biblical years" of 360 days each (which would lead us to the wrong date - in 1934.) Alexander's first major defeat of a Persian army was the Battle of Granicus in 334 B.C. Jerusalem soon greeted him as a hero and the high priest Jaddua showed him in writing how he was fulfilling ancient prophecies. In 1967, the Israeli Army took over East Jerusalem and the ground of the Temple Mount, restoring it to Jewish control – 2,300 years later. To someone who isn't familiar with the historical details or isn't inclined to take Bible prophecy seriously, it may seem like I am picking convenient dates 2,300 years apart and creating a successful prophecy where I want one. But to those who are familiar with the details, this interpretation was clear long before 1967.

In 1825 Adam Clarke wrote in his extensive Bible commentaries: "If we date these years from the vision of the he-goat, (Alexander's invading Asia,) this was A.M. 3670, B.C. 334; and two thousand three hundred years from that time will reach to A.D. 1966, or one hundred and forty-one years from the present A.D. 1825."[19] Clarke obviously applied Daniel's prophecy to the same general chain of events, and suggested a date for its fulfillment which would have been exactly right if he had not mistakenly counted a non-existent year zero. We can use prophecy to predict the timing of future events. When detailed astronomical clues are available, sometimes we can time events to within a few minutes.

One example of such accuracy is the ring ceremony in the heavenly wedding between Jesus and His bride. During a total solar eclipse, the moon can appear to be slightly smaller than the sun and we often see the edge of the sun lit up around the moon. This is commonly called the "ring of fire." In an ancient Hebrew wedding ceremony, one part called the "yichud" gives the groom exactly eight minutes of seclusion with the bride to give her the ring. Since solar eclipses last a maximum of just over seven and a half minutes, I believe the astronomical representation of the yichud part of the Hebrew wedding ceremony is the Sun (representing Christ) giving us, His bride (the Earth) the ring of fire during one such eclipse. Of course such eclipses happen often... but in a few years there is going to be a solar eclipse visible from Jerusalem at sunrise – and the week it happens has astronomical events corresponding to every major step in an ancient Hebrew wedding ceremony in the right order. In <u>End Times and 2019</u>, it takes six pages to cover the detailed astronomical match between the night skies that week, and the week-long events of a Jewish wedding. Christ is returning for His bride, and astronomical signs tell us exactly when it happens.

Isaiah chapter 13 warns us that right before Judgment Day, when "the day of the Lord is near" (verse 13:6) we also read "the sun will be dark when it rises." (verse 13:10) If I am correct, this will happen two days before Judgment Day. My favorite astronomical software, Stellarium, shows that during the eclipse mentioned above – from the point of view of Jerusalem – the moon will be in front of the top portion of the sun from about 5:54AM until 6:35AM, at which point the eclipse is total for over seven minutes. By around 6:42AM the top edge of the sun starts to become visible, even though the moon still blocks out about 99 per cent of the sun. Sunrise is officially 6:37AM – well before the top of the sun becomes visible. "The sun will be dark when it rises." Some Israelis might not have a good view of the eclipse near sea level, but Jerusalem is a mountain city; the Temple Mount's altitude is approximately 2427 feet above sea level – and from high ground one can see a more distant horizon and watch the sun rise earlier. Those in Jerusalem should be able to watch the sun be dark as it rises, just as described in Isaiah. I believe this total solar eclipse – visible at sunrise over Jerusalem – occurs in the middle of the week long Jewish wedding ceremony and corresponds to Christ giving His bride the ring. It's timing, in my opinion, further confirms that the end of the week-long wedding ceremony is on Judgment Day.

Prophecies tell us that certain events happen at the beginning, middle, and end of Daniel's 70th week of years – the last seven years of the world as we know it. Sometimes four or five or six clues point to the same exact day. In End Times and 2019, I focused on the end of the seven years – in December 2019. But events really pick up the pace three and a half years earlier when the Antichrist takes the spotlight in 2016. I have discovered at least five major clues (and some minor ones) pointing to one specific date in June 2016 – when the Antichrist will proclaim himself to be Lord over the earth and demand our worship. This fits perfectly within my timeline of end times events as described in my last book. But this book is focused on WHEN the Antichrist admits his identity, WHERE the Beast's home kingdom of Mystery Babylon is, and WHO will be revealed as the Antichrist.

If you would like to better understand:
What the Antichrist is
What Mystery Babylon is
When the Antichrist will stand in the Temple in Jerusalem
Who the Antichrist might be
And What we should expect to happen to us in the present world
Just continue reading.

NAMES AND TITLES OF THE ANTICHRIST

There are hundreds of names for Christ, each giving unique insight to a particular situation. Despite calling Jesus: the Son of Man, Son of God, Son of Mary, Son of David, Heir of all things, Captain of our Salvation, the Redeemer, the Messiah, the Prince of Peace, King of the Jews, the Lamb of God, the Lion of Judah, the Logos (the Word), the Light of the World, Rabbi, High Priest, Savior, etc. - we know these all apply to Jesus... Some other names and titles are not so obvious. What about "the despised One" or "the One abhorred"? They hardly sound like titles for Jesus – but they are. In Isaiah 49:6-7 God says:

"'It is too small a thing that You should be My Servant to raise up the tribes of Jacob and to restore the preserved ones of Israel; I will also make You a light of the nations so that My salvation may reach to the end of the earth.' Thus says the Lord, the Redeemer of Israel and its Holy One, to **the despised One**, to **the One abhorred** by the nation, to the Servant of rulers, 'Kings will see and arise, princes will also bow down, because of the Lord who is faithful, the Holy One of Israel who has chosen You.'"

The many names of the Antichrist can be even more difficult to recognize and attribute to him, and many scholars question which verses definitely refer to this one final, evil man. The following list should help define and describe the man we are watching for, the one who will soon prove to be our greatest fear incarnate.

"The Antichrist" is a term for a man described by many Bible verses, including 1 John 2:22 "Who is the liar but the one who denies that Jesus is the Christ? This is the antichrist, the one who denies the Father and the Son." "Anti-" means the opposite of, but also instead of. The word "antichrist" means he is both against Christ, the opposite of Christ, and an alternative instead of Christ. The Antichrist is not only the opposite of Christ but a false substitute who will attempt to imitate Him. First he will pretend to be Christ, then he will stand up against Christ. It may also be relevant that on a global level, Islam is the main alternative instead of Christianity.

"The Beast" is the opposite of the Lamb; selfish and heartless, lacking the empathy and other noble qualities that distinguish men from animals. As we see in Revelation 13:4, Satan (the dragon) gives his authority to the Antichrist (the beast): whose followers "worshiped the dragon because he gave his authority to the beast; and they worshiped the beast…"

"The Man of Sin" lives the opposite of Christ's sinless life, for the Antichrist revels in sins. In the King James Bible, 2 Thessalonians 2:3 describes the day when "that man of sin be revealed, the son of perdition."

"The Lawless One" - The same verse in the NASB (2 Thessalonians 2:3) calls him "The Lawless One" – emphasizing his rebelliousness, opposing both human and divine authority. The verse also describes the day when "the man of lawlessness is revealed, the son of destruction." He will make his own laws.

✓ "The Assyrian" is the tool God uses to punish those who do not keep the faith in Israel. Isaiah 10:5-6 reads "Woe to Assyria, the rod of My anger and the staff in whose hands is My indignation, I send it against a godless nation… it is its purpose to destroy and to cut off many nations." in Isaiah 10, God continues: "I will punish the fruit of the arrogant heart of the king of Assyria." Also "My people who dwell in Zion, do not fear the Assyrian who strikes you with the rod and lifts up his staff against you, the way Egypt did. For in a very little while My indignation against you will be spent and My anger will be directed to their destruction." (Isaiah 10:5-7, 10:12, 10:24) God also threatened the King of Assyria with hell in Isaiah 30:31-33. In the ancient past, many of these Assyrian references were fulfilled through the Middle Eastern Kingdom of Assyria (and its capital, Nineveh) around 700 B.C. Not everyone agrees that such verses of Bible prophecy have a second fulfillment yet to come in the future. But very often, a prophecy sees one historical fulfillment early in history, while a second one occurs thousands of

True years later. Sometimes it is hard to tell when a prophet is speaking about the initial historical event that first fulfilled a prophecy or a later fulfillment in the end times, for in their visions they may see events separated by millennia merely as different stages of the same trend. "It is not unusual for biblical prophecies to have more than one fulfillment."[20]

As I write this in June 2014, Assyria is being reborn. Syria and Iraq are coming under the control of a new group of radical Muslim rebels called ISIS – the acronym, in English, for "Islamic State of Iraq and Syria." They have the support of the old Baath party, and anyone else who prefers rule by Sunnis instead of Shiites. Some suggest they are trained and funded by the CIA, with funds and instructions from American intelligence. Will the chaos they bring to the region serve American ends, justifying a larger war? Will the chaos (and arrival of more American troops in the region) serve Obama's goals? Is America dropping food and medicine out of airplanes... or secretly dropping weapons?

The Bible offers an interesting viewpoint. Nahum 1 and 2 tell us about the eventual destruction of Nineveh and Assyria, but before Assyria's destruction, there are (in Nahum 3:3-4) "Many slain, a mass of corpses, and countless dead bodies— they stumble over the dead bodies! All because of the many harlotries of the harlot, the charming one, the mistress of sorceries, who sells nations by her harlotries." As of July 2014, the new Islamic State is executing Iraqis who worked with Americans... sometimes up to 1,500 at a time. Other verses indicate the harlot enabling Nineveh may be America – more on that later. Let us focus on the fact that Assyria is reappearing after about 2600 years as a political entity called the Islamic State – just in time to fulfill prophecy.

Of course, these Muslim rebels do not call this territory "Assyria." They did, however, announce the re-establishment of a new Islamic Caliphate. Such events may have little meaning to readers who aren't clear on what the Caliphate represents, but I think this may be the biggest fulfillment of prophecy since the creation of Israel in 1948 and the establishment of Israeli control over all of Jerusalem in 1967. Though a thorough discussion of the evidence must wait for another chapter, I believe the revived Islamic Caliphate is Daniel's fourth kingdom come back to life – and that this is one of the clearest signs yet that the end times are underway. **?**

As author Joel Richardson describes in books like Mideast Beast and Islamic Antichrist, the Bible's many descriptions of the final empire of the Antichrist does not match a revived Roman Empire, but a revived Islamic Caliphate. Daniel's fourth kingdom was described as destroying and encompassing the three empires before it (Babylonian, Persian, and Greek)?- but the Romans were only in Babylon for a few months from 116-117 A.D., and never conquered Persia. Daniel's fourth kingdom cannot be the Roman Empire. Despite being less centrally important to European and American thinking than the Roman Empire – only the historical Islamic Caliphate fits the Bible's description by having completely incorporated the Babylonian, Persian, and Greek empires.

The old Islamic Caliphate also contained the nations and peoples which the Bible constantly describes as Israel's future end times enemies. A revived

David Montaigne

Caliphate will allow the sons of Ishmael to settle their unfinished business with the sons of Isaac. A revived Roman Empire does not. "The Roman Empire does not sufficiently meet the criteria of the fourth-kingdom text, whereas the Islamic Caliphate fulfills all of the criteria perfectly."[21] Richardson proves with hundreds of scriptural references that we should look to the Middle East for the rebirth of Daniel's fourth kingdom – in the form of a revived Islamic Caliphate – and that a future request by the Antichrist to submit to him and worship Allah fits with the Bible's description of the abomination of desolation.

Time Magazine tells us: "radical Sunni militants on June 29 declared a new Islamic caliphate, a religious superstate, stretching from eastern Iraq to the Syrian city of Aleppo. The group formerly known as the Islamic State of Iraq and Greater Syria (ISIS) is now simply the Islamic State, dropping the names of the two countries whose sovereignty it doesn't recognize."[22] We will cover this Islamic Caliphate more later.

In the end times, these "Assyrian" references may describe the behavior of an Antichrist who is not necessarily of Assyrian origin. The term "grammar Nazi" could be applied to someone today in reference to their arrogant assertion of authority, without anyone thinking the person is German or fascist or anti-Semitic. Likewise, the term "Assyrian" may have been used as a biblical reference to the warlike aggressiveness of a future Antichrist who shares the vicious reputation of the ancient Assyrians – without the future individual being referred to necessarily bringing his forces to Israel from a base in lands that were once Assyrian ("Greater" Syria, a tiny part of eastern Turkey, and the northwest half of Iraq.) Though anyone in control of armies in Iraq or Syria could come to Israel through what was once Assyrian territory – whether they are native to the region, or just the arrogant and aggressive leader of an occupying power dominating the region as America has.

"The Arrogant One" Jeremiah 50:31-34 says "'Behold, I am against you, O arrogant one,' declares the Lord God of hosts, 'For your day has come, the time when I will punish you. The arrogant one will stumble and fall with no one to raise him up; and I will set fire to his cities…. So that He may bring rest to the earth, but turmoil to the inhabitants of Babylon."

"The King of Babylon" is another name used repeatedly for the Antichrist, as in being "against the king of Babylon" in Isaiah 14:4. There are so many references to the King of Babylon and to Babylonians that we cannot fully address the significance in this list of names; it is another topic which must be covered in depth in another chapter. Some scholars are convinced that end times references to Babylon refer to a new city on the same ancient site in what is now Iraq. Proponents of this idea include Arthur Pink, who wrote: "Babylon will be one of the headquarters of the Antichrist. He will have three: Jerusalem will be his religious headquarters, Rome his political, and Babylon his commercial."[23]   Tim LaHaye's Antichrist character in the popular yet fictional <u>Left Behind</u> series, Nicolae Carpathia, rules from a headquarters in New Babylon, also rebuilt in Iraq.

But most scholars point out that "Mystery" is not an adjective but a noun; that the correct wording is "Mystery, Babylon" and that this end times city is not located in Babylon but is a modern city fitting the Bible's many descriptions. As Charles Ryrie wrote: "The Christian will realize by the use of this word 'mystery' that this Babylon is not the city on the Euphrates but a secret use of the word."[24]   I believe New York is the best candidate for Mystery Babylon. This would make the King of Babylon the American President (who also tends to have an army in Iraq, and therefore rule over parts of ancient Babylonia and Assyria as well.) As with the title of "the Assyrian," the "King of Babylon" is in any future fulfillment of prophecy unlikely to actually be from the site of ancient Babylon, and more likely is just the leader of a world empire which fits certain descriptions of the Babylonian kingdom.

Jim thought this too

Babylon was known for having one language and a tower reaching up to heaven, but they lost their tower and lost their unity of language. One could easily argue that New York lost its high towers and has been the main port of entry for immigrants. The English language, once unquestioned as the language of the nation, is no longer viewed as the official language. Spanish dominates huge sections of the United States, and many other languages go unchallenged within their respective enclaves. There are dozens of clues pointing to New York and America as the location of Mystery Babylon: another chapter will analyze the evidence in great detail.

If nothing else, the Antichrist cannot be a future leader who is truly Assyrian and simultaneously truly Babylonian. He is probably neither, yet he and his empire will share traits with both ancient kingdoms. For now we will merely note that the phrase "the King of Babylon" comes up many times in reference to the Antichrist, as in Isaiah 14:4. Near the end of the apocalypse, an angel calls out "Fallen, fallen is Babylon the great!" (Revelation 18:2) Many analysts believe the word "fallen" is used twice to indicate a second, future event repeating the ancient fall of historical Babylon. We must assume that as "King of Babylon" the Antichrist heads a powerful empire, possibly more powerful than any which have come before – until it is suddenly destroyed.

"The King of the North" fights against the King of the South; so does the Antichrist, who probably is the King of the North. Daniel's chapter 11, unfortunately, is quite confusing, and if taken literally, implies that the King of the North is a traitor against his own troops. Daniel 11:11-12 says "The king of the South will be enraged and go forth and fight with the king of the North. Then the latter will raise a great multitude, but that multitude will be given into the hand of the former. When the multitude is carried away, his heart will be lifted up, and he will cause tens of thousands to fall; yet he will not prevail." I think one possible explanation is that a Christian nation will have a leader who is secretly a Muslim, who will betray his nation to its Islamic enemies in battle.

"The Seed of the Serpent" comes from Genesis 3:14-15 after the Serpent has caused Adam and Eve to eat the forbidden fruit: "The Lord God said to the serpent, 'Because you have done this... I will put enmity between you and the woman, and between your seed and her seed.'"

"The Angel of the Bottomless Pit" is considered the same as Abaddon, Apollyon, and The Destroyer. Revelation 9:11 reads "They have as king over them, the angel of the abyss; his name in Hebrew is Abaddon, and in the Greek he has the name Apollyon." Apollyon, in Greek, is the Destroyer. This is probably why author Thomas Horn has picked book titles like Apollyon Rising 2012, which was updated under the title Zenith 2016 – 2016 being the year I conclude the Antichrist will be revealed to all.

"The Destroyer" or "the Spoiler" or "The Extortioner" – Isaiah 16:4 reads "Be a hiding place to them from the destroyer. For the extortioner has come to an end, destruction has ceased." The Destroyer is mentioned again in Jeremiah 6:26... and in both cases is called "the Spoiler" in the King James Bible. Interestingly, "Al-Mumit" is also one of the 99 names of the deity of the Islamic religion, Allah, which many translate as "The Destroyer" or "The Bringer of Death."

"The Nail" or "the Peg" is an unusual reference.... Arthur Pink tells us this falling nail or peg is a reference to the fall of the Antichrist.[25] Some scholars also compare this name to the nails used in the crucifixion... but personally, I believe this falling nail or peg refers to the shifting axis of the earth and the

20

changing North Pole during a catastrophic pole shift. In the NASB, Isaiah 22:25 says "'In that day,' declares the Lord of hosts, 'the peg driven in a firm place will give way; it will even break off and fall, and the load hanging on it will be cut off, for the Lord has spoken.'" In the KJV the verse says: "shall the nail that is fastened in the sure place be removed, and be cut down, and fall; and the burden that was upon it shall be cut off." I suspect this is a reference to "the north nail" mentioned throughout world mythology in regard to a pole shift at the end of the world. (This is covered in depth in <u>End Times and 2019</u>.) In this book we will not digress long on the pole shift topic; it will suffice here to say the Lapps of Finland are one of many peoples who describe an archer like the constellation Arcturus, who uses his bow (Ursa Major) to shoot down the north nail (the pole star) and cause a shift of the entire surface of the earth on the last day.

A pole shift is not unrelated to our understanding of the Antichrist, for his fall coincides with the fall of his North Pole throne and a cataclysmic pole shift that brings on a new heavens and a new earth on the last day of the current world in late December 2019. The pole star is by definition in the extreme north. Isaiah 14:13 tells us of Satan: "But you said in your heart, 'I will ascend to heaven; I will raise my throne above the stars of God, and I will sit on the mount of assembly in the recesses of the north." As my <u>Ryrie Study Bible</u> comments on a reference to "the north" in Jeremiah 50:3 "...out of the north. In Jewish thought, the origin of anything sinister."[26] Satan attempts to have a throne in the extreme north of the sky, where all the other stars in the heavens appear to rotate around the North Pole Star. This is where the L-shaped constellation Draco the Dragon represents Satan, until there is a pole shift and he falls to earth. Draco's "L" shape is the basis of the "twisted serpent" of Isaiah 27:1 and even the Hebrew letter "L" (lamed) and the Arabic letter "L" (laam) and the Arabs' "Allah."[27] This is where the Maya and other ancient cultures place their false god "about to fall from his throne in the polar center."[28]

Even American Christians have a "false god" at the North Pole. He rides a sky chariot like Apollo, and the eight animals attached to his chariot are like the eight planets of the sun god. He steals most of the attention from Jesus on a holiday when Christians should be contemplating their savior's willingness to be born as a human to bring us the message of salvation, and instead we focus on material things like presents. This North Pole deity "knows when we're naughty or nice" and as children we sometimes fear his judgment in late December when he leaves his North Pole throne. The false god is celebrated with a tree (axis) with a bright (pole) star at the top. He comes down the chimney through the fire if necessary, and won't enter through the door of your house – which is especially interesting in light of John 10:9 when Jesus says "I am the door; if anyone enters through Me, he will be saved." And of course the name, Santa, is practically spelled the same as Satan. These are not coincidences; the Santa story has a dark side related to Satan and a pole shift.[29]

"The Branch of the Terrible Ones" is a name which seems to indicate that the Antichrist is a descendant or offshoot or branch of a horrible, troublesome group of people. In the King James Bible Isaiah 25:5 says "The branch of the terrible ones shall be brought low." The phrase is unrecognizable in the NASB or even in Young's Literal Translation. "An abominable branch" can also be found in Isaiah 14:19 in the KJV or YLT, but still not in the NASB) Since the words "terrible" and "terror" and "terrorist" all come from the same root, it is possible that the Antichrist is associated with the group of people known for terrorism. The branch of Ishmael?

"The Prince that Shall Come" - Daniel 9:26 says "the prince who is to come will destroy the city and the sanctuary. And its [or his] end will come with a flood." The Roman general Titus was the first fulfillment of this prophecy. He was the son of Emporer Vespasian, making him a prince at the time. And he did bring an overwhelming "flood" of legions of soldiers who defeated the Jewish uprising and destroyed Jerusalem and the Temple in 70 A.D. Most Americans think that since this verse clearly refers to the Roman prince, Titus – the people of the prince must also be Roman, and that the empire of the Antichrist will be a revived form of the Roman Empire. But in another chapter we will review the evidence that over 90% of the Roman legions involved were local men – Syrians, Egyptians, and Arabians. "The people of the prince" were Arabs.

"The Prince of the Covenant" – The Antichrist is also referred to in Daniel 11:22 as "the prince of the covenant" in regard to the seven year peace covenant he makes with Israel. As he intends to betray Israel halfway through the covenant, it is relevant that in Nahum 1:11 he is called God's enemy and is described as "One who plotted evil against the Lord, a wicked counselor."

"Wicked Prince of Israel" – In Ezekiel 21:25-27 we read "wicked one, the prince of Israel, whose day has come, in the time of the punishment of the end,' thus says the Lord God, 'Remove the turban and take off the crown; this will no longer be the same. Exalt that which is low and abase that which is high. A ruin, a ruin, a ruin, I will make it. This also will be no more until He comes whose right it is, and I will give it to Him.'" At the time of the end, the Antichrist, who had seized control of Israel through deceit and has been the chief king over much of the Earth for over three years, will have his crown (political authority) and turban (headdress indicating religious authority) removed. The land will be a ruin; some versions (like the King James) say "overturned" several times (sounding more like a pole shift) and the kingship over the Earth will be given to one whose right it is – Christ.

The point must be emphasized after considering the last three "prince" names for the Antichrist that if he is a prince of the covenant, then he is not a Jew but one foreign to Israel who comes and makes a covenant with the Jews and their enemies. Likewise, if he is a prince who will come to Israel, he is a foreigner taking Israel over. So when he is the "wicked prince of Israel" we must understand he is foreign to Israel but has seized power there. We should not, from the list of names above, assume that the Antichrist will be Israeli, or Syrian, or Iraqi – even though these regions will play central roles in his rule.

[handwritten note: NOT Necessarily - the "Covenant" could mean the Abrahamic Covenant]

"The Idol Shepherd" will not take care of his people. The NASB says "worthless shepherd" but the common reference is to the King James' "idol *[handwritten: ?]* shepherd." Zechariah 11:16-17 warns us "I am going to raise up a shepherd in the land who will not care for the perishing, seek the scattered, heal the broken, or sustain the one standing, but will devour the flesh of the fat sheep and tear off their hoofs. Woe to the worthless shepherd who leaves the flock! A sword will be on his arm and on his right eye! His arm will be totally withered and his right eye will be blind." This may not literally involve a sword. A sniper may shoot the Antichrist in the head, damaging the left hemisphere of his brain where the right arm and eye are controlled. Revelation 13:3 says of the beast: "I saw one of his heads as if it had been slain, and his fatal wound was healed. And the whole earth was amazed and followed after the beast." Any head shot or otherwise apparently fatal wound to the Idol Shepherd will probably occur three days before his "miraculous" healing and announcement at the Temple. Instead of being killed off, the Antichrist will probably claim he was saved by God so that he could implement a plan to save us from the great crisis the world will be suffering. This healed wound could also refer to his newly restored kingdom.

[handwritten right margin: NIV - "foolish shepherd"]

"The Little Horn" is a name which tells us of the Antichrist's originally marginal status. In Daniel 7:8, right after a fourth beast with ten horns comes out of the sea, "another horn, a little one, came up among them." Daniel

23

David Montaigne

7:23-25 continues to comment on this little horn: "'The fourth beast will be a fourth kingdom on the earth, which will be different from all the other kingdoms and will devour the whole earth and tread it down and crush it. As for the ten horns, out of this kingdom ten kings will arise; and another will arise after them, and he will be different from the previous ones and will subdue three kings. He will speak out against the Most High and wear down the saints of the Highest One, and he will intend to make alterations in times and in law; and they will be given into his hand for a time, times, and half a time.'"

Daniel 8:9-11 says "Out of one of them came forth a rather small horn which grew exceedingly great toward the south, toward the east, and toward the Beautiful Land. It grew up to the host of heaven and caused some of the host and some of the stars to fall to the earth, and it trampled them down. It even magnified itself to be equal with the Commander of the host; and it removed the regular sacrifice from Him, and the place of His sanctuary was thrown down." This "little horn" or "rather small horn" is certainly the Antichrist. Daniel 7:19-20 explains that even Daniel himself sought further clarification of this: "Then I desired to know the exact meaning of the fourth beast, which was different from all the others, exceedingly dreadful, with its teeth of iron and its claws of bronze, and which devoured, crushed and trampled down the remainder with its feet, and the meaning of the ten horns that were on its head and the other horn which came up, and before which three of them fell, namely, that horn which had eyes and a mouth uttering great boasts and which was larger in appearance than its associates.

The horns represent strength and power, the eyes represent intelligence. Arthur Pink says the little horn "refers to the lowly political origin of the Antichrist, and describes him as he is before he attains governmental supremacy."[30] This "little horn" is an important clue, for the 11th little horn king will be different from the ten kings before him; even his empire may be different than previous ones.

Some readers may remember a movie line which helps make a point about the fast rise of this "little horn" in a political career that quickly takes him from obscurity to great power. The line was spoken by the character of Marty McFly's grandfather in the 1985 movie "Back to the Future." After Marty, transported back to 1955, refers to a road as John F. Kennedy Boulevard, his grandfather responds with "Who the hell is John F. Kennedy?" At the time, one might not have known a Senator from another state... despite the fact that just a few years later, he was the most powerful

24

man on Earth. I make this reference just to show how a politician like a Senator could rise from relative obscurity to great prominence and a very high position of power – like President of the United States – or even "King of the Earth" and "Antichrist" in a relatively short number of years.

"The Son of Perdition" is corrupted and damned. John 17:12 says "not one of them perished but the son of perdition, so that the Scripture would be fulfilled."

"The Bloody and Deceitful Man" will do anything to get the power he wants. Starting with breaking his peace covenant with the Jews, he lies and kills on an epic scale. In the King James Bible Psalm 5:6 says "the Bloody and Deceitful Man"; the same verse reads "the man of bloodshed and deceit" in the NASB.

"The Wicked One" will not let rules or human lives get in the way of his ambitions. Psalm 10 also describes him as boastful, blasphemous, denying God, egotistical, deceitful, treacherous, cruel, and proud. This name is from the KJV of Matthew 13:19 and 13:38. He is "the evil one" in the NASB.

"The Enemy" and "The Adversary" will be [SATAN] against God, Christ, and mankind. Psalm 74:10 asks "How long, O God, will the adversary revile, and the enemy spurn Your name forever?"

"The Vile Person" or "Despicable Person" - Daniel 11:21 reads "Vile Person" in the King James, but the NASB tells us "a despicable person will arise, on whom the honor of kingship has not been conferred, but he will come in a time of tranquility and seize the kingdom by intrigue." We already knew the Antichrist would be a master of politics, rising from obscurity through deception and trickery until he leads a great empire, and eventually the world.

There are many other names for the Antichrist as well: The Prince of Tyre, The Unclean Spirit, The Lie, etc. But the list of names expounded on above should give a sufficient description of him, especially in conjunction with the next list that compares and contrasts him with Christ. For although it may already be somewhat obvious what the Antichrist stands for, a brief list of contrasts may further clarify the nature of the Antichrist:

9.

Antichrist – The Lie - "You are of your father the devil… he is a liar and the father of lies." (John 8:44)
Christ – The Truth - "I am the way, and the truth." (John 14:6)

Antichrist – comes up from below. "The beast that comes up out of the abyss." (Revelation 11:7)
Interesting side note – Islam's 12th Imam, the Imam Mahdi whom Muslims expect as an end times savior, is believed by many Muslims to have fallen down a well over a thousand years ago at the age of five… and he is expected to come back out of the well to lead an Islamic Army during the end times. The Qu'ran itself also says in Surah 27:82 "At the right time, we will produce for them a creature, made of earthly materials, declaring that the people are not certain about our revelations." A creature made of earthly materials… sounds like a beast from the earth to me. Various theories suggest it could be a lot of things, from a computer to the Antichrist. Islam clearly promotes the idea that Christians are wrong, and that during the end times Islam's leader will ascend out of a well in the earth, and that some kind of earthly creature will speak against Christ. These facts might prove to be very relevant.
Christ – comes down from above. "I have come down from heaven." (John 6:38)

Antichrist – denies his opposite. In Matthew 4:3 and 4:6 Satan says to Jesus "If You are the Son of God…" then suggests a few tests to prove or disprove it. We know Satan was one of God's highest creations, perfect in wisdom. He knew who Jesus was, yet attempted to question or deny it. Like father, like son. "Who is the liar but the one who denies that Jesus is the Christ? This is the antichrist, the one who denies the Father and the Son." (1 John 2:22) Also: "For many deceivers have gone out into the world, those who do not acknowledge Jesus Christ as coming in the flesh. This is the deceiver and the antichrist." (2 John 1:7)
Christ – acknowledges his opposite. John 5:43 "I have come in My Father's name… another comes in his own name."

Antichrist – "You are of your father the devil" (John 8:44) and "the son of destruction" (2 Thessalonians 2:3) who "comes in his own name." (John 5:43) This "king will do as he pleases, and he will exalt and magnify himself above every god." (Daniel 11:36)

Christ – "the Son of God" (John 1:34) tells us "I have come in My Father's name" (John 5:43) and "I have come down from heaven, not to do My own will, but the will of Him who sent Me." (John 6:38)

Antichrist – "the mystery of lawlessness" or "the mystery of iniquity" – Satan incarnate, as described in 2 Thessalonians 2:6-7 "And you know what restrains him now, so that in his time he will be revealed. For the mystery of lawlessness is already at work; only he who now restrains will do so until he is taken out of the way."
Christ – "the mystery of godliness" – God in human form, as described in 1 Timothy 3:16 "great is the mystery of godliness: He who was revealed in the flesh."

Antichrist – "The Beast" is a ravenous animal that will kill others to satisfy itself. "The beast that comes up from the Abyss will attack them, and overpower and kill them." (Revelation 11:7)
Christ – "The Lamb" is gentle, sacrificing its life for human needs - "Like a lamb that is led to slaughter." (Isaiah 53:7)

Antichrist – "The Wicked Prince" of Ezekiel 21:25: "wicked one, the prince."
Christ – "The Prince of Peace" in Isaiah 9:6 "A child will be born to us, a son will be given to us; and the government will rest on His shoulders; and His name will be called Wonderful Counselor, Mighty God, Eternal Father, Prince of Peace."

Antichrist – "The Destroyer" of Gentiles: "a destroyer of nations" (Jeremiah 6:26) and of the Jews: "suddenly the destroyer Will come upon us." (Jeremiah 4:7)
Christ – "The Savior:" "You will know that I, the Lord, am your Savior and your Redeemer." (Isaiah 60:16)

Antichrist – "The Idol Shepherd" or "the worthless shepherd" of Zechariah 11:17 who does not care about his followers, and only cares about using them to achieve his own goals.
Christ – "I am the good shepherd; the good shepherd lays down His life for

the sheep." (John 10:11)

Antichrist – "Wicked Counselor" - "One who plotted evil against the Lord, a wicked counselor." (Nahum 1:11)
Christ – "Wonderful Counselor" "For a child will be born to us, a son will be given to us; and the government will rest on His shoulders; and His name will be called Wonderful Counselor, Mighty God, Eternal Father, Prince of Peace." (Isaiah 9:6)

Antichrist – "King of Babylon" (Isaiah 14:4) an evil city of trickery and fornication (Revelation 18:2-10)
Christ – "King of Israel" (John 12:13) the Holy Land, "the apple of His eye." (Zechariah 2:8)

Antichrist – "The abominable branch" of Isaiah 14:19 (KJV) is "a rejected branch... Like a trampled corpse." (Isaiah 14:19 - NASB)
Christ – The Glorious Branch "the Branch of the Lord will be beautiful and glorious" (Isaiah 4:2)

Antichrist – defiles the temple with "the abomination of desolation" in Matthew 24:15.
Christ – purified the temple, removing the profane: "and drove them all out of the temple" (John 2:15)

This may be the work of the False Prophet

Antichrist – Forces all to renounce Christianity and accept the mark of the beast or be executed. "He causes all, the small and the great, and the rich and the poor, and the free men and the slaves, to be given a mark on their right hand or on their forehead." (Revelation 13:16) The mark of the beast is used to PREVENT those without it from surviving, as any hidden Christians cannot buy or sell (make a living, buy food – eat) without the mark. Revelation 13:17 warns us "he provides that no one will be able to buy or to sell, except the one who has the mark, either the name of the beast or the number of his name."
Christ – Allows us to choose to accept him in our hearts and minds. "Let the peace of Christ rule in your hearts." (Colossians 3:15) The seal of God is given to a small number who choose Christ and are selected as worthy – the

144,000 end-times Christian converts from amongst the Jews – as a seal of protection. Revelation 7:3-4 "Do not harm the earth or the sea or the trees until we have sealed the bond-servants of our God on their foreheads. And I heard the number of those who were sealed, one hundred and forty-four thousand sealed from every tribe of the sons of Israel." Also the vision of end times wrath in Ezekiel 9:4-6 "Go through the midst of the city, even through the midst of Jerusalem, and put a mark on the foreheads of the men who sigh and groan over all the abominations which are being committed… do not touch any man on whom is the mark."

Antichrist – is a Denier of Food for his enemies: "he provides that no one will be able to buy or to sell, except the one who has the mark" (Revelation 13:17) which leads to starvation not just for the faithful Christians who refuse his mark, but for the world: "for three years and six months, when a great famine came over all the land." (Luke 4:25) "Behold, an ashen horse; and he who sat on it had the name Death; and Hades was following with him. Authority was given to them over a fourth of the earth, to kill with sword and with famine." (Revelation 6:8)
Christ – is the Bread of Life – "I am the bread of life; he who comes to Me will not hunger." (John 6:35)

After reading the introduction, the names for the Antichrist, and the contrasts with Christ, we should have a clear concept of the ultimate evil we will eventually be dealing with. But so far, we are primarily dealing with an idea; it may be harder to assume this biblical reference will prove to be a real man, someone who gives speeches on our televisions and whose voice and face we know – and whose wrath we will fear. Is there any reason to have faith this is someone we already know? Someone real, that will – in the very near future – fulfill end times prophecies?

WHAT IS THE ANTICHRIST?

Webster's New World College Dictionary defines the word "antichrist" as "the great antagonist of Christ, expected to spread universal evil before the end of the world, but finally to be conquered at Christ's second coming."[31]

Simply put, he will be the most impressive human being in almost two thousand years – a multi-talented political superman whom many will see as a political and economic savior in a time of crisis. But unlike the savior Christians know, the Antichrist will be uniquely self-centered, with limitless personal ambitions and no concern for humanity or submission to the will of God. The very crisis that brings him greater power will help free him of all restraint, and we will see his true nature revealed. After achieving great authority he will demonstrate unbridled evil, grasping for more and more power no matter what his actions cost in human lives. Unsatisfied with kingship or dominating the world – he will settle for nothing less than complete submission and loyalty, with all mankind treating him as if he were God. Then his title of Antichrist will be fulfilled, because he will work in opposition to Christ and offer himself as God on earth instead of Christ.

By definition, the idea of the Antichrist is a Christian invention – you can't conceive of an Antichrist without first knowing about Christ. So it is no surprise that the Antichrist is mentioned in the New Testament, but never directly mentioned in the Old Testament of the Jews. The Antichrist is the embodiment of rebellion against God – a sinful rebellion Satan started in heaven and will attempt to finish through his avatar on earth. A rebellion that must be utterly crushed before Christ can purify and redeem the world. But rebellion is exactly what the Jews expected their Messiah to lead – they expected him to be a superman – a glorious political, military, and religious leader who would rebel against foreign rule and free the Jews from the tyranny of oppression. How did this description of a messiah come to be viewed as fitting the evil antithesis to Christ better than it fits the Christian description of the Messiah?

The German philosopher Frederick Nietzsche wrote extensively on both the superman and the Antichrist, and his disgust with the common man and Christian weakness is especially obvious in his book titled: <u>The Antichrist</u>. But in attacking Christian values, Nietzsche can help us understand that

Christianity redefined what it meant to belong to a religious group, and what that group expected its salvation to be like. Many early religions were based on ethnicity and culture and were tied exclusively to a specific people. As Judaism prepared us for Christianity, western culture may be most familiar with these concepts as they applied to the Jews.

Most Christians don't realize just how Jewish Christ is. A simple riddle helps emphasize this point: who "'had a miraculous birth, was sent into Egypt, was sent to his brethren and was rejected by them, was delivered to the Gentiles who put him to death, was in the grave for three days, [and] was raised from the grave on the third day?' The Jews. 'All these things are true of both Christ and the Jews. The nation had its start in the miraculous birth of Isaac; then they went into Egypt for 400 years, they were chosen to be a light to other nations… when they were disobedient God turned them over to the Gentile nations (Times of the Gentiles began), they were scattered for 2000 years (two days), they were raised again on the third day.'"[32] Hosea 6:2 "He will revive us after two days; He will raise us up on the third day." Christ is the ultimate concentration of God's role for the Jews in one man.

Judaism taught them that they were God's special, chosen people, and that their religion and their Messiah applied to them – and no one else. The Israelites were taught that their salvation through a Messiah would involve righting the wrongs their people suffered on earth, in the present, material world – returning their people to a position of strength and freedom and prosperity in an earthly golden age.

Christianity, on the other hand, emphasizes that people are not special – that they are weak, sinful creatures who don't really deserve the perfection of God's heaven on the merits of their own behavior. Success in the present, material world is often viewed with disdain, as if power and wealth is usually gained through compromised morals and ethics. Matthew 19:24 says "it is easier for a camel to go through the eye of a needle, than for a rich man to enter the kingdom of God." Anyone who enjoys wealth and power is suspected of being corrupt and greedy, and is told that they would be better off (in the long run – in the afterlife) if they gave everything away to the poor. Christianity appealed to the oppressed and weak who had no hope of a wonderful life here and now – but who could be convinced that by meekly accepting their lot on earth, they would be rewarded in heaven. The Christian Messiah is meek like a lamb, sacrificing Himself for others. Christ did not come to lead a military rebellion against Roman occupation. He accepted execution like a criminal.

For almost two thousand years, Christians who have accepted Christ as their Savior have wondered why the Jews – who were the only ones expecting a Messiah – generally did not recognize Him or accept Him when He came. Jesus fits the descriptions in the New Testament wonderfully – but He isn't quite a match for everything the Jews expected in a rebel military strongman based on their Torah. Early debates between first century Jews and Christian converts undoubtedly focused on these discrepancies. And in defining what Christ is – and what he is not – these early debates must also have clarified what would define the opposite of Christ.

Such debates and definitions continue into modern times. One cannot read Nietzsche's books without seeing his disdain for Christianity's glorification of weakness and meekness and submission. The God of the Old Testament was a power to be feared, and He inspired those created in His image to be strong. In the New Testament God emphasizes love and pity and grace. In the few sentences of Nietzsche's preface to The Antichrist he describes how (in his opinion) one should become indifferent to truth, have hardness of spirit, see human conditions as beneath oneself, value reverence and love of oneself, and view mankind with contempt. Nietzsche's pride and arrogance is clear from the very first sentence: "This book belongs to the very few. Perhaps not one of them is even living yet."[33]

Was he writing for a future Antichrist? We can see in his writing an extreme sense of superiority, and it is hardly surprising that his philosophy had a huge influence on Nazi ideology and on Adolf Hitler - the man many would say came closest to embodying the spirit of the Antichrist so far. Nietzsche hated Christianity for valuing weakness and having pity on the weak. He felt that we should let the weak die off to breed stronger generations of supermen; but that Christianity had made strength seem evil instead of virtuous.

As he nears his conclusion, on his second to last page, Nietzsche wrote: "If we do not get rid of Christianity, it will be the fault of the Germans."[34] He viewed Christianity as a disease only German culture was strong enough to cure. This certainly sounds like a challenge; one Nazi leadership may have attempted had they won WWII. Nazism certainly shared Nietzsche's disgust with Christianity's slave mentality and its institutional disdain of science and reason. On his last page Nietzsche says "I condemn Christianity. I call Christianity the one great curse, the one great innermost corruption… the one immortal blemish of mankind."[35]

It is men like Nietzsche, who despise Christianity and believe man's strength and independence should not suffer under divine restraint, who will facilitate the Antichrist's rise to power. He would have us choose self-reliance over the values of Christianity. Christ would have us acknowledge God's vastly superior wisdom and submit ourselves to His plans for us. This can be very difficult, for it is the nature of intelligent men to question everything, including God. The Antichrist takes this questioning nature to the next level. He answers the question with the emphatic choice to place himself above God; to follow his own ambitions and rebel against God.

It all boils down to accepting God's perfection and one's role in God's perfect plans. To do this one must accept that all details of the plans are based on God's complete and perfect knowledge and wisdom. Albert Einstein once said "God does not play dice." Events are not left up to chance. Proverbs 16:33 tells us the same thing: "The lot is cast into the lap, but its every decision is from the Lord." Every tiny detail, has been planned in advance. God has seen the end from the beginning. Do we choose to submit to God and accept His all-knowing plans, or try to fight against them?

Satan was once in heaven, and had enjoyed a high position with great power and luxury. As an angel with great intelligence and access to the very throne room of God, Satan should have been wise enough to see the futility in challenging God's infinite wisdom and power.

But the qualities Satan had been given as a blessing made him proud and ambitious, and he coveted God's power and authority. When he acted out his rebellious plan he was cast out of heaven, and as soon as he could he began to meddle with humanity on earth. Satan became the adversary of God, interfering with God's human creations and encouraging them to doubt and question God's motives. When Adam and Eve doubted God's restrictions on eating from the Tree of Knowledge and wanted to become wise like God, they were following in Satan's rebellious footsteps, and they too were cast out. When we contemplate the inherent imperfection in Satan, and wonder why God would create an angel of such a rebellious and evil nature, is our doubt already a sin paving the way towards rebellion? How can we know without questioning things? The Book of Genesis first explored the idea that questioning God to the point of acting on our doubts and breaking His rules is a sin. If sin should be viewed as a new disease that infected humanity way back in the Garden of Eden, then after that we needed a cure – but we were incapable of perfecting one on our own. Christianity teaches us that God sent His Son – Jesus Christ - to redeem us from Adam's mistake.

The Antichrist offers us a very different solution to sin. He does not offer a cure to heal a disease. Instead he is more like a drug dealer pushing increasing doses of product on an addicted population without the strength to get clean. The Antichrist is not sent to bring us back in line with God's plans. He embodies the spirit of Satan, literally and figuratively, as an example that we can enjoy the ultimate sin of rebellion against God's authority. That we do not have to meekly accept an inferior role in God's plans. That we should seek knowledge and power and technological progress to create our own Eden. To borrow a catch phrase from the character Gordon Gekko in "Wall Street:" Satan, and the Antichrist, would undoubtedly say "Greed is Good." Greed and ambition lead to success and advancement. Meek followers of Christ may aspire to worship God and sing His praises eternally in heaven; others may question how boring that could quickly become. What is wrong (the Antichrist will undoubtedly believe) with seeking an alternative to God's plans, such as adjusting our DNA and inventing spaceships that let humanity explore the galaxy – wouldn't we be on a path to become like gods ourselves?

But if God's plans are perfect then any alternative plans are not. We should not make the mistake of viewing Satan as a light-bringer or assuming that he or his "son" are looking out for our best interests. The Antichrist will be entirely self-centered, and he includes others in his plans only to serve his own ambitions. Christ will lead men back to God. The Antichrist will merely lead men to conclude that there are alternatives to God's plans. Everyone on both sides will eventually see Bible prophecies unfolding before them. It would be impossible not to be aware of the final outcome, spelled out in a billion Bibles across the planet. But as he will think he has nothing left to lose by trying, the Antichrist will oppose God and Christ until the bitter end.

Early on, he will be a great political leader, rising from obscurity to head a great people, and eventually the world. The Antichrist must enter politics long before the tribulation, because at the beginning of Daniel's seventieth week he establishes a seven year covenant with the Jews. Daniel 11:16-17 clarifies that "he will also stay for a time in the Beautiful Land, with destruction in his hand. He will set his face to come with the power of his whole kingdom, bringing with him a proposal of peace which he will put into effect." He must already have a high position of power to be internationally recognized at this time as a deal-maker. But initially, Daniel 7:8 mentions that a "horn, a little one, came up among them." If he does rise from obscurity, this rules out potential candidates like Prince Charles or his son William – for although some suggest them as the Antichrist, they have from birth been in line for the British throne.

Some Christians argue that as a mock Christ or imitation of Christ, he must be a Jew, because Jesus Christ was Jewish, and the Antichrist will attempt to mimic Christ in many ways in order to trick people into worshipping him. They note that early Christians assumed he would be from the tribe of Dan, with the snake as its symbol. Hippolytus of Rome (170-236 A.D.) believed that the Antichrist would come from the tribe of Dan and would rebuild the Jewish temple on the Temple Mount in order to reign from it. He identified the Antichrist with the Beast out of the Earth from the book of Revelation. "By the beast, then, coming up out of the earth, he means the kingdom of Antichrist; and by the two horns he means him and the false prophet after him. And in speaking of 'horns like a lamb,' he means that he will make himself like the Son of God, and set himself forward as king. And the terms, 'it spoke like a dragon,' mean that he is a deceiver, and not truthful."[36]

Others add that they assume the Jews would not accept him as their leader if he is not Jewish himself. This seems a little silly to me, as he is not only referred to as the prince of Israel but the prince of Tyre, and much more often as the Assyrian or the King of Babylon. How anyone imagines the Antichrist brokers a covenant with the Jews and their enemies if he himself is Jewish and leader of the Jews – remains a mystery to me. As Walid notes: "Israel undertakes a formal covenant with the Antichrist. If he were one of their own, they probably would not have to actually sign a document."[37] And since Christ embodied the historical experience of the Jews in one lifetime – and the Antichrist will be the opposite of Christ – I assume he will not embody the Jewish experience or ethnicity.

But as the real Messiah was Jewish, and the Antichrist will attempt to mimic Christ, it is possible he will claim at least some Jewish heritage. The true Messiah must be a descendant of King David's royal line; and the Antichrist may falsely claim such descent. Israel is deceived into allowing the Antichrist to reign over them – as are many other nations. The Bible makes it very clear that Israel is not his original homeland, and also that the Antichrist will arise out of "the sea" (Daniel 7:2-3, Revelation 13:1) indicating that he will arise out of the gentile nations, not Israel. Many expect the Antichrist to be Roman, or European, or Arab.

The Antichrist will excel at many things, and show great skill and genius in several areas of knowledge and human relations. He will in many ways imitate Christ at first, pretending to be noble and peaceful. Until the mid-point of Daniel's 70th week of years (what some people call the seven year tribulation) when the Antichrist's behavior is no longer restrained, the first and longest part of his political career is spent pretending to care about mankind, and he often mimics Christ as an apparently virtuous leader. Like Satan in 2 Corinthians 11:14, he "disguises himself as an angel of light."

Despite eventually displaying the fearsome characteristics of all four horsemen of the apocalypse,[38] early on he is represented by only the first one in Revelation 6:2: "I looked, and behold, a white horse, and he who sat on it had a bow; and a crown was given to him, and he went out conquering and to conquer." That horseman doesn't sound so bad – he doesn't even have to arm his bow with arrows. He may conquer peacefully at first. The white horse gives an appearance of purity and nobility, like a white knight in shining armor; like a savior – and the fact that the Antichrist is on a white horse warns us that he is attempting to mimic Christ, and may falsely claim to be Christ, who also appears as the rider of a white horse in Revelation 19:11-14 "And I saw heaven opened, and behold, a white horse, and He who sat on it is called Faithful and True."

But eventually the Antichrist will oppose Christ and offer himself as an alternative to Christ. Halfway through the final seven years, "the Antichrist 'comes out of the closet' with his true beliefs and intentions."[39] This change in his person will occur suddenly, and the difference between the covenant-of-peace-making phase 1 Antichrist will be dramatically different from the unrestrained, bloodthirsty, God-hating phase 2 Antichrist. In the first phase he will seem like a great natural leader of men, so intelligent and wise, so skilled in politics and public speaking, that he will convince the world to give him great power over us. Never satisfying his lust for power and glory, he will eventually convince us he can defy death itself, surviving a seemingly deadly head wound that appears to heal itself and bring him back from death. He will demand that we worship him and his image, and offer our complete loyalty and submission as if he is God. He will be an "incarnation of evil, a 'super-man,' the Antichrist, who will exercise a world-wide rule, deify the state and achieve a union of church and state so that men will be forced to worship him or suffer economic sanctions and death."[40]

Many people mistakenly assume this man will be obviously evil from the beginning, but until the mid-point of the final seven years, he will seem charismatic and admirable. A large portion of the masses will love him and think he is a great leader. Other world leaders will turn to him at a time of crisis and they will allow him to end up ruling over them. Only in his final three and a half years will he demonstrate the characteristics of the last three horsemen of the apocalypse, bringing war, famine, and death.

Even when we study other cultures (not Israel, or neighboring influences) we can still find references to an "Antichrist" remaining normal and calm for the first 3.5 years. In Tantric Buddhism "there is a myth of Kundalini, translated 'Serpent Power' and meaning 'coiled,' which may preserve the same cabala for 1,260. Kundalini 'normally lies asleep in the form of a serpent in three and half coils surrounding a penis in a mythical center or circle.'"[41] Without studying biblical references to the Antichrist, I might overlook such an odd passage. But if the cabala or gematria for "Kundalini" is 1260, that of course reminds me of Daniel's 1260 days. And three and a half coils of a dormant serpent going around a circle sounds to me like three and a half orbits (years) of the peaceful, phase-1 Antichrist before he uses his access to "Serpent Power" and changes to a more obviously evil dictatorship.

Long before reaching the point of assuming absolute leadership over many nations, the Antichrist will already be an impressive man. He will be a well-educated, intellectual genius. Imagine, in modern terms, someone with one or more degrees from an Ivy League University. Before his career in politics, he would probably practice a respected profession like law, or medicine, or be the inventor or engineer of new technologies. He will be the kind of man who wins a Nobel Prize for his great contributions. Some think that references to the King of Tyre apply, as in Ezekiel 28:3 "Behold, you are wiser than Daniel; there is no secret that is a match for you." He will be able to find any answer; he will have great powers of perception and persuasion. Daniel 8:23 says "A king will arise, insolent and skilled in intrigue." All the wisdom the devil can give him will be at his disposal; he will understand and master all subjects – the sciences, the humanities, even the occult. Of course, the full extent of this will not be obvious immediately. Until he is ready to act boldly, he will not want to seem superhuman.

He will be a great speaker. Revelation 13:2 tells us he has a "mouth like the mouth of a lion." Revelation 13:5 "There was given to him a mouth speaking arrogant words and blasphemies, and authority to act for forty-two months was given to him." When he proclaims himself to be God, he will have three and a half years left in power before he is destroyed just prior to the end of the world as we know it.

David Montaigne

He will be financially successful. Personally, he is likely to be a multi-millionaire. The government of his initial nation or kingdom is likely to concentrate power and wealth under his control, such that even if his land is not any more prosperous under his rule, its wealth is centralized and he will gain power from his financial and commercial policies. Ezekiel 28:4-5 "By your wisdom and understanding you have acquired riches for yourself and have acquired gold and silver for your treasuries. By your great wisdom, by your trade you have increased your riches." After he has attained more complete control of the world and its economy, no one will buy or sell without his permission. Revelation 13:16-17 "And he causes all, the small and the great, and the rich and the poor, and the free men and the slaves, to be given a mark on their right hand or on their forehead, and he provides that no one will be able to buy or to sell, except the one who has the mark, either the name of the beast or the number of his name." He will have ultimate financial power and control. It has been suggested that the mark could be an implanted RFID chip or a form of bar code tattoo. The two long lines for calibration at the beginning, middle, and end of every bar code do represent the number six.

Again, I think this the False Prophet

He will be a political genius. Daniel 11:21 says "a despicable person will arise, on whom the honor of kingship has not been conferred, but he will come in a time of tranquility and seize the kingdom by intrigue." Is "the kingdom" merely a reference to his initial nation, or to Israel, or to Christ's Kingdom – the whole Earth? After seizing Israel, the Antichrist will proceed in his attempt to attain the global power he desires. Revelation 13:2 tells us "the beast which I saw was like a leopard, and his feet were like those of a bear, and his mouth like the mouth of a lion. And the dragon gave him his power and his throne and great authority." This could simply mean that the Antichrist will be subtle and graceful like a leopard, strong and ferocious like a bear, bold and confident like a lion, and powerful and fear-inspiring like a dragon. But it seems much more likely that these four animals symbolize the combined power of previous great empires – Greek, Persian, and Babylonian – combined under a final Satanic empire.[42]

If we choose to look for modern representations of these empires, the leopard presents a problem. Many nations have chosen the lion as their national mascot; none have chosen the leopard. If we must associate the leopard with a region, then despite a vast former range – the leopard's current range is just in Africa. Perhaps the beast being like a leopard indicates an African origin? Aside from the lack of leopards or Africans running great empires, we have all heard of the Russian Bear, the British Lion, and the Chinese Dragon. The

Bible usually means Satan when it uses the word dragon, but the term could also apply to the most populous nation of the Dragon Throne, whose military strength and financial influence may already surpass America's. It would not be too much of a stretch to apply the Antichrist animals of Revelation 13:2 to mean that the most powerful nations of the modern world are all united under the Antichrist's control; an African-American President with Russia, Britain, and China allied with him.

It may seem hard to imagine such unity of purpose by these rival nations, but perhaps some global threat by plague, famine, nuclear terrorism, extraterrestrials – or some other Satanic deception – could theoretically achieve such international cooperation. In any case, the four animals signify Antichrist rule over many great nations – either the greatest empires of the modern world, or at least rule over the territories of the great Middle Eastern empires – the Babylonian, Persian, and Greek Empires – which when combined, largely correspond with the empire of the historical Islamic Caliphate. Perhaps the final empire is a "revived" or reestablished Islamic Caliphate? (A revived Islamic Caliphate was officially declared June 29, 2014 as I was writing this.) Many Bible scholars assume the Antichrist's empire will be a composite empire during the end times; that the empires of iron, brass, clay, silver, and gold in Daniel 2 are the same as the leopard, bear, lion, and dragon empires combined in Daniel 7 – and that since Daniel 2:35 tells us that "the iron, the clay, the bronze, the silver and the gold were crushed all at the same time" – that it will be one final empire of the Antichrist, with all the combined lands suffering destruction at the end of Daniel's 70th week.

In addition to political power over his many territories, the Antichrist will seek a religious power and authority greater than that of any prophet or pope – he will eventually want to be worshiped himself. The fourth century theologian Jerome noted in his commentary on Daniel that the Antichrist would be a man "in whom Satan will wholly take up his residence in bodily form," and worship is what Satan has wanted for millennia. Most theologians agree with Jerome, and like Tim LaHaye, assume that the Antichrist "will actually be Satan himself, clothed with the Antichrist's body."[43] Since the Antichrist will be a politician indwelt by Satan, it should not be surprising that he will also want to become a top religious leader. Perhaps he will attempt to be the high priest of a new world religion designed to encourage people to worship him. Or he may take over an existing religion opposed to Christianity – such as Islam – in which religious and political leadership are expected to be combined in one leader.

There are many different interpretations of Daniel 11:37, which tells us: "He will show no regard for the gods of his fathers or for the desire of women, nor will he show regard for any other god; for he will magnify himself above them all." This could mean that he does not acknowledge the one true God, or any previously worshiped god, and that he only exalts himself. The reference to not seeking the desire of women could either mean he is completely focused on his lust for more power and is not distracted by women – or that he may have homosexual tendencies. "The desire of women" has even been suggested to imply the hope of a pregnant Jewish woman to give birth to the Messiah – whom the Antichrist despises. And it could merely be a reference to not caring about nations identified with women – Israel and America.

Another theory, "the Islamic Antichrist" theory, suggests that the Antichrist will be the Caliph of a restored Islamic Caliphate – a confederation of Islamic nations united against Israel and the West. As Caliph, he will be like the Muslim version of the Pope. Muslims will offer him their complete loyalty and submission; they will bow to him and do anything he asks, even if it costs them their life. They will, in effect, worship him as Allah's vice regent on earth. This theory also has an interesting suggestion for who Allah is; but we will cover that more later. Perhaps the Antichrist is Muslim but his "fathers" were not. Perhaps he fills the role of the "father" of a country but pays no attention to the God of its "founding fathers." Disregarding the desire of women would then be a reference to the inferior role of women in Islamic society, for under Islamic Sharia Law, women do not have equal rights with men - they are property owned by men, lacking many freedoms such as the right to vote, travel, or deny sexual advances.[44]

Barack Obama wrote an interesting story related to this in <u>Dreams From My Father</u>, when his mother explained to him: "What your grandfather respected was strength. Discipline. This is why, even though he learned many of the white man's ways, he always remained strict about Luo [Kenyan] traditions.... This is also why he rejected the Christian religion.... he could not understand such ideas as mercy towards your enemies, or that this man Jesus could wash away a man's sins. To your grandfather, this was foolish sentiment, something to comfort women. And so he converted to Islam—he thought its practices conformed more closely to his beliefs."[45] In this quote, Christianity is the desire of women – the idea that Christ can atone for our sins is described as the foolish sentiment of women. Could this be what the Antichrist disregards?

In Ezekiel 21:26, at the end of the Antichrist's reign, God tells him "Remove the turban and take off the crown." This implies he wears both the religious headdress of the priests and the crown of the king. He assumes political and religious leadership. This is not accomplished by the brute force of an overwhelming army. Daniel 11:23 tells us "After an alliance is made with him he will practice deception, and he will go up and gain power with a small force of people." After the seven year peace covenant with Israel has been made, he uses intrigue and deception to attain more power. Verse 11:24 continues "In a time of tranquility he will enter the richest parts of the realm, and he will accomplish what his fathers never did, nor his ancestors." Phrases like "the richest parts of the realm" or "the glorious land" always refer to Israel. The fact that he gains power over Israel with "a small force of people" indicates that they let his forces assume command peacefully, probably as allies and protectors under the terms of the covenant of peoples. The contrast between his "fathers" and his "ancestors" may mean that he was raised by men other than his biological father, who had different ancestry.

He will be a military genius. Revelation 13:4 says "Who is like the beast, and who is able to wage war with him?" The beast may refer to the kingdom and its king – who must head extremely powerful armies. Daniel 8:24 tells us "His power will be mighty, but not by his own power, and he will destroy to an extraordinary degree and prosper and perform his will; he will destroy mighty men and the holy people." Power not by his own power could refer to the idea that God is allowing this final rebellion to play out as part of His own plans. It could refer to power granted to him by the United Nations, or by Satan. Isaiah 14:16 describes the Antichrist as "the man who made the earth tremble, who shook kingdoms." We should not underestimate the power this man will have, as he will be indwelt by Satan, with the power of an archangel. In Matthew 4:5 "the devil took Him [Jesus] into the holy city and had Him stand on the pinnacle of the temple." This is an entity who is interpreted as being able to supernaturally teleport Jesus Christ around.

The Bible describes a war centered on the Middle East. Daniel 11:25 says the Antichrist will prepare "against the king of the South with a large army." Egypt has traditionally been the king of the South. The only land from which one can advance south into Egypt is Israel; so this clue indicates that the Antichrist is commanding forces in Israel at this point. He may have entered Israel under the pretense of protecting it; perhaps a threat of invasion by Egypt or some of Israel's other Muslim neighbors was countered with the installation of troops from the Antichrist's original nation, under the premise that the enemies of Israel would not dare to attack if it would also be viewed as an attack on the forces of the Antichrist.

Daniel 11:25 continues "so the king of the South will mobilize an extremely large and mighty army for war; but he will not stand, for schemes will be devised against him." Again the Antichrist is scheming for more power, this time, to gain control over Egypt – but he is not in control of the entire world, for other nations like Egypt are scheming against him. Verse 11:27 says "As for both kings, their hearts will be intent on evil, and they will speak lies to each other at the same table." The King of Babylon and the King of the South (the Antichrist, and the leader of Egypt) will negotiate and try to deceive each other, but of course no mortal leader is a match for the Antichrist, who does conquer Egypt. Verse 11:28 says "Then he will return to his land with much plunder; but his heart will be set against the holy covenant, and he will take action and then return to his own land."

Habakkuk 2:5 says "he does not stay at home. He enlarges his appetite like Sheol, and he is like death, never satisfied. He also gathers to himself all nations and collects to himself all peoples." Wherever the Antichrist is from, he does not stay there. His greed for power over all the peoples of the earth leads him to distant conquests. Though the Bible clearly describes the regions of Egypt, Assyria, Babylonia, and Israel – if these were his only conquests, he would not have an empire greater than that of previous empires. We must assume that although the Bible focuses on lands known to early Christians (lands near Israel) the Antichrist rules a much larger, more powerful empire. He makes many enemies.

Perhaps after bringing his troops into Israel as protectors while there was still peace, the Antichrist either justifies a "preemptive" attack on Egypt, or maneuvers Egypt into starting the aggression. Perhaps an extremist faction has taken over Egypt and plans to attain nuclear weapons, and the Antichrist invades to prevent it. Perhaps Israel is faced with multiple, simultaneous enemies in Gaza or Egypt, or Syria, or Iran, or the revived Caliphate… the exact reasons are irrelevant here. The bottom line is that the Antichrist establishes his armies in Israel peacefully, as a defensive part of the covenant, then starts to take over nearby nations (at least Egypt) and then returns to his own land – not Israel. Daniel 8:5 suggests that he flies to Israel from the west, "coming from the west over the surface of the whole earth without touching the ground." After returning home, presumably by air and to the west, events cause the Antichrist to return to the South (Egypt) at the appointed time – perhaps an uprising against his forces in Egypt. Daniel

? *alexander the Great?*

42

11:29-30 tells us "At the appointed time he will return and come into the South, but this last time it will not turn out the way it did before. For ships of Kittim will come against him; therefore he will be disheartened and will return and become enraged at the holy covenant and take action; so he will come back and show regard for those who forsake the holy covenant."

Some interpreters argue that these are merely descriptions of events which occurred thousands of years ago. And I agree that they do have a fulfilment in the past. The Seleucid King Antiochus, whose empire stretched from Turkey to Pakistan, twice invaded Egypt – but his second victory was ruined by a threat from the growing Roman Empire that he would be at war with Rome if he didn't leave Egypt immediately. He retreated in shame and vented his frustration on the Jews, defiling their Temple and attempting to eradicate their way of life. The Jews resisted and won a guerilla war against overwhelming odds.

But Bible prophecy has a way of experiencing two fulfillments; one near term (in our ancient past) and one long-term fulfillment (in the end times, in our immediate future.) As Isaac Asimov (of science-fiction fame) wrote in his Bible commentaries, such dual fulfillments are typical of "the parallelism that is the essence of Hebrew poetry."[46]   As Arthur Pink wrote a century ago: "Many, if not the great majority of the prophecies — not only those pertaining to the Antichrist, but to other prominent objects of prediction — have at least a twofold, and frequently a threefold fulfillment. They have a local and immediate fulfillment: they have a continual and gradual fulfillment: and they have a final and exhaustive fulfillment."[47]   He also wrote that some events "received a tragic fulfillment in the past. But like most, if not all prophecy, this one will receive a later and final accomplishment."[48]   Charles Ryrie agreed, as he wrote in the Ryrie Study Bible: "It is not unusual for biblical prophecies to have more than one fulfillment."[49]   Sometimes the distinction between the past and present fulfillments are blurred. Joel Richardson explains that in dealing with "the dual fulfillment of so many prophetic passages" we often see "an intermingling of the historical and the future" and must often wonder "historical or future, oftentimes both elements are intertwined."[50]   So although some prophetic descriptions do match historical events fulfilled long ago, I suspect that history will soon fulfill them again, with Middle Eastern wars involving the Antichrist.

Failure in Egypt is a major turn of events. The Antichrist is not victorious in Egypt this time, because the Egyptians have a naval ally – the ships of Kittim also battle the Antichrist. Kittim literally referred to the island of Cyprus, north of Egypt. Turks and Russians are north of Egypt, and Turkey is the dominant power in Cyprus today. Of course the Russian navy is much stronger. Daniel's reference could see a future fulfillment through interference from Turkey or Russia or another navy in the Mediterranean. To ancient Hebrews the name "Kittim" came to symbolize all the islands of the Mediterranean, and lands of the west in general. The phrase once applied to the Romans, and a second fulfillment regarding "the ships of Kittim" could apply to a variety of modern navies in the near future.

Somehow this alliance against him makes the Antichrist angry about his covenant with Israel. Did the Israelis fail to support him in Egypt? Maybe he realizes that since he already has his armies in Israel, that if he betrays Israel he could have even more complete domination over the Jews, while gaining many Muslim allies for his act of betraying his covenant with Israel. Why, he could just claim that was his plan all along. And since the details of his actions have been written down for thousands of years, it would not be difficult to convince anyone that betraying Israel was planned in advance.

In any case, he is "enraged at the holy covenant" and "he will come back and show regard for those who forsake the holy covenant." What exactly is the Holy covenant about, anyway? The holy covenant was about God's gift of the land of Israel to the descendants of Abraham. It is about the Jewish people's right to exist, in Israel, with Jerusalem as their capital. The Antichrist will initially strengthen a covenant with Israel's moderate neighbors (like Jordan, one of the few Muslim nations which acknowledges Israel's right to exist.) But after the mid-point of the final seven years the Antichrist will act against Israel's right to exist and will be allied with the Muslim nations who seek to destroy Israel.

Daniel 11:31 says "Forces from him will arise, desecrate the sanctuary fortress, and do away with the regular sacrifice. And they will set up the abomination of desolation." As Irenaeus warned us over 1800 years ago: "he who shall come claiming the kingdom for himself... having a name containing the aforesaid number [666] is truly the abomination of desolation."[51] For this to occur in our near future, a Jewish Temple must be erected on the Temple Mount in Jerusalem; for worship and sacrifice in it to be stopped, it must first have started.

As of the time I am writing this chapter, political reality does not make the construction of a Jewish Temple seem likely soon, despite rumors of its preconstruction. But something major like a bitter and decisive war with Iran or another enemy could make Israel care very little about the opinion of the Islamic world. A Hamas rocket launched from Gaza could hit the Dome of the Rock Mosque, removing it as an obstacle. A minor earthquake could collapse the already buckling walls supporting the foundation. Or perhaps the long-lost Ark of the Covenant shows up. This artifact is believed to contain the very presence of God on earth; and its rediscovery could lead to a demand to rebuild a Temple to properly house the Holy of Holies. And a Temple could be erected very quickly if it is more like the tent used during the Exodus and less like the great stone Temple of Solomon. Regardless of the nature of the structure, the Bible indicates that a Temple which reestablishes sacrifices is present at the mid-point of the last seven years – and that the Antichrist ends the sacrifices and defiles the Temple.

This is the mid-point of the final seven years of this world, three and a half "times" or years into Daniel's 70th week of years. (1263 days, if I am correct in assuming an assassination attempt on the 1260th day and an apparently fatal wound being miraculously healed three days later on the more important "resurrection" date.) At this point the Antichrist establishes himself as "the king of Israel" (Hosea 10:15) despite the fact that "the honor of kingship has not been conferred" (Daniel 11:21) willingly by the Jewish people. The Antichrist also demands worship, possibly even suggesting that he is God.

Psalm 55:12-14 tells us "For it is not an enemy who reproaches me, then I could bear it; nor is it one who hates me who has exalted himself against me, then I could hide myself from him. But it is you, a man my equal, my companion and my familiar friend; we who had sweet fellowship together." Some believe these verses describe Jesus talking about His betrayal by Judas; AND a future betrayal of Israel by someone close whom they trusted, who turns out to be the Antichrist. Since Israel has no stronger ally or closer friend than the United States, could America – or at least its leader – be the familiar friend that betrays Israel in the end times? I have seen polls that show most Israelis don't trust Obama. I have heard Israelis in America say "they view him like a god back in Israel" because he has given so much money and weapons to their military. Some believe he supports Israel's hardline Islamic enemies. Others believe he has said "Israel's security is holy to me" (though I can't find such a comment online.) Let's assume that Israeli opinions are mixed, and that some portion love and trust Obama.

It is hard not to think of the tour Obama had in Israel in early 2013, called

"Unbreakable Alliance" in English – and called "A Covenant of Peoples" in Hebrew. This fits with the idea that The United States (and especially its biggest city, New York) is Mystery Babylon – a topic we must explore at length in another chapter. Daniel 8:9 also implies that the Antichrist subdues three kings. Irenaeus' disciple Hippolytus wrote his Treatise on Christ and Antichrist about 1800 years ago and clarified that the three horns or kings plucked by the Antichrist are "the three kings of Egypt, and Libya, and Ethiopia."[52] Egypt's Mubarak and Libya's Khadafi have already been removed from power during Obama's presidency. Will anything happen soon in Ethiopia – or Sudan, as the region referred to by the name Ethiopia at that time just meant the land south of Egypt?

As early as the Book of Genesis and the description of the serpent's deception in Eden, we are told that the Antichrist will receive a head wound. Genesis 3:15 says "And I will put enmity between you and the woman, and between your seed and her seed; He shall bruise you on the head, and you shall bruise him on the heel." The seed of Satan is the Antichrist. Zechariah 13:17 suggests he will be wounded by a sword (we are left to speculate if it is a wound to the head): "Woe to the worthless shepherd who leaves the flock! A sword will be on his arm and on his right eye! His arm will be totally withered and his right eye will be blind."

We would not expect the Bible to have said he is shot with a bullet from a gun, but we should not rule out the idea that this injury does not literally involve a sword. Perhaps a sniper will shoot the Antichrist in the head, specifically damaging the left hemisphere of his brain where the right arm and eye are controlled. But this won't affect him for long; his infernal father Satan will use his powers to heal him. Revelation 13:3 tells us "...his fatal wound was healed. And the whole earth was amazed and followed after the beast." This would probably occur shortly before he enters a rebuilt Jewish Temple in Jerusalem to proclaim himself God and insist that we worship him. 2 Thessalonians 2:3-4 says this is the pivotal event before Jesus Christ returns to fix everything; warning us not to believe the Second Coming has occurred earlier than it really does, and reminding us "it will not come unless the apostasy comes first, and the man of lawlessness is revealed, the son of destruction, who opposes and exalts himself above every so-called god or object of worship, so that he takes his seat in the temple of God, displaying himself as being God." This act of entering the Temple and claiming to be God is the defining act of the Antichrist. It is the ultimate rebellion, and it will mark the mid-point of Daniel's 70th week, leaving just 3.5 years of tribulation to go.

HOW CAN YOU BE SO SURE THERE'S AN ANTICHRIST?

At some point in my research a good friend asked me a question.

"Dave, how can you be so sure there's an Antichrist?"

"I see too many clues pointing to the same date."

"No, Dave. I'm not talking about breaking codes or finding astronomical signs and other clues pointing to a date. I mean, if you don't assume Jesus Christ necessarily existed, then what can possibly make you so sure about the Antichrist? How can you take a relatively minor figure from the religion about Christ, and have conviction he is coming on a certain date – but have less conviction that the Messiah on whom the religion is based even existed? You have to start with Christ to define the opposite, don't you?"

My friend was right. I had been living like a "Christian Atheist," as Craig Groschel titled one of his books. "Welcome to Christian Atheism, where people believe in God but live as if He doesn't exist."[53] I had been living as if Christianity might be right, but not as if I had been convinced conclusively. I was fascinated with end times prophecy, but I lacked religious faith. Why should I care about what the Bible says at all, if I didn't have sufficient faith in Jesus Christ? Was it just one mythological tale among many – and if so, no matter how many astronomical clues I unravel in it – no matter what scientifically plausible cosmic events might be described by it – why assume that a supernatural being like an Antichrist is coming?

It's one thing to recognize patterns of fulfilled prophecies or heavenly alignments that match comments in an ancient book – and to assume that book (or maybe even the religion it describes) merits further study. It is another thing to bypass the main requirement of faith the religion has, having little faith in its central message – yet for some reason, have greater certainty in the existence of another supernatural being the religion mentions. My friend felt I was performing some interesting mental gymnastics to bypass faith in Jesus while taking Bible prophecies about the Antichrist seriously.

I had to admit, it sounded very foolish to have more faith in the Antichrist coming on a certain future date while having less faith that Jesus Christ had definitely existed in the past. By this point in my life I believed in God, but then so does Satan – he just refuses to submit to God's authority. Belief in God is not enough; but I had a very hard time submitting and letting Him rule my life. Were my doubts about the historical existence of Jesus leading me to an essentially Jewish point view – that if Jesus wasn't the Messiah, He just hadn't come yet? (I had not yet found historical records from Roman historians mentioning Christ as early as 49 A.D.[54]) I was placing plenty of faith in future events, yet not so much on past history as the Bible described events surrounding Jesus… yet my faith in the future events was based on the Bible's New Testament, which is focused on Jesus, whom I wasn't very sure about… Mental gymnastics indeed. On what was I basing the "faith" I did have in the Bible?

Don't get me wrong, I was trying to figure out faith in Jesus. I had advanced along my spiritual path enough that I believed in God, I just didn't see why He would need to send an intermediary to give us a message. Was He too busy or unconcerned to interact with us directly? And if He wants to convince us He exists and has a message for us, why not show more supernatural power? Like – all the time? Why make us wonder if He even exists, because there is so little evidence – when there could be a perpetual cosmic spectacle of proof in sight every day? Why do we have multiple religions, and religious disputes, and wars, if there is one right way?

It seemed unlikely to me that God would FAIL so miserably at convincing humanity of His presence, if in fact He had ever tried to send us a message. Were God and Satan and Jesus and Antichrist all just "expansionist creations of the human mind?"[55] This is what I had always assumed Voltaire meant when he said "If God did not exist, it would be necessary to invent him."[56] I had always focused on the part about "inventing him," and assumed that as a philosopher of the French Enlightenment (who got into so much trouble for criticizing the monarchy and the Catholic Church that he was exiled to Britain) Voltaire must have been an atheist suggesting that man had invented God. This was, after all, the same man who had said: "If God created us in his own image, we have more than reciprocated" and "Those who can make you believe absurdities, can make you commit atrocities."[57] But as it turns out, deeper study of Voltaire reveals that I misunderstood him. He only despised the Church, and was suggesting in the first and most famous quote that we need God – that it would be necessary to invent God, if not for the fact that God **does** exist.

It was interesting to realize I had been wrong about something that had seemed so obvious. Could deeper study of God reveal new insights for me, as it had on the less important topic of Voltaire? It seemed unlikely that studying religion and philosophy would remove my doubts, but I accepted Pascal's Wager – an agnostic has nothing to lose by trying to understand God, and it couldn't hurt to better educate myself.

I started studying Christianity anew, not just the prophecies I was most interested in, but the whole religion. I read through the entire Bible, not just certain chapters like Revelation and Daniel. I started reading biographies of intelligent agnostics who had developed faith and converted to Christianity in adulthood. I especially identified with much of what Oxford and Cambridge Professor Clive Staples Lewis had written about Christianity. You might know him by his initials and his fiction, as he also wrote some Chronicles about Narnia... but I identified with his youthful skepticism in books like Mere Christianity and Surprised by Joy: "the impression I got was that religion in general, though utterly false, was a natural growth, a kind of endemic nonsense into which humanity tended to blunder. In the midst of a thousand such religions stood our own, the thousand and first, labelled True. But on what grounds could I believe in this exception?"[58] I identified with his doubts but didn't even have the background of being raised in a Christian family. Would it ever be possible for me to understand or believe that Christianity is right?

At one point it had seemed unlikely to me that God even existed. It still seemed unlikely that He would create us knowing our free will and our flaws and imperfections could never allow us to pass His tests, and that we would need a Savior to fix the problem. I wouldn't create an imperfect system that I knew I would have to provide a fix for later on. As George Carlin said, "If this is the best God can do, I am not impressed." Couldn't God do a little better than that?

The conclusion I have finally come to, is – NO, He couldn't. He couldn't do better than that. Not that God is limited, I just don't think any creation can be as perfect as its creator. As C.S. Lewis pointed out, Hamlet is a wonderful character – and his most noble traits may have been modeled in the image of Shakespeare himself – but Hamlet is not Shakespeare; nor was Hamlet created without limitations and flaws. Hamlet isn't going to find evidence of Shakespeare or deduce Othello or Macbeth from what he can observe. "If Shakespeare and Hamlet could ever meet, [or if Hamlet could ever be made to understand] it must be Shakespeare's doing... The 'Shakespeare' within the play would of course be Shakespeare and one of Shakespeare's creatures. It would bear some analogy to the Incarnation."[59]

Like any created "character" we aren't going to discover or understand all the complexities of our creator. We cannot achieve the all-knowing intelligence or wisdom of our creator. And finite knowledge and wisdom lead to flawed decisions. Couple our limited brains with free will, and there's a recipe for imperfection. When God intervenes on our behalf to provide grace and salvation it is not just to save us but to teach us – to demonstrate that we required it; that no amount of good behavior on our part would ever achieve perfection or allow us to bargain our way into a perfect heaven. Hamlet didn't get himself into a book. We will not, through our own efforts, be perfect enough to get into the Book of Life. We need our creator to write our names in.

Like a child negotiating with parents, most of us, early in our spiritual development, try to set the terms of entry into heaven ourselves. We let God know all the wonderful things we will do, and in return we announce that he should consider that good enough, and let us know heaven awaits us even if that is all the restraint we can muster. But as John Hagee has said, God is not playing "Let's Make a Deal." And if we thought our position in heaven were earned, (as Satan felt he deserved his high station and was entitled to more) we would never be satisfied with it. Only if we understand that what we receive is through undeserved grace could we possibly be content, even with all the infinite amazingness of heaven at our feet. Let me explain my thoughts. My analogies will not work for everyone, but they help my understanding.

I eventually realized that I am a lot like a cell in a body. Early on, I didn't realize this - I was just an individual, surrounded by many other individuals, and like them, I was trying to get ahead in the world. Trying to earn more money and obtain more goods and services for myself. In isolation, this makes sense. But from the perspective of being one cell in a greater body, this is acting like a cancer. Imagine how troublesome it would be if every cell in your body was acting independently, looking out for its own interests and taking limited resources from its neighbors instead of working for the good of the greater whole? Your first order of business would be figuring out how to send a message to your cells, to get them on track. To make them realize they exist only to be a part of you. That you have been giving them all the nutrition they need to survive and flourish. To let them know that you don't want to lose any of them if you don't have to, but that eventually the

Final Treatment will come in the form of chemotherapy, and by then it will be too late for any malignant cells to take your side and realize their rightful place. You want to keep all your cells, as many as possible. You wish no Final Treatment were necessary. It will hurt you too, on a much greater scale.

You might, if you were the brain and had such control over your body, convince a blood cell first – and send that blood cell as a traveling messenger....

Of course the analogy of being like a cell in a greater body, and realizing I was acting like a cancer, instead of part of the greater whole... that idea can only carry me so far. It may be relevant to view myself as a tiny cell, while God is more like the giant trillion-celled brain of the body. I can also accept that in reality God is so immense, so vast, so inconceivably multi-dimensional – that no analogy will do. If God is overwhelming beyond all my mental parameters, even beyond cause and effect and space and time as I know them – then to communicate with human beings, He would have to use an intermediary or a small part of Himself to convey the message. And at that point, what form would be most useful? What better form to take than a human body? And as another friend of mine suggested, choosing to come down to us in human form is not just to match the form we happen to have evolved into, if we were created in His image...

At this point in my thought process, the idea of God sending a part of Himself in human form to communicate with humanity on our level was starting to make a lot of sense to me. I still didn't have overwhelming proof. I didn't all-of-a-sudden believe events had happened exactly as described in the Bible. But at least, for the first time in my life, the possibility made some sense to me.

And during my research on Bible prophecy, I occasionally stumble onto things that really get my attention. Chuck Missler has pointed out an interesting pattern in Genesis Chapter 5. We are given a genealogy, a lineage starting with Adam, Seth, Enosh, Cainan, Mahalalel, Jared, Enoch, Methusaleh, Lamech, and Noah. I had already been fascinated by Noah's flood, and Enoch's "solar" 365 year lifespan (like the 365 days in a year) before – not death – but being translated away, bypassing death as he was taken to heaven. "Enoch walked with God; and he was not, for God took him." (Genesis 5:24) The numbers associated with Enoch are full of clues to astronomical events....

But Missler had a different focus; he pointed out that each name in this genealogy has a meaning. Adam means "man" and is sometimes used as a synonym in phrases like "son of Adam." Seth means "the appointed one" as a substitute for Abel, who was slain. Enosh means "mortal;" and when you put all ten names' meanings in a sentence, you read "Man (is) appointed mortal sorrow; (but) the Blessed God shall come down teaching (that) His death shall bring (the) despairing rest."[60]

This would appear to be a prophecy about the Messiah. One could argue that ancient Jewish rabbis conspired to hide a message central to the Christian Gospel in the first book of their Torah. But that doesn't make a lot of sense. The "sentence" formed by the ten names does not seem to describe the Messiah as the conqueror Jews expected to save them from foreign rule... It seems more likely to me that this is a sign of divine inspiration for the book of Genesis. I cannot explain this away, nor do I want to. I hope to keep finding signs that strengthen my religious faith.

Luke 11:9 says "seek, and you will find; knock, and it will be opened to you." Jeremiah 29:13 says "You will seek Me and find Me when you search for Me with all your heart." I have prayed again and again for God to help me understand and accept as much truth as possible. I don't want to lack understanding or faith. I don't want to write a book about the Antichrist and interpret Bible prophecy for other people if I don't fully understand the Bible myself. There are many different opinions on religion. Could I have it all wrong? Billions of people must be wrong.

It is logical that if one religion is correct all others are wrong, and that great evil may be done in the name of the wrong religion. I suspect many will use this as an excuse to dehumanize individual followers of a certain religion. In the dark times ahead it will be easy to hate those whom we see serving an evil cause. But I think it is important to remember the phrase: "there but for the grace of God go I" and acknowledge that if we had been born "over there" with parents of "that" religion our own beliefs would probably be different. Even the saints of the elect can be misled. (Matthew 24:24) I hope that many good Christians, Muslims, Jews, and others act as their brother's keepers and help save those unfortunate enough to find themselves in "enemy" territory. I hope to help save people, not mislead them.

In addition to studying the Bible and reading many other books related to the Antichrist, I have also read a lot of blogs and forum entries and commentaries, and I have watched a lot of internet videos. One day I was watching a video Jonathan Kleck made about Barack Obama and the Antichrist and near the end Kleck was questioning himself. He explained to viewers that he almost didn't finish his video because it all sounds so crazy, and because he could be wrong, and his ideas might even be used against him to make him seem crazy.... But he called out something like:

"Lord, here's the deal. I'm going to open a big book at random, and if you don't show me something amazing that confirms for me that you are sending me this message and that what I am considering showing people is the truth, then I'm not doing it." He then opened a random book, (a thesaurus) and opened to the entry "evil spirits" with major subheadings like devil and Satan. In his video, he continued to explain: "I could have opened up to... the entry for electricity or some other unrelated entry." But instead he opened to something very relevant and persuasive to him, convincing him to go forward.

This made an impression on me. I understand that it may only be an example of an interesting coincidence, and not necessarily the will of God; and that if he had opened to "electricity" and never made his video I would never have heard his story. We are only told about people's amazing experiences; the ones that lead to not believing and not making a video never reach us. But I was in my office realizing I have the same doubts and concerns this other person has, and that I have prayed many times to God asking Him to simply put a stop to my efforts if I am wrong. "God, I don't need fifteen minutes of fame for this book I'm working on." (I said similar prayers for my last book and again when working on this one.) "Please just give me signs to stop and not publish my ideas if I'm wrong. I don't want to mislead anyone, I don't want to be a false prophet, I don't want to publish wrong interpretations of the Bible." On the other hand, Ezekiel 33:6 suggests a certain duty to continue when I think I have discovered something, for God is not happy "if the watchman sees the sword coming and does not blow the trumpet and the people are not warned."

Just moments before writing this, I prayed, "God, if I'm right, and I know who the Antichrist is, and what I'm writing has merit and should be published, please let me open a big book at random and open to an entry that answers this question for me, and solidifies the idea that you are authorizing me to go ahead with this Antichrist book."

I looked behind to my bookshelves determined to pick the thickest book and randomly open it. Now the thickest book happens to be one of my Bibles (about three inches thick.) I thought, "opening a Bible would be stacking the deck in favor of finding a relevant comment or a divine message." But the nearby dictionary was pretty thick too. So I said, "Lord, I'm going to open this dictionary randomly. I'm not even looking at all the entries on the page. I'm only going to look at one in the middle, right by the spine of the book. Whatever has the biggest entry and stands out first, that's what I'm looking at for a sign that you are actually approving my research and authorizing me to comment on and interpret the Bible."

I opened randomly to page 917 of my <u>Thorndike Barnhart Advanced Dictionary</u>. By far the largest entry was to the right middle of the spine: the entry for "seal" including the definition "something that settles or determines: the seal of authority."

I could have turned to something meaningless, like my second time opening the dictionary to make this very point – where on page 685 the biggest entry on the spine is on the top right for the entry "navigate" with the quote "I can scarcely navigate today. Turtles can navigate from one part of the ocean to another."[61] It would have been grasping at straws for the flimsiest excuse for meaning to get a potential affirmation from God out of that entry. But the first time was different - I could not have asked for a better entry as a sign (or a seal, a divine seal of authorization.)

Two days later I found myself reading Jonathan Cahn's novel, <u>The Harbinger</u>, when a sentence caught my attention on page 11: "'A seal,' he said, 'bears witness to a message that it's authentic or that it's of great importance.'"[62]

Was opening my dictionary to the entry for "seal" a coincidence? Are all the clues pointing to June 6, 2016 just coincidences? I don't think so. I assume, with ever-increasing confidence, that I am on the right track - and that if I am meant to have a greater understanding or faith or a further revelation of future events – that such things will happen soon, so long as I keep searching.

I have been searching. I have been reading – thousands of hours of reading. And thousands of hours of writing. It is time to dive deeper into my research, to the more academic reasoning that has led me to conclusions on this subject.

THE KING OF BABYLON

Babylon is a most interesting topic in our consideration of the Antichrist and the end times. It is a complicated subject because in the name "Babylon" there is an obvious reference to the ancient city which was the capital of the first great empire the Bible describes. Few people realize the Revelation of John also repeatedly refers to "Mystery Babylon" – a future city and empire with many similarities to ancient Babylon. Mystery Babylon wields great power and is completely destroyed in the end times. In Jeremiah 50:42-43 God declares that He will send powerful forces "Against you, O daughter of Babylon. The king of Babylon has heard the report about them, and his hands hang limp." In these verses it is very clear that the King of Babylon rules "the daughter of Babylon" – future, Mystery Babylon – not historical, ancient Babylon.

Could Mystery Babylon merely refer to a modern city to be rebuilt at the site of historical Babylon? If the site of ancient Babylon is the same site as a future city which will be the capital of the Antichrist's kingdom, then Daniel's 70th week and the time of the Antichrist must be far in the future, for in 2014, there is nothing but archeological ruins at the site of Babylon in Iraq. Should any New Babylon be rebuilt there, as it is in the fictional <u>Left Behind</u> series – some time will be needed to accomplish the task. As I conclude that biblical clues on the timing of Daniel's 70th week point to 2016, it seems much more likely to me that an existing great city will be known as the modern Babylon.

We know some cities are occasionally described with unusual names. In modern America most of us recognize "Sin City," "The Big Easy," and "The Windy City" as Las Vegas, New Orleans, and Chicago. New York has many nicknames including "Gotham" and "The Big Apple." How confusing such names could be to someone thousands of years later if taken out of context!

The Bible offers similar confusion over names of cities. Jerusalem has many nicknames – some are well-known like Zion or the City of David, others less known and more confusing, as in Revelation 11:8: "the great city which mystically is called Sodom and Egypt, where also their Lord was crucified." It makes things difficult to understand thousands of years later in another language, if the Bible might mean Jerusalem when it says Egypt. We must keep such difficulties in mind as we consider "Mystery Babylon."

Because the ancient Babylonians conquered Judea and took the Jews as captives to Babylon, the city has a special role in Jewish history, in the Bible, and as an example of God's punishment. But not every biblical reference to Babylon is to ancient Babylon in Iraq. There is also "Mystery Babylon" which we should interpret as the original language implied: "Mystery: Babylon" as if asking us to solve the mystery of what this future Babylon-like city is during the end times. Eventually, this mystery will be solved, as Romans 16:25 describes "the revelation of the mystery which has been kept secret for long ages." It is not ancient Babylon in Iraq. It is similar to what is meant by phrases like "the new Atlantis" or "the modern-day Sodom."

In contemplating possible modern contenders as the solution to this mystery, I searched for clear references to modern power centers that could be the city and empire in question. The richest, most powerful nation in the modern world isn't mentioned by name. But wouldn't it be strange if there are no references to America in the Bible? The New World is home to most of the world's Christians, its current pope, and the most powerful nation in the world – one that has dominated the planet financially, militarily, and culturally. America has given more financial aid and sent out more missionaries than any other nation. America has been the closest ally of Israel, has been home to more Jews than Israel, and the nation was founded on values like "In God we Trust." Yet this nation allegedly isn't mentioned in the Bible. Of course, as 1 Corinthians 2:7-8 hints: "we speak God's wisdom in a mystery, the hidden wisdom which God predestined before the ages to our glory; the wisdom which none of the rulers of this age has understood."

Jeremiah 6:22 also tells us "A great nation will be aroused from the remote parts of the earth." I suggest that America is REPEATEDLY and PROMINENTLY mentioned in the Bible, but its description is wrapped in mysteries; especially that of "Mystery Babylon."

Looking at this mystery backwards, if we were expecting an end times version of Babylon, we should look for signs that it is like the Babylon of old. The new daughter Babylon should be like the original. It should be the clearly dominant city of the dominant world empire. It should have a tower symbolizing many nations and languages and government power over them; but any such tower should be brought down. Mystery Babylon is clearly described as the great center of buying and selling. Revelation 18:3 says "the merchants of the earth have become rich by the wealth of her." Her highest towers might even be associated with global commerce or "World Trade." Its home language should be the dominant language of the world, as in Genesis 11:1 "Now the whole earth used the same language and the same words."

As ancient Babylon built a high tower to try to reach heaven, so the future Mystery Babylon must be known for her attempt to reach into heaven. The tower references point at tall buildings, but Jeremiah 51:53 also says "'Though Babylon should ascend to the heavens, and though she should fortify her lofty stronghold, from Me destroyers will come to her,' declares the Lord." America has tall skyscrapers, and is especially known for very tall ones in New York that are fallen. But America's dominant space program also ascends to the heavens; Americans landed men on the moon and planted a flag there as if claiming it. America has orbiting space weapons to fortify their military supremacy in "her lofty stronghold" where she has dominated the space race. Isaiah 14:13 also says "But you said in your heart, 'I will ascend to heaven; I will raise my throne above the stars of God." More than anyone else, it was an American President who decided to form a space program.

Obadiah 1:4 tells us "'the eagle, though you set your nest among the stars, from there I will bring you down,' declares the Lord." The eagle (the United States) set its nest (its capital city, Washington D.C.) among the stars (the stars originally represented the 13 colonies.) Despite much expansion to the west, the national capital is still nestled in the middle of the original 13 states. From Washington D.C., through the presidency, will the once-great nation be brought down.

Ancient Babylon was located in present day Iraq, but the Bible's prophecies combine to make it clear that end-times Babylon could not also be located there. "Mystery Babylon" of the future is an agricultural powerhouse. Jeremiah 50:16 mentions "sowing" and the "sickle" and the "harvest." Verse 26 says "open her barns." Verse 37 mentions "horses." Verse 45 speaks of "flocks" and "pasture." Jeremiah 51:23 mentions the "shepherd" and "flock" and "farmer." Verse 33 again mentions a "harvest." Revelation 18:13 describes "flour," "wheat," "cattle," "sheep," and other produce. These (and other) signs of great agricultural production attributed to Babylon fit the fertile farms of America much better than the deserts of Iraq. Jeremiah 51:13 also refers to "Babylon" as "you who dwell by many waters, abundant in treasures." Again, this describes America well – the United States has thousands of miles of coastline on the Atlantic, Pacific, Gulf of Mexico, and the Great Lakes – before we even consider Alaska's huge coastline adding the Gulf of Alaska, Bering Sea and Arctic Ocean. Iraq hardly has any coastline at all.

In Zechariah chapter 5 we have a strange story about an "ephah." It would help to know that an ephah was the largest unit of measure for dry goods like grain in ancient Israel. Like the bushel in the 19th century or the barrel (of oil) in the 20th century, commerce has depended on such units of measure. So while an American story's reference to trade and commerce might be symbolized by the movement of bushels and barrels, in the ancient Middle East, Jews knew the ephah.

In a vision in Zechariah 5:7-11, an angel clarifies for him: "'This is the ephah going forth.' Again he said, 'This is their appearance in all the land (and behold, a lead cover was lifted up); and this is a woman sitting inside the ephah.' Then he said, 'This is Wickedness!' And he threw her down into the middle of the ephah and cast the lead weight on its opening. Then I lifted up my eyes and looked, and there two women were coming out with the wind in their wings; and they had wings like the wings of a stork, and they lifted up the ephah between the earth and the heavens. I said to the angel who was speaking with me, 'Where are they taking the ephah?' Then he said to me, 'To build a temple for her in the land of Shinar; and when it is prepared, she will be set there on her own pedestal.'" This is a most interesting set of verses regarding the Whore of Babylon.

The ephah symbolizes commerce. A wicked woman at the center of this commerce is set on a pedestal in the land of Shinar, yet another nickname for Babylon. Zechariah was very specific in various other details in his writing, which date his writing to approximately 518 B.C., well after the Jews had returned to Israel from exile in Babylon. So to suggest that Jewish commerce would be re-established in ancient Babylon seems incorrect after the captivity. Ancient Babylon had already passed its prime.

There is, however, a great statue of a woman, symbolic of its city and its nation, sitting on a pedestal at the entrance to a great modern city which is the center of global commerce and finance, and is also still the city with the most Jews. This verse supports the idea that New York is the city of Mystery Babylon and that America is "Babylonia" (as some Bible translations replace the poetic phrase "the land of Shinar" with "Babylon" or "Babylonia.") As Chris Putnam tells us, "the Antichrist and his 'base of operations' – 'Mystery

Babylon' of Revelation 17-18 is also a commercial center of political power that imposes its will on the world."[63]   America is the only nation that has been imposing its will on the world recently, and its largest city – New York – is the seat of Wall Street stock exchanges, the Federal Reserve, and the gold supplies of most nations. "Dominating global finance, it [Mystery Babylon/New York] stands as the center of world commerce until it collapses."[64]

When Zechariah's prophetic career began about sixteen years after the return of the first Jews from their Babylonian exile, approximately 520 B.C. - Babylon was still a large city and a regional capital within the Persian Empire. Zechariah would not have had to describe the city as unready or unbuilt. Jews routinely travelled back and forth by land to a thriving city in Babylon. His descriptions would not be referring to ancient Babylon; he was telling us that the wickedness symbolized by Babylon in the past, would be re-established somewhere far away in the future – in a great commercial city that wasn't ready yet, and one that required flight to get to.

Revelation 18:21 says "Then a strong angel took up a stone like a great millstone and threw it into the sea, saying, 'So will Babylon, the great city, be thrown down with violence, and will not be found any longer.'"   But ancient Babylon thrived for over a thousand years after it was conquered, and can still be found near Baghdad over 2,500 years after its defeat. Jeremiah 51:41-43 tells us that eventually: "Babylon has become an object of horror among the nations! 'The sea has come up over Babylon; she has been engulfed with its tumultuous waves. Her cities have become an object of horror.'" These verses tell us many things. One, this version of Babylon is not just one city, but an empire including many cities which become an object of horror.   Two, Babylon is engulfed by the waves of the sea, something which never happened to ancient Babylon, which is far inland, not on the coast of the sea.

Jeremiah 51:13 "O you who dwell by many waters, abundant in treasures, your end has come." This rules out ancient Babylon and Iraq. It rules out Moscow, the major city of America's long-time rival. One could argue that China is America's rival superpower at this point, but despite Beijing being sort of near the coast on the Pacific, China does not dwell by "many" waters like the United States. But New York is right on the ocean, and the United States is surrounded by water "from sea to shining sea."

Revelation 17:18 tells us Mystery Babylon is "the great city that rules over the kings of the earth." Few cities qualify as possibilities at all. Financially, New York and (to a lesser extent) London control the world's money. The political capital cities of the greatest military powers like Washington, Moscow, and Beijing must be considered. Through religion, Mecca and Rome exert an international influence.

Once upon a time, it could have been argued that Rome dominated the world (at least the world known to the Jews in Israel) and even today, through the Catholic Church, "Rome" still has great influence over many nations. For centuries, the main city many writers have considered as the modern version of Mystery Babylon was Rome. When Romans crucified Jesus in 33 A.D., destroyed the Jewish Temple in 70 A.D., and persecuted Christians for a few centuries after that – Rome established itself as the enemy. At the time, it was also the greatest military and economic power in the world. Some Christian scholars note that Revelation 17:9 says "Here is the mind which has wisdom. The seven heads are seven mountains on which the woman sits." Many have assumed that the seven hills of Rome are the seven mountains on which the woman riding the beast sits. But reading further along in Revelation, it is obvious that the seven mountains are really seven kings and kingdoms, (or even continents) and not literal hills or mountains at all. This was conveniently ignored during centuries of the Protestant Reformation, when it was politically useful to identify Rome, the Catholic Church, and the Papacy with the Beast of the end times.

Rome has had (and through the Vatican continues to have) a huge influence on many nations. But Rome is not the financial or commercial master of the entire planet. Even within Italy, Milan is more of a financial center than Rome. As for Rome's Jewish population – there are only about 15,000 Jews in Rome, about 1% of the Jewish population of New York.

There is also an interesting prediction from the French prophet Nostradamus about these events. He made an apocalyptic reference to "the King of Babylon" that seems to rule out the Roman interpretation when he wrote in quatrain 10:86:

> "Like a griffin will come the King of Europe,
> Accompanied by those of 'Aquilon':
> He will lead a great troop of red ones and white ones,
> And they will go against the King of Babylon."[65]

Aquilon is the mythical land of the north wind, and I believe from other references to it that Nostradamus meant Russia. So with a King of Europe who is like a griffin (a winged lion, perhaps the Royal Air Force of the British Lion under King Charles or King William…) diverse European forces (red and white to Nostradamus probably meant French and Spanish; and the lion may mean British) Western European and Russian forces fight the Antichrist – the King of Babylon. This Nostradamus prophecy suggests that we should rule out Europe or Russia or a revived Roman Empire as the homeland of the Antichrist. The Antichrist and his empire cannot be European if Europe from Russia to the Atlantic is fighting under a single king, united in fighting against the Antichrist.

John Preacher makes a case for Mecca in The Islamic Antichrist. He suggests that oil is the "wine" of the harlot's fornication on which the kings of the world get drunk, and that Saudi Arabia is the harlot. He thinks the Shiites in Iran will destroy Saudi Arabia, including the holy cities of Mecca and Medina, and move the black stone from the Ka'ba to Jerusalem. But Mecca does not rule all nations, it has no Jews to flee from it, it is not symbolized by a woman, the city does not sit on many waters…. And it would be very unpopular to nuke Mecca, and quite difficult to remove the Ka'ba from Mecca (either before or after nuclear destruction.) Even Saudi domination of the oil market is being replaced by high production in Russia and North Dakota.

To eliminate some possible contenders for Mystery Babylon, let's play "fill in the blank" with a city and consider the phrase: "It doesn't matter unless those in _____ agree." Many cities listed above no longer make sense. Once great power centers like Madrid and Paris and Berlin no longer apply. Only a few great cities are true seats of power, so much so that someone in a different nation cares what decisions are made there. Militarily there are three great powers on the earth – nations do care what is decided on, militarily, in Washington D.C., Beijing, and Moscow. Of the three superpowers, only America and China could be described as making the merchants of the world rich through trade. But the China hypothesis has several flaws, including that China has not provided the main international language, it is not surrounded by many waters, Beijing is not on the coast, it is not known for its fallen towers, China hardly has any Jews, it is not symbolized by a woman, etc. China also has not ruled over many kings. But since WWII, when the United Nations was established in New York, that city has hosted a world-governing body from which ALL nations are influenced. But it is not the political control of the UN that solidifies New York as Mystery Babylon.

David Montaigne

I argue that control of money is the greatest power, and that the golden rule rings true: "Whoever has the gold, makes the rules." The gold deposits of most national banks are (allegedly) still stored in vaults underneath New York. This is because in the 20th century, world finance power shifted to the growing American powerhouse in New York, which still truly reigns supreme in this category. In World War II, all Allied nations agreed that America's isolated location made it safe from Germany and Japan, and that America's safe factories and fields made its economy and currency safe. In 1944 the United States dollar became the de facto world currency for trade. Control of world finance was also handed to the cartel of New York bankers in 1944 when the Bretton-Woods agreement among the Allies agreed that world trade would be denominated in US dollars.

As the head of one of the world's greatest banking families (Mayer Amschel Rothschild) once said: "Let me issue and control a nation's money and I care not who writes the laws." In the 19th century, the Rothschilds dominated world finance from London. But not only did the US economy eclipse that of Britain, it took over the world economy. Right after WWII, the economy of the United States was as large as the economies of all the other nations of the world put together.

CNN's main financial show for over twenty years was called Moneyline, hosted by Lou Dobbs. It was filmed in New York and every show opened with the line: "Live from the financial capital of the world…" Bankers in New York even fund and control politicians in Washington D.C. The US Federal Reserve prints and digitizes an endless supply of "money" into existence, and its leaders don't care who makes the laws of the United States or even the WORLD, because the bankers in New York basically control the world through its money supply.

All world trade is focused on New York. All major corporations have their headquarters (or at least regional offices) there. The biggest stock exchanges and investment banks are there. Revelation 18:23 says "your merchants were the great men of the earth, because all the nations were deceived by your sorcery." I argue that the sorcery referred to is "fractional reserve banking" – the system of mere paper money in which the world trades in dollars created on a whim and backed by nothing.

Dollars used to represent a certain amount of gold or silver. In the 1960s and 1970s, that backing was taken away. The United States now prints and digitizes an almost infinite amount of paper "money" into existence, and the majority of people on the planet don't even understand that without the good intentions of the United States government it is inherently as worthless as "Monopoly" money. Even now, dollars are only redeemable so long as no one tries to redeem any significant amount. If anyone requested that a few trillion dollars of the total owed be redeemed immediately in tangible property rather than digital account balances, the U.S. government would flat out refuse and default on its obligations, or create more "money" out of thin air and hyper-inflate the value of the debt owed to creditors down to nothing. Many of us grew up after the gold and silver backing of dollars was taken away, and we have never known any money except the I.O.U. papers of the U.S. government.

But someday, that government will be less than trustworthy. It will not want to repay holders of its I.O.U.s with anything of value. It will insist that you trust them and that your paper and digital transactions represent real wealth and savings. But the constant creation of money backed by nothing but promises is financial "sorcery." Anyone with a degree in economics understands exactly what is going on and knows New York is financial sorcery central. Any student of the Austrian school of economics who truly understands the Federal Reserve and the Bretton Woods financial system the world has been placed under would instantly recognize this quote to apply to American commerce and finance, dependent on ever increasing promises. The unlimited creation of paper money is a fraud enforced by bankers and the armies of their nations to allow continued domination of global wealth – and New York is the center of this scheme. As Revelation 18:23 describes it "your merchants were the great men of the earth, because all the nations were deceived by your sorcery."

—" *Virgin daughter of Babylon* "

Isaiah 47:11-12 continues "evil will come on you which you will not know how to charm away; and disaster will fall on you for which you cannot atone; and destruction about which you do not know will come on you suddenly. Stand fast now in your spells and in your many sorceries with which you have labored from your youth; perhaps you will be able to profit." Financial spells and sorcery are evil and deceptive, and lead to destruction. But you go ahead, maybe you'll make a profit. Habakkuk 2:68 warns "Woe to him who increases what is not his — for how long— and makes himself rich with loans? Will not your creditors rise up suddenly, and those who collect from you awaken? Indeed, you will become plunder for them. Because you have looted many nations, all the remainder of the peoples will loot you." These verses emphasize that the "sorcery" is related to "profit" and "loans" and "creditors."

This view of the problem is not new and that I'm far from the only one who sees it this way:

"If the American people ever allow private banks to control the issue of their currency, first by inflation, then by deflation, the banks...will deprive the people of all property until their children wake up homeless on the continent their fathers conquered. – Thomas Jefferson

"When a government is dependent upon bankers for money, they and not the leaders of the government control the situation, since the hand that gives is above the hand that takes... Money has no motherland; financiers are without patriotism." – Napoleon Bonaparte

"The few who understand the system will either be so interested in its profits or be so dependent upon its favours that there will be no opposition." – Lord Rothschild

"It is well enough that people of the nation do not understand our banking and money system, for if they did, I believe there would be a revolution before tomorrow morning." – Henry Ford

"These persons or groups who, first, seize the power to create money (be it currency or credit) and then loan it to the government at interest are, indeed, the prime enemies of the nation." – Father Charles Coughlin

"The real truth of the matter is, as you and I know, that a financial element in the large centers has owned the government." – Franklin D. Roosevelt

Revelation 14:8 (NASB) says "fallen is Babylon the great, she who has made all the nations drink of the wine of the passion of her immorality." (KJV) "Babylon is fallen, is fallen, that great city, because she made all nations drink of the wine of the wrath of her fornication." America has invaded and destroyed nations that did not play along with the rule of trading everything (especially oil) in unbacked, inherently worthless I.O.U.s called dollars. Iraq, and other nations, have tried to distance themselves and their oil from dollars, and America has let them know the results.

In his book on The Antichrist, Arthur Pink wrote in 1913 (just before the creation of the Federal Reserve) that Mystery Babylon would not be mentioned so prominently were it not the home of apostate Israel. "It is in this city that the most influential Jews will congregate at the Time of the End. From there, Jewish financiers will control the governments of earth."[66] Pink continues with additional comments which I quote not for their politically incorrect anti-Semitism but to emphasize that this expert on the Antichrist (Arthur Pink) did make connections between New York, financial control, and the Jews: "The love of money outweighs sentimental considerations. Zionism has made no appeal to their avarice."[67] Most Jews do not flee to Israel. "High finance is the magnet which will draw the covetous Hebrews"[68] to New York.

I would argue that most Jews came to New York simply because it was the main port of entry for European immigrants. Mystery Babylon must have a large population of Jews, for at the time of the end, God suggests that they flee the city to escape its destruction. Jeremiah 51:5-6 says: "For neither Israel nor Judah has been forsaken by his God, the Lord of hosts, although their land is full of guilt before the Holy One of Israel. Flee from the midst of Babylon, and each of you save his life! Do not be destroyed in her punishment."

Mecca has no Jews. Rome has only about 15,000 Jews. Most European cities have small Jewish populations because the Jews there died in the Holocaust; and most Arab cities have few Jews left because they chose to flee persecution and move to Israel after 1948. But New York had **two million** Jewish residents not that long ago, and still has over one million Jews today. It is the only city that dominates world finance and trade, it does so through financial "sorcery," and it is the city with the most significant population of Jews that could heed Jeremiah's message and leave before Mystery Babylon is destroyed.

As Charles Ryrie (of the Ryrie Study Bible) has explained in his book Revelation: "Her name is called a mystery. (Note that the word 'mystery' is not an adjective – 'mystery Babylon' – but a noun in apposition with Babylon – "Mystery, Babylon.') The Christian will realize by the use of this word 'mystery' that this Babylon is not the city on the Euphrates but is a secret use of the word."[69] We should understand that the counterfeit system of worshipping the almighty dollar would be categorized as a similar mystery.

Since the harlot is the mother of harlots, we should envision a federation of false currencies - many currencies in a dollar-centric paper money system. A system controlled in New York. "Babylon is both a city and a system... This is much the same as the way Americans speak of Wall Street." In Revelation 19:2 the harlot is judged based on her fornication – New York money interests don't care about America; bankers' interests are international – this is disloyal fornication. And this brings up an interesting point, that the general population of America, the political leadership in Washington D.C., and the banking elite in New York – rarely have the same interests and goals. To have total financial control of the world, the Antichrist – above all else a political leader – must destroy the controlling financial system of the harlot. I again suggest that a president must often be tempted to rid himself of the controlling strings of his puppet-masters in New York banks. If he ever does, perhaps Michael Rood will be right in stating that "the Destroyer himself is revealed as the commander in chief of the New World Order."[70] Many people already conclude that "the President of the United States of America is referred to, Biblically, as 'the King of Babylon.'"[71]

As the largest city of the most powerful nation, New York is also the de facto world capital. This is where the alien ship lands in the 2008 movie "The Day the Earth Stood Still." Mayor Rudy Giuliani hosted Saturday Night Live on November 22, 1997, and ended the opening skit with "Live, from the Capital of the World, it's Saturday Night!" The United Nations is headquartered there. No other city can make such a claim to effectively being the world capital.

Revelation 17:18 says "The woman whom you saw is the great city, which reigns over the kings of the earth." The word "is" clearly means "represents," for a woman is not literally a city. I know of one woman who represents a city - the Statue of Liberty is a symbol of New York – and she has welcomed millions of immigrants through Ellis Island to add to America's melting pot of nationalities. Lady Liberty's crown has seven spikes representing seven seas and seven continents much like the seven mountains associated with the harlot and beast in Revelation. Yet many people wonder what the symbols in Revelation mean, as if no clues are ever given.

Revelation 17:7 "And the angel said to me, 'Why do you wonder? I will tell you the mystery of the woman and of the beast that carries her, which has the seven heads and the ten horns.'" The Antichrist and his kingdom are different than the kings and kingdoms before them. The Antichrist is an 11th one, like the largest spike of the 11 radiating forward from the pedestal on which the Statue of Liberty sits. Revelation 10:1-2 describes an angel whose "face was like the sun" (the Statue of Liberty's crown has seven rays coming out) and "had in his hand a little book which was open" (like the tablet in the statue's left hand.) This angel "placed his right foot on the sea and his left on the land" like our statue standing on the coast. In Revelation 10:5 "the angel whom I saw standing on the sea and on the land lifted up his right hand to heaven" just as the Statue of Liberty is holding up a golden torch, a cup of fire, in her right hand; as in Revelation 17:4 "having in her hand a gold cup."

The Statue of Liberty looks like several other ancient statues – which is no surprise, as she was based on earlier goddesses of the Old World. The sculptor, Auguste Bertholdi, had just attempted to sell his idea for a giant statue to the Suez Canal project – he wanted to build a huge statue of the Egyptian goddess Isis to stand by the canal as a robed woman holding a torch. Isis had influenced the Roman concept of the goddess Libertas (which our Statue of Liberty was based on) – a goddess of liberty, personal freedom, and the very Roman idea of doing whatever feels good, which eventually linked Libertas with prostitution. This is no surprise, as the images of Isis and Libertas are both derived from the Babylonian goddess Ishtar, goddess of prostitution and "Mother of Harlots."

Revelation 17:15 says "the waters which you saw where the harlot sits, are peoples and multitudes and nations and tongues." Ellis Island was the main port for immigrants coming into the American melting pot from many nations, right by the Statue of Liberty – an image we can trace back to the harlot of Babylon. I can't claim to know what John saw in his visions or how clearly he saw it – or understood it – but it sounds like the Statue of Liberty to me.

Zechariah 5:1 "Then I lifted up my eyes again and looked, and behold, there was a flying scroll." I suspect this is the same scroll which has seven seals on it in the Book of Revelation. Zechariah 5:2 "I see a flying scroll; its length is twenty cubits and its width ten cubits." This is a giant magic scroll, approximately 30 feet long and 15 feet wide. Zechariah 5:4 "'I will make it go forth,' declares the Lord of hosts, 'and it will enter the house of the thief and the house of the one who swears falsely by My name; and it will spend the night within that house and consume it.'" I think this means that fiery judgment comes to destroy the house of the blasphemous thief. Any old thief who shoplifted a pack of cigarettes? No, probably someone very important, like the Antichrist who tries to steal God's land and throne. His house is probably the main city of the Antichrist's Mystery Babylon. Fiery judgment by any method? I suspect it could come in the form of a nuclear weapon in a missile or cargo container about 15 feet wide and 30 feet long. Zechariah 5:5-6 continues to describe New York: "Then the angel who was speaking with me went out and said to me, 'Lift up now your eyes and see what this is going forth.' I said, 'What is it?' And he said, 'This is the ephah going forth.'" Where is this all happening? Zechariah 5:10-11 says "'Where are they taking the ephah?' Then he said to me, 'To build a temple for her in the land of Shinar; and when it is prepared, she will be set there on her own pedestal.'" I am again forced to consider the Statue of Liberty, and the nuclear destruction of New York, probably in mid-2016. *↳ didn't happen! 1.1.16*

America was once known as a force for good. Mary Antin described the view of America at least some Europeans had in the late 19th century: "America was in everybody's mouth. Businessmen talked of it... Children played at emigrating... All talked about it."[72] The Statue of Liberty was a beacon of freedom from oppression. The United States later fought Japanese Imperialism and German Fascism. It fought a cold war against Soviet Communism. It established a Peace Corps, performing good works and giving humanitarian aid throughout the world. America took in millions of immigrants from around the world – millions of people year after year who gave up everything they had for a chance to live in the great nation of America. So when Jeremiah 51:41 says "the praise of the whole earth been seized! How Babylon has become an object of horror among the nations!" We should note that the world initially ADMIRED Babylon, and PRAISED it before it BECOMES hated and eventually a destroyed horror. World-dominating superpowers are usually hated, not admired or praised. But America once stood for good.

No longer does America stand for goodness and the defense of righteousness. In WWII, the British were HAPPY to have over a million U.S. troops built up in their land – because our goal was to protect our mother country with which we shared so much in common – and to liberate the rest of Europe from Nazi tyranny. Of course today, no nations occupied by the United States are thrilled to have a controlling American presence.

Jeremiah 50:12-13 says of the future Babylon: "Your mother will be greatly ashamed, she who gave you birth will be humiliated.... everyone who passes by Babylon will be horrified." I am hard pressed to think of a mother for ancient Babylon, or for Rome or the Vatican (or any other potential contender for Mystery Babylon.) But America clearly does have a mother – America was born from Great Britain. Britain is further confirmed as the mother of Babylon the Great in Daniel 7:4 when he describes the British lion, supported by wings of the American eagle. Ezekiel also seems to mention the British lion in Ezekiel 38-39 as the land of "Tarshish", who gives birth to "young cubs". Tarshish is a cryptic reference to a western naval power (The British navy reigned supreme for centuries) and the "young cubs" of this mother lion are America, Canada, Australia, New Zealand, etc. Daniel refers to the mother (Britain) as a lion. The national symbol of England is a lion. The eagle wings on top of the lion may represent American help in both world wars. America's national symbol is the eagle.

Jeremiah 50:23 "How the hammer of the whole earth has been cut off and broken! How Babylon has become an object of horror among the nations!" What nation has been acting as the hammer of the whole earth? Despite decades being praised for supporting freedom – America has established military bases in about 150 countries – and uses them for support when invading places like Iraq and Afghanistan. America has been "the hammer of the whole earth."

Revelation 16:16 announces the beginning of the Battle of Armageddon: "And he gathered them together into a place called in the Hebrew tongue Armageddon." The next three verses record the fall of Babylon the Great. "And the seventh angel poured out his vial into the air...and great Babylon came in remembrance before God, to give unto her the cup of the wine of the fierceness of his wrath." This passage clearly teaches us that the destruction of Babylon will take place near the time of the Battle of Armageddon. Since we know that the Battle of Armageddon occurs at the end of the Great Tribulation, after the reign of the Antichrist and after the Mark of the Beast, it is obvious that Babylon has not yet completely fallen, but is powerful during the end times. I think America's destruction (or at least the destruction of the city of Mystery Babylon) will probably occur in the second half of Daniel's 70th week, somewhere from 2016 to 2019.

Jeremiah 51:55 tells us "For the Lord is going to destroy Babylon, and He will make her loud noise [or voice] vanish." The King James version of the verse says "the Lord hath spoiled Babylon, and destroyed out of her the great voice." New York will no longer have the greatest voice in world policies either through the United Nations, or Wall Street financial control, or the media, or the Federal Reserve.

Jeremiah 50:17 "Therefore thus says the Lord of hosts, the God of Israel: 'Behold, I am going to punish the king of Babylon and his land, just as I punished the king of Assyria." Is this a prophecy of future events still to come, or merely a reference to past events punishing Nebuchadnezzar thousands of years ago? One could make an argument either way. But at the time Jeremiah is speaking of, there are many Jews in "Babylon" and God encourages them to leave. Jeremiah 50:4 clarifies "'In those days and at that time,' declares the Lord, 'the sons of Israel will come, both they and the sons of Judah as well.'" In Jeremiah 50:8 the Jews are told to "Wander away from the midst of Babylon." Jeremiah 51:5-6 also encourages Jews to leave Babylon and avoid suffering the city's destruction: "For neither Israel nor Judah has been forsaken by his God, the Lord of hosts, although their land is full of guilt before the Holy One of Israel. Flee from the midst of Babylon, and each of you save his life! Do not be destroyed in her punishment, for this is the Lord's time of vengeance." Prior to the Persian conquest of ancient Babylon, the Jews COULDN'T leave Babylon. They had been brought into exile against their will without freedom to leave. So God's pleas to flee do not apply to the Jews of ancient Babylon, only the Jews living free in a future Mystery Babylon like New York.

Jeremiah 50:19 says "I will bring Israel back." Jeremiah 50:16 says Babylon will be devastated to such a degree that all immigrants – Jews and non-Jews – who haven't established themselves for a long time yet will want to leave: "They will each turn back to his own people, and they will each flee to his own land." Again the Jews in "Babylon" are warned in Jeremiah 51:45 "Come forth from her midst, my people, and each of you save yourselves from the fierce anger of the Lord." This seems an unnecessary warning for ancient times, as when Zopyra betrayed Babylon to the Persians, the Persian king Cyrus freed the Jews after he captured Babylon, and commanded Jerusalem to be rebuilt.

But as the Bible describes Mystery Babylon's sudden destruction and the smoke of her burning, I suspect New York will be nuked. There might be Iranian involvement; and there might even be another betrayal by a traitor within the land of "Babylon" (America) who makes it possible for Iranians to achieve the nuclear destruction of New York. Jeremiah 51:11 says "The Lord has aroused the spirit of the kings of the Medes, because His purpose is against Babylon to destroy it." The Medes were in Persia, now Iran. This verse should not be considered a reference to the historical Persian conquest of ancient Babylon, when a real Persian king conquered the city and maintained it intact as a regional capital – but to a future event in which that "spirit" of Persian hostility utterly destroys Mystery Babylon. Jeremiah 50:40 tells us "'As when God overthrew Sodom and Gomorrah with its neighbors,' declares the Lord, 'no man will live there.'"

The city may be destroyed as a form of divine retaliation for what the Antichrist does to desecrate the Temple in Jerusalem. Jeremiah 50:28 says "There is a sound of fugitives and refugees from the land of Babylon, to declare in Zion the vengeance of the Lord our God, vengeance for His temple." We are clearly warned that Jews are back in Israel (Zion) as fugitives and refugees from the land of Babylon to point out that Babylon's destruction was vengeance for the King of Babylon's acts against God's Temple. (This could mean that New York is destroyed in June 2016.) One could argue that Jews have returned to Israel before; that in ancient times, the Persians conquered Babylon and allowed the Jews to return to Jerusalem 70 years after the Babylonians destroyed the Temple. But the Jews at that time were not refugees and fugitives. The city of Babylon was still a great city and a regional capital within the Persian Empire. The Jews who left did so willingly, under no pressure. This verse applies to Mystery Babylon. Jeremiah emphasizes this important event by mentioning it again in Jeremiah 51:12 "His purpose is against Babylon to destroy it; for it is the vengeance of the Lord, vengeance for His temple." This must be the same event from verse 50:28, and clearly "Babylon" is destroyed, which did not happen when Persia captured ancient Babylon.

New York is certainly a top contender for Jeremiah's prophecy on a city with lots of Jews being asked to flee. No other city has ever had such a large Jewish population, nor has any city ever seen such a great decline in its Jewish population. Although down from a peak of over 2 million Jews in the 1950s, New York City still has, by varying estimates, approximately 1.1 to 1.2 million Jewish residents. Even after about a million Jews have unknowingly heeded Jeremiah's warning to flee New York City, it still has more Jews than any other city in the world, even more than Jerusalem or Tel Aviv. Many will be too comfortable in America to heed the call before it's too late. I am starting to see headlines like "Obama Stopping Jews From Returning To Israel" and "Obama is trying to keep the Jewish people here in the United States from returning home to Israel."[73]

In Iraq, there are no longer ANY Jews left to flee the site of ancient Babylon. Many Jews stayed in Babylon when the Persians liberated them, and a large Jewish community flourished in Iraq for thousands of years. The entire nation of Iraq had about 130,000 Jews (mostly in Baghdad) in 1945, but anti-Semitism against Jews surged in the late 1940s with the creation of the State of Israel. By 1967 there were only about 3,000 Jews left in all of Iraq, and those Jews were mercilessly persecuted and murdered in the late 1960s around the time of the Six Day War. By 1970, almost all of the surviving Jews had fled. There are believed to be approximately *six or seven* Iraqi Jews left today, all keeping their identities hidden. So another clue that end times Babylon seems unlikely to be in ancient Babylonia (modern Iraq) is that there are been hardly any Jews left to flee from Iraq.

Another very interesting point is made right before the last quote from Jeremiah. In chapter 51 verses 1-4 the Lord says "Behold, I am going to arouse against Babylon… the spirit of a destroyer… do not spare her young men; devote all her army to destruction. They will fall down slain in the land of the Chaldeans." I find this very interesting because Chaldea is just another name for central Babylonia. You wouldn't say the Babylonians are going to be slain in the land of the Babylonians, just as it wouldn't have made sense to say "the Soviet troops will be slain in the land of the Russians" or "the British will be slain in the land of the English." You would just say they will fall in THEIR OWN land. Unless, of course, it is NOT their own land – if the "Babylonian" army that dies in Chaldea isn't really from that land, then it makes sense. If Mystery Babylon is meant to represent New York and America, then the forces of Mystery Babylon (American soldiers) fall in the land of the Chaldeans (Iraq.)

I find it very interesting that the most powerful armies currently in the Middle East are American and that Revelation 9:16-17 tells us "The number of the armies of the horsemen was two hundred million; I heard the number of them. And this is how I saw in the vision the horses and those who sat on them: the riders had breastplates the color of fire and of hyacinth and of brimstone; and the heads of the horses are like the heads of lions; and out of their mouths proceed fire and smoke and brimstone. A third of mankind was killed by these three plagues, by the fire and the smoke and the brimstone which proceeded out of their mouths. For the power of the horses is in their mouths and in their tails; for their tails are like serpents and have heads, and with them they do harm." Instead of glossing over those details, as it is so easy to do when the Bible mentions things we are unfamiliar with, let's take these visions seriously. "The technology and geopolitics had not advanced enough for early Christians to understand many descriptions except as monsters, but these 'monsters' are common, and easily recognized military hardware today."[74]

Revelation 9:2-11 "He opened the bottomless pit, and smoke went up out of the pit, like the smoke of a great furnace; and the sun and the air were darkened by the smoke of the pit. Then out of the smoke came locusts upon the earth, and power was given them, as the scorpions of the earth have power. They were told not to hurt the grass of the earth, nor any green thing, nor any tree, but only the men who do not have the seal of God on their foreheads. And they were not permitted to kill anyone, but to torment for five months; and their torment was like the torment of a scorpion when it stings a man. And in those days men will seek death and will not find it; they will long to die, and death flees from them. The appearance of the locusts was like horses prepared for battle; and on their heads appeared to be crowns like gold, and their faces were like the faces of men. They had hair like the hair of women, and their teeth were like the teeth of lions. They had breastplates like breastplates of iron; and the sound of their wings was like the sound of chariots, of many horses rushing to battle. They have tails like scorpions, and stings; and in their tails is their power to hurt men for five months. They have as king over them, the angel of the abyss; his name in Hebrew is Abaddon, and in the Greek he has the name Apollyon." Their king is the Destroyer, the Antichrist.

The sting of locusts that lasts for five months could be the effect of chemical weapons; the vision of men's faces could be pilots seen through helicopter windshields. Joel 2:2-4 even tells us these mighty warriors only appear "like" horses: "there is a great and mighty people; there has never been anything like it, nor will there be again after it to the years of many generations. A fire consumes before them… Their appearance is like the appearance of horses; and like war horses, so they run."

Ancient prophets lacked the language to describe futuristic technology. Some say that the wheels Ezekiel saw in the sky could have been alien spacecraft. Ezekiel 1:4-5 describes "something like glowing metal in the midst of the fire. Within it there were figures resembling four living beings. And this was their appearance: they had human form." Whatever Ezekiel saw, his language lacked modern words like spaceship or extraterrestrial. We must consider such limitations when we contemplate how ancient Hebrews might describe modern warfare.

As for the colors on the breastplates; fire is red, hyacinth is blue, and brimstones are chalky white. Brimstone is often wrongly associated with yellow sulfur. A Google Image search for "brimstone" mostly shows lemon-yellow butterflies, but search "piece of brimstone" and images of white rocks are found. Real brimstone is WHITE. Keep this in mind when considering that the armies of the Antichrist employ "locusts" that sound like helicopters

Greek does not give a color of either yellow or white — it just says "Brimstone-like"

73

and "horses" which are clearly not actual horses but are tanks or some other war machine with the power to shoot what sounds like artillery. Also note that the riders of these war machines are identified by their flag or breastplate colors of red, blue, and white. This certainly does not rule out the notion that they are American forces with red, white and blue flags.

If the Apocalypse revolves around American armies in the Middle East, then a third world war can't be that far off. The American psychic Edgar Cayce told a boy born in 1939 that "he would live to see a religious war."[75] Nostradamus portrays the apocalypse of WWIII as largely between Christian and Islamic sides. It is not hard for me to see Christian Europe banding together against Islamic nations someday if WWIII starts. It is harder to see Europe united against America... but as I write this in 2014, Russia seems to be annexing parts of Ukraine; Poland, Latvia, Lithuania, and Estonia seem scared of Russian intentions... and if Putin's Russia comes to dominate Europe, the continent's alignment with the United States could end.

German business is aligning towards Russia, and securing supplies of Russian oil and gas will only strengthen that relationship. Germans are already angry at America's NSA eavesdropping on Chancellor Merkel's cell phone and spying on almost all forms of the German population's electronic communications. Decades of surveillance by the Gestapo and the Stasi have left Germany with a strong aversion to such information gathering. A new entry was made in German dictionaries in 2013: "Der Shitstorm"[76] refers to German indignation over American spying.

In France, the same distaste for American surveillance is called "la tempte de merde."[77] Relations have been strained by various revelations from Wikileaks and Edward Snowden, when various allies (not just in Europe) have learned that the NSA views them as "'frenemies' – part friend and part enemy."[78] What if the airliner shot down over Ukraine in 2014 is eventually blamed on the USA? What if some new event makes Europeans angry at the United States? Many unexpected changes could occur - especially if America proves to be controlled by the Antichrist. Then even if Europeans still like the people of America, they may have to fight the Antichrist's government and military of America anyway.

A century ago, Kaiser Wilhelm II, Germany's last monarch, already viewed the liberal trends in the United States and Britain with disdain. Commenting on the English-speaking peoples, he is described viewing them as "the land of Liberalism and therefore of Satan and the Anti-Christ."[79] But Germans today don't merely view America's liberal views as anti-Christian; many Germans have long-expected the Antichrist to be American.

Many Russians agree. While Americans have long viewed them as godless atheists, the reality today is that Christianity is coming back in Russia. While overt Christianity is under attack within the American military, Russian priests now bless the guns of their troops with holy water. "Alexander Dugin, the man known as 'Putin's Brain', believes that the U.S.-led New World Order is the 'kingdom of the Antichrist' and that it is inevitable that it will be destroyed."[80] How many other Europeans share that view?

We have already reviewed small parts of the following large verse, but looking at the larger context is also important. Jeremiah 51:1-13 reads: "Behold, I am going to arouse against Babylon and against the inhabitants of Leb-kamai [New York, and America] the spirit of a destroyer [The Antichrist.] I will dispatch foreigners to Babylon that they may winnow her and may devastate her land; for on every side they will be opposed to her in the day of her calamity. [Illegal immigration is soaring and has been institutionalized as a method of gaining more voters for a certain political party. An unguarded border with Mexico also means smugglers know they can bring in drugs, people, guns, surface to air missiles, and even nuclear weapons.] Let not him who bends his bow bend it, nor let him rise up in his scale-armor; [Border patrol units have been dissolved and remaining guards have been told to stand down.] so do not spare her young men; devote all her army to destruction. [US troops have been slain in Iraq, Afghanistan, etc.] They will fall down slain in the land of the Chaldeans, and pierced through in their streets. For neither Israel nor Judah has been forsaken by his God, the Lord of hosts, although their land is full of guilt before the Holy One of Israel. Flee from the midst of Babylon, and each of you save his life! Do not be destroyed in her punishment, for this is the Lord's time of vengeance; He is going to render recompense to her. Babylon has been a golden cup [Statue of Liberty?] in the hand of the Lord, intoxicating all the earth. The nations have drunk of her wine; [bogus money – the dollar system of trade] therefore the nations are going mad. Suddenly Babylon has fallen and been broken; Wail over her! Bring balm for her pain; perhaps she may be healed. We applied healing to Babylon, but she was not healed; forsake her and let us each go to his own country, for her judgment has reached to heaven and towers up to the very skies. [Were events like 9/11 warnings?] The Lord has brought about our vindication; Come and let us recount in Zion the work of the Lord our God! [The call is made for Jews to leave America for Israel.] Sharpen the arrows, fill the quivers! The Lord has aroused the spirit of the kings of the Medes, [Iranians] because His purpose is against Babylon to destroy it; for it is the vengeance of the Lord, vengeance for His temple. [Perhaps New York is destroyed when the Antichrist desecrates a rebuilt Jewish Temple.] Lift up a signal against the walls of Babylon; post a strong guard, station sentries, place men in ambush! [Terrorists?] For the Lord has both purposed and performed what He spoke concerning the inhabitants of Babylon. O you who dwell by many waters, [America] abundant in treasures, your end has come."

There are many important points made in the lengthy passage above. The spirit of a destroyer raised against Babylon sounds like Apollyon, as referenced in the Book of Revelation. This would make the timing during the end times, not that of ancient Babylon. These Babylonians will fall down slain in the land of the Chaldeans. This is an odd statement, because Chaldea was a part of Babylonia, and it was a Chaldean dynasty that ruled Babylon through Chaldean kings like Nablopolassar and Nebuchadnezzar. Once that dynasty was in control, everyone came to call Babylonia Chaldea. It was the ancient equivalent of calling the Soviet Union Russia, or calling the United Kingdom England. For another example that Chaldea refers to Babylon, we can compare two mentions of "Belshazzar the Chaldean king" in Daniel 5:30 and "Belshazzar king of Babylon" in Daniel 7:1.

So as we already discussed - for Jeremiah 51:4 to tell us that the Babylonians will fall down in the land of the Chaldeans begs the question: why not tell us they fall in their own land? Perhaps because Babylon, in this context, is not the ancient city of the Chaldeans but the modern city of Mystery Babylon - New York – and its empire – America – whose troops will fall in Iraq. There may even be a traitor that intends to weaken America who allows Persia/Iran to destroy New York and American troops in the Middle East.

The Babylon whose end has come intoxicates all the earth with her wealth and luxury and sits on many waters. Babylonia had a small coastline on the Persian Gulf, and the city of Babylon – while on a great river – was far inland. America sits on many waters, has the greatest navy and the biggest economy in the world. New York has been the financial center of the world, and sits on the coast. The spirit of the Medes are against it – Medes are Persians – in modern terms, Iranians. If New York is ever nuked, Iranians will top a short list of potential suspects. At the time I write this in mid-2014, there is a "missing" Malaysian airliner which I suspect might have been taken for the eventual delivery of a nuclear cargo to New York – though a shipping container or missile or box truck could also do the job. Should

New York ever be nuked (as I suspect it will be in 2016) then I also expect that Iran will be blamed.

New York or not, the Bible does seem to describe a coastal city's nuclear destruction in Revelation 10:1-3 "I saw another strong angel coming down out of heaven, clothed with a cloud; and the rainbow was upon his head, and his face was like the sun, and his feet like pillars of fire... He placed his right foot on the sea and his left on the land; and he cried out with a loud voice, as when a lion roars; and when he had cried out, the seven peals of thunder uttered their voices." If John did have a vision of a mushroom cloud exploding over New York, this might be how he would have described it. As described on the second page of "Time No More" (once available on the internet, but no more) "The most unmistakable event in all of Revelation, the destruction of the latter-day city of Babylon, which receives fully twenty-four verses of coverage in chapter 18, shall have come to pass." I believe this will happen right as the second half of Daniel's 70th week begins, as the 3.5 years some call "the great tribulation" begins.

Revelation 14:6-8 says "And I saw another angel flying in midheaven, having an eternal gospel to preach to those who live on the earth, and to every nation and tribe and tongue and people; and he said with a loud voice, 'Fear God, and give Him glory, because the hour of His judgment has come; worship Him who made the heaven and the earth and sea and springs of waters.' And another angel, a second one, followed, saying, 'Fallen, fallen is Babylon the great, she who has made all the nations drink of the wine of the passion of her immorality.'" So once all nations have finally heard the gospel, as the Hour of God's judgment has come, Babylon is "fallen, fallen" – for this is the second destruction of "Babylon." Andrew Simmons, author of Quenched Like a Wick: Revealing the Day America Breathes Her Last, believes this will occur on June 5, 2016.[81]

Ezekiel 7:26-8:1 "'Disaster will come upon disaster and rumor will be added to rumor; then they will seek a vision from a prophet, but the law will be lost from the priest and counsel from the elders. The king will mourn, the prince will be clothed with horror, and the hands of the people of the land will tremble. According to their conduct I will deal with them, and by their judgments I will judge them. And they will know that I am the Lord.' It came about in the sixth year, on the fifth day of the sixth month..."

Jeremiah 51:28 again suggests Iran will lead nations against Babylon: "Consecrate the nations against her, the kings of the Medes, their governors and all their prefects, and every land of their dominion." Since Medes and Persians did fight ancient Babylon, it makes it hard to know for certain whether the Bible is describing literal Babylon (in Iraq) or Mystery Babylon thousands of years later... But most Bible prophecy has two fulfillments. Every land of Persian dominion could mean that fundamentalist Muslims from Iran lead the Islamic world to war against non-Muslims. In Islamic prophecy, Muslim end times armies carrying black flags will come from Khurasan – a province in northeastern Iran. They will be led by the Mahdi – the Muslim savior – and everyone will follow them to Jerusalem.

Isaiah 2:5-7 "Come, house of Jacob, and let us walk in the light of the Lord. For you have abandoned your people, the house of Jacob, because they are filled with influences from the east, and they are soothsayers like the Philistines, and they strike bargains with the children of foreigners. Their land has also been filled with silver and gold and there is no end to their treasures; their land has also been filled with horses and there is no end to their chariots." The House of Jacob is Israel, which has abandoned its people somewhere else, outside of Israel. They have international commerce. There is vast gold and silver. We may be reminded of the vaults of the Federal Reserve Bank of New York, which since WWII has held roughly 25% of the world's mined gold reserves for approximately sixty foreign central banks and international monetary organizations. There is no end to treasures in America, the land is extremely wealthy. Natural resources are abundant. There are many horses and chariots – the military might of this land is unlimited. All of this should make us think of the United States.

In Revelation 18:9 we understand that the whore has fornicated with the kings of the earth, which implies a greater context than just the ten kings under the Beast. The Beast doesn't appreciate that the harlot has independent interests and serves her own needs. In Revelation 17:16 we learn that the Beast and his ten kings come to hate the Harlot and will destroy her: "And the ten horns which you saw, and the beast, these will hate the harlot and will make her desolate and naked, and will eat her flesh and will burn her up with fire." Could this possibly mean that the Antichrist (who I think is the King of Babylon – or President of the United States) will hate "New York City, the great Babylon"[82] – the power center of Wall Street, the banking elite, and the United Nations? What if a president in Washington were to want unlimited power, without being controlled like a puppet by the real masters in New York? Would a president who was egomaniacal, greedy, selfish, and evil be willing to nuke New York and blame it on others to gain dictatorial control?

Would he also be willing to sacrifice American armies in the Middle East? Daniel 11:11 "The king of the South will be enraged and go forth and fight with the king of the North. Then the latter will raise a great multitude, but that multitude will be given into the hand of the former. When the multitude is carried away, his heart will be lifted up, and he will cause tens of thousands to fall; yet he will not prevail." It is not clear at all whether the King of the North is the Antichrist leader of Mystery Babylon or not, but in this particular verse it sounds like the King of the North will lose tens of thousands of troops to his "enemy" and be happy about it! This sounds like a traitorous leader who wants the other side to win. What might explain this? One possibility is a president who is secretly a member of a certain religion, who in his heart, thinks his nation has been a rogue monster that needs to be brought down.

This could explain many of Obama's strange policies, like support of the Muslim Brotherhood in Egypt. "The Egyptian people are astounded. They simply do not understand the Obama Administration's efforts to bring the Muslim Brotherhood back to power.... Amr Adeeb, a prominent Egyptian commentator, argues that the U.S. is helping the Muslim Brotherhood to achieve power, in order to turn Egypt into a magnet for jihadist fighters.... To Westerners, this may seem like a bizarre conspiracy theory, but for Egyptians it helps explain why the U.S. government is supporting an organization that has openly declared jihad against the West.... set hospitals on fire, and murdered Christians in the streets. The Muslim Brotherhood has no respect for the rule of law, but the Obama Administration treats the Egyptian military that removed the group from power as a threat to democracy itself."[83]

Daniel 11:19 says "he will turn his face toward the fortresses of his own land" and Daniel 11:39 might be describing this same event when we are told that the Antichrist "will take action against the strongest of fortresses with the help of a foreign god." As Zopyra betrayed ancient Babylon to the Persians, could an insider work with or allow or blame Iranians for the destruction of the main city of Mystery Babylon? Looking at this reference in the larger context of Daniel 11:37-39: "He will show no regard for the gods of his fathers or for the desire of women, nor will he show regard for any other god; for he will magnify himself above them all. But instead he will honor a god of fortresses, a god whom his fathers did not know; he will honor him with gold, silver, costly stones and treasures. He will take action against the strongest of fortresses with the help of a foreign god." This god of fortresses or fortifications, we are told by theologian Alexander Hislop, was pronounced "Ala Mahozine"[84] which starts off sounding remarkably like "Allah." Are the followers of Allah willing to attack America? Do they include the inhabitants of Persia? Are they often inclined towards war? "The Qu'ran contains at least 109 verses that call Muslims to war."[85]

If any American city is nuked, martial law will be established immediately. Special, dictatorial presidential powers will be granted. Many have noted that the Antichrist will achieve his greatest power after a disaster, an unprecedented crisis that encourages other leaders to cede their power to him on a global level. I constantly hear rumors that this could occur as early as late 2014, but my hunch is that there will be no nuclear events until 2015 at the earliest. On March 25, 2014, President Obama expressed his concerns over "the prospect of a nuclear weapon going off in Manhattan."

If New York is nuked, I would not expect this before 2016. Not only would this fit the description of the destruction of Mystery Babylon, but it would also take out the cartel of elite bankers who finance and control Washington politics. It would destroy the United Nations headquarters and bring the "czars" or governors of the ten FEMA regions into great power. (The Federal Emergency Management Agency exists to handle disaster mitigation and response.) Presidentially appointed "czars" exist in many departments already, and the word Czar comes through Russia, and Byzantium, and Rome – where it started as Caesar. Ten kings, or ten horns, could be the ten governors of the ten FEMA regions which would have great power once martial law is immediately imposed after a major terrorist event. Special presidential powers would be granted to cut through red tape and deal with the crisis quickly. Deuteronomy 28:43 warns us: "The alien who is among you shall rise above you higher and higher, but you will go down lower and lower." This reminds me of Dorothy Rabinowitz referring to Obama as "the alien in the White House."[86] Even now, some perceive "the rise of a totalitarian regime in America – an imperial presidency achieving a new level of control with Barack Obama."[87]

After 9/11, President Bush had sudden and unprecedented global support to act as he saw fit. Could another president suddenly be granted great authority to restore order? Imagine waking up to hear that New York has been nuked; WWIII seems imminent (or appears to have started already) American stock markets are literally vaporized, Asian and European stock markets are opening down 40%, and soldiers are posted at your local supermarket and gas station, where food is almost gone from shelves and gasoline is suddenly over $20/gallon. The president asks for special emergency powers. Does he get them? Of course he does. I think the American people, and most of the rest of the world - would allow any reduction of freedoms and any retaliation as America's response – against anyone who is blamed, guilty as charged with no prolonged debate over evidence. What if the president says it was Iran? What if he says it was a right-wing militia? What if he says it was Israel? No matter who is blamed, I would expect ten very powerful FEMA governors, and an even more powerful president.

Many Bible scholars writing on the topic of ten kings under the Antichrist have thought that Rome is Babylon and that the revived Roman Empire must exist in its final form divided under ten kings for the little horn of Daniel 7:24 to rule. But animal horns grow with age; a little horn represents a young new country and king. America may be relatively young as nations go, and Obama may be relatively young as presidents go, but nothing Roman is new or young. And in Daniel 7:7 this beast empire is "different from all the beasts that were before it." What makes the Roman Empire, or what would make a revived, 21st century version of it so unique?

Modern America, on the other hand, could be viewed as unique because of the way it was founded as a democracy. As Edward Said (one of Obama's professors at Columbia) noted in Culture and Imperialism, "The United States has replaced the earlier great empires and is the dominant outside force" in the Middle East. Daniel 7:23 "The fourth beast will be a fourth kingdom on the earth, which will be different from all the other kingdoms and will devour the whole earth and tread it down and crush it." America is different from all other kingdoms. It is ethnically diverse. It was founded on the principles of democracy, not along ethnic lines. It has military bases and occupying forces all over the world. From its own empire building days that brought in lands from Puerto Rico to Alaska and Hawaii (already a huge portion of the planet) the United States victory in WWII led to the occupation of western Germany, Italy, and Japan. Between WWII and the cold war against the Soviet Union, US military bases were also built in many other friendly nations, with the highest numbers in Germany, Japan, South Korea, Italy, Great Britain, Spain, and Turkey. Add on newer adventures in the Middle East, with many troops in Iraq, Kuwait, and Afghanistan... and lower numbers of troops on American bases in almost 150 other nations – and we can understand why America has been a unique WORLD power.

Let's look at Daniel 7:24 another way "As for the ten horns, out of this kingdom ten kings will arise; and another will arise after them, and he will be different from the previous ones." What if this is a reference to Western Civilization – The West – The First World – NATO – and the powerful kingdom at its head is Postwar America? What if this is the global American empire that came about as a result of victory in Europe and the Pacific in WWII?

Before WWII, The United States was in economic depression and had a pitiful army. America was unquestionably considered weaker than Germany, Great Britain, France, The Soviet Union, or Japan. After WWII American armies occupied half the world, from Germany and Italy to Japan and South Korea. The American economy had an industrial output and economic wealth equal to the rest of the world combined, because other major powers had largely destroyed each other. America was the only nation with the atomic bomb. No nation had ever dominated the world like postwar America, nor has any other nation used its power so often. Jeremiah 25:11-12 may have a very interesting parallel for this: "nations will serve the king of Babylon seventy years. Then it will be when seventy years are completed I will punish the king of Babylon and that nation."

The Jews were exiled in ancient Babylon for seventy years 2,600 years ago. This prophecy was fulfilled already. But many prophecies experience multiple fulfillments, and this one may see a second fulfillment in America. Postwar America has occupied the defeated enemies of WWII. Germany and Japan in particular have been economic powerhouses, producing high-quality merchandise for American consumers. World War II ended with the American occupation of these countries in 1945. Will American economic dominance and the economic servitude of former enemies end about 70 years later, around 2015?

Dinesh D'Souza opens his latest book on Obama with the words: "The American Era, 1945-2016."[88] Germany is shifting into Russia's sphere of influence; Japan is shifting into alignment with China... Andrew Simmons suggests that with the end of the Holocaust and World War II, "1946 saw the branch of national Israel become tender and put forth leaves. But of even more significance, America began her 70-year reign as Babylon."[89]

Daniel 9:1-2 is very interesting. It gives us great insight into Daniel's thinking: "In the first year of Darius the son of Ahasuerus, of Median descent, who was made king over the kingdom of the Chaldeans — in the first year of his reign, I, Daniel, observed in the books the number of the years which was revealed as the word of the Lord to Jeremiah the prophet for

the completion of the desolations of Jerusalem, namely, seventy years."
Notice that Daniel is claiming to understand the prophetic time period as
revealed by God, about (plural) "desolations" of Jerusalem for seventy years,
in the year after Darius defeated Babylon.

Daniel was already a wise old man by the time the Persians conquered
ancient Babylon. He had undoubtedly studied Jeremiah's prophecies many
times, but now, after the Jews were finally liberated after seventy years of
captivity, Babylon was not utterly destroyed as Jeremiah described. This
may have initially been confusing to Daniel, until he realized there is a
second, future fulfillment in which another "Babylon" is also destroyed after
seventy years.

As Andrew Simmons describes it: "Daniel was expecting Babylon to be
completely and utterly destroyed at the end of the 70 years. A 'perpetual
desolation.' But it wasn't. The Medes took Babylon, people died, but life in
Babylon continued. Daniel was undoubtedly confused at this point. Was
Jeremiah wrong? Was Jeremiah a false prophet? No! Daniel, at that point,
began to understand that contained within Jeremiah's prophecies are TWO
desolations of Jerusalem... two 70-year periods... two Babylons... two
commands to restore Jerusalem... and two restorations of God's people to
God's holy land."[90]

Many years ago, my first published book was about the prophecies of
Nostradamus. Despite my focus on a Third World War between Christian
and Islamic nations (which may last the 27 years he described if we consider
this war to span the years from 1991-2018) I mention Nostradamus now
because he wrote about "the new Babylon, miserable daughter increased by
the abomination of the first holocaust, and it will last for only seventy three
years and seven months."[91] In the 1990s, I assumed this referred to Russia.

Godless daughter of Mother Russia, the Soviet Union included many distinct
peoples and was enlarged by territorial gains following the end of World War
II (and apparently, the first Holocaust.) Russia's Duma, it's "congress," was
shut down by Lenin's Bolsheviks on January 18, 1918. The coup against
Gorbachev started on August 18, 1991. These dates are exactly seventy three
years and seven months apart. I still think the Soviet Union fits this
Nostradamus prophecy perfectly.

But the King of Babylon leading Mystery Babylon cannot be Russian if our
earlier Nostradamus reference from quatrain 10:86 was interpreted correctly;

for it has Russians (and western Europeans) fighting the King of Babylon. Of course America was also greatly increased in power after the first use of the atomic bomb at the end of the war in August 1945. Could 2019 mark the end of the United States? Could "Postwar America" be Nostradamus' "New Babylon?"

Roman/European civilization has had many dominant nations as "king" or leader of Europe over the course of history. There were times when no one would dispute the supremacy of the Greeks, or the Romans, or the Spanish, or the French, or the British, or the Germans... It would be easy enough to compile a list of ten dominant European powers. But no one would question that since 1945, the dominant military power in Western Europe has been the Postwar United States. America was spawned by Europe but is not in Europe, it was never a kingdom with a king, and the ethnicity of its people is only about half European. This could be the final power which "will be different from the previous ones."

The differences may apply to the kingdom (Postwar America) and its king (president.) Since the end of WWII, ten similar "kings" arose. Postwar America saw ten new presidents who were indisputably conceived by white parents, indisputably raised under an entirely Christian influence, and indisputably born in the United States who have assumed the presidency: Eisenhower, Kennedy, Johnson, Nixon, Ford, Carter, Reagan, Bush I, Clinton, and Bush II. Then another arose after them, who is in many ways different. Revelation 17:12 "the ten horns which you saw are ten kings who have not yet received a kingdom, but they receive authority as kings with the beast for one hour." If a day is as a thousand years to God, and an hour is one 24th of a day, perhaps it is one 24th of a thousand years - or about 42 years. We could go from late in the Eisenhower administration to early in the Bush II administration in this time frame for those first ten postwar kings.

Barack Hussein Obama is very different in his complexion and ethnicity. Many dispute where he was born. Many dispute whether Obama's religious beliefs are Christian or Muslim. Many dispute whether his policies and goals are designed to help America, or if he views America as a neocolonial monster and designs policies to weaken America's global influence. As the book description for Will Clark's King Obama: America's Greatest Danger very mildly points out: he "doesn't seem to be focused in the same direction as all other American presidents before him."[92] In April 2014, USA Today noted "The idea that President Obama acts as if he is the king of the United States or a tyrant, instead of president, has become a cliché over the past five years."[93] They also released a poll on July 2, 2014 which analyzed all the postwar presidents and titled its article "Poll: Obama 'worst president' since World War II."[94] Such themes are covered in detail in Pamela Geller's The Post-American Presidency: The Obama Administration's War on America.

Some argue that when the little horn arises within the boundaries of a new, revived empire we even have a clue regarding the part of the empire he comes from. Daniel 8:8-9 says "Out of one of them came forth a rather small horn which grew exceedingly great toward the south, toward the east." This leads some to suggest that the Antichrist originates from the north and west of the empire, and that he will eventually grow in power towards the south and east of it. President Obama spent his childhood in America's westernmost state of Hawaii, then entered politics and rose to the rank of Senator in Chicago in the middle North. Going to Washington D.C. he moved south and east to assume power.

Of course, this may not even apply to Obama and America. There is a perfectly good fulfillment of this prophecy in the past. In a larger context: Daniel 8:8-9 reads "Then the male goat magnified himself exceedingly. But as soon as he was mighty, the large horn was broken; and in its place there came up four conspicuous horns toward the four winds of heaven. Out of one of them came forth a rather small horn which grew exceedingly great toward the south, toward the east, and toward the Beautiful Land." This is an excellent description of Alexander the Great, the male goat, as a large and mighty horn (great conqueror) who died at age 33 as soon as he had conquered the known world. He had four generals who divided his (Greek) empire, and the small horn of interest is the Seleucid Dynasty that ruled from Syria. This dynasty begat Antiochus Epiphanes, the evil king who desecrated the Jewish temple, placed a statue of Zeus with his own face in the temple, brought pigs into the temple, and well fits Isaiah's descriptions of the Antichrist as the King of Assyria, as well as fitting Daniel's descriptions of the Abomination of Desolation. The Jews rose up against Antiochus, overthrew his forces and cleaned out the Temple, which has been celebrated ever since with the Jewish holiday of Hanukkah.

I suggest, however, that this was merely the first fulfillment, and that these prophecies will still see another fulfillment in the end times, probably through America. Scotland Yard detective and theologian Sir Robert Anderson agreed on "a primary fulfilment in Antiochus Epiphanes – 'the Antichrist of the Old Testament.' But that it was only a primary fulfilment.... the presumption is clear that the ultimate fulfilment"[95] will help bring closure to the New Testament.

Like Antiochus Epiphanes, Mystery Babylon also has enemies – and identifying these rivals may help determine whether or not America can be Mystery Babylon. Jeremiah 50:9 tells us "I am going to arouse and bring up against Babylon a horde of great nations from the land of the north, and they will draw up their battle lines against her; from there she will be taken captive." North of American troops in Iraq? North of America itself? North of Jeremiah's perspective, writing in Israel? No matter which vantage point we consider, this could point to Russia as a potential enemy of Babylon. A horde of nations from the north could refer to Russia and many former Soviet Republics which Russia may dominate again soon. Battle lines are probably being drawn in Ukraine and other theaters of war as I write.

Unfortunately, the King of Babylon, himself an enemy of the King of the South (Egypt) is sometimes portrayed as the King of the North. Joel 2:20 also says to Israel "But I will remove the northern army far from you, and I will drive it into a parched and desolate land." Is Israel's enemy from the north, and their enemy also from their north? This is very unclear.

Jeremiah 16:14-15 says: "'Therefore behold, days are coming,' declares the Lord, 'when it will no longer be said, 'As the Lord lives, who brought up the sons of Israel out of the land of Egypt,' but, 'As the Lord lives, who brought up the sons of Israel from the land of the north and from all the countries where He had banished them.' For I will restore them to their own land which I gave to their fathers.'" The largest exodus of Jews was their departure from Russia in the late 19th century. Russia could be "the land of the north." But when Ezekiel 38:6 tells us the Antichrist will come "from the remote parts of the north" are these the same location? One possible suggestion is given by answering the question: "how could the King of the North come against Anti-Christ if Anti-Christ is from the North? Answer is simple - in Ezekiel Anti-Christ and Magog comes from the "remote parts of the north" (Ezekiel 38:6) and NOT from the Land of the North."[96] Turkey is north of Israel. Russia is north of Turkey. And continuing right over the pole, one could argue that America is even further north of Russia, or that Russia is north of America. I am not satisfied with the lack of biblical clarity over the many northern references.

Nostradamus tells us that "the Arabs... these Eastern Kings will be chased, overthrown and exterminated, but not altogether, by means of the forces of the Kings of the North."[97] He also says "the principal Eastern chief will be vanquished by the Northerners and Westerners.... Then the Lords of Aquilon [the North], two in number, will be victorious over the Easterners, and so great a noise and bellicose tumult will they make amongst them that all the East will tremble in terror of these brothers, yet not brothers, of Aquilon [the North]."[98]

Nostradamus confirms there are two Kings of the North. One popular idea is that Russia is the main good Christian land of the north, (how ironic, given my view of Russia when I grew up) allied with some other major power that is both northern and western. I think it would be wonderful for America, if it must produce the Antichrist – to rid itself of him early on, staging an uprising against him while he is overseas and letting him stay in his New World Order capital in Jerusalem. I will hope that America eventually frees itself of Antichrist control while he focuses on the Middle East. Then America, even if it is weakened by a limited nuclear war and a civil war first – could rally in the end to be the great northern and western ally of Christian Russia, its brother and ally in every world war, yet hardly its brother in many other ways... Of course, this is just one possible interpretation of the confusion over too many northerners.

Revelation 16:10-12 says "Then the fifth angel poured out his bowl on the throne of the beast, and his kingdom became darkened; and they gnawed their tongues because of pain, and they blasphemed the God of heaven because of their pains and their sores; and they did not repent of their deeds. The sixth angel poured out his bowl on the great river, the Euphrates; and its water was dried up, so that the way would be prepared for the kings from the east." "Babylon" might be different than the actual land through which the Euphrates flows, through which kings of the east will pass through. There is no mention of drought in the kingdom of the Beast; if his kingdom were ancient Babylonia, then drought should be mentioned if the Euphrates River dries up. Another clue to consider his kingdom of Mystery Babylon to be some other land is that the Antichrist kingdom is the dominant military power of its time, with the potential to take over the entire world by force. Yet in Iraq, the Euphrates dries up to allow in the kings of the east. If this were the heartland of the Antichrist kingdom, enemy armies from the east would not march right in so easily. And again, future Babylon's enemies are from its north, not the east. Also if this were Mystery Babylon being overrun, there would be more of a biblical narrative about it – like Joshua crossing the Jordan or Moses crossing the Red Sea. "Biblical writers emphasized what they determined to be important when they gave more expositional space to these matters"[99] – the relative lack of detailed events associated with the huge army crossing the Euphrates implies it cannot be the overthrow of the Antichrist capital or homeland.

Isaiah 47:9 says "two things will come on you suddenly in one day: loss of children and widowhood. They will come on you in full measure In spite of your many sorceries, in spite of the great power of your spells." I suspect that the "sorceries" reference the financial shenanigans New York banking interests have achieved through Congressional approval of the creation of the Federal Reserve – a private company that "prints" as much paper and digital money as they want. Using the dollar as the world's reserve currency already gives American companies a huge advantage, as described in Revelation 18:23: "your merchants were the great men of the earth, because all the nations were deceived by your sorcery." Perpetually creating more money out of thin air compounds the abuse, as every dollar saved is worth less over time. But the bankers get wealthier, and the government gets unlimited money without officially collecting more unpopular taxes (though inflation of the money supply is clearly an indirect form of taxation.) I believe the Book of Revelation describes this unholy alliance between New York bankers and the political leaders in Washington as the woman who rides the beast and gets her authority from the beast. The Federal Reserve was authorized to create money "by order of the President and Congress of the United States, both of whom are the willing or unwilling slaves of its private creators."[100]

Of course the "beasts" in Washington eventually get tired of being controlled by the "harlots" in New York and conspire to rid themselves of the controlling puppet-strings of this financial arrangement, as described at the end of Revelation 17: "The waters which you saw where the harlot sits, are peoples and multitudes and nations and tongues. And the ten horns which you saw, and the beast, these will hate the harlot and will make her desolate and naked, and will eat her flesh and will burn her up with fire. For God has put it in their hearts to execute His purpose by having a common purpose, and by giving their kingdom to the beast, until the words of God will be fulfilled. The woman whom you saw is the great city, which reigns over the kings of the earth." I would not be surprised at a conspiracy to achieve this end. There are too many potential beneficiaries who will enjoy the end of New York's financial domination – from China and Russia to the Middle East to Washington, D.C.

We could occasionally assume that Jeremiah's references to Babylon could describe the ancient city in Iraq, but the end times events in Revelation are definitely in the future. Revelation 18:2-10 says "Fallen, fallen is Babylon the great! She has become a dwelling place of demons and a prison of every unclean spirit, and a prison of every unclean and hateful bird. For all the nations have drunk of the wine of the passion of her immorality, and the kings of the earth have committed acts of immorality with her, and the merchants of the earth have become rich by the wealth of her sensuality.' I heard another voice from heaven, saying, "Come out of her, my people, so that you will not participate in her sins and receive of her plagues; for her sins have piled up as high as heaven, and God has remembered her iniquities. Pay her back even as she has paid, and give back to her double according to her deeds; in the cup which she has mixed, mix twice as much for her. To the degree that she glorified herself and lived sensuously, to the same degree give her torment and mourning; for she says in her heart, 'I sit as a queen and I am not a widow, and will never see mourning.' For this reason in one day her plagues will come, pestilence and mourning and famine, and she will be burned up with fire; for the Lord God who judges her is strong. 'And the kings of the earth, who committed acts of immorality and lived sensuously with her, will weep and lament over her when they see the smoke of her burning, standing at a distance because of the fear of her torment, saying, 'Woe, woe, the great city, Babylon, the strong city! For in one hour your judgment has come.'"

This description seems to fit nuclear destruction of New York City better than any ancient conquest of Babylon. Judgment and destruction come in a single hour, involving being "burned up with fire." Ancient Babylon was never burned. As for modern, Mystery Babylon, a heavenly voice warns the Jews, "Come out of her, my people," so as to avoid sharing in her destruction. Could Ezekiel 22:20-21 also be talking about this event: "As they gather silver and bronze and iron and lead and tin into the furnace to blow fire on it in order to melt it, so I will gather you in My anger and in My wrath and I will lay you there and melt you. I will gather you and blow on you with the fire of My wrath, and you will be melted in the midst of it." This could be a metaphor about regathering in Israel.

Isaiah 14:30-31 "I will destroy your root with famine, and it will kill off your survivors. 'Wail, O gate; cry, O city.'" This verse describes utter and complete destruction without survivors or a name for posterity. Ancient Babylon was still a city for many centuries after its defeat, and thousands of years later we still know its name. Revelation 18:21 reads "So will Babylon, the great city, be thrown down with violence, and will not be found any longer." Not the gradual loss of importance that the city of ancient Babylon felt over the course of many centuries. A violent end, which we are told elsewhere, comes in a single hour, and causes such complete destruction that the city cannot be found afterwards. "This is describing the fall of the United States. This country [America] is described as Mystery Babylon."[101]

Isaiah 13:19-20 also says "And Babylon, the beauty of kingdoms, the glory of the Chaldeans' pride, will be as when God overthrew Sodom and Gomorrah. It will never be inhabited or lived in from generation to generation." If the future Mystery Babylon were in Iraq, and never meant to be inhabited again, it probably would not be part of the blessed land promised by God to be part of an expanded Israel in the future, as in Joshua 1:4 "From the wilderness and this Lebanon, even as far as the great river, the river Euphrates, all the land of the Hittites, and as far as the Great Sea toward the setting of the sun will be your territory." New York, however, could be destroyed and made uninhabitable and not affect God's promise.

A nuclear attack on New York would seem like the destruction of Sodom and Gomorrah, with fire from the sky, complete destruction, and radiation that would prevent future habitation. Isaiah 13 also describes the changes on earth and in heaven that correspond to a pole shift in connection with the destruction of "Babylon's" kingdom: "For the stars of heaven and their constellations will not flash forth their light; the sun will be dark when it rises and the moon will not shed its light. Thus I will punish the world for its evil and the wicked for their iniquity; I will also put an end to the arrogance of the proud and abase the haughtiness of the ruthless. I will make mortal man scarcer than pure gold and mankind than the gold of Ophir. Therefore I will make the heavens tremble, and the earth will be shaken from its place at the fury of the Lord of hosts." This obviously occurs in a future time when the cosmic maelstrom of the tribulation occurs as described in Matthew 24:29, and also, as Isaiah 14:1 continues to explain, after God has returned the Jews to Israel:

Isaiah 14:1-9 "When the Lord will have compassion on Jacob and again choose Israel, and settle them in their own land, then strangers will join them and attach themselves to the house of Jacob. The peoples will take them along and bring them to their place, and the house of Israel will possess them as an inheritance in the land of the Lord as male servants and female servants; and they will take their captors captive and will rule over their oppressors. And it will be in the day when the Lord gives you rest from your pain and turmoil and harsh service in which you have been enslaved, that you will take up this taunt against the king of Babylon, and say, 'How the oppressor has ceased, And how fury has ceased! The Lord has broken the staff of the wicked, the scepter of rulers which used to strike the peoples in fury with unceasing strokes, which subdued the nations in anger with unrestrained persecution. The whole earth is at rest and is quiet; they break forth into shouts of joy. Even the cypress trees rejoice over you, and the cedars of Lebanon, saying, 'Since you were laid low, no tree cutter comes up against us.' Sheol from beneath is excited over you to meet you when you come; it arouses for you the spirits of the dead, all the leaders of the earth; It raises all the kings of the nations from their thrones.'"

These passages seem to indicate that when the Jewish people have been brought back to live in Israel, the king of Babylon will be an enemy whom hell itself is eventually excited to greet, raising the spirits of the dead – perhaps at Judgment Day. With Iraq occupied by American forces, both the ancient Babylon and the Mystery Babylon of New York are both ruled by the King of Babylon, the US President. Could this be the end times enemy of Israel, so evil that hell celebrates his arrival in the underworld?

Isaiah 14 is very clear: the Jews are back in Israel (verse 1); but will be oppressed again (verse 2); God will end their suffering (verse 3); after which they will "taunt against the king of Babylon" (verse 4); that the oppression has ceased (still verse 4); that God has broken the power of the wicked ruler (verse 5); who had subdued the nations (verse 6); but afterwards the whole earth rests (verse 7); no one rises against them any more (verse 8); hell is excited to meet the evil king (verse 9); who was powerful but now weak (verse 10); and is dead and rotting in hell (verse 11) and Satan has fallen (verse 12.) This description sounds like the end times; it is too final to apply to ancient Babylon.

Revelation 16:17-21 makes it sound like Babylon falls at the end of the tribulation: "Then the seventh angel poured out his bowl upon the air, and a loud voice came out of the temple from the throne, saying, "It is done." And there were flashes of lightning and sounds and peals of thunder; and there was a great earthquake, such as there had not been since man came to be upon the earth, so great an earthquake was it, and so mighty. The great city was split into three parts, and the cities of the nations fell. Babylon the great was remembered before God, to give her the cup of the wine of His fierce wrath. And every island fled away, and the mountains were not found. And huge hailstones, about one hundred pounds each, came down from heaven upon men; and men blasphemed God because of the plague of the hail, because its plague was extremely severe."

I suspect that New York may be destroyed earlier, around the middle of the final seven years – but that these verses describe the destruction of America (and most of the world) during a pole shift at the end of the seven years.

~~Isaiah~~ *Rev.* 17:1-18 "Then one of the seven angels who had the seven bowls came and spoke with me, saying, 'Come here, I will show you the judgment of the great harlot who sits on many waters, with whom the kings of the earth committed acts of immorality, and those who dwell on the earth were made drunk with the wine of her immorality.' And he carried me away in the Spirit into a wilderness; and I saw a woman sitting on a scarlet beast, full of blasphemous names, having seven heads and ten horns. The woman was clothed in purple and scarlet, and adorned with gold and precious stones and pearls, having in her hand a gold cup full of abominations and of the unclean things of her immorality, and on her forehead a name was written, a mystery, 'BABYLON THE GREAT, THE MOTHER OF HARLOTS AND OF THE ABOMINATIONS OF THE EARTH.' And I saw the woman drunk with the blood of the saints, and with the blood of the witnesses of Jesus. When I saw her, I wondered greatly. And the angel said to me, 'Why do you wonder? I will tell you the mystery of the woman and of the beast that carries her, which has the seven heads and the ten horns. 'The beast that you saw was, and is not, and is about to come up out of the abyss and go to destruction. And those who dwell on the earth, whose name has not been written in the book of life from the foundation of the world, will wonder when they see the beast, that he was and is not and will come.

Here is the mind which has wisdom. The seven heads are seven mountains on which the woman sits, and they are seven kings; five have fallen, one is, the other has not yet come; and when he comes, he must remain a little while. The beast which was and is not, is himself also an eighth and is one of the seven, and he goes to destruction. The ten horns which you saw are ten kings who have not yet received a kingdom, but they receive authority as kings with the beast for one hour. These have one purpose, and they give their power and authority to the beast. These will wage war against the Lamb, and the Lamb will overcome them, because He is Lord of lords and King of kings, and those who are with Him are the called and chosen and faithful.' And he said to me, 'The waters which you saw where the harlot sits, are peoples and multitudes and nations and tongues. And the ten horns which you saw, and the beast, these will hate the harlot and will make her desolate and naked, and will eat her flesh and will burn her up with fire. For God has put it in their hearts to execute His purpose by having a common purpose, and by giving their kingdom to the beast, until the words of God will be fulfilled. The woman whom you saw is the great city, which reigns over the kings of the earth.'"

The Devil's whore is associated with his capital of Mystery Babylon, as Christ's bride is associated with the New Jerusalem in Revelation 21:10. The whore wears purple and scarlet (Rev 19:4) which are colors representing wealth and luxury. The bride wears white. The bride is the faithful portion of Israel (with gentiles grafted in) so perhaps the whore is the unfaithful portion of the population that rebels against God. New York is a nexus for those who worship Mammon – money – more than a virtuous life. Heaven celebrates the bride's wedding, but celebrates the whore's destruction. The seven great historical empires of the Middle East include five which have fallen: Egypt, Assyria, Babylonia, Persia, and Greece – the sixth one, Rome – the one that "is" in existence at the time of the Book of Revelation, and the seventh one which had not yet come – which could be America – though there is another interesting possibility we will discuss later.

Isaiah 1:21 brings up a fascinating concept, almost worthy of a chapter of its own: "How the faithful city has become a harlot." Babylon was never faithful, even back to Nimrod and the Tower of Babel, ancient Babylon was always about defiance. New York, on the other hand, was founded by the Dutch "with God's merciful help"[102] and there are many colonial references to American states being founded on Christian values:

April 10, 1606 – The Charter for the Virginia Colony read in part: "To the glory of His divine Majesty, in propagating of the Christian religion to such people as yet live in ignorance of the true knowledge and worship of God."

November 3, 1620 – King James I granted the Charter of the Plymouth Council: "In the hope thereby to advance the enlargement of the Christian religion, to the glory of God Almighty."

April 25, 1689 – The Great Law of Pennsylvania was passed: "Whereas the glory of Almighty God and the good of mankind is the reason and the end of government."

July 4, 1776 – the signing of the Declaration of Independence, which includes divine references: "We hold these truths... that all men are created equal, that they are endowed by their Creator with certain inalienable rights... appealing to the Supreme Judge of the world."

1787 – James Madison, the "architect" of the federal Constitution and America's fourth president, said: "We have staked the whole future of American civilization, not upon the power of government, far from it. We have staked the future... upon the capacity of each and all of us to govern ourselves, to sustain ourselves, according to the Ten Commandments of God."

April 30, 1789 – George Washington said at his first inauguration: "My fervent supplications to that Almighty Being Who rules over the universe, Who presides in the council of nations, and Whose providential aid can supply every human defect, that His benediction may consecrate to the liberties and happiness of the people of the United States a government instituted by Himself."

July 4, 1821 – John Quincy Adams wrote: "The highest glory of the American Revolution was this: it connected, in one indissoluble bond, the principles of civil government with the principles of Christianity. From the day of the Declaration ... they (the American people) were bound by the laws of God, which they all, and by the laws of the Gospel, which they nearly all, acknowledged as the rules of their conduct."

1841 – Alexis de Tocqueville wrote in his book, <u>Democracy in America</u>: "In the United States of America the sovereign authority is religious ... there is no other country in the world in which the Christian religion retains a greater influence over the souls of men than in America."

February 11, 1861 – Abraham Lincoln, said in a farewell speech to the people of Springfield, Illinois: "Unless the great God who assisted (Washington) shall be with me and aid me, I must fail; but if the same Omniscient Mind and Mighty Arm that directed and protected him shall guide and support me, I shall not fail ... Let us all pray that the God of our fathers may not forsake us now."

1891 – The U.S. Supreme Court restated that America is a "Christian Nation." "Our laws and our institutions must necessarily be based upon and embody the teachings of the Redeemer of mankind. It is impossible that it should be otherwise; and in this sense and to this extent our civilization and our institutions are emphatically Christian ... this is a religious people. This is historically true. From the discovery of this continent to the present hour, there is a single voice making this affirmation ... we find everywhere a clear definition of the same truth ... this is a Christian nation."[103]

1909 – President Theodore Roosevelt said it was his "great joy and glory that in occupying an exalted position in the nation, I am enabled, to preach the practical moralities of the Bible to my fellow-countrymen and to hold up Christ as the hope and Savior of the world."[104]

But over the course of the next century, something changed in American cities like New York. Maybe people started to shift their faith to scientific advancement. Maybe economic prosperity made people feel less dependent on God – especially in centers of concentrated wealth like New York. By the 1960s, Christianity had seen its peak in big American cities. On October 22, 1965 the cover of New York's Time Magazine prominently asked "Is God Dead?" The New York Times headline including the phrase "God Is Dead" was published on January 09, 1966, leading to the equally famous line "When the New York Times said God is dead" in Elton John's 1971 song "Levon."

Father Charles Coughlin, whose social commentaries reached thirty million radio listeners prior to World War II, had this to say in 1972: "Democracy, as we know it, has degenerated even below the level of atheistic Marxism. In fact the contest in which Moscow and Washington are now engaged is a contest between two atheistic states, one admittedly so, and the other hypocritically so."[105]

Jeremiah 2:9-11 may be especially relevant here: "'Therefore I will yet contend with you,' declares the Lord, 'And with your sons' sons I will contend. For cross to the coastlands of Kittim and see, and send to Kedar and observe closely and see if there has been such a thing as this! 'Has a nation changed gods?'" God is saying to apostate Israel, who has abandoned His laws, that he will deal with them – and their sons' sons. Since the sons are skipped, some interpret this to mean that a second fulfillment of wrath will fall on a future generation. Where? Kittim was a poetic Hebrew term (originally referring to Cyprus) which eventually referred to any western lands far across the sea. For this future wrath, we are told to look to the coast of a land far west of Israel whose behavior begs the question, have they "changed gods?"

America has certainly changed policies. Under Obama, the trends are towards more socialism, more welfare, more immigration, more Islam, more pressure on Israel, more spying, and more centralized government powers.

David Montaigne

Lech Walesa, the former Polish president and leader of the Polish "Solidarity" movement that eventually helped end Soviet domination of Eastern Europe – commented on Obama's America in 2010: "They're getting weak. They don't lead morally and politically anymore. The world has no leadership. The United States was always the last resort and hope for all other nations. There was the hope, whenever something was going wrong, one could count on the United States. Today, we lost that hope."[106]

NASA provides an interesting example into the changes taking place regarding America and God since the 1960s. In 1968, on Christmas Eve, the crew of the Apollo 8 mission circled the moon, and read the first ten verses of the Bible to the people of Earth. Astronaut Bill Anders began with: "We are now approaching lunar sunrise, and for all the people back on Earth, the crew of Apollo 8 has a message that we would like to send to you. 'In the beginning God created the heaven and the earth. And the earth was without form, and void; and darkness was upon the face of the deep. And the Spirit of God moved upon the face of the waters. And God said, Let there be light: and there was light. And God saw the light, that it was good: and God divided the light from the darkness.'" Jim Lovell continued: "'And God called the light Day, and the darkness he called Night. And the evening and the morning were the first day. And God said, Let there be a firmament in the midst of the waters, and let it divide the waters from the waters. And God made the firmament, and divided the waters which were under the firmament from the waters which were above the firmament: and it was so. And God called the firmament Heaven. And the evening and the morning were the second day.'" Frank Borman finished the broadcast with: "And God said, 'Let the waters under the heaven be gathered together unto one place, and let the dry land appear: and it was so. And God called the dry land Earth; and the gathering together of the waters he called seas: and God saw that it was good.' And from the crew of Apollo 8, we close with good night, good luck, a Merry Christmas – and God bless all of you, all of you on the good Earth."

Obama has vastly changed NASA's mission. We are not developing the moon. We are not sending men to Mars. "NASA chief Charles Bolden announced that from now on the primary mission of America's space agency would be to improve relations with the Muslim world" and to "help them [Muslims] feel good about their historical contribution to science and math and engineering."[107] I like my Muslim friends. I'm happy to help them feel good. But this is not a sensible use of my tax dollars. What the heck does making Muslims feel good have to do with NASA's mission?

one of 3 things Obama changed him with —

96

A much more dangerous controversy arose over the appointment of John Brennan as CIA director – when allegations were made that the reason he would not take his oath of office with his hand on a Bible was because he had converted to Islam while in Saudi Arabia. True or not, it is disturbing that he took his oath with a very early copy of the Constitution, before the Bill of Rights were included in 1791. So does that mean we have a potentially Muslim CIA director at the very point in history when America's most active enemies are fundamentalists in the Middle East? One who at least symbolically refuses to acknowledge freedom of speech, freedom of religion, freedom of the press, the right to keep and bear arms, the right to be secure against unreasonable searches and seizures, the right to trial by jury and due process of law – and all the other amendments in the Bill of Rights? If he does support those amended laws, why would he only be sworn in on an old copy of the Constitution before they were added in? It would seem that his decision may reflect a distaste for both the Bill of Rights and the Bible. Should we be surprised? Not really. In June 2007, Barack Obama said "Whatever we once were, we are no longer a Christian nation."

And he is right. Though there are millions of Jews, Muslims, Hindus, Buddhists, and non-believers, even most of the Christians are "Christian Atheists," (as author Craig Groeschel would describe many people in his book titled: The Christian Atheist: Believing in God but Living As If He Doesn't Exist.) American Christians have become incredibly liberal, allowing many cultural changes that early Americans would have considered atrocities. This is very dangerous when faced with a powerful potential enemy like communism was or Islam might become. As Jack Smith explains: "The reason why Americans need to take special notice of Sharia is that America makes herself particularly vulnerable to the threat of Islam's deception. We have elevated multiculturalism, political correctness, and tolerance to be virtues above all others, including truth. Our actions put blinders on the minds of Americans, thereby allowing the deception to succeed because we deny the reality of the danger right before us."[108] I am not suggesting that we bring back McCarthyism or the Crusades or the Inquisition; I am just pointing out the facts.

Many businesses are open every day of the week and millions of Christians work Saturday and Sunday instead of observing a day of rest to go to church. In two landmark decisions, Engel v. Vitale (1962) and Abington School District v. Schempp (1963), the US Supreme Court established the current prohibition on state-sponsored prayer in schools. In 1971 the state of Nevada began licensing prostitutes and brothels. The Supreme Court 1973 decision Roe v. Wade made abortions legal. In 1986 the extremely disrespectful "artwork" known as "Piss Christ" – a photo of a crucifix in the artist's urine – won $5,000 of taxpayer funded prize money from the National Endowment for the Arts. The same year, Judge Butzner of the Fourth Circuit Federal Appeals Court said: "We agree with the District Court that the doctrine taught by the Church of Wicca is a religion." Witches were recognized first, then the Church of Satan. In 2004, Massachusetts became the first state to legalize same-sex marriage after the Supreme Judicial Court's decision in Goodridge v. Department of Public Health in late 2003. California and at least 15 other states have followed their lead. Colorado and California seem to be leading the way for legalizing recreational use of marijuana.

Since 2002, multiple lawsuits have come up in California, Florida, Massachusetts, and other states arguing that the Pledge of Allegiance is unconstitutional because it includes the phrase "under God." In 2002, a federal judge ordered that a granite monument of the Ten Commandments be removed from the Alabama state courthouse. Similar controversies have come up in court over displaying the Ten Commandments in Oklahoma, Florida, Texas, and other states. By 2005, many major corporate and government entities stopped using references to "Christmas" and replaced the term with the more multi-culturally sensitive "holidays."

Major musical performances have gone from wholesome family events to downright evil – and it's not just the old reference to Ozzy Osbourne biting off a bat's head; it's Madonna's allegedly Satanic ritual performance at the 2012 Superbowl halftime, Lady Gaga's allegedly Satanic videos, Katy Perry allegedly summoning Satan at the 2014 Grammy Awards....

I'm not necessarily against the freedom to choose to act as one wishes regarding any of these particular issues – my personal biases here are almost entirely irrelevant. I'm just pointing out that an American in 2014, hypothetically, could work as a prostitute on the Sabbath, and after work she could smoke a joint while being married to her lesbian lover in the Church of Satan, and have an abortion after the ceremony, and as unlikely as this ridiculous set of events may be, all these things are legal.

Contrasted with this, an American today could get fired from their job for saying dangerous, insensitive, and illegal statements at work such as "Merry Christmas," or "I believe the only path to heaven is through our Lord and Savior Jesus Christ." Those statements would be considered politically incorrect, and create an insensitive workplace environment. Does that sound like America is still a Christian nation? No, I think Barack Obama was right when he said "Whatever we once were, we are no longer a Christian nation."

Jeremiah 50:6 warns: "My people have become lost sheep; their shepherds have led them astray."

The following is from a letter by Billy Graham posted some time ago on the Billy Graham Evangelistic Association website: "Some years ago, my wife, Ruth, was reading the draft of a book I was writing. When she finished a section describing the terrible downward spiral of our nation's moral standards and the idolatry of worshiping false gods such as technology and sex, she startled me by exclaiming, "If God doesn't punish America, He'll have to apologize to Sodom and Gomorrah."[109]

Of course, Matthew 10:15 clarifies: "it will be more tolerable for the land of Sodom and Gomorrah in the day of judgment than for that city." New York, and America, will also be severely punished. In Jonathan Cahn's bestselling novel, The Harbinger - a fictional prophet teaches the main character a set of "facts" that seem to make for a detailed correlation between ancient Israel and modern America. Cahn describes the ancient northern kingdom of Israel (which was warned by prophets that it was turning away from God) before it's destruction at the hands of the Assyrian army – and compares them to events surrounding 9/11 and its aftermath in the United States. [Is it relevant that the Jewish Temple was destroyed by both the Babylonians and the Romans on the 9th of Av – the 9th day of the 11th month, a kind of 9/11 date?] Cahn presents many details centered on the verse of Isaiah 9:10 and how it both applies to, and has been quoted repeatedly by, American politicians - without understanding what God really means.

Cahn's basic premise is that America was a Christian nation; that by choosing to be such a nation, we formed a special covenant with God – like Israel once had – and that by shifting away from God and all that is good, America is breaking the covenant and will no longer be blessed. "We drove Him out of our schools, out of our government, out of our media, out of our culture, out of our public square. We drove Him out of our national life."[110] America may have been formed as a Christian nation, but has largely given up its Christian values. How will God respond? We will be warned (9/11 being a major "harbinger" of future doom that will be worse) and then punished severely. The Harbinger describes "a nation that once knew God but then fell away, a sign that America is now the nation in danger of judgment."[111]

If a man accepts Jesus Christ he is grafted on to Israel. If a nation accepts Jesus Christ, will it be grafted into Israel as an entire nation? Will it share the covenants as in Deuteronomy 28:1-15? "The Lord your God will set you high above all the nations of the earth. All these blessings will come upon you and overtake you if you obey the Lord your God:" These verses are followed by specific rewards… but what about punishments for a nation that rebels? America was founded on rebellion against authority… and by the 1960s rebellion against Christian values was a well-established trend.

The Harbinger portrays the events of September 11, 2001 as the first of several divine punishments America receives. Cahn notes that America suffered significant financial collapse exactly seven years after 9/11 in September 2008… and he implies that he may expect another far worse calamity after another seven years in September 2015, though he never actually made such a prediction directly in his book. (On July 31, 2014 I stumbled on a video interview in which Rabbi Cahn says September 13, 2015 should be the crucial day.) It's a fun novel to read for anyone interested in topics like Bible prophecy and America's potential downfall, and while it is merely a fictional novel, September 2015 certainly coincides with the 2014-2015 tetrad of four blood moon eclipses, which could be a sign of major prophetic events.

Unlike Jonathan Cahn, it is not my mission to judge or debate the pros and cons of specific American policies and trends, but anyone can acknowledge that at least some of the following are not positive developments or representative of the actions of a just and upstanding nation:

The United States ENFORCES its policies, to its economic benefit, by military suppression of much of the world. Foreign nations are not free to abandon the American sphere of influence, especially in regard to use of the US dollar for trade. Nations that attempt to sell oil in currencies other than dollars suffer the wrath of American policies and sanctions, followed up by the Air Force and the Army if said foreign leadership resists stubbornly.

America uses financial and military coercion to secure the biggest slice of the pie of money and resources for itself. The USA has about 4 percent of the world's population but uses 25 to 30 percent of the resources. And it wastes them. Americans dispose of more edible food, more functioning products, and more water than most nations consume. When the levels of pollution lead to things like holes in the ozone layer, nation-sized floating trash islands in the Pacific, and reproductive problems for animals like polar bears, shouldn't we question how we are harming the biosphere of the planet?

American schools, in the name of zero-tolerance, have become insanely intolerant of many normal behaviors. When a six year old boy can be suspended from school for acts such as kissing a girl's hand... having an imaginary gunfight with friends while pretending they are playing cowboys and Indians or cops and robbers or humans and aliens... or saying Merry Christmas – who benefits from this?

American schools, workplaces, culture, and government enforce the agenda that all choices are equally acceptable. Regardless of your beliefs on any particular issue or where your preferences lie across the spectrum from worshipping Jesus/Allah/God/Satan/Buddha/Vishnu or nothing at all, or whether you understand or appreciate the merits of socialism, fascism, capitalism, communism or corporatism, whether or not you favor full legalization of abortion, homosexuality, recreational drugs, automatic weapons, pornography, polygamy, prostitution, divorce, bankruptcy, or pre-marital sex – the liberal agenda that all choices are equally good and valid serves one primary purpose – to promote hyper-individualism and undermine the foundations that any group is based on.

I'm not arguing in favor of any particular basis for a state or a culture or a set of laws; but if we disallow basing society on logical presumptions (like the US Constitution, Bill of Rights, Magna Carta, etc.) or religious beliefs (of any religion) or ethnic/national unity then we remove all forms of self-identification. We remove social expectations of what someone in our group is supposed to do, we leave it up to every child to decide on their own what is acceptable – and children are notoriously poor decision makers. Even President Obama, when asked what his definition of sin is, said: "Being out of alignment with my values."[112] This is the easiest path to immorality – individualism taken to an extreme. This is not a uniquely American problem, but as the nation that dominates the cultural influence of young minds around the world through music, movies, and the internet, America is "the major exporter of immorality."[113]

Cardinal Ratzinger (later Pope Benedict XVI) said on April 18th, 2005 that there is a "...dictatorship of relativism that recognizes nothing as definite, and which leaves as the ultimate measure only one's ego and desires."[114] I would rather see my children raised under social/religious/cultural guidelines

I don't believe in that to see them raised under none at all, and I feel like the trend leads to hyper-individualism, self-gratification, a lack of empathy, and a lack of moral and ethical development. I would rather have my children question authority and ask why they are expected to do a particular thing that seems questionable or wrong, then to wonder why no one is ever expected to have to do anything right.

Before this trend began – up until approximately the 1960s – America enjoyed great prosperity, as if it had enjoyed the Lord's blessings as described in Deuteronomy 28:1-15 "Blessed shall you be in the city, and blessed shall you be in the country. Blessed shall be the offspring of your body and the produce of your ground and the offspring of your beasts, the increase of your herd and the young of your flock. Blessed shall be your basket and your kneading bowl. Blessed shall you be when you come in, and blessed shall you be when you go out. The Lord shall cause your enemies who rise up against you to be defeated before you; they will come out against you one way and will flee before you seven ways. The Lord will command the blessing upon you in your barns and in all that you put your hand to, and He will bless you in the land which the Lord your God gives you. The Lord will establish you as a holy people to Himself, as He swore to you, if you keep the commandments of the Lord your God and walk in His ways. So all the peoples of the earth will see that you are called by the name of the Lord, and they will be afraid of you. The Lord will make you abound in prosperity, in the offspring of your body and in the offspring of your beast and in the produce of your ground, in the land which the Lord swore to your fathers to give you. The Lord will open for you His good storehouse, the heavens, to give rain to your land in its season and to bless all the work of your hand; and you shall lend to many nations, but you shall not borrow. The Lord will make you the head and not the tail, and you only will be above, and you will not be underneath, if you listen to the commandments of the Lord your God, which I charge you today, to observe them carefully, and do not turn aside from any of the words which I command you today, to the right or to the left, to go after other gods to serve them. But it shall come about, if you do not obey the Lord your God, to observe to do all His commandments and His statutes with which I charge you today, that all these curses will come upon you and overtake you..." and then curses are listed instead of blessings.

I find it quite interesting that these verses describe America well, right up until the years when the nation really started to renounce God in earnest. Up until the 1960s, America abounded in prosperity. It was the breadbasket of the world; a major agricultural exporter. It was the biggest exporter of oil.

Its manufacturing was considered top of the line. It was the main creditor nation, lending money to other nations. America never lost its wars. As America changed and became less Christian, it became an agricultural importer; an oil importer – even dependent on foreign oil. American technology and manufacturing is no longer considered the best, even in the automobile or computer industries it once created and dominated. America is now the greatest debtor nation, owing trillions of dollars to China and Japan in particular. America lost the war in Vietnam, and it does not seem possible to win a war in Iraq or Afghanistan or on terrorism. Of course, this could just be a coincidence.

Let us contrast America's experience with Russia's experience, and also consider Genesis 12:3 in which God told the Jewish people: "I will bless those who bless you, and the one who curses you I will curse." In the mid 19th century, the Russian Empire had millions of Jews – by far the largest Jewish population on Earth. In 1881 the assassination of Tsar Alexander II was blamed on the Jews. Horrible persecution known as pogroms began, and by 1891 America had taken in two million fleeing Russian Jews. Uncle Sam was portrayed in one political cartoon as the new Moses, parting the Atlantic for Jews to cross. The US government began supporting the cause of a Jewish homeland around Jerusalem. The American military, which had almost no army or navy in 1880, defeated what had been a major European empire in 1898, when America destroyed the Spanish navy and took over Cuba, Puerto Rico, and the Philippines. This was unheard of – defeat of a European Empire by non-Europeans.

In Russia, persecution of the Jews continued. Russia, which had been a major power, had its navy destroyed by an Asian navy – the Japanese – at the battle of Tsushima Strait in 1905. This was unheard of – Europeans losing to Asians. American president Theodore Roosevelt brokered the peace between Russia and Japan, and the deal signed in America gave Japan almost everything they wanted. It was a humiliating defeat for Russia. In the First World War, Russia surrendered again and lost huge territories. The Russian monarchy was murdered and replaced with a communist regime. The church was outlawed as the Russian state became the officially atheist Soviet Union. It was simply announced that the Russian people, suddenly and as an entire nation – no longer believed in God.

While America won the First World War and was recognized as a major power, the Russians lost the war despite having been on the winning side because they surrendered with a separate peace. This was unheard of – being on the winning side, yet losing anyway. They lost about 300,000 square miles of territory with approximately 50 million inhabitants, and followed the losses imposed in the treaty ending WWI with about 7 million casualties of famine. Not long after, the Soviets saw about 25 million more deaths in World War II. America "only" lost about 250,000 men in WWII and emerged from the war as the greatest superpower, with the only atomic weapons and half the world's economic output. This was America's position when Israel needed a friend in 1948, and the United States was the first nation to recognize its existence on the day Israeli independence was declared. The Arabs (backed by Russia) immediately attacked Israel, and an American Army Colonel, David Marcus, went to Israel to head the Israeli military.[115] America was at the peak of its power and influence when Israel needed a friend.

I don't think the topics above are coincidences. As Proverbs 14:34 suggests, "Righteousness exalts a nation, but..." you can guess what happens when righteousness is lost. Like many other authors, "I believe that Babylon the Great that will fall is America."[116] I believe the nation will be punished. I think New York is the city of Mystery Babylon – the one that sits on many waters, has a high Jewish population, dominates world finance and commerce, is symbolized by a woman, and had towers that fell. There are many other less convincing signs I haven't even mentioned: according to R.A. Coombes in America, The Babylon – there are 33 unique Bible references describing America as the end times kingdom of Babylon and 66 clues unique to New York City.

I think New York will be destroyed within an hour, by fire, and that the wealthy traders of the world will weep at her burning. I suspect a nuclear weapon will be used, and that although blame may be placed on Iran – I suspect that someone in charge might be the one orchestrating the event – a false flag event that will lead to martial law and a powerful dictatorship under special presidential powers. This may happen approximately the same day as the revealing of the Antichrist's identity; if so he may gain great sympathy and dictatorial powers. The world community, stunned by the destruction of New York and paralyzed by fear of social upheaval – may leave many other nations looking for a political superman to offer hope and leadership during a time when economic collapse, invasion by Russia and China, and nuclear war are very real threats. I think the most likely man to be revealed to the entire world as the Antichrist in 2016 is the American President Barack Hussein Obama.

TIMING THE FINAL SEVEN YEARS

We have covered the evil characteristics of the Antichrist, especially through names and titles like the King of Babylon. Now that we know what the Antichrist is and what we can expect him to do someday, the top question we have not yet covered in detail is "Exactly when is this likely to happen?" If the date could be established to be centuries or millennia in the future, the person would be a name we don't know from a culture we don't understand. But if the date is coming soon, then the time and identity of the person will be very meaningful to us.

The Antichrist's reign begins in the middle of the final seven years of Daniel's 70th week. Many people refer to this as the seven year tribulation, but I think that the peace covenant which already started this period went largely unnoticed by the general population, and that the first 3.5 years are not going to be viewed as the tribulation until the second 3.5 years are underway. At the midpoint between these two halves of the final seven years the Antichrist enters a Temple in Jerusalem and demands our worship as if he is God on earth – after which he is in the final phase of his career – completely unrestrained, violent, arrogant, and deadly. This second half of the reign of the Antichrist will take up the final years of the present world.

One way to calculate the mid-point date when the Antichrist is revealed would simply be based on knowing the timing of the final seven years. Unfortunately, (for our purpose of clarification) the first few years are uneventful, except for the confirmation of a seven year covenant. And for many reasons, including that the world is not yet meant to understand everything – the details of the covenant are initially kept secret. The only major clue the Bible offers us will not be obvious until long after it occurs.

Bible prophecy may not say much about the start of the final seven years, but there are many descriptions of the climactic end. So when is the end of the world as we know it? What years have various prophecies and other clues led us to focus our attention on? If we can determine the end of the final seven years, we can subtract seven years to reach the beginning, and determine the mid-point three and a half years in to reach the date when the Antichrist can be expected to present himself. One potential clue to the time of the end involves the King of Babylon.

The phrase "the handwriting is on the wall" comes from a miraculous sign in the fifth chapter of the Book of Daniel. In 539 B.C., there was a feast in Babylon the night before the Persian army captured the city. At the feast, the King of Babylon and his guests ate and drank from gold and silver vessels stolen from the Jewish Temple some years earlier. Suddenly, the hand of God appeared at the wall and began writing. The king grew pale and called his wise men to interpret the message, but the Babylonian wise men didn't have a clue. Daniel 5:12 tells us they needed someone with "extraordinary spirit, knowledge and insight" capable of the "explanation of enigmas and solving of difficult problems."

When Daniel arrived he explained to the king: "you have exalted yourself against the Lord of heaven; and they have brought the vessels of His house before you." (Daniel 5:23) For desecrating His Temple in Jerusalem, the king would be punished. Daniel 5:25-30 warned "this is the inscription that was written out: 'MENĒ, MENĒ, TEKĒL, UPHARSIN.' This is the interpretation of the message: 'MENĒ'— God has numbered your kingdom and put an end to it. 'TEKĒL'— you have been weighed on the scales and found deficient. 'PERĒS'— your kingdom has been divided and given over to the Medes and Persians....' That same night Belshazzar the Chaldean king was slain." Within hours, the Persian King Darius conquered Babylon. The exact date is not agreed upon, but it was definitely October of 539 B.C.

One may notice the difference between "PERES" and "UPHARSIN" but I think it is minor. Peres means "is divided" and upharsin means "and dividings." The plurality of "dividings" along with the attention-getting use of two words may imply a second event to a future Babylon.

The Hebrew words of the inscription also have a monetary value. The Babylonian "tekel" was like the Hebrew "shekel." A mena was equal to 50 shekels, and an upharsin was equal to 25 shekels. So the words of the inscription were equal to 126 shekels, and with 20 gerahs per shekel, many have noted that 2,520 gerahs could refer to a judgment upon Babylon of seven years ("biblical years" or "prophetic years" of 360 days, times seven, which equals 2,520.) Many students of Bible prophecy were expecting a major event in 1982 – 2,520 years after the overthrow of the historical Babylon. A parallel event like the destruction of Mystery Babylon and a modern King of Babylon. But nothing critical happened in 1982. Did prophecy fail? Does the handwriting on the wall not lead us to the destruction of Mystery Babylon after a final week of years?

106

I believe it does. I believe that very soon, another "King of Babylon" we will know as the Antichrist will desecrate another Jewish temple in Jerusalem when he is revealed at the mid-point of the final seven years in 2016. And at the end of the final seven years, he will be punished and removed from his throne by the arrival of a much greater King, the King of Kings. My timeline of prophetic events puts the Second Coming of Jesus Christ in late 2019.

Multiply the actual number of days in a year (365.25, not 360) times seven, and we have just under 2,557. Starting in 539 B.C. and counting forward 2,557 years (with no year zero) we come to the year 2019, when the Antichrist who rose to the peak of his power in 2016 will be overthrown and killed. Could this just be a coincidence? Despite providing a nice segue from a chapter on Babylon to a chapter on timing the final seven years – I did not determine that 2019 A.D. is the final year of the world as we know it through "the handwriting on the wall."

But proving the significance of 2019 as the end of my timeline is crucial to convincing anyone about the importance of the Antichrist arriving in 2016. Anyone who has read my previous book, End Times and 2019, is already familiar with some of my research. Even the title of that book – and this book – make it clear that I think 2019 is the year in which Christ returns and the present world ends. Determining the end of Daniel's 70th week of years in December 2019 gave me my first reason to expect the arrival of the Antichrist 3.5 years earlier in June 2016 – and I believe there is a great deal of biblical evidence, largely in the form of astronomical clues, which point to December 2019 as the time of a pole shift – when the entire surface of the planet will move over the core. I believe pole shifts have happened before; that a previous one is described in Genesis, and that the next one described in Revelation is predictable.

I may lose many Christian readers by reviewing the evidence for periodic pole shifts, despite the fact that "the Holy Spirit has not yet completed 'His renovation of the face of the Earth' which long since has been predicted."[117] I understand that while recurring cycles are central to the beliefs of Hindus, Buddhists, the ancient Maya, the ancient Egyptians, and many other groups – they are not consistent with modern Christian theology. But there is massive physical evidence of pole shifts occurring repeatedly, with the most destructive catastrophes at the middle and end of the great cosmic cycles, and less destructive events one quarter and three quarters through the cycle. Should we ignore evidence that doesn't seem to fit with our understanding of

David Montaigne

Christian doctrine? Or is there a way to reconcile science to religion?

I have no problem acknowledging that the planet is 4.5 billion years old while simultaneously accepting that the Earth was created just thousands of years ago. Allow me to explain. This is not Orwellian "doublespeak." I'm not the Queen from Alice in Wonderland claiming "I've believed as many as six impossible things before breakfast." I've simply done enough research to understand what ancient writers meant when they used a phrase.

For example: it is very well established that when early writers used the term "Ethiopia" they meant the land immediately south of Egypt. In ancient Greek geography, this area of the Kingdom of Cush was called "Ethiopia." But Sudan is our current name for the nation south of Egypt; and the nation we now know as Ethiopia is a different land which is farther southeast. So when the Bible mentions "Ethiopia" (as in Ezekiel 38:5) are we supposed to assume it means the nation we call Ethiopia today? NO! But this is hardly intuitive to an American Christian reading an English Bible with minimal knowledge of African geography or ancient Greek cartography.

Likewise, when we read about "the Earth" in ancient texts, we must understand that to our distant ancestors, this phrase only represented the "new" surface conditions since the last pole shift – the current version of the earth. The creation of "the Earth" was mere thousands of years ago, just as the Bible tells us, because it is describing a recent re-creation. *(handwritten: do not agree!)*

Genesis 1:1 tells us "In the beginning God created the heavens and the earth." Isaiah 45:18 tells us "For thus says the Lord, who created the heavens (He is the God who formed the earth and made it, He established it and did not create it a waste place.)" This very clearly says that God "did not create it a waste place." Some other translations include "not empty He prepared it" and "he did not create it to be empty, but formed it to be inhabited." Yet Genesis 1:2 tells us "The earth was formless and void." If the earth was not created as an empty wasteland, how did it get that way just one sentence into the creation story in Genesis?

One top expert on the ancient meaning of Genesis in Hebrew and Aramaic is Arthur Custance. He studied the Book of Genesis before it was corrupted by numerous translations through Greek, Latin, and other languages, and reached us its final but slightly altered form in English. Custance says that in the earliest Aramaic version, Genesis 1:2 should be translated as "the earth was laid waste." He wrote: "After studying the problem for some thirty years and after reading everything I could lay my hands on pro and con and after accumulating in my own library some 300 commentaries on Genesis, the earliest being dated 1670, I am persuaded that there is, on the basis of the evidence, far more reason to translate Genesis 1:2 as 'But the earth had become a ruin and a desolation, etc.' than there is for any of the conventional translations."[118] God's past methods seem to involve pole shifts that cause world-destruction and renewal. With this in mind, Custance's conclusion makes perfect sense: that the correct English translation of the very first words of the Bible in Genesis 1:1-2 should be "IN A FORMER STATE GOD PERFECTED THE HEAVENS AND EARTH; BUT THE EARTH HAD BECOME A DEVASTATED RUIN."[119] While I have many reasons to believe that the last major global disaster involving a pole shift was over 12,000 years ago, a lesser event (which was still catastrophic for the much of the world) did occur approximately 6,000 years ago. *Then he would also have to believe that there were some humans or animals etc. previously because we know that death came thru Adam & Eve's sin.* I can only point out that there have been recurring cycles of global natural disasters in the past, that the Bible describes pole shifts repeatedly,[120] and that I believe they play a major role in our immediate future – despite their complete lack of mention in mainstream Christian teaching. A catastrophic pole shift is not the kind of happy ending which pastors will focus on if they want to keep their flock. Isaiah 28:19-22 describes that "it will be sheer terror to understand what it means.... destruction on all the earth."

If God chooses to make the "new heavens and new earth" of the next pole shift in Revelation the last and final pole shift for this planet, it is certainly within His power to do so. Or perhaps Christianity's "once and done" view of the future is linked to humanity but not to the Earth. Salvation may be eternal and final for us at a "new" location.

We can try our best to theorize about the future, but I can't avoid basing my conclusions on clues from the past. There was nothing eternal or final in the ancient understanding of the future. When Deuteronomy 7:9 tells us "Know therefore that the LORD your God, He is God, the faithful God, who keeps His covenant and His lovingkindness to a thousandth generation" – I can't help but notice that we are not told "forever," we are told "to a thousandth generation." I also notice that Neanderthals went extinct about 26,000 years ago. And that a full cycle of the precession of the earth's axis through all the signs of the zodiac – a cycle so closely linked to pole shift cycles and galactic superwave cycles, lasts about 26,000 years. A thousand generations would be about 26,000 years. Does something about our covenants with God change at the end of a 26,000 year cycle as Deuteronomy 7:9 may imply?

Zechariah 11:9-10 warns of a time when God says: "'What is to die, let it die, and what is to be annihilated, let it be annihilated; and let those who are left eat one another's flesh.' I took my staff Favor and cut it in pieces, to break my covenant which I had made with all the peoples."

As discussed in Douglas Krieger's <u>Signs in the Heavens and on the Earth</u>: "Question: What is the significance of the Mazzaroth spoken of in Job 38:31? Answer: Since the Mazzaroth specifies an interval of time (we know this to be 25,920 years known as the Great Precession of the Equinoxes), any answer to our question that pertains to the Lord asking Job if he can disrupt the time interval..."[121] implies that the cycle will reach its end on schedule.

Evidence forces me to conclude that an upcoming pole shift cataclysm will destroy civilization and change surface conditions so much that we will have a "new earth" as described in Revelation. I believe this event coincides with Jesus returning for His bride, and that the end of the present world at this heavenly wedding is the focal point of Bible prophecy. There is additional information from other ancient cultures and many branches of science – which should, in my opinion, be viewed as supporting evidence. With these issues in mind, please consider some of the many sources – biblical and not biblical – pointing to the end of the world around 2019:

One historically popular theory involves the creation of the world and the seven day week. The book of Genesis tells us the earth was created in six days, and that God rested on the seventh day. We are also taught in 2 Peter 3:8 "that with the Lord one day is like a thousand years, and a thousand years like one day." Many assume God will rest for a seventh millennium after 6,000 years of normalcy since the creation of the world. The most popular date for creation is the one Irish Archbishop James Ussher calculated in the 17th century; based on biblical genealogies, Ussher arrived at the creation date of Sunday, October 23, 4,004 B.C. Many Christians assumed that his calculations were accurate, and that around the start of the new millennium sometime near the year 2000, the world would be 6,000 years old and ready for Christ to arrive and start the millennium of rest.

Ancient Jews also felt that predicting a date for end times events was possible, for they warned that "he who announces the Messianic time based on calculation forfeits his own share in the future."[122] Israel's ancient "Dead Sea Scrolls also contain Hebrew astronomical texts about the 'royal science' including a 'horoscope written in code' and a 'true predictor of destiny.'"[123] Jewish scholarship and culture experienced a renaissance in ancient Babylon, where the Talmud was written as a set of commentaries to clarify and expound upon the meaning of the Torah (the books of Moses: the Old Testament.) The Talmud teaches that the Messiah will come no later than six thousand years after creation, similar to the idea based on Archbishop Ussher's creation date. But the Hebrew calendar is (as of the time of this writing) in year 5774, because the ancient Jews calculated creation of the world on October 7, 3761 B.C. Based on these ancient Jewish beliefs and calculations, the end of the world as we know it will occur no later than our Gregorian calendar year 2240 – though some scholars have tried to reconcile the Hebrew calendar to Ussher's chronology with the addition of "missing years" that would bring the last possible date much closer.

Sir Isaac Newton was one of the greatest scientific minds of all time. Many people know him only as an astronomer, and do not realize that he invented calculus and made enormous contributions to mathematics, astronomy, and physics. Newton spent decades obsessed with the orbital motion of the planets – but he also spent decades applying his intellect to biblical prophecies in Revelation and Daniel, attempting to find and decode hidden messages in the Bible that could clue him in to the timing of the end of the world. John Maynard Keynes found a chest full of Newton's notes on Bible prophecy after he took over Newton's old post as the Provost of Cambridge University. Keynes once said of Newton "He looked at the whole universe and all that is in it as a riddle, as a secret which could be read by applying pure thought to certain evidence, certain mystic clues which God had laid about the world to allow a sort of philosopher's treasure hunt to the esoteric brotherhood... He regarded the universe as a cryptogram set by the Almighty... By pure thought, by concentration of mind, the riddle, he believed, would be revealed to the initiate."[124] Newton assumed God had left us clues to everything, and that if we armed ourselves with math, science, and the Bible, we could decipher all the clues in the universe.

Newton's essay "Observations upon the Prophecies of Daniel, and the Apocalypse of St. John" was published after his death in 1727. The year 2060 is often cited since its 2003 discovery in Newton's 4,500 pages of notes – but in other comments on timing such prophecies he gave ranges of dates which rule out his most famous 2060 date.[125] In reality Newton was "constantly reappraising the date at which the Day of Judgment would come, seeing it as an event that was preordained but at the same time one whose date humans might deduce."[126] Newton never narrowed down his timing for the Second Coming or Judgment Day to his satisfaction, but the range of dates he focused on is in the 21st century.

The early 21st century also coincides with the start of the Age of Aquarius – and the Bible indirectly suggests we should pay attention to this point in time. We are told in Mark 14:13 "Go into the city, and a man will meet you carrying a pitcher of water; follow him." This is quite odd because the only "man" ancient Israelites would ever see carrying a pitcher of water was the constellation of Aquarius in the night sky. Men didn't carry water in ancient Israel. The reference in Mark "seems to suggest an intentional symbolic reference to the zodiacal sign of Aquarius – for in first-century Palestine the carrying of water was strictly women's work."[127]

We can see the strong social rules for this at play in John 4:6-7 "So Jesus, being wearied from His journey, was sitting thus by the well. It was about the sixth hour. There came a woman of Samaria to draw water. Jesus said to her, 'Give Me a drink.'" Jesus Christ waited and sat there until a woman came by. Some think He waited because His only purpose there was to speak with the woman. But he could have met her after she drew water. I suspect part of His purpose was to make a point about not drawing the water Himself. Because of strong social customs forbidding men from carrying or drawing water, He would rather wait for a woman than to satisfy his thirst sooner by getting His own water. Yet we should follow a man carrying water into the house… this would be unheard of – and to men of that time this would have been an obvious reference to the house of Aquarius – the water bearer. If through these conflicting examples the Bible is telling us to go into the house of Aquarius, what can we expect when we enter it?

The second chapter of John describes a wedding at Cana, and though it is unclear precisely who was getting married, some suggest that Jesus may have been the groom. The suggestion that events at Cana could have symbolized the first steps of Jesus' eventual wedding is not as outrageous as it may first sound, for His death is commonly thought of as "paying the bride price" and the entire Bible "is basically the story of a wedding, from start to finish. It is a love story of a loving Father, seeking the perfect Bride for His Son."[128] We see this theme beginning in Genesis, when Abraham seeks the perfect bride for his son, Isaac – and the theme continues through the gospels (Matthew 22:2 "The kingdom of heaven may be compared to a king who gave a wedding feast for his son.") until Jesus returns for His bride in Revelation.

As for the wedding at Cana, John 2:1-2 tells us "the mother of Jesus was there; and both Jesus and His disciples were" too. They would be there if Jesus were the bridegroom. We also know that providing the guests with

L, they would be
there because Jesus
was there – no matter who was getting married.

112

wine was the responsibility of the bridegroom and his family.

In modern times, the father of the bride traditionally pays for the wedding. This is because in medieval Europe, daughters were viewed as an economic burden on their fathers – and the custom of paying the groom a dowry to take a daughter was established. But in ancient Israel the labor and fertility of young women were highly valued, and the groom's family paid the bride price to purchase her from her father. The groom's family also paid for the wine – and all other aspects of the wedding feast – as hinted at above in Matthew 22:2 when the king "gave a wedding feast for his son."

In John 2:3-4, we read that "When the wine ran out, the mother of Jesus said to Him, 'They have no wine.' And Jesus said to her, 'Woman, what does that have to do with us? My hour has not yet come.'" It may be very telling that Mary implied it was Jesus' responsibility to provide wine at the wedding, and also that Jesus did not deny this responsibility. He did not say "I'm not the groom, tell him to provide wine!" Jesus merely commented on timing, as if emphasizing that the wine wasn't due yet because the meaningful moment of His wedding had not yet arrived.

Because He was not the groom! - Geesh!

Perhaps this was because the events at Cana were nowhere near as important as the heavenly wedding when He comes for His bride in the future. Perhaps we should consider that wine is symbolic of transformation, both in the fermentation of juice, or the more obvious turning water into wine – or being spiritually reborn as a Christian – or the entire world entering a new age. Wine is also a symbol for the transformation from the redemptive blood of Christ, and it was not quite time for Him to redeem everyone yet.

But Jesus did soon turn water into wine, providing wine as a bridegroom is supposed to do. John 2:9-11 tells us "When the headwaiter tasted the water which had become wine, and did not know where it came from (but the servants who had drawn the water knew), the headwaiter called the bridegroom, and said to him, "'Every man serves the good wine first, and when the people have drunk freely, then he serves the poorer wine; but you have kept the good wine until now.' This beginning of His signs Jesus did in Cana." There is no mention of anyone else as the bridegroom. No other man says "I provided no such wine, Jesus did." The Bible transitions smoothly from addressing the bridegroom about the wine in verse 10 and attributing the transformation of the wine to Jesus in verse 11. Many interpreters believe that Jesus, having provided the wine, is the bridegroom to whom the headwaiter is speaking.

If we view Jesus as a bridegroom, (as we must do by Revelation, and should consider doing here in John) we should be aware that an Israelite man traditionally took no more than two years to prepare a place for his bride at his father's house. The bride's family would prepare while they were "waiting for up to two years – for the bridegroom to come for the bride."[129] Of course only the father of the groom decided when preparations were complete, but traditionally this took less than two years. Hosea 6:2 also comes to mind: "He will revive us after two days; He will raise us up on the third day." This interpretation relies on the thousand years as a day concept from 2 Peter 3:8. If we assume a thousand-fold increase in the time needed for a heavenly wedding, perhaps Jesus would return after no more than two thousand years (prior to 2033 A.D.)

The great Greek philosopher Plato linked such a divine wedding with the conclusion of half a precession cycle (six of the twelve zodiac ages) and his "Nuptial Number" or "Number of the Bride" as described in The Republic is based on the 12,960 year classical figure for half a precession cycle. At the wedding at Cana, there are six empty stone water jars which had been set aside for purification. They may represent the six zodiac ages which have passed since the last major pole shift cataclysm Earth experienced at the time of the Pleistocene Extinction over 12,000 years ago.

Transforming the water jugs into wine could symbolize the transformation of the earth into a new earth. The Age of Pisces would be the sixth and final Age before the pole shift when the Age of Aquarius begins; the end of the Piscean Age would be represented by opening the sixth jar and pouring out its contents; and opening this sixth and final jar at the wedding would be like opening the sixth seal in Revelation 6:12-14, which sounds very much like a description of a pole shift: "I looked when He broke the sixth seal, and there was a great earthquake; and the sun became black as sackcloth made of hair, and the whole moon became like blood; and the stars of the sky fell to the earth, as a fig tree casts its unripe figs when shaken by a great wind. The sky was split apart like a scroll when it is rolled up, and every mountain and island were moved out of their places."

Plato's description of world-changing events at the end of a regular period of years also sounds like a pole shift. He said "for divine begettings there is a period comprehended by a perfect number"[130] and while his method of reaching the number (of years between catastrophes) is complex, I believe he was focused on a figure of 12,960 years between events. Plato also said about these occasions: "God himself accompanies and helps to wheel the revolving world... when the times are fulfilled, he lets it go, and the Universe begins to roll back... the end of the backward is the beginning of the forward movement, and when the forward ends, the backward begins, and the limits of both are marked by destruction among animals and men. When the backward movement ends, and the forward begins, a few men are left surviving..."[131] Aristotle later commented on Plato's idea "that all things change in a certain cycle: and that the origin of the change is a base of numbers."[132] Based on Plato's timing of the destruction of Atlantis we now are in the ballpark for Plato's very rough expectation of another divine wedding and destruction of civilization. Whose "wedding" did Plato (and Jesus) imply might occur near the end of the Age of Pisces and the start of the Age of Aquarius?

Jesus told the disciples at Cana to fill the six jugs with "water, which, when poured out (again at his direction), is found to have 'turned into wine'. We may interpret the symbols, both numerological and otherwise, to mean that the aqueous or Piscean age initiated by Jesus is supposed to be a preparatory age of purification leading directly to the glories of the expected Kingdom, and that this is destined to commence with the advent of the Aquarian age."[133] Certainly the Age of Aquarius is associated with pouring out the contents of a water jug, and many have associated this zodiac age with the expectation of a future Great Flood. Was Jesus associating this with His future wedding? Daniel 9:26 does warn us of such events that "its end will come with a flood."

Perhaps 1 Corinthians 10:11 is of relevance here when it says "Now these things happened to them as an example, and they were written for our instruction, upon whom the ends of the ages have come." There is no agreement by modern astronomers on when to officially date the end of the Age of Pisces and the beginning of the Age of Aquarius, but the French Institut Geographique National uses 2010 A.D. French author Jean Phaure agrees that the start of the Aquarian Age in the early 21st century sees "the Second Coming of Christ, the Last Judgment. Then a new cycle of humanity begins, probably with a reversal of the poles."[134]

The Mayan culture of ancient Mexico held many beliefs about their sun-god Kukulkan which are amazingly similar to Christian thoughts on the messiah. Mormon President John Taylor once wrote "The story of the life of the Mexican divinity, Quetzalcoatl [the Aztec name for the same god the Maya called Kukulkan] closely resembles that of the Savior; so closely, indeed, that we can come to no other conclusion than that Quetzalcoatl (Kukulkan) and Christ are the same being."[135]   The Maya expected Kukulkan to return to them at a future time to accept kingship over the earth. He would do this when the winter solstice sun (representing Kukulkan) reaches the great throne in the sky at the holy crossroads where the ecliptic crosses the Milky Way at the galactic center.   When did they expect their sun-god to be "crucified" on this heavenly cross?

As the earth orbits the sun, the sun appears to move clockwise through the constellations of the zodiac.   The galactic center is located between Sagittarius and Scorpio, and the sun appears to be near the point of the galactic center at some point every year. But for any certain day of the year, such as the winter solstice on December 21 - there is another, almost imperceptible cycle at play. The sun on any one particular date appears to move counter-clockwise through the zodiac once every 25,800 years. So while an alignment of the sun and the galactic center occurs every year throughout history, it only happens on the winter solstice for a few decades every 25,800 years. 1998 was the central year of this alignment, but due to the fact that the sun is not just a point (it has some size to it, a diameter of about one half a degree in our field of view) the winter solstice sun is still near the galactic center for several years to come.

Kukulkan is supposed to achieve enthronement and kingship over the earth after the winter solstice sun reaches the galactic center throne. Based on the famous Maya ballcourt game, with the sun represented by the gameball, and the galactic center represented by the goal-ring, we might assume that the astronomical alignment is considered complete only after the ball passes completely through the goal – after the sun's entire sphere passes the galactic equator. The Mayan Calendar's Long Count of over 5,125 years ended with great fanfare and hype on December 21, 2012. But John Major Jenkins explains that the end date was chosen within a range of years when Mayan astronomers knew that the alignment of the sun and the galactic center would occur every December 21. The end date "alignment must be conceived as a range extending over at least thirty-six years."[136]

December 21, 2012 may have marked the beginning of a final period of troubles and cataclysms the Maya believed would end with the triumphant return of their god-king after the last year in which the disk of the winter solstice sun still touches the galactic equator in 2018 – meaning 2019's winter solstice could be a significant end-date – December 21, 2019. There is an ancient Mayan drawing symbolizing a near alignment of several planets near the sun and galactic center at the end of the world in the Dresden Codex of the Popul Vuh – and it does correspond to the positions of the planets in December 2019 – not when the Long Count ended in 2012. As we know "from Hebrew tradition the association of angels with planets"[137] this may also correspond to the assembly when "all the angels were standing around the throne" in Revelation 7:11 on the last day.

In Tibetan Buddhism, there is a concept of the Kalachakra "Wheel of Time" which describes the cycles of time and the end of the current cycle. This is the only "end of the world timing" in Buddhist eschatology. Many Tibetans believed that Kalachakra knowledge was introduced into Tibet in 1027 and that end times events would begin 960 years later - when something happens in 1987.[138] Unless this began a series of events I don't know about, it would seem that Tibet's wheel of time hasn't ended yet. But I find the recent article "Dalai Lama Says He Should Be The Last Tibetan Spiritual Leader" very interesting as he says "the institution of the Dalai Lama has served its purpose."[139] What does he know that most people don't? And is this related to Pope Francis being the final pope on Saint Malachy's prophetic list?

Since Buddhism is heavily influenced by Hinduism, it may be relevant that many sources state that the Hindu Kali Yuga Age began in 3012 BC. Perhaps the timing of the Kalachakra Wheel of Time starting something new in 1987 was supposed to coincide with the 5,000th year of the Kali Yuga Age. In Hindu cosmology, at the end of time (which doesn't necessarily come at any certain date) "the Kalki (White Horse) Avatar, the tenth and final incarnation of Vishnu, will arrive. The heavens will open and he will appear on his white horse with his sword 'blazing like a comet.' He will destroy the wicked and restore purity. Entire continents will sink and rise in the process."[140] This reminds me of Christ arriving on a white horse, and also of a pole shift. But no Hindu prophecies exist to time the end of the world, and this does little to clarify what (if any) events began in 1987. Some authors, as early as Jose Arguelles in The Transformative Vision in 1975, choose to add a 25 year time period to the Kalachakra's prophecy for 1987 and reach 2012 (the end of the Mayan Long Count) as a cataclysmic year. This reminds me of the alignment of the winter solstice sun with the galactic center, which could be the "event" that began approximately in 1987. John Major Jenkins said this alignment is in effect for about 36 years – which could take us well beyond 2012, if we began in 1987.

Many people assume that if the "seven year tribulation" were already underway we would know – that it would be obvious if it had started in

December 2012. But the Bible says nothing about a reaction to the covenant that starts the clock ticking; only that after the first 3.5 years the treaty will be broken. The lack of emphasis on events in the intervening years implies a sense of normalcy, even if wars and a worsening economy and a program to build a new Temple should be getting everyone's attention. We should expect no obvious great events or sense of urgency at that time. It is quite possible that the crucial changes involve a secret covenant, with unpopular terms kept hidden from the general population. Matthew 24:38-39 warns us that most people will be blissfully unaware: "For as in those days before the flood they were eating and drinking, marrying and giving in marriage, until the day that Noah entered the ark, and they did not understand until the flood came and took them all away; so will the coming of the Son of Man be."

This all changes after 3.5 years, when scripture suddenly pays great attention to events at the mid-point and end of Daniel's seventieth week. I am reminded of bamboo – as for the first few years, it might grow two inches per year, then suddenly grow eighty feet the next year. The problems of the first 3.5 years may accelerate so slowly that they seem almost normal – until they reach the date when events suddenly accelerate. Perhaps waiting until the end times' fourth year for obvious signs is hinted at in Luke 13:6-9: "And He began telling this parable: "A man had a fig tree which had been planted in his vineyard; and he came looking for fruit on it and did not find any. And he said to the vineyard-keeper, 'Behold, for three years I have come looking for fruit on this fig tree without finding any. Cut it down!'" After three years of nothing, the impatient man saw what he expected in year four. Is this a parable of what we should expect in the final seven years – a hint that the first half of Daniel's seventieth week will not be recognizable as tribulation?

Ancient India also makes a relevant point on this. We previously addressed a longer Hindu quote about the "myth of Kuṇḍalinī, translated 'Serpent Power' and meaning 'coiled,' which may preserve the same cabala for 1,260. Kuṇḍalinī 'normally lies asleep in the form of a serpent in three and half coils.'"[141] This is similar to the Antichrist who is like a serpent, inactive or dormant or at least not yet revealed to us for 3.5 revolutions around the sun during the first half of the final seven years.

The Mayan "end date" in 2012 was so well-publicized that many people will scoff at my suggestion that 12/21/2012 was merely the beginning of the end – the start of the final seven year period of troubles in which the true end date in December 2019 was meant to be understood as more important. But I believe this is the case, both biblically and according to the Egyptians and even the Mayans. Despite the common assumption that the Mayan Long Count ending on December 21, 2012 marked an end, not the beginning of years of trouble – I believe December 2019 is the time which is central to their idea of world-renewal.

At several web sites[142] we can read that Mayan elders consider the focus on 2012 a misunderstanding of "their end date" - and that we only have a focus on "December 2012 FROM THOSE WHO HAVE SPOKEN FOR US. Therefore: We, the Mayans, and in accordance with our calculations, it is our wish that the dates to be considered for the completion of this cycle & the start of the new cycle be the ones signaled in the Mayan Calendar: - OXLAJUJ (13) KEME = COMPLETING this CYCLE of TIME in: 2019."[143]

The Mayan Pyramid of Kukulkan at Chichen Itza, Mexico, is also central to understanding Meso-American thoughts on the timing of the end of the current world age. This pyramid was astronomically aligned to coincide with the early 21st century. The pyramid has 91 steps on each of four sides and one at the top – 365 in all, representing the 365 days in the year in which the earth orbits the sun. Because Chichen Itza is in the tropics, there are two days a year when the sun is directly overhead at noon – directly above the pyramid/throne. But there is only a brief window of years in the 25,800 year cycle of precession when the Pleiades constellation - which according to Mayan mythology, should symbolically crown their sun-god on his coronation – is in the right position directly behind and above the sun on May 23, the first of the two zenith dates.

Interestingly, "the Syriac name for the Pleiades is Succoth, which means 'booths.' In the Middle East, the Pleiades is 'the congregation of the judge, or ruler.'"[144] We should note that many Bible prophecy scholars expect Jesus to return on the Jewish holiday of Sukkot, (The Feast of Tabernacles) when the Lord is expected to dwell with us again. Through this name for the Pleiades, we see that even in Israel the constellation is linked with judgment and crowning the king and the end of the world.

For the Maya, the Pleiades represent the crown and the alignment with the sun and the Pleiades in the zenith directly above the pyramid/throne is pivotal for timing the coronation of their god-king. The proper alignment over the Pyramid of Chichen Itza, with the sun and Pleiades directly in the zenith, only achieves the proper alignment for one brief span of years every 25,800 years. "Kukulkan's pyramid is a precessional clock with its alarm set for the twenty-first century."[145] So in Job 38:31 when God asks: "Can you bind the chains of the Pleiades?" perhaps He is suggesting that we cannot delay the inevitable end of the great cycle.

Egypt's Great Pyramid may also confirm this timing. Above ground, the Great Pyramid represents the northern hemisphere of the Earth at 1/43,200 scale. If we imagine the tunnels and chambers below to be an underground mirror image of equal size, then the entire shape represents the entire planet. Right now the pyramid is incomplete – the top is not built up to a point – symbolizing that the world is not complete. Many images, including the Great Seal of the United States (as shown on the back of the one dollar bill) show the Eye of Ra (or Horus, or God, or Masonry's "Great Architect") looking down on us from where the top of the pyramid would be, as if suggesting that we aspire to reach God. Even ancient India's Rg Veda texts mention "He, the first origin of this creation... Whose eye controls this world in highest heaven."[146] If the stone top of Egypt's Great Pyramid were completed, it would be 5780 inches high. Several British archeologists believed that the inch is an ancient measurement and that measurements within the Great Pyramid are prophetic timelines with inches equal to years. The height in inches may refer to Hebrew calendar year 5780, which corresponds with December 2019 and may represent "completion of the world" or the end of the world as we know it in 2019.

David Flynn, author of <u>Temple at the Center of Time: Newton's Bible Codex Deciphered and the Year 2012</u>, reached similar conclusions based on measurements around the Temple in Jerusalem, and the notes from decades of research and analysis of Bible prophecies by Sir Isaac Newton. His final seven years begin in late 2012 and end in late 2019. As the end of an online pdf file summarizing Flynn's conclusions words it: "Based on the numbers, it looks more and more clear that the time between the end of 2012 and the beginning of 2020 encompasses the last week of Daniel."[147]

Televangelist Jack van Impe also suggests that 2019 could be the last year of our present world. Though several references to a generation indicate that the Bible intends us to assume a length of 40 or 70 years, van Impe calculates a number in between the two common answers. He notes that Matthew chapter 1 describes the generations from Abraham to Christ as 2160 years, and that if you divide this by 42 generations, you get between 51 and 52 years per generation. He adds 52 years to the historically pivotal year 1967, when the Israelis recaptured eastern Jerusalem, and took possession of the land of the Temple Mount for the first time in thousands of years – and reaches 2019. One could also take the 4000 years from Adam to Christ and divide by 77 generations to get approximately 51.9 years per generation.

Jack van Impe's reasoning behind adding the 52 years (a generation) to 1967 is based on Matthew 24:32-34 "Now learn the parable from the fig tree: when its branch has already become tender and puts forth its leaves, you know that summer is near; so, you too, when you see all these things, recognize that He is near, right at the door. Truly I say to you, this generation will not pass away until all these things take place." The fig tree is generally understood to represent Israel, and the territorial expansion of Israel following victory in the Six Day War in 1967 is Israel growing, or the fig tree putting forth its leaves. Others would argue that Psalm 90:10 tells us a generation is 70 years "As for the days of our life, they contain seventy years." But this fits as well, because Israel was created as a nation in 1948; and the war of independence against their Arab neighbors started in 1948 and ended in 1949... therefore the firstfruits of Israel – the first generation of young men conceived in 1948 and born in 1949 in the new nation of Israel – these were the soldiers liberating the Temple Mount in 1967, and they will be turning 70 in 2019, 70 years after Israel's war of independence ended.

There are certainly enough clues indicating that we are at approximately the right moment in history for the biblical end times. Ussher's estimate points near the year 2000. The Hebrew calendar would suggest the end must be before 2240. Isaac Newton focused on the 21st century. The Maya focused on astronomical alignments in 2012 and 2019. Daniel's "handwriting on the wall" may point to 2019. Egypt's Great Pyramid hints at 2019. Israeli history plus the length of a biblical generation points to 2019. If we assume the end of Daniel's 70th week is in 2019, then 3.5 years earlier would be the mid-point of the seven years when the Antichrist enters a rebuilt Jewish Temple and proclaims himself to be God – sometime in 2016, depending on how late in the year 2019 we assume the 70th week of years ends.

Can we narrow it down a little better than that? Of course we can. I have already made the case for December 21, 2019 as the last day of Daniel's 70th week, and have explained the reasoning for this conclusion at great length in End Times and 2019. The concept of periodic, cataclysmic pole shifts is central to my case. Despite many biblical references to them, so far in this book I have tried to keep pole shift references to a minimum. It may not seem that way to Christian readers who consider the idea alien to biblical teaching – but to fully understand the end of the present world, I believe we must dive far deeper into the biblical evidence of pole shifts.[148]

David Montaigne

We have already discussed Arthur Custance and his translation of the beginning of Genesis: "IN A FORMER STATE GOD PERFECTED THE HEAVENS AND EARTH; BUT THE EARTH HAD BECOME A DEVASTATED RUIN." I believe Genesis describes a previous pole shift, while Revelation describes the next one. Revelation 16:18-20 says "there was a great earthquake, such as there had not been since man came to be upon the earth, so great an earthquake was it, and so mighty. The great city was split into three parts, and the cities of the nations fell. Babylon the great was remembered before God, to give her the cup of the wine of His fierce wrath. And every island fled away, and the mountains were not found." Many verses describe global earthquakes, global flooding, the destruction of all cities and nations, the sky appearing to roll up like a scroll, etc.

Isaiah 24:1 sounds like a pole shift: "Behold, the Lord lays the earth waste, devastates it, distorts its surface and scatters its inhabitants." Job 9:5-6 tells us "It is God who removes the mountains, they know not how, when He overturns them in His anger; who shakes the earth out of its place, and its pillars (poles) tremble." Nahum 1:5-6 says "Mountains quake because of Him and the hills dissolve; indeed the earth is upheaved by His presence, the world and all the inhabitants in it." Hebrews 12:26-27 explains "Yet once more I will shake not only the earth, but also the heaven. This expression, "Yet once more," denotes the removing of those things which can be shaken." The Bible even comments on its mention of "yet once more" to emphasize that this has happened before, and will happen again! The Book of Genesis describes past pole shifts; Revelation describes the next one.

There are also some very interesting verses in non-canonical books – books which we know existed, but did not make the final cut for inclusion into the Bible we know today. The Book of Jasher was referenced in 2 Samuel 1:18 and in Joshua 10:13 in regard to the sun standing still in the sky. Jasher 6:11 tells us: "And on that day [the day of the Flood] the Lord caused the whole earth to shake, and the sun darkened, and the foundations of the world raged, and the whole earth was moved violently, and the lightning flashed, and the thunder roared, and all the fountains in the earth were broken up, such as was not known to the inhabitants before." Noah 65:1 says "Noah saw the Earth had tilted and that its destruction was near." 2 Esdras 2:4 says "nations will be in confusion; the movement of the stars will be changed."

Alan Kurschner summarizes: "toward the end of the great tribulation a cluster of unique celestial disturbances will cause an upheaval and global blackout."[149] Charles Ryrie commented on this and noted the description like a new world "rising from the decay and wreck of the old world" and "literally this [description in Revelation] indicates a complete change in climactic conditions."[150] John Shorey wrote that it is "as if every continental plate on the earth is moved out of place at the same time."[151] As Bruce Killian of scripturescholar.com says: "Pole shifts are recorded in the Bible, if you know how to look for them, from the very beginning."[152]

The Bible is not the only ancient book describing pole shifts. Many books around the world give us mathematical and astronomical hints at the recurring, periodic cycles of destruction. Since Hamlet's Mill it has "come to be generally recognized that ancient myths encode a vast and complex body of astronomical knowledge."[153] Ernest McClain offers "a persuasive explanation of crucial passages in texts of world literature — the Rg Veda, the Egyptian Book of the Dead, the Bible, Plato — that have defied critics of the separate concerned disciplines. All these passages deal with numbers. What sounds like mathematical nonsense or literary gibberish has"[154] meaning when we apply the ancient warnings to pole shifts. Our ancestors understood what had happened before and have warned us about what will happen again. Over 2,600 years ago, Solon and other Greeks were told by the Egyptian priesthood: "there have been, and there will be again, many destructions of mankind.... you remember one deluge only, whereas there were many of them."[155] Jay Weidner, co-author of <u>The Great Cross of Hendaye</u>, explains that our ancestors have warned us that "an angry sun" is involved in "a periodic catastrophe"[156] that repeatedly affects our planet.

Even Nostradamus suggests in Quatrain 2:81 of his prophecies that at a time with "fire from the sky... the urn threatens Decaulion again" (the biblical flood) "after Libra will leave her Phaethon" which refers to the Greek myth of the sun veering off course in the sky. Nostradamus also wrote: "the great translation will be made and it will be such that one would think that the gravity of the earth has lost its natural movement and that it is to be plunged into the abyss of perpetual darkness."[157]

There is also physical evidence of pole shifts all over the world, if you know how to look for it. Bands of ancient coral reefs criss-cross the earth, marking the unusual orientation of many former equators. There are oil fields and fossilized forests deep underneath deserts and oceans and ice sheets. The land west of Hudson Bay is rising from "isostatic rebound" at a rate that indicates it was under the center of a polar ice cap over 12,000 years ago. The Pleistocene Extinction occurred approximately 12,500 years ago, (10,500 B.C.) when something killed off mammoths, saber-toothed tigers, giant sloths, New World horses, and so many other animals that it is believed to be the biggest loss of species since the dinosaurs died. North Atlantic Ocean temperatures rose over ten degrees in just a few years just after this. A wave of human migration from Asia to Alaska followed.

Lava flows have magnetic ions solidified in the rock, oriented to magnetic north at the moment of solidification. Analysis of the lava flows at Steens Mountain, Oregon concludes that magnetic north moved approximately 36 degrees in no more than six days[158] – a minimum of six degrees per day if it took 6 days (which would fit the biblical timeline for creation of the world) or even faster if it wasn't spread out so evenly over six days. Similar testing on lava flows at Battle Mountain Nevada show two flows one year apart – with 53 degree changes at some point during the year in between.[159]

In the science of dendrochronology, tree-ring evidence is well established through about 10,460 B.C.[160] This is consistent with the Pleistocene extinction and a cataclysm near 10,500 B.C. washing most forests away. Egyptologists who know astronomy and archeo-astronomy have determined that the pyramids at Giza are aligned to the stars as they appeared around 10,500 B.C.[161] This is roughly one half precession cycle in our past, and may be the approximate date of the last major pole shift. A much lesser catastrophe may have occurred one quarter cycle back, just over 6,000 years ago. The biggest cataclysms may happen every full precession cycle, like the one that helped eliminate Neanderthal Man about 26,000 years ago – and like the one we are due for now as we enter the Age of Aquarius.

Could being kicked out of Eden, and Noah's Flood be descriptions of pole shifts? Could the tree with a serpent in it be a metaphor for the world axis pointing to the constellation Draco the dragon? Could Adam and Eve's sudden need for clothing indicate a change to a cooler climate in their original homeland? Could the description of Eden blocked off by a flaming sword in the sky describe a borealis seen over their old, abandoned homeland – just like the extreme north and south of the earth see at night today?

Many Christians are quick to point out "the rainbow covenant" because they believe God will never flood the earth again, and that a pole shift would flood the earth and is therefore ruled out by this covenant. As I believe this covenant is misunderstood, let's inspect Genesis 9:11-17: "'I establish My covenant with you; and all flesh shall never again be cut off by the water of the flood, neither shall there again be a flood to destroy the earth.' God said, 'This is the sign of the covenant which I am making between Me and you and every living creature that is with you, for all successive generations; I set My bow in the cloud, and it shall be for a sign of a covenant between Me and the earth. It shall come about, when I bring a cloud over the earth, that the bow will be seen in the cloud, and I will remember My covenant, which is between Me and you and every living creature of all flesh; and never again shall the water become a flood to destroy all flesh. When the bow is in the cloud, then I will look upon it, to remember the everlasting covenant between God and every living creature of all flesh that is on the earth.' And God said to Noah, 'This is the sign of the covenant which I have established between Me and all flesh that is on the earth.'"

The people of that time had never experienced rain - so they had never seen a rainbow until after the flood.

There is no mention of a "rainbow" in Noah's story. It is also implied that this is a new kind of bow/cloud combination not seen before, one that God sets up after the flood as a sign to calm down future generations afraid to leave the mountains they survived in to repopulate the lowlands where civilization was destroyed. I suggest that "the cloud" is not a regular cloud at all, but the incoming cloud of cosmic dust associated with the arrival of a galactic superwave emanating from the center of our galaxy.

Ezekiel 32:7-8 warns "And when I extinguish you, I will cover the heavens and darken their stars; I will cover the sun with a cloud and the moon will not give its light. All the shining lights in the heavens I will darken over you and will set darkness on your land." The sun and its solar wind will eventually push the dust out back out of the solar system, but I think we can count on at least three days of darkness.

Pole shifts are very likely triggered by the impact of periodic outbursts from the black hole at the center of our galaxy. In End Times and 2019 I devoted an entire chapter to the theories of Dr. Paul LaViolette. In Earth Under Fire, he explains how the center of every spiral galaxy, including our own, goes through periodic phases of activity. We see nothing for thousands of years, then like clockwork – or a cosmic version of "Old Faithful" – we suddenly notice an explosion of light, radiation, and gravity waves.

I am reminded of 1 Kings 19:11-12 "And behold, the Lord was passing by! And a great and strong wind was rending the mountains and breaking in pieces the rocks before the Lord; but the Lord was not in the wind. And after the wind an earthquake, but the Lord was not in the earthquake. After the earthquake a fire, but the Lord was not in the fire."

When such a superwave does reach us, it energizes our sun and all the planets, including Earth. We experience the complex effects of a global catastrophe involving a pole shift, flooding, and cosmic dust pushed into the inner solar system. This activates the Sun into a T-Tauri stage in which it puts out more light, heat, radiation, and "extinction-level solar flares"[162] which were a major cause of the loss of many species during the Pleistocene Extinction almost 13,000 years ago.

There are a few such spherical shells of radiation and gravity waves expanding outwards from the center of all spiral galaxies all the time, including our own. We can clearly see the effects of such superwaves in Andromeda, our neighboring galaxy – because we are far off to the side. We have indirect evidence of the last major superwave in our own galaxy, because several major supernovae were set off by the arrival of the same superwave.[163] But we can't see them approaching directly in our line of sight in our own galaxy before they arrive because they aren't solid objects – they are bands of radiation moving at the speed of light. "Even though a nearing superwave would have left the Galactic center 23,000 years ago, we are essentially blind to determine such future events through our normal senses. When we feel earthquakes and see its signs in the sky, it will have already arrived and our time to prepare will have run out."[164] We use reflections of light to see things, but we cannot see a reflection off light itself before it arrives. Because of this inability to observe superwaves as they are coming (coupled with the desire of governments to hide evidence of a coming catastrophe) Dr. LaViolette's theory on gravity waves and galactic superwaves is based on evidence of prior events thousands of years ago and has not been widely accepted. One of his online comments on the arrival of the next superwave suggests that "large tidal forces appearing with the wave's arrival could cause a substantial torquing of the Earth's spin axis."[165]

To put the power of these events in perspective – do not compare the incoming superwave to any wave you have seen in the ocean. It is not like a wave of water ON the earth. The more valid comparison would be between a wave on the beach and a grain of sand – for the earth is tiny compared to such a galactic superwave – it is an expanding sphere approximately 46,000 light years in diameter when it arrives here. This is approximately 270 quadrillion miles wide; as wide as 34 trillion Earths or 312 billion suns placed side by side. It is incomprehensibly large and although its punch has been thinned and weakened as it spreads out, its arrival will still be strongly felt – and will be likened to the presence of God. Its arrival will dominate human history for a thousand years.

When the event horizon of such an outburst reaches us, we will first be hit with a dangerous burst of gamma rays, then gravity waves, then the center of the galaxy will appear to have a bright blue light. This blue light, approximately 20-30 times brighter than Venus or Jupiter – will be bright enough to be visible even during the day. Over the next few centuries, light reflected off dust and gas clouds "near" (within a few hundred light years of) the galactic center will illuminate a larger and larger oval area around the central blue "star." The Hopi described it as the arrival of the Sasquasohuh or Blue Star Kachina. The Egyptians called it "the eye of Horus." India's Hindus referred to it as "The Seat [or Navel] of Vishnu." Islamic prophecies describe the "emergence of the Tariq Star which will trigger switching of the Poles of the Earth and major changes in the environment."[166] This occurs on "The Day when the earth will be changed to a different earth, and so will be the heavens; and (men) will be marshalled forth before Allah."[167] In the Bible it was described as "the Shekinah Glory," and we should not overlook the connection to the appearance of a special "star" at the birth of Jesus Christ. Ezekiel 1:2-27 said "over their heads there was something resembling a throne, like lapis lazuli [Hebrew: "eben-sappir – sapphire] in appearance; and on that which resembled a throne, high up, was a figure with the appearance of a man… and there was a radiance around Him." Exodus 24:10 also emphasizes the blue color of God's location: "they saw the God of Israel; and under His feet there appeared to be a pavement of sapphire." Within a few centuries this glowing blue region in the sky will be quite large at night, and will be visible for approximately a thousand years – likely corresponding to "the Millenium."

As the galactic center appears to be near the tip of the arrow held in the bow of the constellation Sagittarius, the recognizable arrangement of stars set in the glowing cloud after the minor superwave before Noah's flood (and after the next major superwave event) would be the bow and arrow of Sagittarius. About a thousand years after Noah's flood, the cloud would no longer be visible. As described in Genesis chapter 9, if the sign of the covenant is gone, the covenant is no longer in effect. But many thousands of years ago, knowing that another similar event would not happen as long as they saw the bow in the cloud was extremely reassuring to people who still saw the evidence of God's world-destroying wrath when they visited coastal lowlands and cautiously hesitated to repopulate the fertile but recently annihilated river valleys.

Such devastation from superwaves and pole shifts is reflected in the Book of Genesis from the very beginning – and we would expect "the beginning" to begin at the point of the most recent new creation during a pole shift event. But perhaps the most obvious clue that we should look at "the beginning" in Genesis as one of many periodic pole shifts is found in Jeremiah 4:23-26 "I looked on the earth, and behold, it was formless and void; and to the heavens, and they had no light. I looked on the mountains, and behold, they were quaking, and all the hills moved to and fro. I looked, and behold, there was no man, and all the birds of the heavens had fled. I looked, and behold, the fruitful land was a wilderness, and all its cities were pulled down before the Lord, before His fierce anger." This clearly describes a pole shift AFTER men have built cities (and a pole shift reduces them to rubble) and AFTER there are mountains to quake and birds to flee... when the earth is "formless and void" and described with the same phrases as in the beginning of Genesis. Isaiah 14:21 also sounds like God was against man's repopulating the world after a pole shift when He said "They must not arise and take possession of the earth and fill the face of the world with cities."

I believe that pole shifts occur repeatedly and regularly, as part of a periodic cosmic cycle, and that our ancient ancestors understood this cycle. The Bible gives numerous prophetic clues about the date of the next such event. They all line up for one particular day.

Haggai 2:18-22 tells us "from the four and twentieth day of the ninth month... I am going to shake the heavens and the earth..." Kislev 24 is the night before Hanukkah, and is also the anniversary of the laying of the foundation of the Lord's Temple. In 2019, Kislev 24 is our December 21. Matthew 24:20-22 tells us "pray that your flight will not be in the winter, or on a Sabbath. For then there will be a great tribulation, such as has not occurred since the beginning of the world until now." Which makes sense, because the pole shift they are warning us about last happened the last time the world was "destroyed" and "recreated" with vastly different surface features. In 2019, Kislev 24 and December 21 are the same day, when the Sabbath (Saturday) is also the first day of winter. This is the shortest day of the year, and we know the celestial disturbances described for the end times begin when God cuts the days short. Matthew 24:22 tells us: "Unless those days had been cut short, no life would have been saved; but for the sake of the elect those days will be cut short."

Mark Biltz assumes these warnings about the end times Sabbath and winter will coincide with Hanukkah.[168] Assuming he believes in the significance of the four blood moons he wrote a book about as well – and that end times events will occur somewhat near the dates of the blood moon eclipses in

2014 and 2015 – then he must realize that the only year in the near future in which the eve of Hanukkah on Kislev 24 aligns appropriately with the Sabbath and the winter solstice is 2019. Indirectly (very indirectly, without sticking his neck out) I think Biltz is telling us he assumes the end is due in 2019. Biltz also noted that the peak of Noah's flood, after the forty days of rain, was on Kislev 27[169] – which means that what very well may have been the last global catastrophe peaked at the same day of the year as the middle of our upcoming pole shift in 2019.

Most impressively, the positions of the sun, moon, and planets act out all the major steps of a week-long ancient Jewish wedding ceremony from December 21-28, 2019, coinciding with Hanukkah. The Jewish holiday of Hanukkah has been commercialized but it is not just a "Jewish Christmas" for giving gifts. The holiday was created to celebrate the successful Jewish uprising against the Seleucid King Antiochus, who oppressed the Jews and defiled their temple by placing a statue of Zeus (with his own face) in the temple to be worshipped. He tried to eradicate the Jewish religion and culture, which would have destroyed them as a distinct people. Antiochus is often described as an early version of the Antichrist; and even his name (ANTI-oCHus) shows similarities. I must conclude that the overlap of a holiday based on cleansing and rededication of the Temple after victory over an evil, Antichrist-like leader – along with astronomical alignments correlating to all the major steps in a Jewish wedding is no coincidence, and that the planets are meant to be seen as signs of the Bible's most crucial wedding – that of Christ coming for His bride – in late December 2019.

I believe these alignments, and the wedding in the sky, and the pole shift – will begin immediately after the Antichrist is destroyed by the Son of God. Joel 2:30 tells us "I will display wonders in the sky and on the earth… Before the great and awesome day of the Lord comes." The week from December 21-28, 2019 will host the most impressive events in history. Astronomically, as one author writes, there "will be a cluster of disturbed celestial bodies portending the impending wrath of God. It will be unprecedented so the world will not mistake it."[170] This is described briefly in Matthew 24:29, when Jesus Himself says that "immediately after the tribulation [ending 12/21/2019] of those days the sun will be darkened, and the moon will not give its light, and the stars will fall from the sky, and the powers of the heavens will be shaken." This is described in great detail for over six pages in End Times and 2019; we will only do a brief review here. Some of the most impressive correlations which require little explanation include:

David Montaigne

The Hakafot – in this wedding ritual, the bride circles the groom at the altar seven times before the wedding ceremony starts. Astronomically, Jesus/the groom is the sun, and we on the earth are the bride. The earth circles the sun for seven orbits (exactly seven years) during Daniel's 70th week of years right before the final week in which the wedding pole shift take place. The concept of destruction after circling seven times and the passage of a week is foreshadowed in Joshua 6:4-5 "seven priests shall carry seven trumpets of rams' horns before the ark; then on the seventh day you shall march around the city seven times, and the priests shall blow the trumpets. It shall be that when they make a long blast with the ram's horn, and when you hear the sound of the trumpet, all the people shall shout with a great shout; and the wall of the city will fall down flat."

Another fascinating step in the ancient Jewish wedding ceremony is the yichud – the name of a short reprieve in the middle of the ceremony, and also the name of the private seclusion room which the bride and groom enter for eight minutes, during which the groom gives the ring to the bride. On December 26, 2019 there is a total solar eclipse visible from the Middle East at sunrise. Isaiah chapter 13 warns us that right before Judgment Day, when "the day of the Lord is near" (13:6) and "the earth will be shaken from its place" (13:13) we also read "the sun will be dark when it rises." (13:10) My favorite astronomical software, Stellarium, shows that from the point of view of Jerusalem, the moon will be in front of the top portion of the sun from about 5:54AM until 6:35AM, at which point the solar eclipse is total, and the moon – appearing somewhat smaller than the sun, allows us to see what is commonly called "the ring of fire" – the sun's corona showing around the edge of the moon. A total solar eclipse lasts a maximum of just over seven and a half minutes, corresponding to the eight minutes the groom has to give a bride a ring in the yichud step of the wedding.

By around 6:42AM the moon will still be about 99 per cent in front of the sun, but towards the bottom, with the top edge of the sun starting to become visible. But sunrise in Jerusalem is officially 6:37AM, while the eclipse is still total. Some Israelis will not have a good view of the eclipse near sea level, but Jerusalem is a mountain city; the Temple Mount's altitude is 2427 feet above sea level – and from high ground one can see a more distant horizon and watch sunrise earlier. They should be able to watch the sun be dark as it rises, just as the prophecy in Isaiah 13:10 describes.

At this time of year (late December) the sun happens to be crossing the Milky Way – the bright band of stars which seems to divide the heavens in half. In Genesis 28:12 "a ladder was set on the earth with its top reaching to heaven; and behold, the angels of God were ascending and descending on it." Jacob's Ladder describes the stars of the Milky Way as they appeared in a vertical column in the night sky. In John 1:51, Jesus describes a similar end times sign: "Truly, truly, I say to you, you will see the heavens opened and the angels of God ascending and descending on the Son of Man." This sign involves the column of stars we call the Milky Way, with the Sun at the bottom of the column. We could only see the stars above if the sun on the horizon were dark, as it will be on December 26, 2019.

One of the final steps of the week-long wedding celebration involves the best man. After the newlyweds have consummated their marriage in the honeymoon chamber, the best man would hover just outside the door, waiting for a knock and voice from the groom inside to let him know the couple was ready to come out momentarily – officially as husband and wife. Soon, the great feast of the wedding supper would begin. But first, with great fanfare and excitement and trumpet blowing, the best man would loudly announce that the married couple was about to come out. Astronomically, Elijah/John the Baptist is represented by Jupiter as the best man. From our point of view, Jupiter is right at the edge of the sun's corona on 12/28/2019, repeatedly disappearing and reappearing from view by "the door." In John 10:9 Jesus (represented by the sun) told us "I am the door."

Since I believe this solar alignment with Jupiter happens on Judgment Day, I have investigated the symbolism of Jupiter thoroughly. In Greek mythology, it was Zeus/Jupiter who overthrew the old order of the gods and becomes the new King of the Gods. Jupiter is known as "King of the Planets." Perhaps more importantly, the Hebrew words for "king" and "Jupiter" are "melech" and "Zedek." This sounds a lot like Melchizedek, as in Hebrews 7:1 "Melchizedek, king of Salem, priest of the Most High God, who met Abraham." If Abraham was the first Jew, before Moses, before the Old Testament was written, before Judaism began, how was there already a King of (Jeru)Salem, who was "priest of the Most High God"?

Let's look at the larger context of Hebrews 7:1-3 "For this Melchizedek, king of Salem, priest of the Most High God, who met Abraham as he was returning from the slaughter of the kings and blessed him, to whom also Abraham apportioned a tenth part of all the spoils, was first of all, by the translation of his name, king of righteousness, and then also king of Salem, which is king of peace. Without father, without mother, without genealogy, having neither beginning of days nor end of life, but made like the Son of

God, he remains a priest perpetually." This hardly sounds like a mortal king or priest. It definitely sounds more like an immortal or everlasting angelic being or heavenly body like a planet.

Hebrews 2:17 explains that one reason Jesus took human form was "so that He might become a merciful and faithful high priest." Melchizedek was a great high priest. If he is a description of Jesus Christ, why does the name associate him with Jupiter? Is there something amazing that Jesus' main heavenly representation (the Sun) does in conjunction with Jupiter? I believe so – on Judgment Day – December 28, 2019 – when Jupiter is, from our viewpoint, spending a rare day behind the sun.

Some astrophysicists believe that the force of gravity is conveyed by a certain type of subatomic particle called a muon neutrino. Normally travelling in a straight line, these "gravitons" are scattered when passing through the multi-million degree temperatures of the solar corona. What does this mean to us? There is a measureable gravitational change on Earth when Jupiter appears to go behind the edge of the sun's at its corona. Like everything else in the universe, Earth is in an ever-changing gravitational balance between heavenly bodies. Visual brightness has nothing to do with gravity, but because gravity and apparent brightness both have a lot to do with the size and distance of heavenly bodies, the brightest objects in our skies do (coincidentally) have the largest gravitational influence. The sun and moon exert the strongest tugging on Earth's motion, followed by very, very distant runner ups Jupiter and Venus and Saturn.

When a planet appears to go behind the sun's corona, and the gravitational tugging of its muon neutrinos are scattered, it is as if a hypothetical rope is suddenly let go in a game of tug of war. Because the huge ropes in this three dimensional tug of war – the sun and moon – still remain strong, the overall balance is only slightly affected. Imagine a giant boulder with a woodpecker pecking at it. Usually nothing is affected. But if that boulder is precariously balanced, the woodpecker could be the final straw that breaks the proverbial camel's back and topples the boulder.

I believe that on December 28, 2019 the Earth will already be suffering from a rare but predictable gravity wave from the galactic center. I believe that the combination of the imbalanced ice accumulated hundreds of miles off-center in Antarctica (estimated at 19 quadrillion tons) – coupled with the incoming galactic superwave and Jupiter's multiple passages through the sun's corona will provide enough torque to induce a major readjustment of the Earth's crust over its interior – a pole shift.

One of the many ancient warnings about such events may involve the two witnesses of Revelation. Let us consider the idea that Enoch and Elijah are described as witnesses… to a pole shift.

The early theologians Irenaeus and Hippolytus may have been the last heirs to the uncorrupted oral tradition of the Apostles, and both of them said that Enoch and Elijah were the two witnesses. The Bible tells us that Enoch lived a total of 365 years. This lifespan brings two obvious ideas to mind: first, that no one normally lives that long – and second, that the years of Enoch's life match the number of days in a year. If this is meant to draw our attention to the number of days it takes for the earth to orbit the sun, what other astronomical clues might we take from the story of Enoch?

Enoch's life is broken down into two portions: at the age of 65 he fathered Methuselah, then continued to live another 300 years before he "walked with God" and was "translated away so that he did not see death." (Hebrews 11:5) The word "translated" comes from the Greek "metatithemi" which means "taken to another place." Because I have spent many years researching topics like pole shifts, this makes me think the story of Enoch may incorporate a coded message about a pole shift event in the distant past when the sun (symbolized by Enoch in this story) would have been positioned in the sky next to the galactic center (representing God) when the sun suddenly shifted its apparent position in the sky and was "taken to another place."

I also suspect that the way the Bible breaks down Enoch's life into two unequal portions might be similar to the way the Maya broke their year down based on the dates on which the sun passes directly overhead in the zenith. Every spring equinox in March, the sun is directly above the equator at noon. Lands north of the equator and south of the Tropic of Cancer witness the sun directly overhead at noon at some point prior to the first day of summer. At Chichen Itza, where the Maya built the great Pyramid of Kukulkan, the sun is directly overhead on May 22. The sun appears to keep moving north until summer, then starts to fall southwards again. Chichen Itza experiences a second solar zenith on July 19. At the Mayan city of Izapa where this pattern was first recognized, the latitude is different and the two zenith dates are 105 days apart. The people there broke the year into 105 and 260 portions based on the spread of the zenith passage dates at Izapa's latitude. What latitude, I wondered, would experience zenith passage dates 65 days apart as potentially indicated by Enoch – and could such zenith dates point us to the previous position of Jerusalem, before the last pole shift?

A little research led me to a chart labelled "Zenith passage dates of the Sun for Observers in Different Latitudes" in Anthony Aveni's <u>Skywatchers of Ancient Mexico</u>.[171] Just below 20 degrees north there are 65 days between zenith dates. Could this be the latitude the holy site we now know as Jerusalem used to be located at prior to the last major shift of the earth's crust relative to its axis of rotation? Could this possibly even explain why the Maya had a special term for the 65 day period (Aveni calls it the Cociyo) when neither Izapa nor Chichen Itza experience zeniths 65 days apart?

At first glance, this seems to be a dead end and a bad theory, because we know from other data that the previous North Pole was located on the west side of Hudson Bay. When the North Pole was there, the land that is now called Jerusalem was approximately eleven and a half degrees north latitude, not just under twenty degrees north latitude. However, I soon noticed that the change in latitude – the northward movement Jerusalem experienced as a result of the last pole shift – is approximately 19.8 degrees. Which means that Enoch's being taken away in a "translation" and the years of his life may be astronomical clues to a pole shift after all.

I believe that cosmic events emanating from the galactic center cause recurring, periodic, and predictable pole shifts on earth. I believe the sun will appear to be dark (Revelation 6:12 "the sun became black as sackcloth") for three days, at the point in the year when it appears at the crossing point of the galactic axis and the ecliptic – the apparent path of the sun and planets. I suspect it is no coincidence that Jesus died on a cross and was dead for three days and that we are told the sun went dark when he died. Jonah was in darkness in the belly of the whale for three days, and I believe this is a reference to the sun going dark as it passes through the cosmic leviathan of the Milky Way's central bulge along the galactic axis. I believe these correlations are intentional biblical clues to past and future events.

The Book of Enoch mentions "the sun... and the chariot in which it rises" (Enoch 72:5) and we know Elijah encountered "a chariot of fire." We can safely assume Elijah represents another heavenly body which encountered the sun. "And Elijah went up by a whirlwind into heaven" just after he walked past Bethel (Beth-El = the house of God = represented astronomically by the galactic center) and crossed the Jordan River (the Milky Way) and encountered the chariot of fire (the sun.) So this occurred when the sun (and some other heavenly body – I suggest Jupiter) had just passed the galactic center and the axis of the Milky Way. 2 Kings 2:17 describes the men sent out to look for Elijah after he disappeared – "They searched three days but could not find him." This is another symbolic reference to the three days of darkness and confusion.

And then one of the even stranger comments in the Bible appears in 2 Kings 2:24 "Two female bears came out of the woods and tore up forty-two lads" from Bethel who had previously mocked Elijah's son.

Now I have been to that part of Israel. I have stood in the Jordan River. Large and dense forests from which bears could emerge and suddenly surprise anyone are rare. And even if we grant that there had been thick woods and a pair of real bears, can you imagine 42 young men not scattering and running off in different directions? Surely a pair of bears could kill a lad or two, but forty-two of them? As C.M. Houck commented in The Celestial Spheres: Keys to the Suppressed wisdom of the Ancients: "How could two bears possibly manage to outrun, catch, and destroy forty-two terrified, hyperactive juvenile delinquents? They couldn't. This is sacred language."[172] And what I think he means is that this is another astronomical reference, this time to the two "polar bears" – the constellations Ursa Major and Ursa Minor – the Big Bear and Little Bear near the celestial North Pole. I suggest that during the last pole shift, it was noticed that these "bears" seemed to suddenly move faster and farther than usual into the sky, corresponding with the sudden disappearance of 42 visible stars moving in front of them which unexpectedly fell below the opposite horizon.

In my previous book, End Times and 2019, I conclude that the Bible, the Maya, and the Egyptians all left clues pointing to the next pole shift coinciding with the end of the Tribulation and Judgment Day in late December, 2019. I suggest that Jupiter is the astronomical representation of the prophet Elijah, that the Sun represents Jesus, and that the conjunction of Jupiter and the Sun on Judgment Day represents Elijah anointing Jesus Christ as King. I believe that Enoch and Elijah have been portrayed as witnesses to a previous pole shift, and that their stories give us clues about that last pole shift. I believe they may be the two end times witnesses of the tribulation, and that they will witness the next catastrophic pole shift in December 2019.

Jupiter will appear to hover at the edge of the sun, just as the best man hovers by the door of the bride and groom's chamber a week into an ancient Jewish wedding ceremony. And on that day, those on the earth will hear what sounds like the biggest trumpet blasts in history when the wedding ends and the door opens at the culminating peak of the Judgment Day pole shift. The Bible describes it repeatedly, including:

Revelation 4:1 "After these things I looked, and behold, a door standing open in heaven, and the first voice which I had heard, like the sound of a trumpet."

1 Corinthians 15:52 "at the last trumpet; for the trumpet will sound, and the dead will be raised."

1 Thessalonians 4:16 "the Lord Himself will descend from heaven with a shout, with the voice of the archangel and with the trumpet of God, and the dead in Christ will rise."

Many other cultures also describe a trumpet blast at the end of the world:

In Hindu myth, the destroyer god Vishnu blows on a conch-shell trumpet called a sankh to announce his arrival on the final battlefield at the last day.

Muslims expect a trumpet blast during final events that sound like a pole shift at the end of the world: "when the Trumpet is blown, a single blast; and the earth and the mountains shall be borne away and crushed with a single crushing; on that Day shall happen the Great Event; and the heaven shall cleave asunder." (Qu'ran Surah 69:13-17)

In Norse mythology, the earth loses its shape after great earthquakes, the stars fall, the seas rise, and when the giants gather for the final world-ending battle of Ragnarok, Heimdall – the watchman of the gods – summons all the gods for battle by blowing the ringing trumpet/horn Gjallarhorn, which will be heard throughout earth, heaven, and hell.

Even in the Babylonian "Enuma Elish" creation story, at the end the participants look forward to the eventual trumpet-like sound that announces re-creation: "May his beneficent roar ever hover over the earth." (Tablet 7, line 120)

This Last Trumpet will be blown on "the last day" mentioned repeatedly throughout the Bible, which this author has concluded will be on December 28, 2019 – when "the stars will be falling from heaven" (Mark 13:25) at the end of a week-long heavenly wedding ceremony that corresponds with a pole shift which destroys the surface of the planet as we knew it and creates "a new heavens and a new earth." As John Preacher wrote: "the only way" (stars could fall) would be "a Polar shift or Polar Reversal.... This won't be a slow axis shift."[173] *It could simply be referring to "shooting stars" i.e. meteor showers*

The pole shift starts on the 24th day of the Hebrew month of Kislev. Haggai 2:18-22 tells us "from the four and twentieth day of the ninth month... I am going to shake the heavens and the earth..." Kislev 24 is also the anniversary of the laying of the foundation of the Lord's Temple, which is very significant if a future pole shift starting that day is what creates the new earth/New Jerusalem/new Temple on the anniversary of the old Temple. December 21, 2019 is also the night before Hanukkah starts, allowing the week of heavenly wedding events and pole shifting to overlap the holiday representing freedom from religious oppression and the restoration of the proper worship of God - right when Christ destroys the Antichrist at the end of the final seven years. December 21, 2019 is also the date when the Maya foresaw the winter solstice sun finishing its alignment with the galactic center, with their sun-god Kukulkan taking the throne on the holy crossroads in the sky and becoming King over the Earth.

And in case that alignment still doesn't seem very relevant to you as a Christian, please remember Psalm 89:37, when God describes the Davidic throne of the Messiah as "his throne as the sun before Me." This does describe an alignment with the sun near the galactic center. Also note Psalm 19, which is so relevant to this "Mayan" astronomical alignment that I will quote both the KJV and the NASB. Psalm 19:1-5 (KJV) "The heavens declare the glory of God; and the firmament sheweth his handywork. Day unto day uttereth speech, and night unto night sheweth knowledge. There is no speech nor language, where their voice is not heard. Their line is gone out through all the earth, and their words to the end of the world. In them hath He set a tabernacle for the sun, which is as a bridegroom coming out of his chamber." Do you see the references to a line drawn out by the stars, declaring God's handywork through their signs just as speech or words could do? Do you see how their "line" points to "the end of the world" at the time when the Sun is in position where God "set a tabernacle for the sun, which is as a bridegroom coming out of his chamber?"

If you didn't see the same astronomical clues that I did, or that the Maya did, or that our ancient Israelite writers did, please look at the NASB version of Psalm 19:1-5 as well: "The heavens are telling of the glory of God; and their expanse is declaring the work of His hands. Day to day pours forth speech, and night to night reveals knowledge. There is no speech, nor are there words; their voice is not heard. Their line has gone out through all the earth, and their utterances to the end of the world. In them He has placed a tent for the sun, which is as a bridegroom coming out of his chamber." This very clearly tells us that the sun coming out of its appointed set path/place is as the bridegroom exiting the bridal chamber at the end of the wedding.

I know of one biblical bride who became Queen by marrying the King on a known date. Esther married the Persian King Ahasuerus (Xerxes) on the first day of the month of Tevet, as hinted at in Esther 2:16. Christ is the King of Kings, and if I am correct, Christ's bride will reign as Queen on the first of Tevet as well, which is now the seventh day of Hanukkah, and falls on December 28 in the year 2019.

If the wedding and the pole shift last for a week – as the pole shift which created the Steens Mountain magnetic evidence did – and the week of creation in Genesis did – and the week of an ancient Jewish wedding ceremony did – then the end of the pole shift coincides with the astronomical clues for Judgment Day on December 28, 2019.

This wraps up our summary of the evidence pointing to a pole shift in late December 2019 as the end of Daniel's 70th week of years (see <u>End Times and 2019</u> for much greater detail) and brings us back full circle to the Antichrist – for once we have calculated the end of the final seven years of the world as we know it, we can deduce a date for the beginning, and more importantly the middle – when the Antichrist enters a rebuilt Temple in Jerusalem, proclaims himself to be God, and starts the horrible second phase of his career as the fully revealed Antichrist. Subtract seven years from 12/21/2019 to reach 12/21/2012 – which not coincidentally, is the exact end date of the 5125 year Mayan Long Count. This is the start date of the final seven years of troubles. This is when the Antichrist should have started a seven year covenant of peace with Israel, which he should break after three and a half years when he reveals himself.

Psalm 55:20-21 "He has put forth his hands against those who were at peace with him; he has violated his covenant. His speech was smoother than butter, but his heart was war."

The strengthening of the seven year peace covenant cannot be blatantly obvious or Christians would all know the politician in charge is the Antichrist; but he cannot be revealed until 3.5 years later. I believe the key date for the start of this covenant was December 21, 2012 – but it is a gradual and continuing effort, including the more obvious "Covenant of Peoples" tour that had Obama in Israel in March 2013. The covenant will be ongoing for 3.5 years. There is no benefit to suddenly and obviously portraying it as the covenant Christians have been expecting. Governments will also want to keep the treaty details quiet because there could be chaos if the population felt we were entering the tribulation. In <u>End Times and 2019</u>, I said that only a small number of very aware prophecy scholars will be aware of events "on December 21, 2012. Shortly after this date, probably in early 2013, there should come a day when huge signs are witnessed including the start of a seven year peace treaty with Israel brokered by the antichrist."[174]

On March 20, 2013, despite some very anti-Israel policies and behind the scenes hostility, Obama stood in Jerusalem and said: "The United States is proud to stand with you as your strongest ally and your greatest friend.... I see this visit as an opportunity to reaffirm the unbreakable bond between our nations, to restate America's unwavering commitment to Israel's security and to speak directly to the people of Israel and to your neighbors." Such speeches are part of an ongoing strengthening and reaffirming of the covenant. This peace covenant, and its timing, are described repeatedly by the prophet Daniel, as in Daniel 9:27 "He will make a firm covenant with the many for one week, but in the middle of the week he will put a stop to sacrifice and grain offering; and on the wing of abominations will come one who makes desolate, even until a complete destruction."

Several points should be emphasized regarding the making of this covenant. We can assume that Israel's right to exist will be acknowledged by at least a few of its Muslim neighbors. It is possible that the status of Jerusalem will be decided, and that Israel's choice of Jerusalem as its capital city may also be accepted. But the main thing the Jews must gain from this agreement is apparently the globally recognized right to rebuild a Temple on the original site in Jerusalem and initiate sacrifices there to worship God as their ancestors did in Old Testament times. The central point of Daniel's 70th week of years is the arrival of the Antichrist at the reestablished Temple; so the Jews must be allowed to set up a Temple beforehand. It seems logical that this would be part of the covenant. Since the Muslim populations of Israel and the rest of the Middle East could be expected to react very poorly to this, the Israelis must be pressured to give up something huge in return that would compensate – like the creation of a newly independent Palestinian nation. The exchange of land will probably wait until the Temple is completely ready for assembly, and only then will the covenant, made much earlier, be publicized to populations who will not appreciate its compromises.

We should also note that in English, the text in Daniel does not convey the hardball coercion used by the Antichrist in forcing this deal through. The Hebrew verb "gabar" can be translated as "confirm," "but the sense behind the Hebrew may better indicate oppressing, imposing, or coercing."[175] This implies an obvious fact – that the Jews must give in to a very unpopular requirement of the covenant in order to make it and secure international acceptance of their upcoming Temple – such as Palestinian nationhood with indefensible, reduced Israeli borders.

Due to the unpopular opinion Israeli Jews have on giving up land for peace - as it has never worked before for them, or Native Americans, or anyone else – the Israeli government may insist on keeping the details of such an agreement secret until the Temple has been completely pre-assembled and is ready to put together. I agree with Tim Lahaye and Jerry Jenkins when they say "The Tribulation officially begins when the Antichrist signs a seven-year covenant with Israel"[176] as described in Daniel 9:27. But as Alan Kurschner asks in his book on the Antichrist: "Will we recognize the signing of the covenant when it happens and thereby know that we have entered the seven-year period? I do not think we can be certain that we will."[177]

Tim LaHaye describes the signing of this end times covenant in his fictional Left Behind series of books. Though he was only writing popular fiction, he also suggests the covenant will not be understood for what it really is at the time it is signed. "And the signers of the treaty – all except one – were ignorant of its consequences, unaware they had been party to an unholy alliance. A covenant had been struck. God's chosen people, who planned to rebuild the temple and reinstitute the system of sacrifices until the coming of their Messiah, had signed a deal with the devil. Only two men on the dais knew this pact signaled the beginning of the end of time. One was maniacally hopeful; the other trembled at what was to come."[178]

"Maniacally hopeful" reminds me of Israeli Defense Minister Moshe Yaalon's assessment of John Kerry. He called Kerry "obsessive" and "messianic" in his stubborn pursuit of certain American goals for a peace treaty. Nothing the public knows justifies this. Of course, secret deals about a new Temple being built on a rushed timeline could be viewed as messianic, if since December 2012 Kerry has been pushing in that direction to make sure the Temple is ready for his master on time. Yaalon said: "Secretary of State John Kerry – who came here very determined, and operates based upon an unfathomable obsession and a messianic feeling [...made sure that] throughout the recent months, there is no negotiation between us and the

Palestinians – but rather, between us and the Americans. The only thing that can 'save' us is that John Kerry will get a Nobel peace prize and leave us alone.... The American security plan that was presented to us is not worth the paper it was written on."[179] Why are Kerry's/Obama's terms more important than Palestinian (or Israeli) interests? What does Yaalon know?

Important details of the peace covenant are being withheld from the public, and one reason is so that we do not recognize the beginning of the final seven years. Events at t+his moment in time is not described by Jesus, or Paul, or Daniel, or John's Book of Revelation. Their lack of emphasis on the beginning of the final seven years implies a lack of importance, at least as the events (or lack thereof) at this time are viewed by Jesus, Paul, Daniel, and John. We should expect no obvious great events or urgency at that time. Regardless of our level of interest in recognizing the start of the final week of years, and knowing what is coming and when, the lack of biblical descriptions of the start date indicates that the prophets were much more concerned with events we will recognize 42 months later. Although some Christians will recognize the signs before the middle of the seven years, only then can the Antichrist be made obvious to the world.

When the covenant is signed, the Antichrist's identity will remain unknown to most of the world for another three and a half years. History tells us it is a simple task for an evil politician to hide his true nature from us. The following quote provides a good example: "When I see, as I so often do, poorly clad girls collecting with such infinite patience in order to care for those who are suffering from the cold while they themselves are shivering with cold, then I have the feeling that they are all apostles of a Christianity – and in truth of a Christianity which can say with greater right than any other: this is the Christianity of an honest confession, for behind it stand not words but deeds." – Adolf Hitler, 1937. Hitler made many statements supporting Christianity and its values, and few viewed him as a monster that would eventually be responsible for tens of millions of deaths. Likewise, the Antichrist will not yet be widely recognized when the covenant begins.

Writing again in July 2014, I now know a bit more than I did prior to December 2012. President Obama nominated John Kerry as Secretary of State and put him in charge of the Arab-Israeli peace process on – you guessed it – December 21, 2012. In February 2013 it was revealed that Obama would make a special trip to Israel in March. The official American name for Obama's visit in English was "Unbreakable Alliance." The official name for Obama's tour in Hebrew, in Israel, was "A Covenant of Peoples."

A COVENANT OF PEOPLES. What day do you think Kerry started working on Obama's "Covenant" tour plans? What kind of agreement was made with the Israelis on that "Covenant" visit?

In The Final Babylon the authors wrote: "President Obama announced an 'Unbreakable Alliance' between Israel and the United States, in Jerusalem during Holy Week, 2013. For those who watch prophetic matters closely, the parallels with the most common interpretation of Daniel 9:24-27 of a covenant"[180] to be broken during the final seven years are hard to ignore.

On his "Covenant of Peoples" tour in Jerusalem, on March 20, 2013 President Obama described "how the United States can play a constructive role in bringing about a lasting peace and two states living side by side in peace and security." On December 7, 2013, Obama's Secretary of State and Peace Process front man John Kerry said he was tasked with achieving "a two-state solution in which Israelis and Palestinians are living side-by-side in peace and security." On March 3, 2014 Obama said he wanted to "…create two states - a Jewish state of Israel and a state of Palestine - in which people are living side-by-side in peace and security." Hillary Clinton, John Kerry, Israeli Prime Minister Benjamin Netanyahu, Secretary General of the United Nations Ban Ki-Moon, the Iranian President Mahmoud Ahmadinejad, President Obama, and many others have said "peace and security" in regard to a two-state solution. We hardly need to wonder what might be a central concession of the covenant – it has to involve an independent nation for Palestinian Arabs. Christians know that any territorial concessions go against God's covenant with the Jews, which promises an extensive Jewish homeland. This is why the agreement is doomed to failure and is described as "a covenant with death."

Isaiah 28:10-18 warns: "For He says, 'Order on order, order on order, line on line, line on line, a little here, a little there.' Indeed, He will speak to this people through stammering lips and a foreign tongue, He who said to them, 'Here is rest, give rest to the weary,' and, 'Here is repose,' but they would not listen. So the word of the Lord to them will be, 'Order on order, order on order, line on line, line on line, a little here, a little there,' that they may go and stumble backward, be broken, snared and taken captive. Therefore, hear the word of the Lord, O scoffers, who rule this people who are in Jerusalem, because you have said, 'We have made a covenant with death, and with Sheol we have made a pact. The overwhelming scourge will not reach us when it passes by, for we have made falsehood our refuge and we have concealed ourselves with deception.' Therefore thus says the Lord God,

'Behold, I am laying in Zion a stone, a tested stone, a costly cornerstone for the foundation, firmly placed. He who believes in it will not be disturbed. I will make justice the measuring line and righteousness the level; then hail will sweep away the refuge of lies and the waters will overflow the secret place. Your covenant with death will be canceled, and your pact with Sheol will not stand; when the overwhelming scourge passes through, then you become its trampling place.'"

I think these verses describe a legal document or covenant with orders and lines, through which the Jews ignore God's will for their land and attempt to secure peace through an agreement with an evil human protector. But it fails, the Jews are betrayed, and they suffer at the hands of betrayer. I can't see Israel abandoning territory and making a covenant with evil without getting a huge concession themselves – something like the right to construct the Third Temple – which must exist before the Antichrist can enter it.

1 Thessolonians 5:3 warns us that the Antichrist will betray the Jews during a period of peace and attack Israel when they are certain of their safety and security. "While they are saying, 'Peace and safety!' then destruction will come upon them suddenly like labor pains upon a woman with child, and they will not escape." (NASB) Other versions like the Douay-Rheims (Catholic) Bible say "Peace and Security!" Several internet videos show how many times Obama has talked about Israel's "peace and security."[181]

Daniel 7:25 "He will speak out against the Most High and wear down the saints of the Highest One, and he will intend to make alterations in times and in law; and they will be given into his hand for a time, times, and half a time." Alterations in times and law could be a switch to the Islamic calendar and Sharia law, if the Islamic Antichrist theory is correct. The time, times, and half a time is generally understood to indicate a year, plus two years, plus half a year – often reckoned as 42 months of 30 days, or 1260 days. Adding Daniel's next number of 1290 days gets us within a few days of an exact seven years in total - but it still leaves us with an extra 3 days of death and resurrection to add to each half to reach an exact seven years of 2556 days for Daniel's seventieth week.

The end of the second half of the 70th week might see the death and resurrection of the two witnesses in Jerusalem. Revelation 11 tells us these witnesses will not be harmed until they are finished witnessing, then they will be dead three and a half days. The general population of Antichrist followers, long tired of the message of the witnesses, celebrate their deaths and give each other gifts. Revelation 11:9-10 says "Those from the peoples and tribes and tongues and nations will look at their dead bodies for three and a half days, and will not permit their dead bodies to be laid in a tomb. And those who dwell on the earth will rejoice over them and celebrate; and they will send gifts to one another, because these two prophets tormented those who dwell on the earth." It is not normal to send gifts to each other in celebration of anyone's death; so this could be a clue to the time of year, for it is normal to buy gifts for others right before Christmas, or Hanukkah. Assuming these 3.5 days are at the end of the second 3.5 years (which end December 21, 2019) then buying gifts for the upcoming holidays is normal. Hanukkah starts December 22, 2019, and Christmas is just three days later.

I suspect there will be a similar three day period of interest at the mid-point of the final seven years from June 3-6, 2016. With just a few similarities to events in the <u>Left Behind</u> series' <u>Assassins: Assignment – Jerusalem, Target – Antichrist</u> – I would expect a failed assassination attempt on the Antichrist, in Jerusalem, exactly 1260 days into Daniel's 70th week on June 3, 2016. As the Antichrist will mimic Christ whenever possible, we may hear that he is dying from his wounds on June 4, which just happens to be Ascension Day. He will appear to be mortally wounded at first, but in a tragic mockery of Christ's resurrection, he will rise three days later, "miraculously" revived and fully healed on June 6, 2016. 2 Thessalonians 2:8 says "Then that lawless one will be revealed whom the Lord will slay..." He may even start speaking as if suddenly under the influence of Holy (or unholy) Spirit... He may claim "that God has healed him and given him an assignment of bringing salvation to the world and to usher in peace on earth."[182] To claim that he has been sent by God, and to simultaneously present himself at the Temple in Jerusalem demanding worship may seem like an impossible combination. But if Joel Richardson and the "Islamic Antichrist Theory" are correct, then the Christian Antichrist could present himself as the Muslim savior – and as Caliph of the Islamic world (and in their minds, of the entire world) he would demand our worship as Allah's representative on Earth.

What applies to the king may also apply to the kingdom; the nearly fatal wound, when healed, could also mean that an empire of the Beast has been restored. What if the Antichrist's allegedly holy message of hope and salvation is that we must reach it through Islam? What if New York and the United Nations were just destroyed, and the Antichrist wants to reestablish rule over all nations in another city, one sacred to many religions and at the geographical center of the world – in Jerusalem? What if what he attempts to create is a new Islamic Caliphate?

REACHING 2016

Day of the Antichrist

The previous chapter covered the evidence which led me to conclude that Daniel's 70th week – the final seven years of the present world – runs from December 21, 2012 to December 21, 2019. Starting in late 2012 and adding 1260 days as the prophet Daniel describes brings us to the date I anticipate an attempted assassination on the Antichrist – on June 3, 2016. Three days later, miraculously healed by Satan and ready to take over the world, I expect the Antichrist to be fully revealed and understood by the entire world as he makes his big announcement from the Temple in Jerusalem on June 6, 2016. What other evidence leads to this date?

Well, this didn't happen! JG 8-22-16

The Third Secret of Fatima

In 1917, the most credible and well-documented visions of the Virgin Mary were received by three young cousins in Fatima, Portugal. Several times that year, always on the thirteenth day of the month, the children experienced trance-like visions in which they claimed the Holy Mother spoke to them. At the last of the Fatima apparitions on October 13, 1917, an estimated 70,000 people witnessed what was described as the Miracle of the Sun. Perhaps at least partially due to the many witnesses, the Catholic Church officially recognizes the appearance of the Virgin Mary at Fatima.

On July 13, 1917, the children were given three secrets – three prophecies about horrible things to come. The first two secrets describe aspects of hell, WWI and WWII, and the importance of Russia as a Christian nation. The Third Secret of Fatima may involve an apocalyptic third world war, but we don't know for certain, because the Vatican refuses to come clean.

What topics are so dangerous that the Vatican needs to bury the truth about them? Cardinal Ratzinger (later Pope Benedict) was always tight lipped about the Fatima prophecies, and Pope John Paul II placed him in charge of them. The cardinal commented in 1984 that "the prophecies contained in this Third Secret correspond to what Scripture announces" and also that they refer to "de nivissimis" – a Latin phrase for the end times.

By late 1943, two cousins had already died, and Lucia was sick. The Bishop of Leira ordered her to write down the Third Secret, which the Virgin Mary had told her not to do. Lucia justified it because Catholics are taught that orders from the Church are meant to be viewed as orders from God. Lucia wrote down the Third Secret, with instructions from the Virgin Mary that it should be publicized in 1960, because more would be understood then. But in 1960 Vatican officials wrote in a press release that the information was so horrible that it was "most probable the Secret would remain, forever, under absolute seal."[183] Cardinal Ottaviani related that Pope John XXIII placed the Secret "in one of those archives which are like a very deep, dark well, to the bottom of which papers fall and no one is able to see them anymore."[184]

Starting in 1961, four girls alleged that there were new apparitions of the Blessed Virgin Mary in Garabandal, Spain. The Vatican has not officially recognized Garabandal events as a legitimate miracle, though many famous Catholics, including the now canonized Saint Padre Pio emphatically supported its legitimacy. The Garabandal visions are said to have occurred from 1961 to 1965 to schoolgirls in the rural village of San Sebastián de Garabandal. They claimed that Saint Michael the Archangel came alone at the first vision on June 18, 1961, and was also present with the Virgin Mary on future occasions through the last vision on June 18, 1965. Allegedly, they had come to give us an additional warning in 1961, as the Vatican had disobeyed the instructions to release the Third Secret of Fatima in 1960. At Garabandal, the children were told that someday there would be a great miracle for the whole world to see above the grove of pines in Garabandal – and that less than a year before the miracle, there would be a great warning, as if every human being could see all the sins they had ever committed, and see hell itself, the consequence of sinning without accepting salvation.

As for the Miracle of Garabandal, it is supposed to occur: at 8:30PM on a Thursday; on the feast day of a martyr of the Blessed Sacrament; on a feast of great ecclesiastical importance; in the month of March, April or May; and the last clue is that one of the girls (Conchita Gonzalez, born in 1949) has been told by the Virgin Mary to reveal the exact date of the upcoming miracle eight days beforehand. As one analyst writes: "The next time there will be a Feast of truly great ecclesiastical importance on a Thursday in March, April or May, and which coincides with the Feast of a martyr of the Blessed Sacrament is Maundy Thursday 13 April 2017.... That date is also remarkable in that, as well as being exactly 100 years since the Fatima visions in 1917, it is one of the few times when Maundy Thursday, the great

Feast of the Institution of the Blessed Sacrament, coincides exactly in both the Eastern and the Western churches. It will also coincide with the Jewish Feast of the Passover. We shall know if this is correct because Conchita will confirm the date, 8 days before, there will be a permanent sign at the pine grove in Garabandal and it will be preceded by the Warning. We can expect the Warning within a year of that date and thus any time after 13 April 2016."[185]   Ronald Conte, author of <u>The Secrets of Medjugorje and Garabandal Revealed</u>, feels that his analysis agrees: "this timing tends to support the year 2016 as the year of the Warning."[186]

Padre Pio, the seers of Garabandal once said, would live to see the Miracle before he died. He died in 1968. Case closed – his death disproves the legitimacy of the Garabandal claims, right? Not entirely, because he apparently wrote a letter just before dying that the Virgin Mary had allowed him to see the miracle. Joey Lomangino, who had lost his eyes in an accident in 1947, was told he would gain his sight and see the miracle – and he just died on the anniversary of the visions, on June 18, 2014. Will someone turn in a message from Joey, claiming he saw the miracle? Or does his death discredit the claims? I don't claim to know if the Garabandal visions are legitimate or not, any better than the Vatican does. But I find it interesting that the Warning could coincide with the Antichrist in 2016.

As for the Third Secret of Fatima not being released in 1960 – the alleged reason for the Garabandal visitations... the Vatican finally succumbed to pressure in the year 2000 and released... something. They claimed the Third Secret was about the 1981 assassination attempt on Pope John Paul II. Few believed that the first secrets were on big subjects like hell, world wars, and the spread of communism – but that a mere failed assassination was the horrible secret that couldn't be revealed for so long. *That was my thoughts exactly!*

Bishop Joao Venancio disputes that official explanation. He says he saw Lucia's original paper, handwritten with about 25 lines on one page with small margins – and that what the Vatican released in 2000 was 62 lines on four pages with no margins – and not authentic. We also have interesting comments from Pope John Paul II, who commented on the Third Secret while speaking in Fulda, Germany in 1981: "It should be sufficient for all Christians to know this: if there is a message in which it is written that the oceans will flood whole areas of the earth, and that from one moment to the next millions of people will perish, truly the publication of such a message is no longer something to be so much desired."[187]

David Montaigne

Since I assume there is a pole shift coming soon, I am willing to assume that Pope John Paul II knew what he was talking about, and that the Third Secret of Fatima refers to horrific events at the end of the world. Other famous Marian apparitions have also hinted at this: "a chastisement which has been described at apparitions such as that of our Lady of Akita, in northern Japan, as worse than the Flood"[188] of Noah. I can't avoid thinking of Jesus' warning in Luke 21:25-26 "There will be signs in sun and moon and stars, and on the earth dismay among nations, in perplexity at the roaring of the sea and the waves, men fainting from fear and the expectation of the things which are coming upon the world; for the powers of the heavens will be shaken." I assume that the official Vatican explanation of Fatima's Third Secret given on May 13, 2000 is a deception.

Cannot be worldwide; due to God's promise in Genesis

On March 13, 2013, the Archbishop of Buenos Aires, Cardinal Jorge Mario Bergoglio, became Pope Francis, the first pope from the Americas. The Patriarch of Lisbon, Cardinal José Policarpo, soon announced that Pope Francis twice asked him to consecrate his papacy to Our Lady of Fatima, and this was done on May 13, 2013 – on the 96th anniversary of the apparitions of the Virgin Mary to the three shepherd children. Pope Francis obviously takes the secrets of Fatima seriously, and publically acknowledges this by having his papacy consecrated this way.

Father Malachi Martin has written several books on the Fatima secrets and has said that "the Third Secret is your worst nightmare, multiplied exponentially."[189] In an interview in 1997, he explained that "I was shown the Text of the third secret in February 1960. I cooled my heels in the corridor outside the Holy Father's apartments, while my Boss, Cardinal Bea, was inside debating with the Holy Father (Pope John XXIII), and with a other group of other bishops and priests, and two young Portuguese seminarians, who translated the letter, a single page, written in Portuguese, for all those in the room..... on the content of the Third Secret, Sister Lucy one day replied: 'It's in the Gospel, and in the Apocalypse, read them.' We even know that one day Lucy indicated Chapters 8, 13 of the Apocalypse.[190]

During a radio interview on "Coast to Coast" in December 1997, Art Bell asked "Can you tell us, in a way that we can read between the lines, with regard to the third prophecy, is there a timetable that you are aware of, but cannot speak of, that we can read between the lines on?" Father Martin replied "Yes, and no. There is a... it is not 200 years away, it is not 50 years away, it is not 20 years away..."[191] He then expressed the view that major portions of end times events would be underway before the centennial of the

Marian apparitions at Fatima (before the spring of 2017.)

Lucia apparently mentioned Revelation chapter 8 in her letter; a chapter that opens the seventh seal. The sixth seal, which sounds like a pole shift, had just been opened in Revelation 6:12-14 "I looked when He broke the sixth seal, and there was a great earthquake; and the sun became black as sackcloth made of hair, and the whole moon became like blood; and the stars of the sky fell to the earth, as a fig tree casts its unripe figs when shaken by a great wind. The sky was split apart like a scroll when it is rolled up, and every mountain and island were moved out of their places."

The seventh seal in Revelation 8:1-9 describes the sun's reaction to the likely cause of it temporarily being black like sackcloth – an incoming cosmic dust cloud that eventually provokes a massive flaring up, as when sawdust is sprinkled on a fire: "When the Lamb broke the seventh seal... another angel came and stood at the altar, [the angel at the altar could be Jupiter at the edge of the sun, on Judgment Day, as I described at length in End Times and 2019] holding a golden censer; and much incense was given to him... And the smoke of the incense... went up before God out of the angel's hand. Then the angel took the censer and filled it with the fire of the altar, and threw it to the earth; and there followed peals of thunder and sounds and flashes of lightning and an earthquake. And the seven angels who had the seven trumpets prepared themselves to sound them. The first sounded, and there came hail and fire, mixed with blood, and they were thrown to the earth; and a third of the earth was burned up, and a third of the trees were burned up, and all the green grass was burned up. The second angel sounded, and something like a great mountain burning with fire was thrown into the sea; and a third of the sea became blood, and a third of the creatures which were in the sea and had life, died; and a third of the ships were destroyed." This sounds like a massive solar flare or CME (coronal mass ejection) hits the earth when the sun flares up in response to incoming dust and "the light of the sun will be seven times brighter." (Isaiah 30:26)

Lucia also mentioned that the Third Secret of Fatima involves Revelation chapter 13, which describes the Antichrist and ends with "Here is wisdom. Let him who has understanding calculate the number of the beast, for the number is that of a man; and his number is six hundred and sixty-six." If Father Malachi Martin was right that some of these events would be underway before 2017 – the timing coincides with my conclusion that the Antichrist is revealed in 2016.

David Montaigne

No Vatican officials have commented specifically on the Antichrist in relation to the Third Secret. But Pope John Paul II did talk about massive flooding and pole shift type events killing many people. I believe the next North Pole will be in Siberia, northwest of Lake Baikal, near the borders of Russia, China, and Mongolia. There is a large magnetic anomaly there. The famous Tunguska blast event of 1908 occurred there. The Magnetic North Pole is already moving in that direction. And one of the main founders of the pole shift theory, Professor Charles Hapgood (author of books like <u>Path of the Pole</u>, <u>Earth's Shifting Crust</u>, and <u>Maps of the Ancient Sea Kings</u>) also felt this was the likely location of our next North Pole.

Assuming a pole shift occurs – after the tidal waves, earthquakes, volcanoes, and contamination from wrecked nuclear plants, chemical plants, and oil refineries are dealt with, survivors will face the loss of civilization, with niceties like doctors, food, and technology disappearing fast. On top of that, they will face major climate change. Atlanta will be on the new equator; the entire continental United States – and almost everyone in Canada – will be living in the tropics. What will that do to the people of Russia and China? Most of their nations would become uninhabitable arctic wasteland. We may already think of Siberia that way; imagine it even closer to the North Pole.

Now look in context at what Pope John Paul II said right before commenting on huge floods killing millions: "Given the seriousness of the contents, [of Fatima's Third Secret] my predecessors in the Petrine office diplomatically preferred to postpone publication so as not to encourage the world power of Communism to make certain moves. On the other hand, it should be sufficient for all Christians to know this: if there is a message in which it is written that the oceans will flood whole areas of the earth..."

Pope John Paul II suggested that World Communism – the major powers of which are Russia and China – would make some hostile moves if they knew the secret. Father Malachi Martin agreed and wrote in his book <u>The Keys of This Blood</u>: "were the leaders of the Leninist Party-State to know these words, they would in all probability decide to undertake certain territorial and militaristic moves."[192] I think they would decide to conquer new lands farther from the upcoming new North Pole to provide suitable new homelands for their populations. South Asia, the Middle East, and Central Europe would probably be invaded by Russia and China. Perhaps in Revelation 9:16 when an army of 200,000,000 comes to the Euphrates from the east – it is because the imminent pole shift has become obvious and the Chinese are fleeing a homeland they know will be uninhabitable by the end of 2019. Such invasions of the Middle East will be easy to justify if the Antichrist has already taken over the region in 2016, and Father Martin suggests that the events of the Third Secret will be underway before 2017.

Blood Moons

In 2008, Pastor Mark Biltz was analyzing NASA's astronomical data on lunar eclipses when he noticed that on rare occasion there are four total lunar eclipses in a row, with no partial eclipses in between, within two years. This pattern of four consecutive total lunar eclipses can be referred to as a tetrad. During lunar eclipses, the Earth's atmosphere refracts the sun's light around our planet and onto the moon, while it tends to filter out wavelengths other than orange and red. The moon appears to be blood-red during such an eclipse, and these eclipses have been referred to as blood moons. Biltz noticed that occasionally – just eight times in the last 2,000 years – a tetrad of blood moon eclipses all occur on the Jewish Feast holidays of Passover and Sukkot (Tabernacles.) But what really got Biltz's attention was the close timing of these eclipses near major events in the history of the Jewish people.

I happen to agree with Biltz on many points, including the significance of astronomical signs and Jewish holidays as markers for future events. Biltz wrote that "God says He created the sun and moon and the stars for signals"[193] clearly referencing Genesis 1:14 "Let there be lights in the expanse of the heavens to separate the day from the night, and let them be for signs and for seasons and for days and years." Biltz also says that the word we see in English Bibles as "seasons" is translated incorrectly and that the same Hebrew word in Leviticus is translated as "feasts." The sun and moon in particular are used to establish the timing of Jewish holidays. The spring feasts, including the crucifixion on Passover, have already had their prophetic events unfold. I agree with scholars who anticipate the unfolding of end times events like the Second Coming on the Fall Feasts like Tabernacles – and astronomical details let me know this will occur in 2019.

In Psalm 89:37 God tells us: "as the sun before Me. It shall be established forever like the moon, and the witness in the sky is faithful." Here the sun and moon are faithful witnesses, and aligned properly with the earth, their positions lead to eclipses which may be signs. Scoffers will point out that in the last 2000 years there have been eight such tetrads of blood moon eclipses lined up on Jewish feast days, and only the last three have been near significant events in the history of the Jewish people. I would counter that even three such occurrences establish a new trend; that the trend has been in effect for over 500 years, and that it may be worth keeping in mind as the fourth such set of eclipses occurs in 2014 and 2015. Total lunar eclipses occur on Passover and Sukkot, the holidays associated with Christ's death and birth, in both years. This will not occur again for over 400 years.

Perhaps I am biased to take these potential celestial omens seriously because my own research concludes that the most important prophetic warnings are often linked to astronomical signs, and that the reestablishment of some form of Third Temple in Jerusalem is crucial by June 2016 if an Antichrist is going to be revealed to the world from it. The focus of historical events linked to tetrads of blood moons on Jewish holidays also fits this idea.

Although Biltz does not make a claim that the Third Temple will be rebuilt near this tetrad of eclipses, many others do. In John Hagee's book: Four Blood Moons: Something is About to Change, he asks: "What historical event will take place during their occurrences that is significant to Israel and the Jewish people?"[194] Let's consider the narrowing geographic focus of events associated with the only tetrads of total lunar eclipses falling exclusively on Passover and Sukkot since the 15th century:

The World – In 1492 the Jews were expelled from Spain, the Spanish officially discovered the Americas, and the Jews spread out to live in many new countries. This worldwide diaspora included the United States, where eventually there were more Jews than in Israel. Within one year of these historical events there was a holiday tetrad of blood moons in 1493 and 1494.

The Nation of Israel - Israel was re-established as a nation in 1948, and within a year of this independence there was a blood moon tetrad on the Passovers and Sukkots of 1949 and 1950.

The City of Jerusalem – Israelis reunited all of Jerusalem under Jewish rule after recapturing East Jerusalem and the Temple Mount in 1967. Within a year, there was a similar tetrad in 1967 and 1968.

The Temple – Some Israelis have wanted to build a new Jewish Temple on the Temple Mount ever since 1967. With Hamas rockets being fired from Gaza into Jerusalem as I write this, the possibility exists that one could destroy the Dome of the Rock Mosque. If it is destroyed, whether by war or a fanatic or any other cause, such destruction would remove the main obstacle to Jewish claims over the entire Temple Mount. Or perhaps the lost Ark of the Covenant is discovered, prompting the establishment of a Temple to properly house it. My research points to the reestablishment of some form of Third Temple in Jerusalem no later than June 6, 2016. This would be within a year of the tetrads of holiday blood moons in 2014 and 2015 and seems to fit the increasingly focused geographical fulfillment of prophetic events near blood moon tetrads.

The Number of the Beast

Revelation 13:18 "Here is wisdom. Let him who has understanding calculate the number of the beast, for the number is that of a man; and his number is six hundred and sixty-six."

Everyone knows the number 666 is associated with evil, and Satan, and the Antichrist. Many people have applied gematria to the names of famous leaders like Nero Caesar and claimed to add the ancient letter values of their names to 666. Others have made claims based on three names of six letters each like Ronald Wilson Reagan and suggested that someone is the Antichrist. The inventors of the "bar code" that identifies retail merchandise through a laser scan of a series of vertical lines may have had this number in mind when they made sure every bar code has a set of two long and narrow lines at the beginning, middle, and end (each pair representing a "6") for calibration. Some think this bar code is the mark of the beast that no one will be able to buy or sell without, as in Revelation 13:17 "he provides that no one will be able to buy or to sell, except the one who has the mark, either the name of the beast or the number of his name."

A few naysayers would argue that the whole 666 interpretation of the number of the beast is incorrect. On May 1, 2005, scholars revealed that a newly discovered fragment of the oldest surviving copy of the New Testament, dating from the third century, indicating that the Number of the Beast might really be 616. David Parker, professor of New Testament textual criticism and paleography at the University of Birmingham, has said that the numerical value of The Beast given to John in Revelation might actually be 616. Even if there is merit to this new idea, June 2016 is still 6/16. But most researchers believe there was an early error in transcribing a single letter to a bad copy which ended up with the slightly different letter "iota" representing a one in the "tens" part of the number. This was even commented on in the first century after Christ.

The apostle John taught Polycarp the gospel without inserting his own interpretations. Polycarp taught the same unadulterated message to Irenaeus, who wrote <u>Against Heresies</u> around the year 180 A.D. The words "heresy" and "heresies" didn't have negative connotations before Irenaeus. The Greek word "haeresis" simply meant "school of thought." Irenaeus was angry that as the apostolic tradition was handed down through the first few generations after Christ, interpreters were already modifying the messages, replacing Hebrew idioms with Greek philosophy, and adding their own interpretations. The point Irenaeus was trying to make is that the traditional oral messages of Jesus, given through the apostles, was divinely inspired, and not just "a school of thought" like that of Jewish Essenes or Greek Stoics. And Irenaeus made it very clear that John personally conveyed to Polycarp, who accurately conveyed to him [Irenaeus] that the Antichrist would be an individual man, indwelt by Satan, and that the name of the Antichrist would "possess the number six hundred and sixty-six."[195] He clarified that "reason also leads us to conclude that the number of the name of the beast, [if reckoned] according to the Greek mode of calculation by the [value of] the letters contained in it, will amount to six hundred and sixty-six."[196] Irenaeus even commented on the 616 mistake already in some written copies: "I do not know how it is that some have erred following the ordinary mode of speech, and have violated the middle number in the name, deducting the amount of fifty from it."[197]

But I also suspect that the number 666 refers not only to the name of a specific man, but also to a specific date. Even Nostradamus may have referred to this in quatrain 2:89 of his prophecies. He warned that "One day" when "the new land will be at its high peak to the bloody one the number recounted." I don't think there is much time left for America to be considered at its high peak.

Readers may also be familiar with the fictional character Damien Thorn from the movie "The Omen." Damien's character was the young Antichrist, and the creator of the character chose to have him born at 06:00 a.m. on June 6. This date is an obvious representation of the number of the beast from Revelation 13:18. Such a date is "his" type of date, and just might be inferred from 2 Thessalonians 2:6, when we are told "in his time he will be revealed." A 6-6-6 type date is "his" time to be revealed.

If I were writing fiction, I would pick this date for the Antichrist. If I had to pick one date in my seven year timeline from 2012-2019 that seemed most appropriate for the Antichrist and the number 666, it would have to be during the year ending in 6 (2016) and be on the sixth day of the sixth month of that year. The only 6/6/6 type of date available would be June 6, 2016.

But I am not writing fiction. This date just happens to be 42 months into Daniel's seventieth week of years, 1260+3 days after the start of a seven year timeline when I expect the Antichrist to be healed from a head wound which would normally be fatal without supernatural intervention. And there just happens to be a rare and appropriate astronomical alignment that same day.

As Above, So Below

Many cultures believed that events on earth are mirrored by events in heaven. In Joel 2:30 God tells us "I will display wonders in the sky and on the earth." Tim LaHaye wrote that sometimes "action takes place in heaven but causes a response on earth."[198] Ancient Egyptians built the three main pyramids at Giza next to the Nile River in a way that accurately represents the belt stars of the constellation Orion next to the Milky Way – an attempt to replicate heaven on earth. But recently I was more interested in finding something astronomical that would mirror the Antichrist entering the Temple in Jerusalem. For such an important event in biblical prophecy – which I believe is riddled with astronomical clues – I was certain something in the sky would correspond to this event.

A new Venus cycle has long been associated with the birth of the Aztec god Quetzalcoatl and my first thought was that the planet Venus probably represents the Antichrist. Isaiah 14:12 says "How you have fallen from heaven, O star of the morning, son of the dawn!" (NASB) The King James version says "How art thou fallen from heaven, O Lucifer, son of the morning!" "This is the only mention of Lucifer by name in the Bible. He is clearly described as Venus, the morning star."[199] If we look up "Lucifer" in the dictionary we can see definition one is "a name of the devil" and definition two is "the planet Venus when appearing as the morning star."[200] Viewing Venus this way also fits the etymology of the word planet: "The word deceive is πλανοσ, (planos) from which we get the word planet, meaning wandering star. It means to mislead or cause to wander."[201]

There is an ancient association of the Sun with the Son of God, well established in many cultures, at least as far back as Babylon. In the Enuma Elish creation story, the highest God Ea says in lines 101 and 102: "My little son, my little son! My son, the Sun! Sun of the heavens!" In Christianity, the fiery altar of the Temple sounds like the Sun, which represents Jesus Christ astronomically.

On June 6, 2016 – 1260 (+3) days into Daniel's 70th week of years – Venus is directly behind the sun from Earth's vantage point. "As the Sun is Christ and Venus is on the opposite (anti-) side we have our astronomical anti-Christ."[202] The full quote of Isaiah 14:12-14 also seems relevant here: "How you have fallen from heaven, O star of the morning, son of the dawn! You have been cut down to the earth, You who have weakened the nations! But you said in your heart, 'I will ascend to heaven; I will raise my throne above the stars of God, and I will sit on the mount of assembly In the recesses of the north. 'I will ascend above the heights of the clouds; I will make myself like the Most High.' At the time the Antichrist will proclaim himself to be God, the month will be June, and the sun will be near its highest point in the sky. But Venus will, from Earth's perspective, be BEHIND the sun – even higher than the sun.

One of Nostradamus' prophecies may be relevant to this. Quatrain 3:34 warns us:

"When the eclipse of the Sun will then be,
The monster will be seen in full day:
Quite otherwise will one interpret it,
High price unguarded: none will have foreseen it."[203]

If a solar eclipse is meant, as Leoni's translation assumes, then this does not apply to 2016. But if the medieval French word "du" is simply translated as "by" instead of "of" in the first line then it might refer to a planet being eclipsed **by** the sun. As light of full day is described, the light of the sun is apparently not being blocked as it would be during an eclipse "of" the sun. At the moment of this alignment (eclipse of Venus by the Sun?) "the monster will be seen" and this could easily be taken to refer to the Antichrist being revealed. Most will have failed to foresee that this man was in fact the Antichrist, and many will suddenly pay a high price for not being on guard against him.

This occultation of Venus behind the sun is a rare event; it only happens 9 times every 105 years - the next time being June 6-7, 2016. Seven years could easily pass by without Venus being occulted by the sun. The odds of Venus going behind the sun on any given day are about 9/(105*365.25) –

odds of about 1 in 4,261. It only happens on a 6-6-6 date one day out of every 15,563,302 days. That means on average it would not happen again on such an interesting date for about 42,611 years. The combination is a VERY rare sign. As it also happens about 3.5 years into my timeline for the final seven years (after exactly 1260 days, plus 3 days to heal, after an assassination attempt) I cannot ignore the appropriate astronomical lineup as mere coincidence. It would be especially difficult to ignore as a coincidence when so many other clues point to the same exact date.

Jubilees

Leviticus 25:1-10: "The Lord then spoke to Moses at Mount Sinai, saying, 'Speak to the sons of Israel, and say to them, 'When you come into the land which I shall give you, then the land shall have a sabbath to the Lord. Six years you shall sow your field, and six years you shall prune your vineyard and gather in its crop, but during the seventh year the land shall have a sabbath rest, a sabbath to the Lord.... Count off seven sabbaths of years for yourself, seven times seven years, so that you have the time of the seven sabbaths of years, namely, forty-nine years. You shall then sound a ram's horn... and proclaim a release through the land to all its inhabitants. It shall be a jubilee for you, and each of you shall return to his own property.'"

As a punishment for ignoring these cycles, the Jews were exiled to Babylon for 70 years, so that the land could experience all the sabbaths which had been ignored. Based on these verses in Leviticus, the forty-nine year cycles of jubilees seem pretty important to God. Some people misunderstand jubilees as occurring every 50 years, but year 50 is just year 1 of the next 49 year cycle, much like an 8th day is the first day of a new seven day week. "The 50th year is simply the first year of the next jubilee cycle."[204] The year after every 49th year was to be a jubilee year when there would be "a release through the land to all its inhabitants." What exactly does that mean? Why is it relevant to calculating the date on which the Antichrist will be revealed?

All sales of land in ancient Israel were really leases. The "sale price" of property was based on how many years were left before the next jubilee at the time of the transaction, because the property would revert back to its original owner (or his family) at the jubilee. God Himself had divided the land of Israel into twelve tribes, and the people felt it was important that the land stayed with the tribe it belonged to. Any "sales" violating the God-given tribal delineations would be rectified every jubilee. In addition, all debts were to be forgiven and all slaves would be freed at the jubilee year. This served as a reminder to the Jewish nation that both the land and the people belong to God, not to human owners – and that any ownership we think we have is temporary.

Many Jews expected the Messiah would come at the end of a jubilee cycle; especially when they lived under foreign domination and yearned to have the land and the people freed and reclaimed by God. The prophet Elijah is quoted in Jewish commentaries on the Old Testament known as the Talmud: "Elijah told Judah, the brother of Sala Hasida, 'The world will endure not less than 85 Jubilees, and on the last Jubilee the Son of David will come.'"[205] 85 jubilees of 49 years each would mean a minimum of 4,165 years must transpire before the messiah could come. Perhaps one reason Jews were not inclined to accept Jesus as Messiah is because less than 3800 years had elapse in their calendar between creation and the ministry of Jesus. "When the Prophet Elijah set a time for the Messiah's arrival, he meant to say as follows: 'Until that time, the eighty fifth Jubilee cycle, do not even hope for him, for he will surely not come before then. But from then on, you may indeed hope for his arrival."[206]

Many Christians also expect Jesus to return at the end of a jubilee, because of Luke 4:18-19, when Jesus was at Nazareth and read to the crowd "The Spirit of the Lord is upon Me, because He anointed Me to preach the gospel to the poor. He has sent Me to proclaim release to the captives, and recovery of sight to the blind, to set free those who are oppressed, to proclaim the favorable year of the Lord." This was based on Isaiah 61:2 "To proclaim the favorable year of the Lord and the day of vengeance of our God." A "favorable year" releasing captives could be a jubilee. Daniel 9:25, if partially quoted out of context, could also lead to such an expectation: "from the issuing of a decree to restore and rebuild Jerusalem until Messiah the Prince there will be seven weeks" or forty-nine years. Others point out that Daniel's 70 weeks (70 * 7 = 490) of years are the same as 10 jubilee cycles. So the Messiah does come at the end of a jubilee cycle, right?

Not when we consider the huge and indeterminate gap of years prior to the 70th week of seven years. Daniel 9:26 clarifies that the messiah is killed after seven and sixty-two weeks.... Since then almost 2000 years have already passed. This gap makes it impossible to find a start date for a jubilee cycle 42 years before the 70th week, to make a full 49 years when it ends. Revelation 11:2 sheds some light on jubilees and the gap of years between

True– But that doesn't make it impossible for Christ To come on a Jubilee year. I Think He will; We just won't know it.

Daniel's 69th and 70th week: "do not measure it, for it has been given to the nations." Although some scholars claim we could deduce when jubilee years would have been if anyone had been keeping track of them – I do not believe the ancient dates of jubilees are relevant to the Second Coming, and I believe we are instructed not to worry about counting the years for jubilee cycles.

It seems almost impossible to do so anyway – to know when such a 49 year cycle last began - because no one has been keeping track of jubilees for about 2500 years. They are only relevant when the twelve tribes are in Israel. Leviticus did not say that Moses should start counting years right away; he was told "When you come into the land which I shall give you" then he should start counting years. The jubilees were primarily for keeping the land properly divided amongst the twelve tribes.

But the Assyrians had conquered the northern kingdom of Israel and carried off almost the entire population of the ten northern tribes into captivity by around 718 B.C. (These are commonly referred to as the "Lost Tribes" because they never returned from captivity; they were either assimilated, killed, or relocated.) Some Jews in the remaining kingdom of Judah already felt that jubilees had become irrelevant because ten out of twelve tribes were not there to benefit from the land ownership restoration of jubilees anymore. After the Babylonians took the last two tribes of Judah and Benjamin into captivity in 584 B.C. – the Second Temple was destroyed, the rabbinical Sanhedrin was disbanded – and no one kept counting years for jubilees. Most scholars do not feel there is any value in trying to calculate when jubilees would have been, because without the twelve tribes present in the land, the jubilees simply have no purpose.

Other scholars who want to keep track of jubilees believe the last reference to a jubilee year was made by the prophet Ezekiel, referring to approximately 574 B.C. If we count 17 jubilee cycles back from 574 BC, the first jubilee cycle would have started in 1406 B.C. If this was the year that the Israelites entered the Promised Land after the Exodus from Egypt, it also corresponds with Thiele's (but not Ussher's) date of 931/930 B.C. for the start of the divided kingdom into Israel and Judah – based on 1 Kings 6:1 "Now it came about in the four hundred and eightieth year after the sons of Israel came out of the land of Egypt, in the fourth year of Solomon's reign over Israel, in the month of Ziv which is the second month, that he began to build the house of the Lord." Since these two methods agree, they might lead us to correct dates for past jubilee years. But if the correct interpretation of Leviticus is that jubilees only matter when all twelve tribes live in Israel, then the jubilees

Like the feasts of Israel, the Jubilees are always
important to God + are a picture of Christ returning
David Montaigne
To free His bride + the earth from the "curse"

have been irrelevant for thousands of years, and would only be relevant again after the Messiah "corrects everything" and ALL the tribes of Israel (not just the Jews of the former kingdom of Judah) are brought back to Israel.

Without the twelve tribes living in Israel, there is no biblical reason to keep track of jubilees. And without the Sanhedrin, who announced the jubilee by blowing the ram's horn trumpet – no one exists to make the start of a jubilee cycle official. Just for the heck of it, however, these dates would imply a jubilee year (if it mattered, and if anyone had been counting) in 35 B.C., 15 A.D. (no year zero) and 64 A.D.

If the old count of jubilees did matter in regard to the Messiah, they certainly did not line up with Jesus Christ's birth, crucifixion, or even the start of His ministry. The last jubilee would have been in 1975 – when nothing noteworthy happened in Israel – and the next jubilee would be in 2024. Misguided calculations have led to other dates, however, and there are many people who believe "2016 is EXACTLY the 120th Jubilee."[207] Such people are expecting the Second Coming in 2016, and if anyone with miraculous powers shows up in 2016 on global television broadcasts claiming to be the Messiah, many people will listen. *If you calculated correctly*

Personally, I agree with most other scholars – that despite the common expectation that Daniel's 490 years refer to ten jubilees and the idea that Christ might return at the end of a jubilee cycle – I think the jubilees have not been relevant for at least 2700 years. They may become relevant again after being restored in the future, but that doesn't help us date Christ's return based on when a jubilee would have ended if anyone were still counting years. At the end of the final seven years Christ will arrive and claim kingship over the earth and that will begin a new set of jubilee cycles.

However, we should expect the Antichrist to attempt to mimic Christ and act like he is fulfilling Bible prophecies so that people will worship him. Daniel 8:23 tells us that "In the latter period of their rule, when the transgressors have run their course, a king will arise, insolent and skilled in intrigue." First off, we should not ignore that this hints that the insolent king will arise (be born?) near the end of the 2300 years of gentile rule over Jerusalem which Daniel had just mentioned, and refers to "the latter period of their rule," which ended in 1967. This insolent king may have been born not long before 1967. Of the few famous leaders sometimes mentioned as candidates for being the Antichrist, we should note that Vladimir Putin was born in 1952, Pope Francis in 1936, Mahmoud Ahmadinejad in 1956, ISIS leader and

160

Caliph al-Baghdadi in 1971, Prince William in 1982, and Barack Obama's birth around 1961 seems to make him the best fit for this particular clue.

Most people correctly assume that Daniel's "insolent king" refers to the Antichrist, even if they merely think it means he will be skilled at political doublespeak. The NASB version of the verse above notes that intrigue could be replaced with "ambiguous speech." But the King James version of Daniel 8:23 says "in the latter time of their kingdom, when the transgressors are come to the full, a king of fierce countenance, and understanding dark sentences, shall stand up." Darkness implies something hidden. Proverbs 1:6 in the NASB suggests that we make efforts "to understand a proverb and a figure, the words of the wise and their riddles." The King James does not say riddles; it says "understand a proverb, and the interpretation; the words of the wise, and their dark sayings." As D.W. Miller explains, "dark sentences" and "dark sayings" are mentioned repeatedly in the Bible and the phrases refer to prophecies.[208]   *That would be any politician!*

If this interpretation is correct then it means the Antichrist will be aware of prophecies; the very ones we are analyzing – and he will do what he can to appear to fulfill messianic prophecies, and appear to be worthy of the worship he demands. Though the date of his big arrival on the scene (when he announces who he really is at the Temple in Jerusalem) must be over three years shy of the end of Daniel's 70th week, the Antichrist does not care about truth in general or the actual relevance of jubilees. But one way the Antichrist could attempt to mimic Christ and deceive those people who aren't experts on the subject – one way to help make people think he is the messiah - is to convince people that his grand appearance is at the end of a jubilee cycle. As Arthur Pink once wrote: "In blasphemous travesty of this Satan will send forth the mock messiah to usher in a false millennium."[209] As we are told in 2 Thessalonians 2:11 "God will send upon them a deluding influence so that they will believe what is false."

There will be many people theorizing about the 49 years after the Israeli entry into East Jerusalem. Even Isaac Newton, in his notes on Bible prophecy, commented that one day Israel would be restored as a nation, and that there would be a particular day when the Jews begin to rebuild Jerusalem. "This part of the Prophecy being therefore not yet fulfilled, I shall not attempt a particular interpretation of it, but content myself with observing, that as the seventy and the sixty two weeks were Jewish weeks, ending with sabbatical years; so the seven weeks are the compass of a Jubilee, and begin and end with actions proper for a Jubilee, and of the

David Montaigne

highest nature for which a Jubilee can be kept: and that since the commandment to return and to build Jerusalem, precedes the Messiah the Prince 49 years…"[210] I will emphasize again this 49 year period ending in 2016 is not the correct match for either the ancient jubilee cycle or the Second Coming in 2019, but especially if early June is newsworthy for assassination and war and the apparent revival of the Antichrist claiming to be the Messiah, millions will believe.

A major element of jubilees is the emphasis on Israel, and how slaves are freed and land "purchases" return to their original owners at the end of these 49 year periods. This is a reminder that people do not permanently own other people, or the land – that God is really the owner of people and land. Remember that the ancient Greek letter "stigma" (no longer in the modern Greek alphabet) not only was the sixth letter, used to represent sixes… it was also a mark put on slaves, a mark of ownership like a cattle brand. As E. W. Bullinger wrote in Number in Scripture: "the word stigma means a mark, but especially a mark made by a brand as burnt upon slaves, cattle, or soldiers, by their owners or masters; or on devotees who thus branded themselves as belonging to their gods."[211]   What better time for the Antichrist to reveal himself and claim to be God, and claim ownership of the people and land – than exactly 49 years after the Israeli Army reclaimed East Jerusalem and the Temple Mount? What better time to force Israel to give up land than when they might believe Leviticus 23:10 is being put into effect: "It shall be a jubilee for you, and each of you shall return to his own property."

The Israelis entered East Jerusalem on June 6, 1967… though the Temple Mount was officially secured early the next morning… so let's say the relevant liberation spanned the night from June 6 to June 7. Venus goes behind the sun June 6 to June 7, 2016 as a heavenly ("as above, so below") correspondence to the event of the Antichrist proclaiming himself to be God in the Temple on June 6, 2016… exactly 49 years after the Israelis entered East Jerusalem to end the time of the Gentiles and establish Jewish control for the first time in thousands of years. I do not think the end of the 49 years from 1967 to 2016 will usher in the Second Coming. But I do think it will usher in the appearance of the Antichrist, and that many people will be fooled into thinking that he is their savior when he most certainly is not.

I believe that the Temple must be rebuilt by June 2016. At that point, as Daniel 9:26 tells us: "the people of the prince who is to come will destroy the city and the sanctuary." Hippolytus clarified these prophecies and commented about 1800 years ago on the Antichrist and the Temple: "he will

did not happen!
VC 8-22-16   162

raise a temple of stone in Jerusalem."[212] If this is correct, not only will the Temple be rebuilt, but the Antichrist may even be instrumental in achieving its construction. And I just heard a rumor in June 2014 that the Israeli government has decided to build the Temple to the side of the Dome of the Rock Mosque; so that Islamic holy sites will not have to be demolished first. This could explain why John was told in Revelation 11:2 "Leave out the court which is outside the temple and do not measure it, for it has been given to the nations; and they will tread under foot the holy city for forty-two months." The outer court of the upcoming Jewish Temple may have the Dome of the Rock Mosque on it. This makes sense to me, as all my research indicates the original Temple was north of the Dome of the Rock. There are three main theories:

A – The Jewish Temple was exactly where Islam's Dome of the Rock Mosque stands today near the southern end of the Temple Mount.
B – The Jewish Temple was South of it.
C – The Jewish Temple was north of it.

I believe that the northern theory, often described as Asher Kaufman's theory – is the correct one. Not only have there been historical records, archeological digs, and even infrared thermal scans supporting this (sunlight heats the pavement of the Temple Mount evenly during the day, but at night the cooling is very uneven, revealing subsurface anomalies like **foundations** by around 11PM) but the Bible gives many clues, such as Ezekiel 43:1-5:

"Then he led me to the gate, the gate facing toward the east; and behold, the glory of the God of Israel was coming from the way of the east. And His voice was like the sound of many waters; and the earth shone with His glory. And it was like the appearance of the vision which I saw, like the vision which I saw when He came to destroy the city. And the visions were like the vision which I saw by the river Chebar; and I fell on my face. And the glory of the Lord came into the house by the way of the gate facing toward the east. And the Spirit lifted me up and brought me into the inner court; and behold, the glory of the Lord filled the house."

These verses clearly describe entering the Temple through the Eastern Gate. Most ancient temples faced east to welcome the rising sun; even Jesus is expected to enter Jerusalem through the Eastern Gate (also called the Golden Gate.) This is the only entrance to the old walled city that gave direct access to the Temple Mount, and it has been sealed shut by the Muslims for over a thousand years, just in case the Christians are correct about Jesus entering it

✱ — *Don't see this happening in view of today's political climate in 163 Israel; However, it could very well be part of the "covenant" confirmed by the Antichrist.*

at the end of the tribulation.

In 1917 the Ottoman Turks still controlled Jerusalem. On the exact day the workmen were about to ruin the ancient stone gate, Muslim control over Jerusalem ended with the entry of the British army. Fifty years later in the Six Day War, some Israeli soldiers suggested surprising the Jordanian defenders of Jerusalem by not entering directly from the west, but circling around and demolishing the sealed Eastern Gate. But an Orthodox Jewish officer protested, reminding his men that according to tradition, the Eastern Gate can only be opened at the arrival of the Messiah.

Matthew 24:27 "For just as the lightning comes from the east and flashes even to the west, so will the coming of the Son of Man be" from the east. Zechariah 14:3-4 says that at the end of the tribulation "Then the Lord will go forth and fight against those nations, as when He fights on a day of battle. In that day His feet will stand on the Mount of Olives, which is in front of Jerusalem on the east." When Jesus touches down just east of Jerusalem on the Mount of Olives it makes sense that He will enter through the Eastern Gate into the Temple.

It also makes sense that the Holy of Holies was located on a rock outcropping where the bedrock reaches above the pavement level. There are only two such possibilities. One is the Rock in the Dome of the Rock Mosque. The Second is the very unassuming little structure known as the "Dome of the Tablets" or "Dome of the Spirits." This is far north of the Dome of the Rock, but is on a direct east-west line between the existing Eastern Gate and the site of the ancient Western Gate. The Dome of the Rock is 348 feet too far south, and covers an uneven outcropping on which the Ark of the Covenant could not have been set down. The Dome of the Tablets/Spirits covers a rock outcropping which is flat and level. It also fits an ancient description of the site of the Temple from the Hebrew Mishnah in Middot 2:1 stating that the greatest portion of the outer court lay to the south, with the second greatest portion to the east. This would mean the Temple has stood closest to the northern edge of the Temple Mount, and second closest to its western edge – as the Dome of the Tablets does. Of course the name – the Dome of the Tablets – also describes the contents of the Ark.

One of the flights of steps at the northwest edge of the raised platform supporting the Dome of the Rock Mosque provides another major clue. It is not aligned parallel to the Mosque platform like all the others and is built of larger stones – because it is part of the original Temple walls. This would place "the Rock" of the Dome outside the original Temple of Solomon.

I know people who claim to have touched the stones that will soon be used in a new Temple. I hear rumors that the Israelis are in possession of the Ark of the Covenant. I am told a new Temple will be built very soon on the Temple Mount with German help... If this is true, then prophecy is unfolding before our eyes, and the Temple will be ready 49 years after 1967.

Interestingly – the last time Jerusalem and its holy sites changed hands was just over 49 years before 1967, when the British captured Jerusalem from the Turks during Hanukkah in December 1917. The Turks fled at the appearance of British aircraft, perhaps as described in Isaiah 31:5 "Like flying birds so the Lord of hosts will protect Jerusalem. He will protect and deliver it; He will pass over and rescue it." And there was also an Arab prophecy that "When the Nile flows into Palestine God's Prophet from the west will drive the Turk from Jerusalem."

As unlikely as that may have sounded prior to the 19th century: in 1917 the British government sent General Edmund Allenby to capture Jerusalem. One of the first things his men did was to build a canal from the Nile River in Egypt east into Palestine. Allenby also had propaganda pamphlets dropped over Jerusalem from airplanes. The message he had written in English was of course translated into Arabic, and he signed his name – Allenby - which read "Allah Nebi" in Arabic - "God's Prophet." Jerusalem was surrendered to the British on December 9, 1917 – the first day of Hanukkah, the day which celebrates the recapture of the Temple by the Macabees in 165 B.C. General Allenby fulfilled prophecy by taking Jerusalem this way, and he did so just a few months over one jubilee before June 6, 1967 – when Israeli forces took over Jerusalem. I believe another change in control of the city is coming on June 6, 2016.

This pair of June 6 dates would not cap the ends of one of God's jubilees as described to Moses and Joshua. But with a 49 year duration and great relevance to the land of Israel, this historical time frame of the first 49 years of Israeli rule over a united Jerusalem will undoubtedly be used by the Antichrist as an alleged sign of his divinity. Over 1800 years ago, Irenaeus warned us in <u>Against Heresies</u> that the Antichrist would rely on "wickedness, **false prophecy**, and deception." Many will be fooled into believing him.

David Montaigne

The Great Apostasy

Another clue regarding the June 2016 time frame for the actions of the Antichrist involves the significance of Passover.   Daniel 7:25 tells us the Antichrist "will speak against the Most High and oppress his holy people and try to change the set times and the laws. The holy people will be delivered into his hands for a time, times and half a time."

Moses received the law on the 50th day after Passover, the Jewish holiday of Shavuot. The significance of this is compounded by Pentecost, when the Holy Spirit descended on the Apostles on the 50th day after Jesus' last Passover. Passover in 2016 starts on April 22, one of the latest possible dates it could ever have in our Gregorian calendar. 50 days later will be June 11, 2016 – just a few days after the most important date of June 6 when the Antichrist declares himself Lord of the Earth. I would expect a new set of laws (Sharia Law, perhaps?) for the planet to be announced by the Antichrist and the False Prophet soon after they seize power in Israel and begin to take over the world in earnest. I think this will probably be announced on June 11, 2016 in another attempt to mimic God's past actions – in this case, giving the Law to Moses fifty days after Passover.

Since June 11, 2016 is a Saturday, it may seem unlikely as a day for "new laws." In America, I think Monday would be more likely, as the first day of our workweek. But remember that Friday is the Islamic Sabbath, and if the Antichrist is imposing Sharia Law, he may very well impose an Iranian style weekend (half days on Thursday, and all of Friday off) with the new work week commencing on Saturday – which would make the new times and laws especially insulting to Jews, forcing them to start work weeks on the Jewish day of rest.

Why does Passover give us a clue pointing to June 2016, and not some other year? In order to give the world new laws, the Antichrist must already have seized power and been revealed in Jerusalem.   Passover always begins on the 15th day of the Hebrew month of Nisan, which is rarely late enough in our Gregorian calendar year to be within fifty days of June 6. To mimic the past "giving of the law" to Moses accurately, the Antichrist should force new laws on us fifty days after the first day of Passover. In 2013 Passover began March 25 and 50 days later it was only May 14 – far too early to give us new laws after seizing power on a 6/6 type date like Damien was born on in The Omen. In 2014 Passover began on April 14; but 50 days later still fell a little short of June 6. In 2015 the dates are April 3 and May 23; finally in 2016

Passover is very late (starting April 22) so June 6 is only 45 days later. In 2016 the Antichrist could seize power on the date like the number of the beast and still be able to give "the law" to people with the date of the new legal proclamation exactly 50 days after Passover. Starting in 2017 Passover's timing doesn't allow the right scenario again; the dates are April 10 and May 30. All Passover dates are too early for several years to come until 2024. So while the timing of Passover in our calendar does not specify 2016 as the only possible year the Antichrist could be revealed, it does allow the Antichrist to mimic the giving of the law at the right time in 2016, whereas this is not possible in most other years.

In reality, the coming of the Antichrist will offer us no new laws from God. His arrival will merely be a foreshadowing of more to come, similar to the Morningstar – Venus. As morning star, Venus is seen shining brightly on the eastern horizon just before sunrise – as if making the first announcement that the sun is soon to come. In the end times, Venus makes special alignments that serve as warnings.

It seems obvious that the "crescent moon and star" symbol of Islam is meant to indicate a crescent moon with the planet Venus at the center of the edge of the dark portion of the moon. (Although the sun is not depicted in the image, it is implied by the orientation of the crescent of the partially visible moon that the sun, moon, and Venus are in a straight line.) One could easily argue that this is the symbol of Allah. It is the same Islamic symbol of the crescent moon with the huge "star" at the edge of the dark portion of the moon which is depicted on the flag of the old Ottoman Caliphate, or on the modern flag of Turkey, or Pakistan, or many other Islamic nations. This is the main symbol of Islam; and it is prominently displayed on the tops of all mosques.

Revelation 13:2 tells us the Antichrist gets his power from Satan. In Isaiah 14, the Hebrew words used for Lucifer are "Heylal Ben Shahar." Heylal or hilal means "morning star" in Hebrew which we now know is the same as the "evening star" and both are really the planet Venus when the sun is just below the horizon. Even our English word for planet is based on the deceiver we associate with Venus. In Greek, "the word deceive is πλανοσ, (planos) from which we get the word planet, meaning wandering star. It means to mislead or cause to wander."[213] Not that the fallen angel Lucifer is the only heavenly being associated with a planet.

"Shahar," means "dawn" but in Hebrew this is almost identical to "sahar." "Sahar" literally means "moon" but is often used in Hebrew poetry to mean "crescent moon." In Arabic the word "sahar" means "a time just before dawn," (which is when Venus is visible as the "morning star") and it is the word heylal or hilal that means crescent moon in Arabic. In Hebrew, "heylel" (הילל) translates as "noun masculine appellative. 'shining one,' epithet of king of Babylon."[214] The Hebrew gematria value of the word is 75, and may be linked to the 75 days at the end of Daniel's 70th week when the Antichrist is dealt with – or even to the 75 days from Purim to June 6, 2016 – which we will discuss later.

The Hebrew word "ben" means "son of." "Heylal Ben Shahar," could be translated as "morning star son of crescent moon." One has to wonder if "Antichrist, son of Allah" is an analogy worth considering. Of course this is not how it has been translated in any English Bible. Young's Literal translation of the phrase is "shining one, son of the dawn." And the NASB I generally use says "star of the morning, son of the dawn." But "morning star, son of crescent moon" is at least as credible a translation as The King James Bible has when it says "Lucifer, son of the morning." Has Satan placed his "name" above every Islamic mosque? This is a very relevant question as we approach the final 3.5 years and a false religion persecutes Christians and Jews… (It is also relevant that Isaiah is discussing the King of Babylon just before mentioning Lucifer.)

The Islamic symbol of the crescent moon and Venus is somewhat similar to the Earth-Sun-Venus alignment of June 6, 2016. But does a crescent moon with Venus at its edge alignment ever actually occur?

Yes it does. They are rare, but the next possible sighting will be April 6, 2016. Does it mean that Satan or the Antichrist will do something two months before his big announcement? As with the blood moons in 2014 and 2015 – it doesn't necessarily mean anything will happen then, but time will tell soon enough. Alignments in the heavens often parallel events on the ground on earth – so when Allah's symbol is in the sky on April 6, 2016 – we might see a major historical event involving Islam. It could be the start of a new war in the Middle East, or perhaps a major terrorist event. Perhaps the Antichrist will give a speech in which few realize he is foreshadowing events in the near future.

None of these thoughts change my expectations regarding the Antichrist and the Venus alignment on June 6, 2016. That is when Venus helps deliver the greatest warning of all, when the Antichrist will make his false claims in the Temple and there are just 3.5 years of Tribulation to go before Judgment

Day. For millions of people who weren't paying attention before this event, Venus will help give the first sign that the Son is soon to rise.

Unfortunately the Antichrist must come first. Remember 2 Thessalonians 2:2-5 "with regard to the coming of our Lord Jesus Christ and our gathering together to Him, that you not be quickly shaken from your composure or be disturbed either by a spirit or a message or a letter as if from us, to the effect that the day of the Lord has come. Let no one in any way deceive you, for it will not come unless the apostasy comes first, and the man of lawlessness is revealed, the son of destruction, who opposes and exalts himself above every so-called god or object of worship, so that he takes his seat in the temple of God, displaying himself as being God."

The apostasy, the great falling away of many previously faithful Christians, will undoubtedly begin in earnest when the Antichrist is revealed. This is not a general or gradual decline in religious faith like Christianity has already experienced in the 19th and 20th centuries; this is the apostasy, a specific event involving the Antichrist and leading to widespread breach of faith – abandonment of faith – and defiance of authority.

Many Christians, including most in America, believe in a pre-tribulation rapture. Michael Rood suggests: "They have a false hope that Jesus is legally bound to appear before the time when man's and Satan's wrath are escalated."[215] You may not need to worry about God's wrath – but unless you make a deal with Satan by taking the mark of the beast, you do have to worry about the Antichrist's wrath. I believe that the seven seals in Revelation are terrible events that eventually unseal the scroll belonging to God and Jesus. I agree with the many authors who conclude that too many scriptures tell us we are not raptured away before the Great Tribulation.

Despite what I and many others have concluded, (that the idea of a pre-tribulation rapture is not supported by the Bible) that doesn't stop church leaders from preaching the reassuring pre-tribulation theory people want to hear. 2 Timothy 4:3-4 warns "For the time will come when they will not endure sound doctrine; but wanting to have their ears tickled, they will accumulate for themselves teachers in accordance to their own desires, and will turn away their ears from the truth and will turn aside to myths." Perry Stone says in a video on "The Bloodline of the Antichrist": "Americans don't know the Bible. They don't know what it says. A lot of them are getting preached a lot of pablum and sugar and ice cream."[216] Drew Simmons, the author of Quenched Like a Wick, says "(The pastors and end-time teachers,

* already happening w/ The gospel of "self-esteem, Name it & claim it, & "God wants you to be rich."

David Montaigne *?*

the drunkards of Ephraim) have built up this case for a pre-trib rapture, but it's not scripturally sound."[217]   It does not make sense to me for Christ to arrive at the middle of the 70th week and do nothing to interfere with the Antichrist at the peak of his power.

But the truth is that suffering and persecution is crucial – it is God's method of judgment. As Tertullian said many centuries ago, "For what is the issue of persecution, what other result comes of it, but the approving and rejecting of faith, in regard to which the Lord will certainly sift His people?"[218]

Revelation 3:10 refers to "…the hour of testing, that hour which is about to come upon the whole world, to test those who dwell on the earth."

2 Thessalonians 1:5 indicates we must be tested "so that you will be considered worthy of the kingdom of God, for which indeed you are suffering." *Bible also tells us we cannot be Worthy on our own (works) but only thru the blood of Christ*
1 Peter 4:12 says "Beloved, do not be surprised at the fiery ordeal among you, which comes upon you for your testing, as though some strange thing were happening to you."

Revelation 6:9-11 describes martyrdom of the saints "When the Lamb broke the fifth seal, I saw underneath the altar the souls of those who had been slain because of the word of God, and because of the testimony which they had maintained; and they cried out with a loud voice, saying, 'How long, O Lord, holy and true, will You refrain from judging and avenging our blood on those who dwell on the earth?' And there was given to each of them a white robe; and they were told that they should rest for a little while longer, until the number of their fellow servants and their brethren who were to be killed even as they had been, would be completed also." Dead tribulation saints are requesting vengeance (God's wrath) but there is no wrath or rapture of the faithful yet. *We have to separate who the "Saints" are – are they Jews? or Christians?*
Revelation 6:12-14 describes the breaking of the sixth seal and the pole shift which does not start until the end of the seven years on December 21, 2019: "I looked when He broke the sixth seal, and there was a great earthquake; and the sun became black as sackcloth made of hair, and the whole moon became like blood; and the stars of the sky fell to the earth, as a fig tree casts its unripe figs when shaken by a great wind. The sky was split apart like a scroll when it is rolled up, and every mountain and island were moved out of their places." There is still no rapture as the pole shift begins, and Matthew

24:29 confirms this is at the end of the seven years: "immediately **after the tribulation** of those days the sun will be darkened, and the moon will not give its light, and the stars will fall from the sky, and the powers of the heavens will be shaken." But soon after, in Matthew 24:31, "He will send forth His angels with a great trumpet and they will gather together His elect."

Again - Who is the Elect? The Jews? Or Christians?

The pole shift at the end of the tribulation is also at the same time frame as the end of the great war known as the Apocalypse, the Ezekiel War, or the Gog-Magog War. Ezekiel 38:17-20 reads: "Thus says the Lord God, 'Are you the one of whom I spoke in former days through My servants the prophets of Israel, who prophesied in those days for many years that I would bring you against them? It will come about on that day, when Gog comes against the land of Israel,' declares the Lord God, 'that My fury will mount up in My anger. In My zeal and in My blazing wrath I declare that on that day there will surely be a great earthquake in the land of Israel. The fish of the sea, the birds of the heavens, the beasts of the field, all the creeping things that creep on the earth, and all the men who are on the face of the earth will shake at My presence; the mountains also will be thrown down, the steep pathways will collapse and every wall will fall to the ground."

Ezekiel 39:7 "My holy name I will make known in the midst of My people Israel; and I will not let My holy name be profaned anymore. And the nations will know that I am the Lord, the Holy One in Israel." This one verse tells us two crucial things. First, after the Gog-Magog war, God will never let His holy name be profaned again. Based on that alone, the Gog-Magog war (or Ezekiel 38-39 war) cannot be an event prior to the time of the Antichrist and Armageddon. The verse also ends with the words "the Holy One **in** Israel." The phrase, "the Holy One **of** Israel" is used 31 times in the Bible, but Ezekiel 39:7 is the only instance using "**in** Israel."[219] If He has appeared in Israel in person at the end of the Ezekiel War, it is the final war, and the battle of Armageddon has been fought.

Many Christians have been taught that these are separate wars, but consider that: both Gog and the Antichrist use a false peace and invade when Israel feels secure. (Ezekiel 38:12-13, Daniel 8:25, 9:27, 11:24, Isaiah 10.20, 1 Thessalonians 5:2-3) Both the armies of Gog and the Antichrist are destroyed by a great earthquake. (Ezekiel 38:19-20, and Revelation 16:18-20) Both armies are devoured by birds and beasts. (Ezekiel 39:17-20, and Revelation 19:17-18) Both armies are from the same nations. (Ezekiel 38:5, and Daniel 11:43) Both Gog and the Antichrist die from the "sword" of the Lord. (Ezekiel 38:21, and Revelation 19:15-21) After both deaths, the Lord is never blasphemed again. (Ezekiel 38:23, 39:7, and Revelation 20:2, 21:8) Gog falls in the open field (Ezekiel 39:5) and the Antichrist falls in the plain of Israel. (Revelation 20:9) Some would argue that Gog is buried (Ezekiel 39:11) and the Antichrist is "thrown alive into the lake of fire." (Revelation 19:20) But Isaiah 14:11 says the world celebrates the death of the King of Babylon when he has "been brought down to Sheol; maggots are spread out as your bed beneath you and worms are your covering." Verses 18-20 suggest that the Antichrist is first buried in a grave and then his soul is brought out because he doesn't even deserve burial: "you have been cast out of your tomb like a rejected branch, clothed with the slain who are pierced with a sword, who go down to the stones of the pit like a trampled corpse. You will not be united with them in burial, because you have ruined your country." Joel Richardson makes a more extensive comparison of the "two wars"[220] and I agree – there is just one last war at Armageddon.

Revelation 7:2-4 tells us an angel "cried out with a loud voice to the four angels to whom it was granted to harm the earth and the sea, saying, 'Do not harm the earth or the sea or the trees until we have sealed the bond-servants of our God on their foreheads.' And I heard the number of those who were sealed, one hundred and forty-four thousand sealed from every tribe of the sons of Israel...." *The Bible never says that Jews will be Raptured (unless they are "completed" Jesus · Christians.* Obviously those faithful Jewish servants have not been raptured away if they still require sealing to keep them safe; and they need the seal to keep them safe as they start (yes, START) to evangelize and teach Christianity during the tribulation. "Why would God want to take His army home when the greatest opportunity to win the lost will be during this time?"[221]

The gospels also tell us that Satan is the ruler of the present world. John 16:11 tells us "the ruler of this world has been judged." We are living in a world which has belonged to Satan, and until that changes, we aren't going anywhere. "How can anyone enter the strong man's house and carry off his property, unless he first binds the strong man?" (Matthew 12:29, and Mark 3:27) I believe there is no rapture until the end of the tribulation, when the Antichrist is defeated.

This is after the first six seals of Antichrist, War, Famine, Death, and Martyrdom, have already been broken and released in chapter six – this is when survivors will be ready to come back to the Lord. The sealed 144,000 Jewish evangelists are also the ones referred to in Revelation 14:4 "These are the ones who follow the Lamb wherever He goes. These have been

[margin handwritten note: We have no way of knowing exactly who the 144,000 will be]

purchased from among men as first fruits to God and to the Lamb." So these are the special select group saved first, they are first fruits, yet they follow Jesus wherever he goes, meaning they are still evangelizing even after the Second Coming, but before the Last Day.

Luke 21:27-28 even says "Then they will see the Son of Man coming in a cloud with power and great glory. But when these things begin to take place, straighten up and lift up your heads, because your redemption is drawing near." Even when Jesus returns near the end of the tribulation, it is still not quite time for the rapture immediately, though it will be "drawing near" by that point.

There is a strong case for the sudden arrival of a great crowd in heaven being interpreted as the rapture in Revelation 7:11-14: "And all the angels were standing around the throne and around the elders and the four living creatures; and they fell on their faces before the throne and worshiped God, saying, 'Amen, blessing and glory and wisdom and thanksgiving and honor and power and might, be to our God forever and ever. Amen.' Then one of the elders answered, saying to me, 'These who are clothed in the white robes, who are they, and where have they come from?' I said to him, 'My lord, you know.' And he said to me, 'These are the ones who come out of the great tribulation, and they have washed their robes and made them white in the blood of the Lamb.'" So one moment the angels and elders were bowing down to worship God, and then in that moment while they bowed and prayed a great multitude of souls arrived in heaven. Those bowing and praying finished, said "Amen," stood up, and suddenly realized they were surrounded by a great number of new arrivals in heaven. Since there were also the "four living creatures" who represent Taurus, Aquarius, Leo, and Scorpio – the cardinal constellations of the zodiac that defined "the plane of the earth" to the ancients – falling on their faces, bowing down – I think this indicates the pole shift is in progress and is the likely method of several billion deaths on the same day in a rapture.

Good grief !!

Daniel 7:21-22 sums it up well: "I kept looking, and that horn was waging war with the saints and overpowering them until the Ancient of Days came and judgment was passed in favor of the saints of the Highest One, and the time arrived when the saints took possession of the kingdom." The saints suffer horrible persecution on earth under the little horn (Antichrist) until after the Second Coming happens AND Judgment is passed. *again who are " the Saints"?*

Perhaps Jesus sums it up even better in Matthew 13:36-43 "Then He left the crowds and went into the house. And His disciples came to Him and said, 'Explain to us the parable of the tares of the field.' And He said, 'The one who sows the good seed is the Son of Man, and the field is the world; and as for the good seed, these are the sons of the kingdom; and the tares are the sons of the evil one; and the enemy who sowed them is the devil, and the harvest is the end of the age; and the reapers are angels. So just as the tares are gathered up and burned with fire, so shall it be at the end of the age. The Son of Man will send forth His angels, and they will gather out of His kingdom all stumbling blocks, and those who commit lawlessness, and will throw them into the furnace of fire; in that place there will be weeping and gnashing of teeth. Then the righteous will shine forth as the sun in the kingdom of their Father. He who has ears, let him hear." *So, we see here that there is more than one gathering – I think there are*

First the tares – the lawless ones are burned. Then the righteous are harvested. This must come after the lawless ones persecute the saints.

Most American Christians believe in the idea of an early rapture. They know, as 1 Thessalonians 1:10 says, we can count on "Jesus, who rescues us from the wrath to come." They hope that statement is all-inclusive. They hope to be rescued from all the end times suffering described in the Bible. But the important thing is to be rescued from the wrath of God and eternal damnation, not the wrath of the Antichrist.

It is not within the scope of this present book to argue the timing of the rapture at greater length. If the evidence were one hundred per cent clear the debate would have been settled centuries ago. I must suggest that the idea of a pre-tribulation rapture is incorrect; and that when all hell breaks loose, and the Antichrist is revealed, and there is a huge expansion of war, and famine, and plague – and Christians see the tribulation is happening and affecting them – many who believed they were going to be raptured away before these events will lose faith, rather than adjust their expectations to allow for suffering through years of horrific events. Those who doubted and had weak faith before the tribulation may give up what faith they had and give in to satisfying their immediate needs. 2 Peter 3:3-4 warns us "that in the last days mockers will come with their mocking, following after their own lusts, and saying, 'Where is the promise of His coming?'"

There will be pressure from governments pushing some form of physical ID mark. I hear rumors that some people already have a mark in their hand. There are already pastors telling their flock that it is OK to take the mark as long as you renounce it and express true faith in Jesus before the Last Day.[222]

There may not be time to think straight. Isaiah chapter 21:2-4 describes a person's anxiety around the time when Babylon is falling: "The treacherous one still deals treacherously, and the destroyer still destroys.... Pains have seized me like the pains of a woman in labor. I am so bewildered I cannot hear, so terrified I cannot see. My mind reels, horror overwhelms me." But this is when we need to be alert and watch for signs, as the Lord says in Isaiah 21:7 "pay close attention, very close attention."

Imagine the following extreme example: Your family is kneeling down outside with hands behind their heads like everyone else who was just rounded up in your neighborhood. All are being asked to renounce God and Jesus and acknowledge allegiance to the Antichrist and accept the mark. Young girls are being raped at gunpoint. The decapitated heads of faithful neighbors you just spoke with so recently lie silent in a puddle of blood. Your young, terrified children are crying and pleading with you to tell the soldiers whatever they want to hear. You vaguely remember some of Revelation 20:4 "And I saw the souls of those who had been beheaded because of their testimony of Jesus and because of the word of God, and those who had not worshiped the beast or his image, and had not received the mark on their forehead and on their hand; and they came to life and reigned with Christ...." but you are not given enough time to remember the entire verse. You are filled with hate and fear, but are powerless before the soldiers in front of you who, in a thick foreign accent, give you five seconds to make a decision while they hold bloody swords ready at the necks of your children, awaiting your answer.

Matthew 24:9-12 describes what will happen: "Then they will deliver you to tribulation, and will kill you, and you will be hated by all nations because of My name. At that time many will fall away and will betray one another and hate one another. Many false prophets will arise and will mislead many. Because lawlessness is increased, most people's love will grow cold. But the one who endures to the end, he will be saved." I would have thought that only the strongest-willed Christians who made a firm decision ahead of time will resist. C.S. Lewis wrote in Mere Christianity that in such a situation "I must not deny my religion even to save myself from death by torture."[223]

But Mark 13:11-13 says: "When they arrest you and hand you over, do not worry beforehand about what you are to say, but say whatever is given you in that hour; for it is not you who speak, but it is the Holy Spirit. Brother will betray brother to death, and a father his child; and children will rise up

175

against parents and have them put to death. You will be hated by all because of My name, but the one who endures to the end, he will be saved."

Luke 21:12-17 is also similar: "But before all these things, they will lay their hands on you and will persecute you, delivering you to the synagogues and prisons, bringing you before kings and governors for My name's sake. It will lead to an opportunity for your testimony. So make up your minds not to prepare beforehand to defend yourselves; for I will give you utterance and wisdom which none of your opponents will be able to resist or refute. But you will be betrayed even by parents and brothers and relatives and friends, and they will put some of you to death, and you will be hated by all because of My name."

When wars, depression, famine and other forms of suffering make Christians realize they were not raptured away before tribulation, they will be stunned – dismayed – shocked – and vulnerable. In 584 B.C. the ancient Jews experienced a similar religious crisis. Most Jews believed they had an unbreakable covenant with God, which would keep their Temple and their capital Jerusalem safe, and continue the royal line of David forever[224] as in 2 Samuel 7:12-16 "Your house and your kingdom shall endure before Me forever." But the city was sacked, the Temple was destroyed, and the king and his sons were executed as the population was dragged to Babylon. Lamentations 2:2-5 describes how the people felt betrayed by God: "The Lord has destroyed without mercy... The Lord has become like an enemy." The prophet Jeremiah advised that after seventy years of atonement and exile there would be a new covenant. This may have done little good for Jews whose expectations and faith in God had been shattered. Many gave up and were assimilated into Babylonian culture.

If many Jews lost their faith during the Babylonian captivity; if Germans were desperate for a savior after defeat in WWI – Christians who survive the start of the tribulation will be that much more desperate because the suffering will be far worse. A deceiver far worse than Hitler will have more power and technology at his disposal to convince them they need to follow orders. Imagine the personal crisis in the mind of a suddenly homeless Christian, fleeing one of several nuked cities with millions of other refugees, unemployed, hungry, cold, possibly separated from family and friends, and surely forever separated from any sense of security he ever had.

Christians may be questioning God and their religious views while being told that although New York and the United Nations have been destroyed, the most powerful men on the planet have made their New World Order capital in Jerusalem. One claiming to be Jesus says Christianity had it all wrong (obvious now, right?) and that Islam is the true religion and that the Mahdi is the true Savior. Both are proclaiming Islam and denouncing Christianity as corrupted and misunderstood. There are offers of free food and shelter in a nearby refugee camp if you just accept the mark of submission and acknowledge the Mahdi as your Caliph, your supreme leader and Allah's representative on Earth.

Will the average starving and disillusioned Christian be able to keep his faith and admit that he must have misunderstood the relative timing of the rapture? With the faith and patience of a Job or a Jeremiah, will the average Christian endure the wrath of the Antichrist without losing his faith in God's grace and salvation through Jesus Christ? Or will he listen to the indoctrination from the forces of the Antichrist, and justify his actions with internal dialogue like: "I'll just get one meal from them for my starving family, even if we have to nod in agreement while eating." Or maybe "We'll just stay here a little while for the kids to regain their strength, even if I have to pretend they are convincing me the Bible is wrong." Or "I'll just let them tattoo their ID# on us to get the food, it doesn't really change what we believe." How long can anyone stand on that slippery slope before he renounces Christianity and bows down in prayer to Allah and his great representatives on earth? Many a former Christian will consciously abandon their religion.

Few will understand that even Jesus' death was a relief after life had been filled with sacrifice and suffering. Few will take 2 Corinthians 5:8 to heart: "We are of good courage, I say, and prefer rather to be absent from the body and to be at home with the Lord." Many will take the mark of the beast in order to put food in their starving bellies and save the lives of their children and themselves. This will be the great apostasy.

The Antichrist seems likely to initiate the final 3.5 years of great tribulation while standing at a Jewish Temple in Jerusalem on June 6, 2016. It does not seem like a coincidence that he will do so within hours of exactly 49 years after the Israeli liberation of all of Jerusalem - when the ground of the Temple Mount reverted back to Jewish control. Daniel 11:39 warns "with the help of a foreign god; he will give great honor to those who acknowledge him and will cause them to rule over the many, and will parcel out land for a price." Will the Antichrist redistribute all land to his supporters? Will the families of those Arabs who left Israel in 1948 be offered "the right of return" their leaders have been pushing for? Some will argue this is what

Leviticus 23:10 refers to when it says: "It shall be a jubilee for you, and each of you shall return to his own property." Will all of Israel be given over to Muslim control in June 2016? The timing is especially appropriate in regard to an alleged jubilee if the Antichrist is attempting to justify the return of such land from Israel to what claims is its "rightful owner" – Allah.

The Temple and The Great Pyramid

Revelation 11:1 "Then there was given me a measuring rod like a staff; and someone said, "Get up and measure the temple of God and the altar, and those who worship in it." Although this task is meant for John, we might find some interesting clues if we assume this command may also have been meant for us. There are a few possible numbers which could be clues towards proper measurement of the temple. The word used here for "temple" is the Greek "naus," the letters of which have a gematria value of 321. We also have a possible clue in 2 Chronicles 3:1 "Then Solomon began to build the house of the Lord in Jerusalem on Mount Moriah, where the Lord had appeared to his father David, at the place that David had prepared on the threshing floor of Ornan the Jebusite." Such a threshing floor would have had a circle at its center, defined by the width of the oxen used to do the work. Any online image search of the words "threshing floor" will show a circular one.

David Flynn (author of <u>Temple at the Center of Time</u>) suggests that in an attempt to measure the size of the "temple of God" from Revelation 11:1, it may be relevant that if we assume the radius of the circle is 321 units (from the gematria value of the word "naus") and multiply by 2*Pi using the imprecise value 3.14 for Pi, we get a circumference of 2015.88 units, which we can assume the ancients would have rounded off to 2016. A more precise value of Pi extended to more decimal places (3.14159) leads to a circumference of 2016.90 units. Without knowing exactly how precise a value of Pi the ancients may have used, we can't convert this measurement to an exact date in our calendar, but it is interesting that it might be a clue to the significance of the year 2016 to the Jewish Temple.[225]

This idea prompted me to look up Flynn's book online. The top book review on Amazon mentions some additional noteworthy "coincidences" Flynn noted, such as the 1948 nautical miles between London and the Temple Mount in Jerusalem – relevant because the British granted independence to

Israel in the year 1948 – and that there are also 666 nautical miles from the Temple Mount to the Ka'aba Cube in Mecca – which is especially relevant if Islam is the religion of the Antichrist. The distance from The Temple Mount to the Statue of Liberty at the edge of New York City is 5706 statute miles, which is 5040 (symbolic of perfection) plus 666. As I believe the Statue of Liberty helps clarify that New York is Mystery Babylon, and that America was once a great land but is now ruled by a top candidate for the title of Antichrist – these distances might just be divine clues. David Flynn seemed to indicate that measuring distances from Solomon's Temple indicates an evil end times link between New York and Islam and the Antichrist, and that 2016 may be a crucial year for such end times events.

Revelation 11:2 also has a numerical clue about measuring the temple, and it is even more clear this clue pertains to time: "Leave out the court which is outside the temple and do not measure it, for it has been given to the nations; and they will tread under foot the holy city for forty-two months." The 42 months is universally viewed as 1260 days. Another way to view the 1260 measurement could refer to the outer court of the temple. If it is a square with sides of 1260 units, it would be 5040 units around its perimeter. 5040 is an amazing number, easily and evenly divisible by the first ten numbers, by 12, and by dozens of other numbers. $1*2*3*4*5*6*7 = 5040$. Plato revered it as the ideal number and based the measurements and divisions of his ideal city of Magnesia on 5040. John Michell points out in The Dimensions of Paradise that 5040 was also known as the combined total of the earth's radius and the moon's radius in miles: 3960+1080.[226]

David Flynn describes many additional numbers that he thinks are relevant to measuring the Temple in Jerusalem, including subtracting the 3024 foot perimeter of the Great Pyramid in Egypt from 5040 and arriving at 2016. While I don't agree with the significance of all the possible clues he details, the online pdf file that served as my initial introduction to his ideas concludes with "Based on the numbers, it looks more and more clear that the time between the end of 2012 and the beginning of 2020 encompasses the last week of Daniel"[227] – and I do thoroughly agree with that.

In 2013 I heard rumors that the blocks of the Third Temple have been completed and are sitting, waiting, ready to be assembled quickly when the political decision is made to move forward. We know the Temple Mount in Jerusalem was retaken in 1967. I believe the Temple will be in place for the Antichrist to enter in 2016. And there might already be a Temple already largely pre-assembled and ready to go by 2013. In which case John 2:20 is

VERY interesting: "The Jews then said, "It took forty-six years to build this temple, and will You raise it up in three days?" There are 46 years for building from 1967 to 2013, and three more to 2016 for raising. When the decision is made to put the blocks together no later than mid-2016, how fast can it possibly be done?

Tim LaHaye (and many others) have suggested that stone blocks have been cut, priests descended from Levites have been trained, red heifers bred and sacrificed, and worship utensils "have been prefabricated in preparation for the day that permission is granted to begin construction of the third temple."[228] I just spoke to an Israeli who confirms this is true and that he has touched the blocks and seen 93 other temple utensils. Rabbi Goren, the former Chief Rabbi of the Israeli Defense Forces – the rabbi who blew the shofar (ram's horn trumpet) just after the Israeli recapture of the Western Wall and the Temple Mount in June 1967 – said in a 1981 interview with Newsweek Magazine that "the secret location of the Ark [Could it be the lost cave where Jeremiah allegedly hid the ark in the Apocrypha's 2 Maccabees 2:4-6?] will be revealed just prior to building the Third Temple."[229] Did Rabbi Goren merely have beliefs about the Ark of the Covenant, or did he know something?

The Royal Chronicles of Ethiopia tell us that Prince Menelik was the son of the Queen of Sheba and King Solomon of Israel. Menelik was raised by Solomon after the queen left, and was educated by Temple priests until age 19, when (as the Ethiopian national epic, the Kebra-Nagast tells us) the Queen of Sheba died, and the Ethiopian court sent for Menelik to come to Ethiopia as king. Their story claims that Solomon made Menelik a replica of the Ark, as he would be too far from Jerusalem to worship at the Temple. But Menelik was concerned with the growing apostasy in Israel, and (allegedly) with the help of like-minded priests, switched the replica with the real Ark and took it to what he believed would be a safer location in Ethiopia, where many people believe it remains to this day – in the Church of Zion of Mary in Aksum.[230] I am reminded of Joshua 22:28 "See the copy of the altar of the Lord which our fathers made, not for burnt offering or for sacrifice; rather it is a witness between us and you."

Ethiopian Falashas ("Falasha" means "exile" in the Amharic language) claim Jewish descent from David and Solomon through Menelik and his Israelite companions. Ethiopian Emporer Haile Selassie (who was overthrown by a communist coup in 1974) claimed such royal lineage and his family still claims royal Davidic descent. Ezekiel 39:21 (in some versions, like the King

James) tells us that God said "I will set my glory among the heathen." Could this be a reference to the Ark of the Covenant, which was the seat of the Shekinah Glory, being hidden in Africa?

Isaiah 18:1 mentions a land "which lies beyond the rivers of Cush" (Ethiopia) and later (in 18:7) suggests that from this land "At that time a gift of homage will be brought to the Lord of hosts from a people *tall and smooth" (*literally – "drawn out.") There are over 120,000 Ethiopian Falasha Jews in Israel today, already having been "drawn out" of Ethiopia. Could this group of African Jews eventually deliver the Ark of the Covenant? Could they have done so already? I have heard rumors from the intelligence community that they have already brought the Ark to Israel.

And while on the topic of Falashas, at least one internet rumor claims Barack Obama has a Falasha ancestor: "Immigration records show that Sen. Barack Obama's grandfather… was an Ethiopian 'Falasha' Jew, who changed his surname when he moved to Kenya."[231] While I suspect this internet rumor is not true, in theory, Obama could use such a pretext to claim descent from the royal line of King David. This is a lineage the Messiah must have, and the Antichrist will probably claim at least a little Jewish ancestry when he stands at the Temple in Jerusalem in 2016, if he wants to mimic Christ in every conceivable way.

What of an even more ancient great temple? Isaiah 19:19-20 tells us of the end times "In that day there will be an altar to the Lord in the midst of the land of Egypt, and a pillar to the Lord near its border. It will become a sign and a witness to the Lord of hosts in the land of Egypt; for they will cry to the Lord because of oppressors, and He will send them a Savior and a Champion, and He will deliver them." Douglas Krieger agrees that our ancient ancestors "built the Great Pyramid as a monument to God at Giza."[232] To the ancient Hebrews like Isaiah, an altar was a pile of rocks. There is a very impressive "pile of rocks" that served as an ancient altar in Egypt. We know Moses was taught its hidden wisdom; for Acts 7:22 says "Moses was educated in all the learning of the Egyptians." The wisest Greeks were honored to be taught by Egyptian priests. When Alexander the Great wanted to start a new city with a great library and university he founded Alexandria in the ancient land of wisdom – in Egypt.

Jesus grew up learning in Egypt; Matthew 2:13 tells us "an angel of the Lord appeared to Joseph in a dream and said, 'Get up! Take the Child and His mother and flee to Egypt, and remain there until I tell you.'" Luke 2:52 says

"And Jesus kept increasing in wisdom and stature, and in favor with God and men." Giza is also at the border of Upper and Lower Egypt. Similar to Berlin when I was a child, (at Germany's center, yet also on its most prominent frontier border of East and West with the well-known "Checkpoint Charlie") the Great Pyramid is both in the heart of (modern, unified) Egypt and on her (divided, ancient) frontier between Upper Egypt and Lower Egypt – just as Isaiah describes it.

Isaiah tells us in the near future, the Great Pyramid there will be understood as an altar to the Lord – perhaps because the revelations encoded in its measurements will be recognized and understood. The scientific knowledge revealed by a study of the pyramid's measurements tells us the ancient Egyptians knew the precise size of the earth, sun, and moon, and the size of the orbits of the moon around the earth and the earth around the sun. They knew the duration of the year as 365.242 days, and the precession cycle as 25,826.4 years. The Egyptians understood and linked time and distance/space in ways we are only starting to comprehend. They must have had advanced science, astronomy, and construction skills.

Many researchers also see a connection to the ancient brotherhood of Masons – Freemasonry. Masonic origins clearly go back to the Knights Templar. Do they extend a few thousand years farther into the past? In their own stories of the Masonic past, the great architect and master mason Hiram Abiff designed the Temple in Jerusalem and was murdered in a botched attempt to steal his secret knowledge. Most see this allegory about the Temple in Jerusalem as a veiled story about the Great Pyramid in Egypt. Masons, of course, are skilled stonecutters. Two main tools, the square and the compass, are used in their trade – and historically, these were the tools used by the gods to measure heaven and earth, as depicted in images from the ancient Middle East to China, where the twofold Chinese creator god Fu Hsi holds a square and compass.

The square base of the Great pyramid is related to its height in the same 2 Pi ratio as the perimeter and radius of a circle. The pyramid, though square, represents our round Earth – and "squaring the circle" is one of the greatest accomplishments of Freemasonry – quite possibly a reference to building the pyramid with so much ancient knowledge of the Earth in its measurements. Another topic of major interest to Masons is "the son of the widow." Generally assumed to be Horus, son of Isis and the deceased Osiris – what if Isaiah 54:47 is more relevant, with Israel as the widow and Jesus as the Son? Remember, Jesus may have been a stonemason. His youth was spent learning wisdom in Egypt. Jesus could be the great initiate, initiated inside the Great Pyramid. And many believe that Masons have a prophetic timeline pointing to 2012 and 2016 and an Antichrist. How might this be tied to the Great Pyramid? Or to an even greater Pyramid in prophecy: the New Jerusalem, with dimensions proportional to and representing the (new) earth: its 1500 mile sides are 7920 thousand yards, like the earth is 7920 miles in diameter. Revelation 21:17 says "according to human measurements, which are also angelic measurements." This could refer to the two ways of using "7920" in the measurements of both the New Jerusalem and the Earth, with lesser and greater units being human and angelic but both really signaling that the same object is being measured either way.

These measurements in the Book of Revelation are important on earth and in heaven. As Charles Ryrie pointed out, an angel makes sure John is not just paying attention but that he is actively involved in the measuring process to make certain he fully appreciates the significance. "John is no longer merely a witness. He is instructed to measure."[233] And many note that although some have assumed the New Jerusalem's shape to be a cube, a sphere like the Earth also has equal length and width and height, as could a pyramid. "It is probably preferable to consider it a pyramid, as this explains how the river can flow down its sides as pictured in Revelation 22:1-2."[234] *No - it says that it will flow down the middle of the great street to the city, i.e. - Main st.!!*

Back to the Great Pyramid and 2016 - Masons often refer to the year with two numbers, for example the year 2000 was 2000 A.D. (Anno Domini, or years after the alleged year of Jesus' birth) and was also 6000 A.L. or "Anno Lucis" (years after the creation of the present world as we know it – or after the gift of "Lucis" or LIGHT from the light-giver or light-bringer. Some will recognize the association of the latter with Lucifer.)

The United States was created in 1776 A.D. – or 5776 A.L. to Masons. (The Illuminati was also formed in Bavaria in 1776.) In the Hebrew Calendar, year 5776 would correspond with early to mid-2016 A.D. Some authors state the height of the Great Pyramid, if completed to the top, would be 5776 inches, and correspond to 2016 A.D. Are these ancient and modern Masonic ways of linking pyramid prophecies, the creation of the United States in 1776 A.D., and the coming of the Antichrist in 2016 A.D.? John Preacher explains: "the pyramid is a representation of all the empires of the world culminating in the final empire ruled by Satan himself as the capstone."[235]

Most lower-level Masons whom we may count as friends and relatives would honestly deny this. True or not, lower level Masons know nothing of the higher truths of the craft, it is hidden from them. The famous Confederate General Albert Pike wrote several books on Freemasonry and explained that low ranking Masons – the overwhelming majority – do not understand the symbols of the brotherhood that refer to astronomy or measuring space and time: "Part of the symbols are displayed there to the initiate, but he is intentionally misled by false interpretations. It is not intended that he shall understand them; but it is intended that he shall imagine he understands them. Their true explication is reserved for the Adepts, the Princes of Masonry."[236] Having spent several years as a member of a Masonic lodge myself, hoping in vain that I might learn new and insightful teachings on such topics… I left the brotherhood none the wiser.

I even went to the Library of Congress in Washington D.C., hoping they had copies of certain nineteenth century masonic books with titles that hinted at contents describing astronomy and symbolism… (as the Library of Congress should have a copy of ALL books published in the United States) but all twelve of the interesting titles I wanted had been stolen. Perhaps a century ago it was permissible to speculate on these topics, but someone doesn't want such information available as the crucial times approach.

Manly Hall, author of The Secret Teachings of All Ages and Freemasonry of the Ancient Egyptians, also described the poorly understood origins of the Masonic brotherhood in the brotherhood of Egyptian priests, and again suggests that very few understand the extended history or astronomy or the deeper symbolic mysteries of Freemasonry. Most American Masons also do not know that in Scottish Rite Freemasonry, only 3760 years are added to an Anno Domini date to reach an Anno Lucis date. Those Masons basically adopted the Hebrew calendar, which is 3760 years and a few months ahead of our Gregorian calendar. So while the founding of the United States was in 5776 Anno Lucis to most American Masons, it is the year 2016 A.D. that is 5776 A.L. to Scottish Rite Masons.

Are there other Masonic/Illuminati links between the two dates? Consider the pyramid drawn on the back of an American one dollar bill. The one with some supernatural entity's all-seeing eye hovering above the unfinished pyramid like the missing capstone that will complete everything. At the bottom of the pyramid the foundation is inscribed with "MDCCLXXVI," the Roman numerals for 1776. Twelve decreasingly sized levels of pyramid blocks are above those numbers before the thirteenth potential level of the all-seeing eye in the sky.

Some associate these levels with the final 12 "Katuns" in the last "baktun" of the Mayan calendar's "Long Count." The Long Count covers a period just over 5,125 years, and ended on December 21, 2012 – I date which I believe is biblically significant, as the start date of Daniel's final seven years. The Long Count is divided into 13 baktuns of 144,000 days each (another biblically significant number) and within that unit are katuns of approximately 19.71 years each (the time between conjunctions of Jupiter and Saturn.) A new katun started at the beginning of June, 1776 A.D., shortly before the Declaration of Independence. Twelve katuns later the Long Count ended on December 21, 2012. If the pyramid as drawn on the dollar bill was influenced by secret societies and the levels of the pyramid blocks do represent katuns beginning in 1776, then the years following 12/21/2012 are represented by these societies' supernatural entity with the all-seeing eye at the top. If we round up from 19.71 years per katun and make each row of blocks equal to twenty years, as some suggest, we get to early June, 2016.

Perhaps an even more relevant interpretation would be to include the pyramid foundation level with the Roman numerals and say there are thirteen levels to the pyramid. This would better represent the original thirteen colonies which became the United States. The 14th level, the all-seeing eye, could represent the missing 14th part of the body of Osiris. In Egyptian mythology, Osiris is the chief god, but his evil brother Set killed him and chopped him into 14 pieces which were thrown in the Nile. Osiris' wife, Isis, finds 13 parts, but not the last one. It is an ancient god like Osiris or Appolyon which Thomas Horn suggests is the evil destroyer coming to reign over the United States around 2016 in <u>Zenith 2016</u>. Either way, (counting 12 or 13 levels under the eye in the seal on the dollar bill) there is only one person I expect at the "top" of the United States in 2016 – President Obama.

Speaking of the presidency, there is an Egyptian-style monument to this office right in front of the White House. The Washington Monument is the tallest building in the District of Columbia; the law says no other building there can be taller. It has a pyramid-shaped capstone on top, an observation deck 500 feet high, and it is just over 55 feet wide, and over 555 feet tall. Although there is symbolic, end-of-the-age meaning behind all the fives in its measurements in feet, it is the measurements in inches that get my attention more. Just short of being 666 inches wide, and over ten times as high, the obelisk is already complete with an aluminum capstone. Is this a symbolic message to presidents that they don't quite measure up to the number of the beast? Perhaps its Masonic builders are the only ones to fully understand the symbolic measurements.

And in case anyone thinks it's a stretch to assume the measurements have important Masonic symbolism, let us remember that Freemasonry began where the Knights Templar ended, in Paris. London eventually took over global supremacy of Masonry, and then America. There were originally 30 obelisks in Egypt. Thirteen were taken to ancient Rome. Then one went to Paris, and in 1878 and 1881, a twin pair built by Thutmoses III were moved to London and New York. Those three are all called "Cleopatra's Needle." The obelisk-shaped Washington Monument is many times larger but was built from granite in Maryland. Why was there a frenzy to erect such obelisks in Western power centers in the 19th century? Were top Masons intentionally summoning some supernatural protector? Some authors believe "America knowingly and intentionally invited the spirit of Antichrist into our land"[237] and that "the final Babylon of the Bible's prophets is New York City while the land of Babylon (Chaldea) is the United States of America."[238] According to R.A. Coombes in America, The Babylon – there are 33 unique Bible references cluing us in to viewing America as the end times kingdom of Babylon and 66 clues describing New York City.

Thomas Horn, author of Apollyon Rising 2012: The Lost Symbol Found and The Final Mystery of the Great Seal Revealed and Zenith 2016: Did Something Begin In The Year 2012 That Will Reach Its Apex In 2016? has written a great deal on symbolism of the Great Pyramid, the Mayan calendar, the Great Seal of the United States, and other related prophetic topics. He has suggested that "The year 2012 could therefore represent in Christian eschatology the beginning of Great Tribulation, with 2016 representing the 'midst of the week' when Apollo (Antichrist) presents himself as God and enters the temple in Jerusalem.... That the year 2012 marks the beginning of the Great Tribulation not only could fit with Bible prophecy, as it is in the "midst of the week"—three and one-half years into the Great Tribulation period—when Antichrist enthrones himself as God in the temple, this would also conform well with the Masonic and Great Seal prophecies forecasting the return of the Great Architect and Hiram Abiff (Apollo/Osiris/Nimrod), who enters the finished temple as god, in this case, mid-2016."[239] In Zenith: 2016 Horn also named the book's final chapter "Final Part of the Last Mystery: 2012-2016, 2019, and the End?" On page 372 he wrote: "Does this mean that the year 2019 – exactly seven years after 2012 – would mark the year that Jesus Christ returns with the armies of heaven to establish His rule over Earth?" I think the answer is yes.

The Great Pyramid is also linked to Solomon's Temple through creation dates. Take the pyramid's approximate height (I have seen estimates anywhere from just under 481 feet to 483 feet) if completed to the top – of 481 feet and double it because the above ground portion we see merely represents the northern hemisphere... imagine an equally large inverted pyramid underground representing the southern hemisphere, with a diameter of about 962 feet for their scale model of the planet Earth. Some scholars date Solomon's Temple dedication to 962 B.C. Others note the reign of Israel's King David first began rule over a united Israel in 1006 B.C. By adding the pyramid's approximately 3023 foot perimeter, we reach 2016. Since the pyramid represents the earth and we are squaring the circle, we also notice the circumference (3023 feet) divided by the double height or double radius (over 962 feet) equals the ratio Pi very accurately.

The American Psychic Edgar Cayce was once asked to comment on Davidson and Aldersmith's analysis of the Great Pyramid and their claim that "the object of the Pyramid's Message was to proclaim Jesus as Deliverer and Savior of men, to announce the dated circumstances relating to His Coming, and to prepare men by means of its Message."[240] Cayce said that only an initiate will fully understand.

The extreme antiquity of the Egyptian pyramids also makes it hard for me to imagine that any prophecies about our time could have been foreseen so far back, before the Flood of Noah. "The genesis date indicated by astronomy for the site as a whole is 10,500 B.C. That is what the layout of the Pyramids says, even if they themselves are younger."[241] Why I have no problem assuming a prophecy can be given 3,000 years in advance, but 12,500 years makes me hesitate – I don't know. But at one point I was ready to dismiss the alleged prophetic connection to the pyramids entirely because some of the facts seemed difficult to believe. Over time, I put more pieces of the pyramid puzzle together and became convinced of its significance.

In 1977 Peter Lemesurier published <u>The Great Pyramid Decoded</u>, an amazing analysis of the internal and external measurements of the Great Pyramid in Egypt. He felt that periodic cycles of destruction regularly destroy human civilization, and that the Great Pyramid was the single greatest example proving "civilizations have already existed on earth whose scientific achievements were equal or superior to our own"[242] who have given us warnings about the future in monuments and legends and prophecies. At times, Lemesurier comments as if periodic destruction is cyclical, and the ancient builders are explaining the future "saying not so much 'This is what will happen' as… 'This is what always happens,'"[243] in every cycle of such events. He wrote that the Great Pyramid warns us about a future event similar to "what in ancient Egypt was called the Destruction of Mankind; in Mexico and Peru, The Destruction of the World; and in Babylonia, Assyria, and China, The Deluge."[244] He asks "what serious purpose is a doomed civilization likely to have in trying to communicate with its successors? The most obvious aim would seem to be the transmission of some kind of warning or advice designed to help the later civilization."[245]

But at other points in his book, Lemesurier clearly states that the pyramid's warnings go hand in hand with the Bible; and that they help us know the dates of future end times events through "semi-secret communications for 'those who have ears to hear' – code-messages, as it were, from initiate to initiate."[246] Its measurements and astronomical alignments are the keys to understanding hidden ancient wisdom. He even says that "the Great Pyramid contains a detailed prophecy in mathematical code – a prophecy whose main purpose appears to be the validating of just such a redemptive or Messianic plan for mankind as appears to have been outlined by Jesus of Nazareth."[247] Of course he does clarify that the Bible is just one of many sources of warnings that point to the same events. On his first page he even makes note of American psychic Edgar Cayce's 1932 comments that the main purpose of the pyramids at Giza are to warn future generations about "that period when there is to be the change in the earth's position and the return of the Great Initiate to that and other lands for the folding up of those prophecies that are depicted there."[248]

Did Jesus himself give us a clue to investigate the Great Pyramid? In John 21, the resurrected Christ appears to His apostles for the third time at the Sea of Galilee. They are fishing, but not catching any fish. (Thinking, but not understanding?) Jesus directs them where to cast their nets (tells them where to look for insight) and they catch 153 fish in John 21:11 "Simon Peter went up and drew the net to land, full of large fish, a hundred and fifty-three." They could have written "many fish" or "a lot of fish" or over a hundred fish." There would normally be little reason to count them accurately. The very words were chosen for their gematria: the Greek words for "fish" (ichthyes) and "the net" (diktuon) both have a numeric value of 153 times 8. Perhaps the number meant something?

Indeed, the number 153 is interesting. Some call it a "triangular number." Three is the first such number; make a dot, center a row of two dots below it and you have a little triangle of three dots. Add three dots in a row below them and you make a bigger triangle of six dots. A series of such numbers continues with 10, 15, 21, 28, 36, 45, 55, 66, 78, 91, 105, 120, 136, 153... By the time you reach the 17th row of 153 dots you have made quite a triangle – or pyramid. Perhaps it meant something to those who were familiar or "initiated" with the Great Pyramid and its measurements – for the King's Chamber is 153 inches long, and is 153 courses of masonry below the summit platform. The sarcophagus in the King's chamber – which was always empty – implies a "missing" body and hints at resurrection... and the number itself has a Christian association with enlightenment.[249]

I find Lemesurier's references to events from 2010 to 2020 the most interesting, including a "river of fire"[250] somewhere around 2017, depending on what scale he uses to interpret internal measurements. My first thoughts of this were either volcanic lava or nuclear fire, but one day I noticed in Daniel 7:10 "A river of fire was flowing and coming out from before Him; thousands upon thousands were attending Him, and myriads upon myriads were standing before Him; the court sat, and the books were opened." This may refer to the stars of the Milky Way when the eruption of the galactic center becomes visible to us as Isaiah 26:21 describes: "the Lord is about to come out from His place to punish the inhabitants of the earth for their iniquity." Lemesurier also wrote that "figures point specifically to a time of dire crisis around A.D. 2020... delineated by the Great Pyramid's chronograph as the 'time of ordeal.'"[251] Elsewhere he describes "world-wide collapse predicted for the early twenty-first century."[252]

This corresponds to another comment in which I pointed out that completing the Great Pyramid by adding the missing capstone at the top would lead to a height of approximately 5780 inches. This height, representing completion of the pyramid, completion of the world, the end of the age and the coming of the Messiah – could be transferred from 5780 inches to Hebrew calendar year 5780, which corresponds to my calculated end date in December 2019.

Years after reaching that conclusion, I learned that Lemesurier shared similar views: "If the builders of the Great Pyramid deliberately omitted to add the capstone to their great symbol for the planet Earth, then that omission could conceivably symbolize an incomplete world... There is some evidence in the ancient texts that the eventual addition of the capstone (and thus the completion of the pyramid to its full design) was seen by the initiates as symbolizing the return of Light to the world in the Messianic person."[253] This could easily refer to the same cornerstone – capstone – Messiah that Jesus himself referred to from Psalm 118:22 when he was quoted in Matthew

21:42 "The stone which the builders rejected, this became the chief corner stone." A typical rectangular building has four equal corners. If the Messiah were represented by one of these, then He would be sharing the foundation with three others. But a pyramid top – now that is a "chief" cornerstone, and one that the builders left behind, or rejected, in purposefully leaving the pyramid incomplete. Since the pyramid represents the world, completing its top with a chief cornerstone may be similar to the Messiah coming to complete the world. Douglas Krieger suggests that "the capstone represents the ultimate New Jerusalem."[254]

Jeremiah 51:25-26 even describes an evil mountain that will not be a cornerstone – the Antichrist and his homeland – in similar terms: "'Behold, I am against you, O destroying mountain, who destroys the whole earth,' declares the Lord, 'and I will stretch out My hand against you, and roll you down from the crags, and I will make you a burnt out mountain. They will not take from you even a stone for a corner nor a stone for foundations, but you will be desolate forever,' declares the Lord." This seems to say that while Jesus does become the chief cornerstone even though people had rejected Him, God Himself rejects His opposite and will not allow the Antichrist to become the chief cornerstone.

Lemesurier also noted that "The descent of the ark upon the mountain in Ararat corresponds closely in symbol to the 'descent' of the final capstone upon the incomplete Pyramid, and thus signifies the return of the Great Initiate himself to physical existence at the onset of the Final Age."[255] (We should also consider the analogy to Exodus 19:11 when the Lord said to Moses: "and let them be ready for the third day, for on the third day the Lord will come down on Mount Sinai in the sight of all the people.") The Lord and the Law coming down onto the mountaintop is like the ark coming down onto a mountain. Noah's ark floated on water 15 cubits above the mountaintops. It is no coincidence that the capstone of the pyramid would be 15 cubits high. The ark represents a capstone on a mountain at the creation of a new world (and the destruction of the old.) Jesus was resurrected on Nisan 17, the same date that Noah's ark came to rest on dry land. Besides the size and height of the capstone, there are many, many other astounding measurements of the Great Pyramid which reveal highly advanced scientific achievement thousands of years ago – and warnings left in stone for future generations. Put simply: "The Great Pyramid contains a detailed prophecy in mathematical code."[256]

But before I digress too far, the main reason I purchased Lemesurier's The

Great Pyramid Decoded in late 2013 (though I now wish I had stumbled onto it years earlier) was because of an online reference to comments I made about my then upcoming book on the Antichrist. I have several clues pointing to the day when the Antichrist goes into a Temple in Jerusalem and proclaims himself to be God. This is June 6, 2016. Someone online commented on one of my posts about this and said that Peter Lemesurier had written about this date (June 6) as well, having an end times connotation hinted at by the Great Pyramid. And he does link this date to a connection between the pyramid and Bethlehem/Jerusalem, which gives one more potential clue pointing to the date I have already reached.

Lemesurier explains: "The designed angle of descent and ascent of its [the Great Pyramid's] sloping passages is 26*18'9.7" – an angle significant... If that same angle is laid off from the Pyramid's east-west axis in a northeasterly direction, for example, the rhumb-line so produced marks the bearing... of the Jewish town of Bethlehem."[257] So the angle of the internal ascending passageway of the Great Pyramid – the indicator of ascent to something higher – points to Christ's birth in Bethlehem. (I am reminded of Hosea 11:1 "out of Egypt I called My son.")

This is not the only angle of interest in which the pyramid points to Christ. A reflection of sunshine off the polished limestone that once covered the pyramid's four sides also would have illuminated a cross shaped pattern on the sand when the sun was high in the sky slightly south of the Great Pyramid... and an outstretched triangle on the sand east of the pyramid every morning. The angle of such a reflection depends on the ever changing position of the sun. But this outstretched triangle of light on the desert sand did point to Jerusalem at sunrise every April 1 – which was the date of the crucifixion in 33 A.D.

If nothing else, the reflection of the pyramid pointing at Jerusalem on the date of the crucifixion at Passover is a remarkable coincidence. The reflections off all four sides forming a giant cross of light in the sand would be an awesome sight. And the angle of the ascending passages pointing to Bethlehem and the birth of Jesus is also amazing. But because of the topic of this book, I am even more impressed that the same angle of 26*18'9.7" in the ascending passageway matches the angle in the descending passageway, and probably points to the Antichrist.

Lemesurier comments that the descending angle or "inverted Messianic triangle" could "be taken to refer to some kind of anti-Messiah."[258] We used an ascending angle to go above the line marking the latitude of the Great Pyramid and went east/northeast to reach the site of the Messiah's birth in Bethlehem. If we take a descending angle to go below that same line of latitude we would head east/southeast to reach Arabia and the birthplace of Islam. The same angle off the longitude of the pyramid could take us south/southeast to another birthplace in Kenya...

But I find it even more interesting that the same exact line drawn on the Pyramid's passageway angle which pointed to the Messiah in the direction of Bethlehem points to Jerusalem as well; the two sites are just a few miles apart. So I find it extremely interesting that this angle points to the summer sunrise over Bethlehem and Jerusalem. Remember the Sun has some width; it takes up half a degree in our field of view – enough to rise from behind both sites as viewed from Giza. The angle of the passageways "clearly has both an astronomical and a chronological significance... [it] marks the bearing of the summer sunrise... specifically, that of sunrise on 6th June... it is possible that the sunrise bearing marked at some date the exact rising of Venus... the datings for this event might well prove to be significant."[259]

In case any of this was not clear – one could reasonably argue that the Pyramid's descending angle is a clue pointing at the Antichrist. Such an angle, heading southeast instead of northeast, arguably points to Arabia and/or Kenya. But even Lemesurier pointed out that the angle of the Pyramid's descending passageway implies an anti-Messiah as it points to Bethlehem and Jerusalem and the Sun on June 6 – and he suggests that at one time it also points to Venus, and that this date might be significant. Venus hardly ever appears behind (or even in front of) the sun on June 6. In our lifetime (the rest of 21st century, anyway – that's as far as my chart lists such events[260]) this lineup occurs just one more time on June 6 – in 2016. We merely have to follow the angle from the Great Pyramid toward the sunrise over Bethlehem and Jerusalem on June 6, 2016, for an extremely rare lineup of pyramid, descending passageway angle, Jerusalem, Antichrist, Sun, and Venus alignment. Another coincidence? If so, it is one of a growing list of coincidences pointing to June 6, 2016.

The Day Before – June 5, 2016

The day before I might have turned in the manuscript for this book to my anticipated publisher; as I thought I was putting the final touches of editing on my book, I happened to be killing time on a break at my day job. I did a search for "June 6, 2016" on Google, expecting that most entries would be ones I had written myself on various web sites. But I secretly hoped that someone else had reached similar conclusions to my own, and that somehow I just hadn't discovered them yet, despite years of research. I was not to be disappointed, for I stumbled onto the thoughts of Andrew Simmons.

As I am already past my deadline, I do not have time to order and read his undoubtedly relevant book titled: <u>Quenched Like a Wick: Revealing the Day America Breathes Her Last</u>. But Simmons' blog and other internet commentaries provide many insights which I believe are in harmony with my own conclusions. Simmons believes that "The destruction of Babylon (America) begins the tribulation. And the destruction of America must happen during the spring." Specifically, he reaches the date of June 5, 2016.[261] I cannot ignore a theory which pins great importance on a date just one day before I believe the Antichrist is revealed.

Simmons agrees that New York and America are the city and empire of Mystery Babylon. He points out many clues which he feels point to the nuclear destruction of New York on June 5, 2016.

One clue is to look one jubilee after Israel spreads out like a budding fig tree. Matthew 24:32 says "Now learn the parable from the fig tree: when its branch has already become tender and puts forth its leaves, you know that summer is near." I had already concluded that the 49 years after the Israelis entered the Old City in East Jerusalem on June 6, 1967 was an important clue on the revealing of the Antichrist. Simmons notes that the war in which this happened started one day earlier – the Six Day War began on June 5, 1967 – and he believes war involving Mystery Babylon will start on June 5, 2016.

Habakkuk 3:17 suggests that it will happen at the same time of year as when the fig tree (Israel) spread its leaves, but that "the fig tree should not blossom and there be no fruit on the vines." Everything will be interrupted in June. Isaiah 18:5 may confirm this: "For before the harvest, as soon as the bud blossoms and the flower becomes a ripening grape, then He will cut off the sprigs with pruning knives and remove and cut away the spreading branches." Israel will suffer at this time of the year.

Daniel 9:25 says "So you are to know and discern that from the issuing of a decree to restore and rebuild Jerusalem until Messiah the Prince there will be seven weeks." Simmons interprets this a little differently than I do. We agree the seven weeks are weeks of years, or 49 years like a jubilee. We agree this period began with the Six Day War, though he starts his count with the first day of the war, and I start a day later with Israeli entry into East Jerusalem. I assume this will incorrectly lead some people to believe that this 49 years were an actual, divinely sanctioned jubilee – and that the Messiah arrives 49 years later when it is really just the Antichrist. Simmons seems to feel that the 3.5 years of tribulation which begin after these 49 years are "The Day of the Lord" and that this fulfills the prophecy.

Hosea 5:7 suggests that a land which is against God will see destruction for bearing illegitimate children. Could this refer to America interfering with the Middle East and helping to spawn new governments and new nations? "They have dealt treacherously against the Lord, for they have borne illegitimate children. Now the new moon will devour them with their land." There is a new moon on June 5, 2016. The odds are only 1 in 29.

Ezekiel 8:1 says "It came about in the sixth year, on the fifth day of the sixth month." Could it really refer to the 5th of June, in the sixth year of our current decade, in our Gregorian calendar, and not in the Hebrew calendar? What is the "It" Ezekiel is even referring to?

Quite possibly, events at the middle of the tribulation. Could it mean that there is an assassination attempt on our politician in Jerusalem on June 3, that Mystery Babylon is nuked on June 5, and that the miraculously revived Antichrist is revealed on June 6? Let us consider the previous paragraph at the end of Ezekiel Chapter 7:

"The land is full of bloody crimes and the city is full of violence. Therefore, I will bring the worst of the nations, and they will possess their houses. I will also make the pride of the strong ones cease, and their holy places will be profaned. When anguish comes, they will seek peace, but there will be none. Disaster will come upon disaster and rumor will be added to rumor; then they will seek a vision from a prophet, but the law will be lost from the priest and counsel from the elders. The king will mourn, the prince will be clothed with horror, and the hands of the people of the land will tremble. According to their conduct I will deal with them, and by their judgments I will judge them. And they will know that I am the Lord."

There are many other clues which Simmons cites online, and I haven't even read his book, which undoubtedly cites many additional clues. Even without a full reading of his book, I felt his ideas were worth mentioning.

I also thought it was worth looking up his June 5 date to try and find other clues. I already expected an assassination attempt on the Antichrist on June 3, 2016 – and noted that when he will appear to lie dying on June 4, it is Ascension Day (40 days after Easter, when Jesus – the true Messiah – rose to heaven) and that an analogy to the Messiah may be made on that day... and of course I have been focused on June 6... but what of June 5?

I wondered if Obama had been inside the Great Pyramid seven years earlier... He did give his famously pro-Muslim speech in Cairo on June 4, 2009. But a little research showed Obama went in the very pyramid that helps warn us about him on the same day (June 4) when he saw an image of a face in the hieroglyphs and said: "That looks like me! Look at those ears!"[262] I was curious to see if the date was an exact seven years away from June 6, 2016 in the Hebrew or Islamic calendar – when I stumbled on Ramadan.

Ramadan

The word Ramadan is from the Arabic root "ramida" or "ramad" which means "scorching heat" and is often associated with fire and burning. Ramadan is the holiest month in the Muslim year, and perhaps the only Muslim holiday most Americans know by name. In 2016, the first day of Ramadan is given as June 6, though technically it starts at sundown on June 5. Because of the time zone difference between, say, New York and Mecca – it will still be June 5 in New York when June 6 begins in Mecca. What was that scorching and burning all about in regard to Ramadan? Could it be the nuclear destruction of New York?

Ramadan is also about re-evaluation and purification. Will eliminating New York be viewed as purifying the world? For many who dislike America, or freedom, or the Jews, or the financial elite, or the United Nations, perhaps the answer is yes. Usually Ramadan's purification is directed inward, as each person fasts and purifies their thoughts and actions. But I suspect on this date in 2016, some jihadis may be considering purifying the world by ridding it of Jews and Christians.

One Muslim blogger writes: "Ramadan is about fire. Ramadan is about sharpening your sword. For Ramadan is about war. Ramadan is Jihad.... Ramadan allows you the sharp sword and blazing fire that you may shred and burn the oppressive world and REMAKE THE WORLD.... Ramadan is the training for Khalifa."[263] [establishing a Caliphate; unifying the Islamic world and subjugating the rest of the world.] If this is Ramadan, please forgive my lack of enthusiasm.

If I hadn't already expected the Islamic world to be celebrating the Antichrist rising against Israel and claiming the land for Allah at this time I might not have thought much about Ramadan... but for this Islamic holiday to begin at just the right moment, I must ask myself: is this yet another coincidence, or is it confirmation? I don't claim to know the exact date the city of Mystery Babylon is destroyed. But I suspect it will be New York, sometime in early June of 2016.

Last Precondition – The Removal of the Restrainer

Although a few of the most zealous seekers of knowledge will study Bible commentary enough to know who the Antichrist is early on – the general population is not allowed to know until the appointed time. There is a "restrainer" who prevents the Antichrist from obviously revealing himself or attempting to take over before his time. This restrainer has been holding back the unveiling of the identity of the Antichrist and will continue to do so until God tells him to stand back and let it happen. Only then is the Antichrist's identity convincingly revealed to the entire world.

2 Thessalonians 2:6-9 tells us "And you know what restrains him now, so that in his time he will be revealed. For the mystery of lawlessness is already at work; only he who now restrains will do so until he is taken out of the way. Then that lawless one will be revealed whom the Lord will slay with the breath of His mouth and bring to an end by the appearance of His coming; that is, the one whose coming is in accord with the activity of Satan, with all power and signs and false wonders." In the King James Bible, lawlessness is translated as iniquity, and many know the phrase "the mystery of iniquity" without necessarily understanding that it means the identity of the Antichrist remains a mystery until God is ready to remove the restrainer and completely unleash the Antichrist.

There has been much debate over this restrainer. Many have suggested that the Church has been the restraining force that encourages evil men to restrain themselves, by threatening them with eternal damnation for sins. They might argue that when the power of organized religion is taken away, that modifying influence, that restraining influence on our behavior – will be gone. Such arguments assume an early rapture, pre- or mid- tribulation, accomplishing the removal of the church and its restraining influence.

Others argue that government is the restrainer; that the enforcement of laws and the threat of being put in jail or executed is what holds back criminal or sinful behavior. And there is some merit to this as well – for regular mortals. But we are not merely talking about an influence on human behavior. We are talking about the demonic spirit that is the Antichrist being restrained – and for such a powerful supernatural entity to be held back from something he wants to do - something – or more precisely, someone – of at least equal supernatural strength and ability must be up to the task. *exactly*

In 2 Thessalonians 2:7 the Bible refers to the restrainer as "he" not "it" or some organization or set of beliefs. This rules out the United Nations or U.S. Congress or government in general as the restraining influence. The personal pronoun "he" also rules out the idea that the saints (a multitude of people) hold back the restrainer until a pre-tribulation or mid-tribulation rapture removes their restraining influence. It rules out the idea that the church is thereby removed at the rapture as a restrainer.

The King James Bible in particular helps portray the restrainer, the "he" - the "Mystery of Iniquity" that restrains the person who is the Antichrist from boldly announcing who he is – as the Holy Spirit. At least this suggestion is both singular and supernatural. But the idea that we will be abandoned by the Holy Spirit at the time of our greatest need is a false doctrine. Let's consider a few verses:

In John 16:7-11 Jesus says: "But I tell you the truth, it is to your advantage that I go away; for if I do not go away, the Helper will not come to you; but if I go, I will send Him to you. And He, when He comes, will convict the world concerning sin and righteousness and judgment; concerning sin, because they do not believe in Me; and concerning righteousness, because I go to the Father and you no longer see Me; and concerning judgment, because the ruler of this world has been judged."

Four major players are involved in this passage. "I" and "Me" refer to Jesus Christ. "The Father" refers to God. The judged "ruler of this world" is Satan. Leaving a fourth "He" who is "the Helper." Few individuals qualify to be discussed at such a level of importance in the course of events that they are listed together with God, Jesus, and Satan.

John 14:16-17 previously clarified "I will ask the Father, and He will give you another Helper, that He may be with you forever; that is the Spirit of truth." This is the Holy Spirit, sometimes thought of as God's active force (as "sunshine" here gives us light and warmth while the "sun" it comes from is too intense to have right here with us) or as an integral part of the godhead/trinity. More importantly, these verses portray the Helper as the Holy Spirit and the "He" who will "be with you forever." Does this sound like "he" will leave us when we need him most? Note also that the Holy Spirit always has a capitalized letter H in "He" (being part of the divine godhead/trinity) but the restrainer, who is not, has a lowercase letter h in "he" and must be a separate individual.

In Joel 2:28-32 God tells us after we start to see the signs of the Last Day "It will come about after this that I will pour out My Spirit on all mankind.... I will pour out My Spirit in those days. I will display wonders in the sky and on the earth, blood, fire and columns of smoke. The sun will be turned into darkness and the moon into blood before the great and awesome day of the Lord comes. And it will come about that whoever calls on the name of the Lord will be delivered." This does not sound like the Holy Spirit has been taken away in the end times; it sounds like the time when the greatest outpouring of Holy Spirit occurs.

Peter repeats this message in Acts 2:17-21 "'And it shall be in the last days,' God says, 'That I will pour forth of My Spirit on all mankind.... I will in those days pour forth of My Spirit and they shall prophesy. And I will grant wonders in the sky above and signs on the earth below, blood, and fire, and vapor of smoke. The sun will be turned into darkness and the moon into blood, before the great and glorious day of the Lord shall come. And it shall be that everyone who calls on the name of the Lord will be saved.'" Once again, it does not sound like God or the Holy Spirit abandon us.

King David wrote in Psalm 23:4 "Even though I walk through the valley of the shadow of death, I fear no evil, for You are with me." Psalm 139:7-8 says "Where can I go from Your Spirit? Or where can I flee from Your presence? If I ascend to heaven, You are there; If I make my bed in Sheol, behold, You are there." Even in hell, God (with all His pronouns capitalized) is there. We cannot get away from God or the Holy Spirit.

Revelation 7:13-14 says "'These who are clothed in the white robes, who are they, and where have they come from?' I said to him, 'My lord, you know.' And he said to me, 'These are the ones who come out of the great tribulation, and they have washed their robes and made them white in the blood of the Lamb.'" These are the "tribulation saints" who were saved after the wrath of the Antichrist is underway. How were they saved? 1 Corinthians 12:3 tells us "no one can say, 'Jesus is Lord,' except by the Holy Spirit." NO ONE is saved except through the Holy Spirit. Therefore the Holy Spirit – "the Renewer of the Face of the Earth"[264] – cannot have abandoned us during the tribulation, when these saints are saved.

But if this popular view that the Holy Spirit is the "he" who is "the restrainer" is wrong; then who is the removed restrainer that allows the Antichrist to reveal himself? Since the Antichrist is a supernatural being of great power, the restrainer must be at least his equal. Revelation 17:8 tells us "The beast that you saw was, and is not, and is about to come up out of the abyss and go to destruction. And those who dwell on the earth, whose name has not been written in the book of life from the foundation of the world, will wonder when they see the beast, that he was and is not and will come." The Antichrist spirit existed in ancient times, was locked up in the abyss, and will soon be unleashed again. Likewise the restrainer has been restraining the Antichrist for ages because he was, is not, and is to come.

When John wrote in the first century A.D. the Antichrist already was "not." One interpretation is that the Antichrist is an evil demonic spirit, possibly Satan himself - who has possessed/indwelt men in the past. I am reminded of comments on Nebuchadnezzar in Daniel 4:16 "Let his mind be changed from that of a man and let a beast's mind be given to him, and let seven periods of time pass over him." Perhaps the Seleucid King Antiochus was possessed by the spirit of Satan; he defiled the Temple around 168 B.C. with his own image as if he were a God. The Bible also indicates that Judas was indwelt; Luke 22:3 says "And Satan entered into Judas who was called Iscariot." Since the death of Judas, this Satanic spirit has apparently been restrained.

The Antichrist's restrainer must be a powerful spirit being capable of chaining demonic spirits in the abyss. The great angel of Revelation 20:1-3 fits the bill: "Then I saw an angel coming down from heaven, holding the key of the abyss and a great chain in his hand. And he laid hold of the dragon, the serpent of old, who is the devil and Satan, and bound him for a thousand years; and he threw him into the abyss, and shut it and sealed it over him." This is a future event, but whoever "he" is, if he can handle Satan himself, and chain him in the abyss, he could be the restrainer of the Antichrist.

The prophet Daniel was once visited by a great angel. Daniel 10:4-6 reads "while I was by the bank of the great river, that is, the Tigris, I lifted my eyes and looked, and behold, there was a certain man dressed in linen, whose waist was girded with a belt of pure gold of Uphaz. His body also was like beryl, his face had the appearance of lightning, his eyes were like flaming torches, his arms and feet like the gleam of polished bronze, and the sound of his words like the sound of a tumult." I am always alert to astronomical references, and when Daniel lifts his eyes (looks up at the sky) and sees a great man composed of flaming torches (stars) with a belt (the constellation Orion with its well-known belt stars) near the great river (The Milky Way) I do not have to wonder what astronomically represents this "man" – it is the manlike constellation Orion. We also know this is the Archangel Gabriel from Daniel 9:20 "Gabriel, whom I had seen in the vision previously, came to me" to help interpret his visions.

Daniel 8:15-17 earlier stated: "When I, Daniel, had seen the vision, I sought to understand it; and behold, standing before me was one who looked like a man. And I heard the voice of a man between the banks of Ulai, and he called out and said, 'Gabriel, give this man an understanding of the vision.' So he came near to where I was standing, and when he came I was frightened and fell on my face; but he said to me, 'Son of man, understand that the vision pertains to the time of the end.'"

Daniel saw a second angel, "one who looked like a man," one who was with the Archangel Gabriel, and who apparently had authority to tell Gabriel what to do, suggesting/ordering Gabriel to give Daniel understanding. We know the Archangel Gabriel spoke to Daniel; he is named specifically. Is anyone else of at least archangel rank so named?

Returning to Daniel 10, there is another powerful helper with Gabriel again, and this time he has a name. Daniel 10:9-13 says "as soon as I heard the sound of his words, I fell into a deep sleep on my face, with my face to the ground. Then behold, a hand touched me and set me trembling on my hands and knees. He said to me, 'O Daniel, man of high esteem, understand the words that I am about to tell you and stand upright, for I have now been sent to you.' And when he had spoken this word to me, I stood up trembling. Then he said to me, 'Do not be afraid, Daniel, for from the first day that you set your heart on understanding this and on humbling yourself before your God, your words were heard, and I have come in response to your words. But the prince of the kingdom of Persia was withstanding me for twenty-one days; then behold, Michael, one of the chief princes, came to help me, for I had been left there with the kings of Persia.'"

Daniel is knocked unconscious by the power of Gabriel's speech. Gabriel explains that Daniel prayed to God, and that he, Gabriel, was sent "in response to your words" (prayers to God.) Gabriel had been supernaturally holding back (restraining) the prince of Persia, who presumably was indwelt by a powerful demonic spirit, as he was withstanding the archangel Gabriel for three weeks. When Gabriel needed help to overcome this powerful evil spirit, he received that help from the chief prince of the angelic realm, Michael - the Archangel Michael.

Daniel 10:20-21 "I shall now return to fight against the prince of Persia; so I am going forth, and behold, the prince of Greece is about to come. However, I will tell you what is inscribed in the writing of truth. Yet there is no one who stands firmly with me against these forces except Michael your prince." Gabriel returns to fighting the Satanic prince of Persia. Gabriel refers to the future Greek conqueror, Alexander the Great, who will defeat and destroy the Persian Empire some centuries later. But it is not this Greek, human, future prince on whom Gabriel waits for help. The Archangel Gabriel relies only on "Michael your prince." We should view him as Israel's guardian angel. In Jewish traditions, Michael protected Abraham, Sarah, Issac, and Jacob on separate occasions, and even advocated on behalf of the Jews during the Exodus, when the devil said they had worshipped idols and should be drowned in the Red Sea.

The entire chapter of Daniel 11 seems to talk about the actions of the Antichrist, including Daniel 11:36: "the king will do as he pleases, and he will exalt and magnify himself above every god and will speak monstrous things against the God of gods." But Daniel Chapter 12 again tells us who will help: "Now at that time Michael, the great prince who stands guard over the sons of your people, will arise. And there will be a time of distress such as never occurred since there was a nation until that time; and at that time your people, everyone who is found written in the book, will be rescued." Again it is the great prince of God's angels, Michael, who will oppose the Antichrist and his evil forces.

Who did God use to confront Satan in the past? Jude 1:9 tells us: "But Michael the archangel, when he disputed with the devil and argued about the body of Moses, did not dare pronounce against him a railing judgment, but said, 'The Lord rebuke you!'" God did not tell Michael to take action against

Satan yet at that time. Even the Archangel Michael, and Satan, and the Antichrist are restrained to play their roles on God's timeline.

In the future, Revelation 12:7-10 again puts Michael in charge of other angels and shows him as the captain of God's army against evil forces: "And there was war in heaven, Michael and his angels waging war with the dragon. The dragon and his angels waged war, and they were not strong enough, and there was no longer a place found for them in heaven. And the great dragon was thrown down, the serpent of old who is called the devil and Satan, who deceives the whole world; he was thrown down to the earth, and his angels were thrown down with him. Then I heard a loud voice in heaven, saying, 'Now the salvation, and the power, and the kingdom of our God and the authority of His Christ have come, for the accuser of our brethren has been thrown down, he who accuses them before our God day and night.'"

The archangel Michael is clearly the leader of heavenly forces against evil, clearly the angel holding the key to the abyss, clearly the angel capable of restraining Satan himself on the supernatural level, and therefore clearly the restrainer holding back the revelation of the person of the Antichrist in Jerusalem until God's appointed time. Jehovah's Witnesses and Seventh-Day Adventists make a strong case for Michael and Jesus being one and the same; that Michael is Jesus Christ pre- incarnate and post-incarnate. They note that Michael fills the role of Jesus in many ways. But the quote above from Revelation 12:7-10 seems to draw a distinction between Michael and Christ. Michael waged war, but Christ has authority – and it seems very unlikely that separate names would be used for the same individual just a few sentences apart. Also, the lack of a capital H for "Michael and his angels" confirms that the sentence is not meant to describe Michael as Jesus Christ.

Likewise, the original passage that got us started on the restrainer makes a distinction as well. It is more subtle, but pay attention to the pronouns and capitalization ✴watch when "he" "his" and "him" are and are not capitalized in 2 Thessalonians 2:7-9 regarding the one who "restrains him now, so that in his time he will be revealed. For the mystery of lawlessness is already at work; only he who now restrains will do so until he is taken out of the way. Then that lawless one will be revealed whom the Lord will slay with the breath of His mouth and bring to an end by the appearance of His coming." Jesus Christ's pronouns are capitalized. Michael the restrainer's are not.

Astronomically, unnamed angels are often likened to planets, while specific beings are usually references to constellations, except for Christ (who is most

✴ Not sure, but I don't believe the ancient Hebrew used capitals; I know it didn't so separate verses + did not use punctuation —

202

often likened to the Sun.) While we digress into astronomical identities, let us not forget how Gabriel was described. "His eyes were like flaming torches" (Daniel 10:6, NASB) or in the King James Bible "his eyes as lamps of fire." We English speaking readers may forget as we read words that have been translated repeatedly, at least through Hebrew and Greek to Latin to English – that John is writing poetry, often favoring similes and metaphors over concise words or names... but the Bible is clearly telling us Daniel "lifted his eyes" (looked at the sky) and since there is not much to see in the sky in the daytime, and Daniel 7:2 tells us "Daniel said, 'I was looking in my vision by night'" we can assume he saw STARS. Gabriel, who is composed of lamps of fire and is seen by looking up at him at night, was also described like a man wearing a belt standing by the river - like the constellation Orion with its three belt stars, by the Milky Way.

Because Michael was also with Gabriel, and he was also standing by the river, and is also an archangel, and also looked like a man – perhaps Michael may also be represented by another man-like constellation by the Milky Way. As Isaac Asimov noted, "'One like the Son of Man' can be paraphrased, 'a figure in the shape of a man.'"[265]

It seems very relevant that the constellation Ophiuchus (The Serpent Handler) not only is located opposite of Gabriel/Orion by the other end of the Milky Way, but is the celestial image of a man holding a huge serpent (the constellation Serpens) – perhaps, an archangel restraining the serpent or dragon-like spirit of Satan and Antichrist. In Greek mythology, Ophiuchus also represents the father of medicine, Aesclepius – who made a potion from the serpent's venom which gave man "access to immortality." The staff of Asclepius is always depicted with a serpent coiled around it (usually three and a half times) and is the basis of the symbols of medicine and of the World Health Organization. Numbers 21:8 is interesting in light of this association "And the Lord said unto Moses, 'Make thee a fiery serpent, and set it upon a pole'" (KJV) or "on a standard." (NASB)

In the Greek myth, Hades, the Greek god of the underworld, complained to Zeus about the potion's elimination of death, and Aesclepius was struck down with a thunderbolt from Zeus. Since the constellations of Ophiuchus and Serpens are locked together in battle, and any falling out of heaven while they hold each other must happen to both of them simultaneously – this may be related to Luke 10:18's description of Jesus perceiving Satan like lightning falling from heaven. But since the two figures are stuck together in the sky – what, if anything, could make it seem as if one constellation, shaped like an angel or a man, is releasing his grip of restraint on another serpent-shaped constellation – or dropping it – when the stars representing them will always be together?

The brightest stars of these constellations – Alpha Ophiuchus and Alpha Serpentis – both rise to a peak height almost 71 degrees altitude above the horizon as viewed from Jerusalem's latitude of 31.78 degrees North. They reach the same height every day of the year, rising in the east with Ophiuchus on his back and the serpent head above him, then level with each other near the zenith, and setting in the west with Ophiuchus on top, pushing the serpent down. There is no date on which this constellation appears uniquely suited to represent the removal of restraint on the serpent.

But Ophiuchus is on the zodiac, on the band of the ecliptic, which means the sun appears to pass through the constellation once a year. Therefore there are times of year when the apparent proximity of the sun prevents us from seeing Ophiuchus at all, centered on the dates in early December, when we might say the sun is "in" Ophiuchus. So during the time from November through January we cannot see Ophiuchus at all. The opposite is true of the opposite "side" of the year. Spring and summer in general, and especially early June, would be an ideal time to see the constellation Ophiuchus. Every night in June Ophiuchus appears on his back in the east as the sun sets, rises to about 71 degrees high in the sky near midnight, and sets in the west pushing the serpent down first at sunrise.

Short of a pole shift that reverses the rotation of the earth, I cannot think of any event that would reverse this process or otherwise make it appear that the Serpent was getting the upper hand or being released from the grip of Ophiuchus as the night progresses – and I do not anticipate a pole shift of any kind at the mid-tribulation point when this removal of restraint should occur. I mention it only because in Islamic eschatology, this is exactly what happens. The Qu'ran tells us that a reversal of the poles, with the sun suddenly rising in the west and setting in the east – comes directly before other end times events. Such a polar reversal (not that I am expecting a 180 degree reversal) would also cause the great serpent/dragon Draco (and all other familiar constellations) to appear to fall out of the heavens for any survivors in the northern hemisphere. Survivors in lands that were in the northern hemisphere would then see constellations which had been visible only in the southern hemisphere. (The reverse is also true; for Australians, Draco would rise into view for the first time.)

We should understand the "midst of the throne" (Revelation 4:6 or 5:6 for example) as the throne room of God, a closed courtroom in which God is the judge, Christ is the defense attorney, Satan is the prosecution, and we the defendants – are not present. Satan is described, depending on the translation or the verse, as being "in the midst of the throne," "In the center of the throne," and "in the middle of the throne," with the throne having "four beasts," "four living creatures," or, as in Revelation 4:7 "The first creature was like a lion, and the second creature like a calf, and the third creature had a face like that of a man, and the fourth creature was like a flying eagle." This is the zodiac, with the four cardinal constellations of Leo, Taurus, Aquarius, and Scorpio (the most ancient zodiacs depicted Scorpio as an eagle instead of the scorpion we know today.) Draco, the dragon, is in the northern center of the zodiac, high above them all in northern skies. From this part of the sky, earth is occasionally blasted with an impressive meteor shower known as the Draconids. I am reminded of Ezekiel 28:16: "I have destroyed you, O covering cherub, from the midst of the stones of fire." I think this implies that Satan was the angel "covering" the earth from Draco's central location in the northern sky.

Satan's heavenly representation – Draco – achieved this polar position as the result of the earth's axis of rotation. Someday, if the rotation of the core of the earth changes – or if a pole shift relocates your formerly northern homeland south of the new equator – Draco may appear to fall to earth during the next pole shift. But as intriguing as such a future pole shift may be, based on my calculations of when a pole shift occurs and how many degrees the poles are likely to move – it cannot be our explanation for anything in 2016. It will not explain anything about Ophiuchus restraining the serpent, and it does nothing to pin down a mid-tribulation date.

Daniel 12:1, however, is somewhat relevant to pinning down a date: "Now at that time Michael, the great prince who stands guard over the sons of your people, will arise. And there will be a time of distress such as never occurred since there was a nation until that time." Assuming Ophiuchus is the heavenly representation of Michael as the restrainer, then Ophiuchus MUST be highly visible in the sky at the mid-point of the tribulation when the Antichrist is revealed. Ophiuchus MUST be seen to "ARISE" and to "STAND GUARD OVER THE SONS OF YOUR PEOPLE."

Ophiuchus cannot be seen at all in the months near December. The mid-point of the tribulation, based on this information, CANNOT be between November and January, when Ophiuchus is completely invisible to us. The sun is "in" Ophiuchus' legs from December 6 to December 16. The midpoint would have to be during a time when Ophiuchus is highly visible; and the most perfect upright view of the constellation at midnight happens around June 6 to June 16.

Midnight is a biblical time for a warning of end times events. Matthew 25:6 reads: "At midnight a shout, 'Behold the bridegroom!'" Could midnight be a clue to when we see Michael/Ophiuchus directly overhead? There is little reason to assume that midnight timing is the crucial factor, despite fitting my theory well. There is more reason to acknowledge that in the Greek Septuagint, the word "paperchomai" in Daniel 12:1 can be defined as "to pass by" or "to pass over," which Ophiuchus will do most directly at the midnight hour. "And at that hour Michael, the great angel who stands over the sons of your people, will pass by." In English, "passing by" seems uneventful, as when we pass by a location without stopping or doing anything. But perhaps part of the intended meaning is that Michael's sign in the sky is passing by directly **overhead**.

Let's focus again on the first sentence of Daniel 12:1 "Now at that time Michael, the great prince who stands guard over the sons of your people, will arise." It would make sense to interpret this to mean that the mid-tribulation point when the restrainer releases the serpent happens when Ophiuchus is first seen to rise in the sky, and most sources say the constellation first becomes visible in June. This depends on when you are awake to look. If you wake up early enough, and look up at the sky an hour before dawn, you could (barely) see Ophiuchus a few months sooner. In March he would be lying on his back before sunrise, which would blind us to him before he rises high in the sky and stands upright. But Daniel describes him as STANDING so this is too early. By April one can see Ophiuchus standing, but only faintly and briefly, right before dawn. By May it is possible to see Ophiuchus standing by about 2am, and by June Ophiuchus can be seen standing upright near midnight. Later in the year, the timing regresses earlier in the night until autumn when he is too close to the setting sun. So based on seasonal variations in the visibility of Ophiuchus standing upright in the sky, May through September are the best times to view the constellation. Based on Daniel's suggestion that he first arises at the time of the mid-tribulation events, this would most likely indicate late May or June. If we assume midnight is important, then the June 6 date is perfect.

While this line of thinking is not as specific as some of the other clues we have pointing to a June 6 date in 2016, it is still highly supportive of that general time of the year. Michael/Ophiuchus stands most upright at midnight from June 6-16, and we can completely rule out the opposite time of the year near December, when Ophiuchus is invisible to us.

I believe the facts about restraining the Antichrist as presented above yield several very meaningful conclusions. First, despite a popular misconception involving the Holy Spirit - the restrainer is not the Holy Spirit, nor is the Holy Spirit abandoning us at the time of the Antichrist. Despite the popularity of the opinion that it is the Holy Spirit which is removed from the earth, it makes more sense that the restrainer is the Archangel Michael – who, if freed from restraining the Antichrist, will be available to organize the armies of God for the war in heaven of Revelation 12:7. Astronomically, Michael, the restrainer of the Serpent, seems to be represented by the constellation Ophiuchus, and this astronomical interpretation corresponds with (and helps support) a mid-tribulation date around June 6.

On such a late spring day Michael gives Satan the key to the abyss, who opens it to release the Antichrist. Revelation chapter 9 continues to say that supernatural locusts swarm out of the abyss. They are like a cross between men and women and iron and horses and chariots and lions and sting like scorpions and have the Destroyer as their leader. Revelation 9:11 "They have as king over them, the angel of the abyss; his name in Hebrew is Abaddon, and in the Greek he has the name Apollyon."

Considering the warlike imagery of these followers of the Antichrist, and the fact that he breaks his peace covenant with the Jews at this very moment 42 months into Daniel's final seven years, when he is freed to boldly proclaim himself to be God – we should not be surprised "if all hell breaks loose" in the form of an apocalyptic war at this point. Daniel 8:25 says "he will destroy many while they are at ease" – it will be a surprise attack. This is "the time of Jacob's trouble" of Jeremiah 30:7 "Alas! for that day is great, there is none like it; and it is the time of Jacob's distress, but he will be saved from it."

Revelation 9:14-18 continues to say "'Release the four angels who are bound at the great river Euphrates.' And the four angels, who had been prepared for the hour and day and month and year, were released, so that they would kill a third of mankind. The number of the armies of the horsemen was two hundred million; I heard the number of them. And this is how I saw in the vision the horses and those who sat on them: the riders had breastplates the color of fire and of hyacinth and of brimstone; and the heads of the horses are like the heads of lions; and out of their mouths proceed fire and smoke and brimstone. A third of mankind was killed."

If you read a definition of brimstone, you read about sulfur, and are misled to think this represents the color yellow. If you look up images of pieces of brimstone, you will see a crumbly, white, chalky substance – as natural brimstone is found in the Middle East. So the colors of the breastplates of those troops led by the Antichrist in battle are red (fire) blue (hyacinth) and white (brimstone.) The Euphrates runs through Iraq, where military forces representing the red, white, and blue of the United States of America have dominated the battlefield since at least 2003. Although many people believe America is not mentioned in Bible prophecy, I believe Revelation 9:18 is just one of many verses describing America's central role in end times events. I suspect that on June 3, 2016, there will be an assassination attempt on the not yet revealed Antichrist, the American president. Corresponding events of war and terrorism, possibly including the nuclear destruction of New York, may occur at approximately the same time. The events might be blamed on Iran, or other Islamic fundamentalists, or even Israel. And the full fury of the American military, which may be bound near the Euphrates in Iraq in 2016, might be unleashed to retaliate against whoever may be blamed for the attacks with all its power. The Antichrist will be revealed to the world from Jerusalem on June 6, 2016. There may even be a nuclear war in June 2016.

There are four "angels" bound at the Euphrates in Revelation 9:14 that are released at a certain day and month and year they were prepared for, to kill a third of mankind. Could these four "angels" be nuclear weapons? In my first book, Nostradamus, World War III, 2002 – I suggested that the French prophet Nostradamus had predicted the West would be at war with Islam by 2002 (possibly for the 27 years from 1991 to 2018). I also pointed out that in paragraph 44 of his letter to King Henry II, that Nostradamus predicted the special destruction of four cities. As the French prophet also predicts "there will be unleashed live fire, hidden death, horrible and frightful within the globes, by night the city reduced to dust by the fleet"[266] in Quatrain 5:8, I interpreted this as a limited nuclear war destroying four major cities.

Nostradamus also wrote: "In the Adriatic will arise great discord, and that which was united will be separated. To a house will be reduced that which was, and is, a great city, including the Pampotamia and Mesopotamia of Europe at 45, and others of 41, 42, and 37 degrees."[267] Nothing about Yugoslavia or the nations it became when it collapsed ever made me think of it as a primary target of nuclear war. But since Nostradamus seems to be indicating that Belgrade shares utter destruction with three other cities, I must consider the possibility.

Yugoslavia's coast was on the Adriatic Sea, and it was united, but is now separated into Serbia, Croatia, and other nations. Much of the Islamic world hates the Serbs for the ethnic cleansing/genocide of Bosnian Muslims as the nation disintegrated in the early 1990s. The former Yugoslavian capital of Belgrade sits between two rivers and therefore is a Mesopotamia, as the word literally means "land in the middle of rivers." It is in Europe, it is at 45 degrees latitude, and it ruled the Adriatic nation when it was united. If the Islamic world wanted to demonstrate its ability to nuke a European city without directly incurring the wrath and response of a major nation, Belgrade could make a sensible target. Could the four numbers of degrees Nostradamus mentioned represent Belgrade and three additional cities to suffer nuclear destruction in WWIII, and would this correspond to the four angels released from the Euphrates to kill a third of mankind?

If so, what are the other three cities? Manhattan is 40.8 degrees north latitude and New York could certainly be the city at 41 degrees. That would fit with the destruction of Mystery Babylon. Istanbul is another interesting possibility, as it was the capital of the Islamic Caliphate through the end of WWI, and 41 degrees latitude runs right through it. Some believe a future Islamic Caliphate could again be ruled from Istanbul, but not if the city is nuked... and that would make rule from Jerusalem easier.

Obama's "home city" of Chicago is at 41.84 degrees north latitude, and could certainly be the one at 42 degrees. But Rome, Italy is also almost 42 degrees north – and in an apocalyptic war that may largely be fought between Islam and Christianity, Rome could be the more likely target. And Nostradamus also wrote in quatrain 2:41

> "For seven days the great star will burn,
> The cloud shall make two suns to appear:
> The big mastiff will howl all night
> When the great pontiff changes country."[268]

A nuclear fireball could look like a second sun. There would be a mushroom cloud above it. A destroyed city might burn for a week. And the destruction of Rome would require the relocation of the papacy to a new country.

Athens, San Francisco, Seoul, and Algiers are all relatively close to 37 degrees north latitude. Teheran, Iran is not quite even 36 degrees latitude.

David Montaigne

All other Middle Eastern cities are even further out of range. The cities suggested above are not the ones I would be most concerned with if I were the Antichrist. But Washington, Moscow, Beijing, London and other major capitals are not at the right latitudes. The cities marked for nuclear destruction could be chosen for reasons that make no sense today. And perhaps Nostradmus' list of latitudes has nothing to do with nuclear war or the four angels released to kill much of mankind in Revelation. You still won't find me in New York, or Rome, Belgrade, or any major city in June 2016. (But it would be interesting to watch this all play out in Jerusalem.)

Some Additional Comments on Timing

The seven years from 12/21/2012 to 12/21/2019 is exactly 2556 days – 6 days more than the 1260 and 1290 day periods as described by the prophet Daniel. Many people might assume "Oh, they must have been using the Hebrew Calendar" – but in the Hebrew calendar, it's even worse – Hanukkah in 2012 was December 9-16, so to get from the day before on 12/8/12 to 12/21/19 it's 19 days extra beyond Daniel's 2550 day total. Seven "biblical" 360 day years is 2520 days which is even further off. It would certainly be more satisfying if seven years were exactly 2550 days, but this simply isn't the case. My best explanation is that a six day discrepancy is explained by two three day gaps, one for each half, with each three day period representing a death and resurrection. I suspect the Antichrist will suffer an apparently fatal assassination attempt exactly 1260 days after 12/21/2012 – on June 3, 2016 – and after the world expects him to die, he will "miraculously" be revived and fully healed.

In reality he will be indwelt and healed by Satan, and announce his kingship over the earth on June 6, 2016 – imitating the three days Jesus Christ lay dead before His resurrection. There are many things I expect the Antichrist to do in his attempt to mimic Christ and portray himself as the Messiah – so it seems very unlikely he would not imitate three days of death – for that is the only sign Jesus said we would get. Matthew 12:39-40 "But He answered and said to them, 'An evil and adulterous generation craves for a sign; and yet no sign will be given to it but the sign of Jonah the prophet; for just as Jonah was three days and three nights in the belly of the sea monster, so will the Son of Man be three days and three nights in the heart of the earth.'" I believe the Antichrist will mimic this when he survives an assassination.

210

This seems like a good time to emphasize I am not encouraging this attempt at assassination. Even if one could be 100% certain who the Antichrist is, murder or attempted murder doesn't look good on one's record down here – or up there. And I think we'll be facing judgment "up there" pretty soon. Besides, the Bible is clear that this attempted assassination fails. Daniel 8:25 says: "he will be broken without human agency." 2 Thessalonians 2:8 says the "lawless one will be revealed whom the Lord will slay with the breath of His mouth and bring to an end by the appearance of His coming." I think the Antichrist will survive the assassination attempt on June 3 and appear fully healed to enter the Temple and demand our worship on June 6, 2016.

That still leaves the problem of the second half of the seven years being three days short. The easy explanation is another three day gap added on for another death and resurrection - of the two witnesses. This would get us from 2550 to 2556 days, or exactly seven solar years. Problem solved, right?

Even that leaves some potential unanswered questions. If, for a moment, we ignore the beginning of the second times, times, and half a time, and focus on the end of Daniel's time frames, it is very interesting that he mentions time frames of 1260, 1290, and 1335 days. Some scholars believe the tribulation ends with the end of the 1335 days. This leaves 30 day and 45 day gaps which might correspond to judgment and wrath. And there is a 75 day gap between my calculation for one astronomical alignment representing the Second Coming on the Feast of Tabernacles on October 14, 2019 – and my calculation of other alignments for Judgment Day at the end of the week long wedding in the sky, end of the pole shift, and Hanukkah on December 28, 2019. If Daniel's 75 day difference fit entirely into the second half of the final seven years, everything would make perfect sense, and Daniel's 75 days would correspond with my 75 days.

Of course, periods of 30 and 45 days adding to 75 days are somewhat common. President Obama was reelected November 6, 2012. The Mayan Long Count ended, and Daniel's 70th week began, on December 21, 2012. Obama was inaugurated on January 20, 2013. Where I found this online, the blogger said: "I am by no means suggesting that this 75 day period is the same one mentioned in the Bible, as it cannot be; however, I am suggesting that this is a prophetic "mirror" or "type" which should turn our eyes to both America as Babylon and to Obama as potentially the nation's final King."[269] I would hope to reconcile my 75 days at the end of my seven year timeline as more than just a mirror.

But Daniel 12:11 says "From the time that the regular sacrifice is abolished and the abomination of desolation is set up, there will be 1,290 days." This seems pretty straightforward: there are only 1290 days remaining after the events involving the Antichrist at the Temple in Jerusalem…. But 1290 days until what, precisely? A rapture? The Second Coming? Judgment Day? All on the same day? And if there are only 1290 days, who remains to blessed upon reaching 1335 days, which I assume must be 45 days later? Daniel 12:12 "How blessed is he who keeps waiting and attains to the 1,335 days!" Is that only for survivors of the pole shift who are "left behind"?

These 75 days between major events are very significant and should not be ignored; yet how do we reconcile them with the first half of the final seven years ending in June 2016? If we overlay my 75 day gap with Daniel's, then Judgment Day should be day 1335. That puts my date for the Second Coming on day 1260. So far so good. But if we count back 1335 days from Judgment Day at the end of the week long wedding on December 28, 2019 we arrive at May 2, 2016. Not June 6, 2016. Jerusalem, we have a problem.

1335 days before December 21, 2019 is even farther back, leading us to April 25, 2016. Neither calculation brings us to what I assume is the "right" date of June 6, 2016. This creates a huge overlap of over a month between the two halves of the final seven years. That seems to make no sense, despite the convenient lineup of time frames at the end of the 1260 and 1335 days with the Second Coming at the Feast of Tabernacles and Judgment Day during Hanukkah. Is there another way we should be looking at this?

Another possibility is to assume that only Daniel's 1290 days is within the seven years, and that the 45 days comes after it. Daniel 12:11 by itself says "From the time that the regular sacrifice is abolished and the abomination of desolation is set up, there will be 1,290 days." Obviously he expects a major end times event 1290 days after the second half of the final seven years begins. But he also expects a blessing upon those "who attain the 1335 days." If we start with June 6, 2016 and go forward 1290 days (plus 3 extra days again) we reach December 21, 2019 – the end of the 70th week of years – the time when I expect a pole shift and the astronomical representation of Christ's wedding to His bride is starting. I must assume that the final 45 days come AFTER this date. But this still feels wrong because then Daniel's 75 day gap does not line up with my own 75 day gap. Overlapping mirroring 75 day periods are not as satisfying as a precise match.

Another possible explanation for the 45 day problem involves Mark 13:19-20

"For those days will be a time of tribulation such as has not occurred since the beginning of the creation which God created until now, and never will. Unless the Lord had shortened those days, no life would have been saved; but for the sake of the elect, whom He chose, He shortened the days." Such a shortening of the days may be the biblical way to tell us the first "half" and second "half" of the final seven years don't work out perfectly if we try to line them up end to end without overlapping. But I think this idea also feels like a weak argument – to suggest that the math doesn't have to add up or that the two halves partially overlap. I think it is much more likely that Daniel would have given us different numbers that are accurate, than to give us numbers which don't add up correctly. Is there yet another possibility?

Again, the closest match for reaching seven years in total is to add three days to the 1260 days and add three days to the 1290 days. With a little death and resurrection added on to each half, we have exactly seven solar calendar years. But that still leaves those pesky 45 days from the end of 1290 days to reach the final number of 1335 days. Even if they are after Judgment Day, they must be significant, and we should have an explanation for them.

I believe the 45 days are for cleansing the new Temple. Forty-five days is exactly how long it took to cleanse and rededicate the Temple in the past. 2 Chronicles 29 explains that Judah's good king Hezekiah replaced the bad king Ahaz. He decided that the evil ways of the previous reign had defiled the temple, and they were going to cleanse it. 2 Chronicles 29:17 says "Now they began the consecration on the first day of the first month" and they finished after "they slaughtered the Passover lambs on the fourteenth of the second month." (2 Chronicles 30:15) So it took 44 days to clean the Temple, meaning that on the 45th day it would be purified for normal use. This would undoubtedly be necessary again after the 1290 day reign of the Antichrist, which is why Daniel 12 ends with "From the time that the regular sacrifice is abolished and the abomination of desolation is set up, there will be 1,290 days. How blessed is he who keeps waiting and attains to the 1,335 days! But as for you, go your way to the end; then you will enter into rest and rise again for your allotted portion at the end of the age." This clearly puts the final 45 days of temple re-dedication "at the end of the age." How blessed is he who reaches the end of that 1335 days, when the Antichrist's reign of terror has ended, AND 45 days later the temple is fully restored!

Since Hanukkah is a holiday about rededicating the Temple, and the New Jerusalem is in effect a new WORLD (created for us via pole shift) and a new TEMPLE (Jesus' Millennium Temple) then the 45 days to dedicate the new world-temple must begin with the pole shift and Hanukkah and follow the end of the seven years. As I described at length in End Times and 2019, there is one more VERY special astronomical alignment just AFTER the end of the world as we know it in December 2019. In late January 2020 – the heavens recreate a rare "tree of life" pattern. The book of Genesis tells us that after Adam and Eve ate from the Tree of Knowledge, God decided to prevent mankind from also eating from the Tree of Life, and becoming like gods. I speculate that our current civilization is very advanced technologically (we have "eaten from the Tree of Knowledge") and we are getting close to preventing our DNA from aging (achieving immortality, or "eating from the Tree of Life") and that our civilization will, once again, be prevented from reaching the Tree of Life – which in the near future, is astronomically represented by an extremely rare alignment representing the Tree of Life as depicted in the Hebrew Kabbalah. I've looked for this alignment in past and future skies, and January 2020 is the only time it happens within my 5,000 year search.

But just because our civilization will not reach the Tree of Life (late January 2020) intact, this does not mean that righteous survivors of God's pole-shift-wrath will not reach it. Revelation 22:15 says "Blessed are those who wash their robes, so that they may have the right to the tree of life, and may enter by the gates into the city." The city, of course, is the New Jerusalem – which is the new earth. Daniel 12:10-12 also indicates that some people will be blessed 45 days after the last 1290 days and that "those who have insight will understand. From the time that the regular sacrifice is abolished and the abomination of desolation is set up, there will be 1,290 days. How blessed is he who keeps waiting and attains to the 1,335 days!"

If the old Earth was destroyed in a pole shift, there will be a lot of debris. Think of all the chemical plants and oil refineries that would be destroyed, and all of the corpses lying unburied. We may need 45 days of decomposition and rain to help cleanse our new Earth, and this may correspond to cleansing the Temple. If the New Jerusalem is the new Earth and this is the new Temple, this makes sense to me. Perhaps everything settles down and washes out by the time of the astronomical representation of the Tree of Life in late January 2020, and 45 days of cleansing after the pole shift in December 2019, everything completely stabilizes and the world/temple is dedicated anew. This would be a new golden age of purity here on earth, right where the ancient Jews expected the Kingdom of Heaven. As Tim LaHaye wrote in Revelation Unveiled, "the new earth will be the Christian's heaven."[270]

ACCEPTING GOD'S PLANS

When I was young, I had trouble believing in God. As I matured, the concept of God the Creator eventually made sense to me, but I didn't see why he would need to send a Son as an intermediary. As I searched and developed spiritually, I acknowledged that God is so vast, existing beyond our confines of the dimensions of time and space, that He cannot be perceived and understood by us in full. To interact with us, He would have to limit Himself, and communicate with us as a partial shadow of His complete self. The logical conclusion on such topics is that if God would communicate with us, sending His message – The Word – in human form makes sense. This allows the easiest interaction with us, and the clearest example for us. In reaching this conclusion, I was on the cusp of understanding Christianity. But I still didn't have evidence. I could not just ignore my doubts and believe "without committing intellectual suicide."[271]

We humans are limited and imperfect. We know there are rules given by politicians and prophets and we justify following some and not others. Most people readily agree with "thou shalt not kill" and manage to avoid killing anyone. But as we go down the list of laws most of us pick and choose; even the best of us can easily justify all sorts of things from jaywalking to recording a football game without the express written consent of ABC Sports and National Football League. We fail to focus on what is right, and do not even consistently follow those few rules we agree are reasonable. We make mistakes. We cheat. We harm each other. We demonstrate that humans are incapable of following all the laws given to Moses. Our sins disgrace ourselves and our creator.

And from the perspective of the rest of the universe, it's a good thing that we humans have very little power, limited by a short span of time in which we briefly exist in just three dimensions. We are but flawed shadows of the heavenly realm of God, who exists in more spatial dimensions than we can comprehend. He also exists outside and beyond our confines of time, for past, present, and future are all one whole to Him, knowing the end from the beginning.

There is nothing we mortals can do to merit ascending to an eternal, multidimensional existence with God. It is normal, because of our limited existence in linear time, to attach too great an importance on "good works," as our lives revolve around cause and effect. But Romans 9:11 clarifies that God's decision to offer us salvation was made before we even existed, when we were "not yet born and had not done anything good or bad, so that God's purpose according to His choice would stand, not because of works but because of Him who calls." Good works will be one result of understanding God's offer of salvation, but works are not to be considered a required down payment. We are incapable of purchasing our own redemption through good behavior or good works because we could never be perfect enough to enter heaven on our own merit.

We humans have a tendency to dislike this lack of complete control. God is beyond our limitations of time and space, making incomprehensible decisions about us before we are born. The whole process reeks of predestination, and many believe that if God knows the end from the beginning then free will is just an illusion. I argue that we do have free will, and that God's knowledge is somewhat like our knowledge of history. My knowing what Napoleon did in the past does not mean that he lacked free will and that the only decisions available to him were the ones I know as established facts. My position in time merely locks in the choices which Napoleon (and everyone else in my past) already made. I did not control Napoleon or take away his free will through reading about him. And I would argue that God's ability to transcend time and know our future as we know the past also does not rule out our free will. But for those of us bound by cause and effect within linear time, the concept of God knowing the results of our choices before we are born without limiting those choices is not simple to grasp.

It doesn't seem fair that we were created with confusion and imperfections and limitations, when so much more is possible. Perhaps this is why God invites us to experience heaven, so long as we understand and accept his grace and authority. That is Christianity. Accepting our limitations, asking for forgiveness for our behavior, asking not to be judged worthy of more based on our own actions but understanding that we can be offered more through unmerited grace, and acknowledging that entry into the perfection of heaven is conditional upon accepting God's rules and authority.

Accepting that God sent His instructional message of salvation in the human form of His Son Jesus Christ was intellectually impossible for me as a young man; but as I searched and matured I finally see that this is the most logical way God would communicate this message to us. He sent a divine message in human form to the only nation of monotheists who believed in a single God at a point in history when they were anticipating a messiah who would save them from persecution. He made sure His message was understood and accepted by at least a few people who would then spread it around the world.

Why does God even care? We are an imperfect stain on His creation, and Christianity teaches us that before we are even born we are judged to be inherently unworthy of heavenly immortality because of the limitations and imperfections that come with being human. To God, we are like the bacteria of an infection in our human bodies. But if I believe that all life has meaning, and that somehow I could communicate with lower forms of life – I would send the bacteria in my infection a message. I would inform them that their actions are self-serving in the short run and fatal in the long run. Because they only exist in MY body, and if I judge their existence to be counterproductive, I will treat them like a problem to be eliminated. There will be a great and final disinfection. Their only chance of survival is to accept my rules of operation and fall in line. Bacteria that work with our bodies are welcome additions. Many bacteria help our cells process sugars and perform other useful functions. They become a part of us, and have been passed down from mother to child.

I believe that all of us, the entire universe, are a part of the body of God. I believe God chose to send us a message, and that it made sense not to just send a magic book but to come in the form of an interactive human messenger. I believe He embodied the Logos, the divine Word, in a human version of Himself. I believe that man was Jesus Christ. I believe He suffered to descend to this form of existence to offer us salvation – a way to escape the normally inevitable death sentence which results from our limitations and imperfections in human form. I acknowledge Jesus Christ as my Lord, as He is a form of God and I must follow His rules to be granted full acceptance in His creation. I acknowledge Christ as my Savior, as we can never achieve perfection or merit entry into heaven without divine grace – which is what Christ was sent to offer us if we will only acknowledge and accept these basic ideas.

I feel excited and energized to finally understand and accept Christianity in my mind and in my heart. But my understanding and belief does carry a price – any wants and desires I had before, which are not consistent with God – they have to go. In accepting Christ as my Lord, I acknowledge there is no longer "my way" just "His way." My past sins and imperfections are forgiven, but I must be "born again" and live for God and His Message, which came in the form of Jesus Christ. If we truly accept God's authority, and know we are saved, we will behave accordingly. Once we truly accept God's rules, we are not judged again. We were judged and sentenced already. If we truly believe, we accept God's authority and grace and we are eternally pardoned – we are saved from ourselves.

After decades of searching, the basic message of Christianity is the conclusion I feel I have finally and logically reached. I had always thought that the gospels taught to avoid trying to reach faith through logic. Luke 18:17 says "whoever does not receive the kingdom of God like a child will not enter it at all" – and many well-intentioned Christians have tried to get me to "stop overthinking it." But I now see that the request to come as a child does not mean to avoid logic or to be ignorant and accept anything blindly or without understanding – coming as a child just means to have unquestioning faith and trust in my heavenly Father, like I had in my human father when I was a child. For me to have faith, I needed understanding. I have finally grasped what is described in 2 Timothy 3:15 - "the wisdom that leads to salvation through faith." It may not be the path most people take to get here. But this is the path that worked for me.

Although it may not matter, I know the exact moment I finally felt and understood this. I was reading a book on "simple steps to salvation" (which I did not assume would help accomplish anything when I started reading it) when I "got it" - and looked up at the clock to note the time, and started writing down my thoughts. Normally I wouldn't recommend paying much attention to someone who sounds like they were born yesterday... but I was just born again yesterday, at 9:11 PM EST, Monday June 9, 2014.

Is it my duty as a Christian to push my beliefs on others? I don't think it is, especially when I spent a lifetime in doubt and have only very recently accepted the message of Christ. But I did title this little chapter "Accepting God's Plans." I believe the evidence points to horrific events coming soon. I believe your faith in God and His plans will be very important soon. So I would be negligent if I did not at least suggest to any readers who lack faith – think long and hard about what you believe. If I am wrong in my conclusions on timing, perhaps there is no rush. But if I am right, there is very little time left to clarify your beliefs. Some of you, right now, are having trouble judging God. I believe that no later than December 28, 2019 – God will be judging us. If you haven't found God yet, keep searching. I don't think He is hiding from us. Once our minds are open to the idea that there is a power greater than ourselves and we have "eyes to see," finding

God is even easier than spotting the red and white striped shirt in "Where's Waldo?" Evidence of God is all around us. I think He is patiently waiting, hoping you will "find" Him while there is still time.

Romans 12:2 "Do not be conformed to this world, but be transformed by the renewing of your mind, so that you may prove what the will of God is, that which is good and acceptable and perfect."

IS OBAMA REALLY THE ANTICHRIST?

In September 2011, Obama said on the campaign trail: "Don't compare me to the almighty, compare me to the alternative."[272]   Challenge accepted. Perhaps Obama meant his potential Republican opponents, and not Satan or the Antichrist, but why phrase it that way? Was it really just a poor choice of words?

I don't think even Joe Biden could make so many poor choices unintentionally. Here is another zinger, first noted in the April 2007 edition of <u>Men's Vogue Magazine</u>: as Morgan Freeman approached Obama at a fundraiser, Obama said: "'This guy was president before I was,' says Obama, referring to Freeman's turn [role] in Deep Impact and, clearly, getting a little ahead of his own bio. Next, a nod to Bruce Almighty: 'This guy was God before I was.'"[273]   How modest and unassuming Senator Obama was. No hint at all there that he might one day stand in the Temple and claim to be God.

At a pre-election rally at Dartmouth in 2008 Obama said to voters: "A beam of light will come down upon you, you will experience an epiphany, and you will suddenly realize that you must go to the polls and vote"[274] [for him.] Funny, I didn't experience that.

At a White House Correspondents Dinner on April 30, 2011 Obama said "Tonight, for the first time, I am releasing my official birth video"[275] and he played the scene introducing Simba in the movie The Lion King. The one where all the animals bowed down to the King of Beasts. Just what is he trying to suggest that time?

In October 2012 (always in jest, of course) Obama told us "Contrary to the rumors you have heard, I was not born in a manger, I was actually born on Krypton and sent here by my father Jor-El to save the planet Earth."[276]   Has any other president, joking or otherwise, ever claimed to be a savior for the planet? And should we overlook the symbolism? The "El" part of the names in Jor-El and Kal-El was an ancient name for God, still recognizable in names like Beth-El (House of God.) Watch the original Superman movie or look up an image of Marlon Brando as Jor-El, in front of the three criminals in the rotating rings. Jor-El is played by the God-father. He wears a black suit with a pentagram (associated with Satanism) emblem on the chest with a serpent (associated with Satan in Genesis) inside the pentagram. Obama is the one who said it: "my father Jor-El." Just what is he claiming to be the son of?

On July 22, 2014 President Obama commented on world affairs and said "the old order is over and the New World Order is coming."[277] Such comments never make me feel warm and fuzzy. When spoken with such authority and intent from a powerful politician like Obama they sound even worse to me.

As other authors have already suggested about the Antichrist: "he is alive today – and he is an American."[278] I suspect that Barack Obama will prove to be the Antichrist. Some readers may find this hard to believe – but roughly 40 million Americans suspect it and another 40 million already believe it. A survey in 2013 showed that 13 per cent of Americans already thought Obama might be the Antichrist and another 13 percent believed that he is definitely the Antichrist.[279] If Obama does prove to be the Antichrist (and I obviously believe there is evidence to support the idea) then we are running out of time. Even if I had no clues on timing prophecy but his identity – his term in office alone tells us the time is soon. I don't think he will allow elections in 2016 that replace him with a new president. It seems less likely that the Antichrist would bring on the apocalypse after leaving office and relinquishing power – and much more likely that he will make his move while still in control of a powerful empire. [Of course I also suspect that Obama has no intention to leave the presidency....] *PAST nothing happened*

So far we have reviewed the evidence for the timing of the Antichrist's *1/8/16* public appearance and demand for worship coming on June 6, 2016. We have studied the evidence for America as Mystery Babylon. We know that one of the primary titles for the Antichrist is the "King of Babylon." So it makes sense that whoever is the President of the United States in June 2016 is the Antichrist. There is no election until November 2016 (if one is allowed to happen then) so I assume Obama will be in power in June 2016.

As Chris Putnam asks: "Is America the final Babylon? If you believe that the return of Jesus Christ is within the next decade or so then this conclusion seems inevitable."[280] As Dr. Bob Thiel noted in his book, Barack Obama, Prophecy, and the Destruction of the United States: "simply by the virtue of his timing as the 44th U.S. President, Barack Obama was destined to aid in the fulfillment of end-time biblical prophecies.... There are reasons to believe that the rising of the final ten-horned beast power and the destruction of the United States will take place under the Obama administration."[281] Televangelist Jack van Impe suggests Obama is being groomed for this role, and author John Shorey agrees that "the President of the United States... could become the antichrist."[282] But is there anything specific that describes Barack Obama?

Unfortunately, while there can be a thousand hints, the evidence cannot be overwhelmingly convincing prior to the removal of the restrainer. Some will know, but most will not. If the Antichrist's identity is not revealed to the world until June 2016, then there simply cannot be enough evidence to convince everyone prior to that date. Something supernatural is at work to limit our understanding, or the evidence itself, until the appointed time.

I dislike the excuse that heaven itself prevents me from making too strong a case for the theory that Obama could be the Antichrist, but as weak as that excuse may sound, I cannot override the will of God or Jesus or the Archangel Michael. Even the prophet Daniel was told to "conceal these words and seal up the book until the end of time" when the Archangel Gabriel gave him a vision of the future in Daniel 12:4. I have received no visions, I am no wiser than Daniel, and I enjoy no freedom of the constraints on revealing prophecy. Although I feel like my book has a seal of approval, I suspect that the evidence available to the world at the time I am writing is meant only for the few with eyes to see and ears to hear.

No one on earth is going to clearly prove the Antichrist's identity to the world before the appointed time. As Isaiah 47:13 suggests, "Let now the astrologers, those who prophesy by the stars, those who predict by the new moons, stand up and save you from what will come upon you." We can only point out the signs. I can't save the world from the inevitable by pointing out my interpretations.

If I correctly understand the limitations on attempting to prove and reveal the Antichrist's identity, I face at least one of the following three problems: No one can

1 – PROVE his identity CONVINCINGLY

2 – TO THE WORLD, ONLY TO A SMALL PORTION OF THE POPULATION,

3 – PRIOR TO JUNE 2016.

Hopefully, I can make my case somewhat well before June 2016. But then, at best, my case will be convincing to a small portion of people – or minimally convincing to a larger number. No one is going to defy these limitations.

There is some merit to what Irenaeus wrote in <u>Against Heresies</u>: "if it were necessary that his name should be distinctly revealed in this present time, [written around 180 A.D.] it would have been announced by him who beheld the apocalyptic vision."[283]   That being said, there are many interesting clues that point to Barack Obama. Some are more convincing than others. You can decide for yourself what may or may not be important.

Did Jesus give us the name of the Antichrist?

Luke 10:18 says "And He said to them, 'I was watching Satan fall from heaven like lightning.'" I wish the English version alone made the truth obvious – but as John Walvoord noted: "because of imperfect translations, some important truth is hidden to the one who only reads the English text of the Bible."[284]   Several internet videos explain that the translation of this phrase into Hebrew or Aramaic leads to the name Barack Obama, and that the original words of Jesus would basically be that he perceived Satan as Barack Obama. Of course we should never take amazing claims at face value without investigating their accuracy, so I looked up some English to · Hebrew dictionaries.

The first translator I saw was at Lexilogos.com and you can use it to verify this yourself online. Enter "lightning" in English and translate it to Hebrew. The result is בָּרָק – pronounced like B-ah-R-ah-K. But don't take my word for it. Copy the Hebrew text from Lexilogos and paste it in the search bar of a site like forvo.com. It will play the audio of any word you enter in any modern language. The top audio choice in the list for בָּרָק is spoken by an Israeli male and clearly sounds like "BAH rock."

Strong's Hebrew Dictionary entry 1300 for "baraq" (baw-rawk') defines it as "lightning."[285]   It is derived from "from 'baraq' (1299); lightning; by analogy, a gleam; concretely, a flashing sword:--bright, glitter(-ing sword), lightning." In the Greek translation of this verse the word "ουρανός" ("ouranos") means heaven or sky, but also means heights or high places.

David Montaigne

Which meaning was originally spoken by Jesus before being translated to Greek? Greeks would generally use the word "παράδεισος" (paradise) to mean heaven in the religious sense; and when reverse translating "ouranos" to English the main translation is sky, not heaven. Young's Literal Translation reads this word as "heaven," the King James says "air," and the NASB reads "air" with a note that the word literally means heaven. This does bring the Hebrew/Aramaic source word that was translated as the Greek "ouranos" into question. But none of this conclusively leads me to "heights" or "high places" and none of it is Hebrew or Aramaic either.

So I looked up Luke 10:18 in Hebrew – biblegateway.com has a Habrit/Hakhadasha version of the Bible. I copied part of the phrase (as you can at home yourself to verify this) from verse 18 "מן נופל השטן את ראיתי כברק השמים" and pasted it into the "reverse translator" (Hebrew to English) at reverso.net and received the English translation as "I saw the devil falls from the heavens as Barak." I can tell one Hebrew word is "shamayim" – the heaven of God. But the Habrit Bible I get this from is itself a translation from Greek, and may just be the first possible definition of "ouranos" but not the original word we need. As some videos suggest, Jesus spoke the phrase in Hebrew or Aramaic, then Luke was written in Greek, then translated to (Latin and) English – and also for Habrit Bible purposes, back into Hebrew as the "shamayim," but that might not be the original Hebrew word we started with in 33 A.D. Assuming that Jesus was speaking Hebrew in the first place. (While He could have spoken any language of the time, some argue that He may have primarily spoken Greek.)

The videos portraying Obama as the Antichrist suggest that from context in other uses of the Greek word "ouranos" as in Luke 8:5, we should assume the Hebrew word for "heights" was used. This would correspond with Satan's own description of where he aimed to be in Isaiah 14:14 when he boasted: "I will ascend above the heights of the clouds; I will make myself like the Most High." Strong's Hebrew dictionary entry 1116 is the Hebrew word "bamah" and is defined as "an elevation:--height, high place." Some videos also claim that in between these words the prefix "o" or "u" would have been used for the English word "from" or "of." But the Hebrew preposition is a varying prefix depending on the word it is attached to, and often has the equivalent of an "M" sound like it does in "meel;" which means "from" or "out of" something. I can't find any Hebrew preposition like the sound "o" or "u." But I have seen other critics of this video state that one of the few points they recognize as correct is that the proper Hebrew preposition often was transliterated as an "o" or "u" sound. And in reference to another Hebrew word in Daniel 5:25, Walter Kenaston wrote: "'U' is a prefix meaning "and, but, since" etc. which depends on context and interpretation."[286]

What if Jesus had been speaking Aramaic? I looked up Luke 10:18 through http://www.v-a.com/bible/ where Vic Alexander describes his efforts to translate an ancient Aramaic version of the Bible to English. He suggests that the verse should read: "He then told them, 'You should have seen Satan as he fell like lightening from heaven.'" The beginning of that phrase sounds odd to me, as does his "e" in "lightening." So I checked Dr. George Lamsa's Aramaic Bible translation at lamasbible.com, where Luke 10:18 reads: "He said to them, I saw Satan falling like lightning from heaven." Peshitta.org even shows Aramaic script, and the word for word translation is a little out of order compared to English sentence structure, but reads "He and said to them I did see him Satan falling like lightning from heaven." But the Aramaic word "from" looks similar to the Hebrew letters for "M" and "L" and I don't know if they would have been transliterated with an "o" or "u" vowel sound.

Of course the problem on the preposition "from" may only represent proper grammar, and not how anyone would have actually spoken. In phrases like "this and that" or "fish and chips" no one enunciates the "and" clearly; everyone says and hears "this 'n that" and "fish 'n chips." And "o'clock" is the abbreviation of the phrase "of the clock" used in England centuries ago – a current example in which we reduce "of the" down to "O." It seems plausible that the ancient Hebrew preposition (of which there are several possibilities), when actually spoken, could have been reduced to a "O" sound, and not necessarily pronounced as spelled. The original Hebrew or Aramaic version of the phrase about perceiving Satan as lightning falling could have been lightning from the heights, and the sounds "Baraq" "O" "Bamah" could have been spoken together by Jesus in this context.

If Jesus had clearly said He perceived Satan's descent to earth (perhaps to indwell someone as the Antichrist) as "baraq 'o bamah" the words might not have been understood as a name by Luke or the other apostles. There are names like plays on words, such as SafeAuto's "Justin Case." Just possibly, Luke himself might have heard Jesus say "Barack Obama" and thought "Jesus' pronunciation was a little strange just now, but I'm pretty sure He said "lightning from the heights." Or the similarity could just be a coincidence. You decide.

There are many vague biblical clues about the Antichrist which seem to fit Obama, along with most other politicians. We can ignore those for not being

David Montaigne

specific enough. Others portray Obama well.

Verses like Daniel 8:9 indicate the Antichrist starts small and rises quickly. Obama went from community organizer to president in just twelve years. He went from the Illinois Senate to the presidency in just over four years.

Revelation 13:7 says that "authority over every tribe and people and tongue and nation was given to him." The rotating chairmanship of the U.N. Security Council occasionally goes to the United States, and normally the U.S. Ambassador to the United Nations takes the gavel. On rare occasion a higher official visiting the United Nations may act as president of the Security Council. But Article 9 of the US Constitution says the president cannot accept authority or titles over any foreign state or governing body, and Obama may have violated this by presiding over the United Nations when he put himself in charge in 2009. But he set a precedent, being temporarily in charge of the U.N.'s most powerful body, the Security Council, which put him in charge of:

international peace and security
mediating disputes and the terms of settlement
the establishment of a system to regulate armaments
determining the existence of a threat and recommending a response
taking military action against an aggressor
recommending the admission of new members
the appointment of the Secretary-General and, together with the Assembly, to elect the Judges of the International Court of Justice.

In 2009, his power was temporary, and he did not abuse it. I suspect there will be a future crisis during which he will mention already having had that authority, and that he will use it more thoroughly in the future.

Daniel 7:11 tells us the Antichrist is arrogant and boastful. We have heard Obama compare himself to the Lion King, to Superman, and even to God. On September 11, 2011, President Obama read a long quote from Psalm 46, including the words "know that I am God." Normally I would just assume it was a poor choice to quote... but many assume Obama chose this because he believes he is The One.

Obama's campaign logo has been an image of the sun rising over America. America represents the West; Japan is the land of the rising sun in the East. But Islamic prophecy describes the sun rising in the West just before the last day. The rising sun is also the translation of "SUBUD," the name of an Indonesian cult named after its founder, Mohammad "Subud" Soebarkah. Our president grew up in Indonesia. Obama's mother, Stanley Ann Dunham, was apparently a member of SUBUD, as was Loretta "Deliana" Fuddy, a former chairwomen of Subud USA's National Committee and the appointed Director of the Hawaii Department of Health who certified Obama's very questionable birth certificate to be legitimate (and who died mysteriously in a plane crash soon after.)

The SUBUD cult has its international headquarters in Chicago, where Obama formed his political base. Far more intriguing - Obama's mother wrote her son's name as Barack Hussein Obama Soebarkah on a passport renewal in Indonesia in 1969, then crossed out the amended name. Obama looks suspiciously similar to the cult's founder – a far stronger resemblance than to Barack Obama, Sr. I don't know what the SUBUD connection means, but there are too many coincidences for me to assume that Obama's years in Indonesia mean nothing.

If you thought the Vietnam War was unpopular within the United States, imagine the impression it made on a young Barack Obama, growing up in Southeast Asia (Indonesia is very close to Vietnam) when his stepfather was a Muslim Indonesian and his mother hated right wing American policies. In July 2013, Obama said: "Ho Chi Minh was actually inspired by the U.S. Declaration of Independence and Constitution, and the words of Thomas Jefferson."[287] You must understand, while no other American president has viewed that enemy leader well, Obama views him as a freedom fighter against American imperialism. No other president has apparently viewed America from an anti-colonial perspective, but that is the main premise made by Dinesh D'Souza in The Roots of Obama's Rage, in which the author concludes: "President Obama is conducting a war against what he considers to be the biggest rogue state of all: The United States of America…. The Obama approach seems to have been both ingenious and largely successful in doing what it set out to do: reduce the power of the neocolonial United States."[288] No other president has treated America as if it is a rogue state or an imperial empire that needs to be brought down. I wish D'Souza's book was assigned reading for all Americans, because I agree with him that "Obama's dream is actually an American nightmare."[289] As one Christian blogger concludes: "it appears that it is his duty to bring down America and bring in the New World Order."[290]

Obama's policies have been so bad for America that many people think he is in over his head or that he has no idea what he is doing. Walter Russell Mead suggests that Obama is "the least competent manager of America's Middle East diplomatic portfolio in a very long time."[291] Obama has been called the "Bungler-in-chief" and one writer said "the presidency of Barack Obama is a case study in stupid."[292] But they probably only say such things because they mistakenly assume that he intends to improve and enrich the nation he controls, despite making policies that fail to achieve such ends. Aaron Klein's <u>The Manchurian President</u> suggests that Obama secretly works for some kind of anti-American cabal. Kevin Hassett wrote that it is "puzzling that he would legislate like a Manchurian candidate."[293] It's not puzzling, it's brilliant! He has helped enemies and alienated allies, and most importantly, by adding trillions of dollars in debt, Obama will achieve the Marxist goal of giving the capitalists the rope they will hang themselves with. "Obama is getting precisely the results he wants" when you consider his anti-colonial worldview: America is the final and most oppressive rogue state, the apex of western colonialism, and he aims to "correct" the imbalance of power and wealth by reducing America's diplomatic, financial, and military advantages.

Daniel 7:24 tells us the Antichrist will be different from the previous kings of his country: "another will arise after them, and he will be different from the previous ones." No other president seems to want to reduce American dominance. "Never before in American history have we had a president who seeks decline, who is actually attempting to downsize his country."[294] Unlike a typical liberal democrat/socialist who merely wants to redistribute wealth from rich to poor within America, Obama seems to want to redistribute global wealth from North to South and from West to East. No other president seems determined to eliminate America's "unfair" advantages.

Daniel 7:20 (KJV) had just pointed out one difference from the previous kings is that the Antichrist's "look was more stout than his fellows." A stout is a strong, dark beer. In addition to being strong and dark, stoutness is also synonymous with large, heavy, and determined. Obama is certainly dark, tall and determined. As for being different – no other president appears to be of African descent or to have experienced a Muslim upbringing.

I know, President Obama has said "I was raised by my mother. So, I've always been a Christian. The only connection I've had to Islam is that my grandfather on my father's side came from that country. But I've never practiced Islam."[295] But as Maury Povich might say, "That was a lie."

[Legal Disclaimer: I am not stating that President Obama definitely is a Muslim. But there is a lot of evidence pointing in that direction, and we need to consider it – especially in light of the Islamic Antichrist Theory.]

In The Audacity of Hope, Obama wrote about his mother's religious beliefs: "I was not raised in a religious household ... My mother's own experiences ... only reinforced this inherited skepticism. Her memories of the Christians who populated her youth were not fond ones ... And yet for all her professed secularism..." she was very spiritual – but hardly Christian. She introduced her son to many religions: "in our household the Bible, the Koran, and the Bhagvad Gita sat on the shelf alongside books of Greek and Norse and African mythology."[296] Does that sound like the Christian Bible held any special respect in that house – or does it sound like they were all considered mythology?

Obama also said in a speech on September 27, 2010: "I'm a Christian by choice. My family didn't—frankly, they weren't folks who went to church every week. And my mother was one of the most spiritual people I knew, but she didn't raise me in the church. So I came to my Christian faith later in life."[297]   Also consider another comment Obama made regarding his Christianity in The Audacity of Hope: "The Christians with whom I worked recognized themselves in me; they saw that I knew their Book and shared their values..." but he was "an observer among them."[298]   This implies that the Bible is "their book," but not his book. While this quote is hardly firm evidence of anyone's current religious views, (as they could have changed in the last twenty years) does this sound like something a Christian would say, or more like something a Muslim might say?

How about the opinion of Obama's own Christian pastor, Jeremiah Wright? The Washington Times (online edition, 5/17/12) gave Wright's view that: "Obama possessed an 'Islamic background' and despite his conversion to Christianity has never abandoned his Muslim roots."[299]   Another source discussing Wright's opinion on Obama's religious views says: "When he first met Barack Obama in 1987, he was immediately impressed by how much Obama then knew about Islam, by contrast with Obama's slender knowledge about Jesus. Asked if he had converted Obama from Islam to Christianity, Wright replied: 'That's hard to tell. I think that I convinced him it was okay for him to make a choice in terms of who he believes Jesus is. And I told him that it was really okay and not a put down of the Muslim part of his family or his Muslim friends.'"[300]

Realistically, we have reason to doubt ANYTHING said by ANY politician of high rank. But Obama gives us reason to doubt almost EVERYTHING he claims. Glenn Beck said "The president's life is pure fiction... it seems as though everything that Barack Obama has said about his family has been carefully calculated... almost none of it is true."[301] So when Obama has given us so many reasons to doubt what he says about his background, why would we automatically believe him about religion?

Which of his self-contradictory comments should we believe? "I've always been a Christian" or "I came to my Christian faith later in life" or that he was just "an observer among" the Christian majority? Should we consider how he brought up "my Muslim faith" in an interview with George Stephanopoulos in 2008? Stephanopoulos interjected the correction: "Christian faith" which Obama then repeated. Obama supporters try to play the slip of the tongue as a gaffe rather than an accidental admission... but no matter how convoluted one's conversation, no matter how a man's brain and mouth may not cooperate while speaking, I must conclude that no one accidentally says "my Muslim faith" if they are really a Christian. As Madonna said just before Obama's re-election at a concert on September 24, 2012: "For better or for worse, we have a black Muslim in the White House."[302]

I'm not suggesting that it is inherently evil to be a Muslim. But since President Obama has told us "I've always been a Christian" when it seems obvious he hasn't... I don't like the duplicity and I have to ask why. Is it just to hide a politically unpopular truth about his past, or is it to hide the reason for an unpopular agenda in the future?

Daniel, Thessalonians, and Revelation all tell us the Antichrist will be blasphemous. Obama has mocked taking the Bible seriously in several speeches, pointing out slavery in Leviticus and stonings in Deuteronomy and suggesting the whole book shouldn't be taken too seriously. On April 4, 2012 Obama referred to Jesus as "a Son of God" instead of "the Son of God." This might not be a significant insight, if not for the fact that he has previously suggested that there are many paths to salvation and that various religions are on an equal footing. Denying the unique role Jesus has in our salvation is the only thing the Bible tells us about "the antichrist" the one time he is mentioned by this title in 1 John 2:22 "This is the antichrist, the one who denies the Father and the Son." And I will repeat and emphasize that Obama said of Morgan Freeman's cinematic role as God: "This guy was

God before I was." That has to be the most blasphemous presidential comment of all time. (Though I also considered Obama's response when asked what his definition of sin is and he said: "Being out of alignment with my values."[303] I thought sin was being out of line with God's laws.)

1 Thessolonians 5:3 warns us that the Antichrist will betray Israel during a period of peace and attack when they are certain of their safety and security. "While they are saying, 'Peace and safety!' then destruction will come upon them suddenly like labor pains upon a woman with child, and they will not escape." (NASB) Many other versions like the English Standard Version or the Catholics' Douay-Rheims Bible say "Peace and Security!" Look up Youtube or any other source of internet videos and you will be amazed at how many times Obama has talked about Israel's "peace and security."[304]

Daniel tells us the Antichrist will sit in the Temple and claim to be God, and that many will claim he is the Messiah. We already covered Obama's quotes about being sent here by his father in the heavens to save the planet Earth – and how Morgan Freeman was God before he was. But that's just Obama talking himself up. What do other people say?

Nation of Islam leader Louis Farrakhan referred to Obama as "the Messiah." TV magnate Oprah Winfrey compared Obama to the Messiah and said "He is the One. He will help us evolve." Oprah Winfrey also put together a video after asking many celebrities to make a pledge of support to Obama – and at the end Demi Moore and Ashton Kutcher encourage others to follow them in saying, "I pledge to be a servant to our president."[305] (It's almost like the Muslim oath of loyalty to a Caliph!)

Director Spike Lee has referred to him as "Black Jesus" and the "Savior" on CNN. Lee also said "Time shall be measured Before Barack and After Barack." Actor Jamie Foxx called Barack Obama "our Lord and Savior." Hardball's Chris Matthews said "Obama is writing the New Testament." Newsweek editor Evan Thomas called him "a sort of God."

If I thought the creators of the web site http://www.obama-christ.com/ truly believed their motto "Barack Obama: Our Lord and Savior" (instead of assuming the site is a twisted attempt at humor) I would expect some of the people named above to be converts to their "church."

Has any leader of any nation been portrayed this way before? How relevant is this? You decide.

Looking back at a book published in 2005, author Thomas McShea made some very interesting predictions in describing his own theories and timetables: "let's look at some rough figures. 1) In three years, the Antichrist becomes president of the United States, in 2008. 2) In four more years at the very least, he will have too much power and will be a dictator, in 2012? In 2015? 3) In four more years, he will rule a lot of the world, in 2016? In 2019?"[306]

I think McShea's The Antichrist is Here was remarkably on target for someone writing in 2005. He also wrote "In the meantime, a federal law will have to be passed so that a foreigner can be president, as it is now, according to the law, only a U.S.-born citizen can be elected president."[307]   McShea never names his prime suspect. From his descriptions, he might have meant Arnold Schwarzenegger and not Barack Obama. But he didn't name anyone, certainly not an unknown Illinois State Senator. Yet he did repeatedly state that he expected the Antichrist to be foreign-born and to run for president and be elected in 2008 – and for that prediction, made in 2005 – I must take note.

666 – The Number of the Beast

Revelation 13:17-18 warns us "…no one will be able to buy or to sell, except the one who has the mark, either the name of the beast or the number of his name. Here is wisdom. Let him who has understanding calculate the number of the beast, for the number is that of a man; and his number is six hundred and sixty-six." I'm pretty sure Barack Obama would dismiss any wisdom in Revelation, because he referred to the entirety of the "apocalypse" as "religious baggage."[308]   Or maybe he just wants to discourage people from studying it, as much of it may apply to him.

Obama's dismissal aside, when John wrote the Book of Revelation he obviously suggested that those with understanding should calculate the number. Since he gives us the number 666, and we don't need to calculate it, perhaps the idea of a number and gematria is misleading. Perhaps 666 is not supposed to be calculated as a number, or perhaps we are supposed to contemplate the number's significance to find additional meaning.

Isaac Asimov wrote in his Bible commentaries that "666 [is] a number which had its own mystic significance, for it fell short of the mystic perfection of 7 three times. For that reason 666 was the acme of imperfection and a suitable number with which to represent Antichrist."[309]

Other researchers claim that the origin of the supernatural beliefs about the number 666 is from ancient Babylon. Babylon is the first culture known to have divided the circle into 360 degrees and they also divided the sky into 36 "decans" of ten degree range. Each of these decans was "ruled" by a "god" to be feared, and in ancient times many superstitious people wore amulets on a necklace with a six by six grid of the numbers one through 36, to show they had acknowledged all the gods of the 36 decans of heaven and were protected by them.

The first 36 numbers add up to 666, a number understood to represent all the pagan gods. Talismans big enough to clearly display the grid of 36 numbers may have eventually been replaced by smaller ones that required less precious metals and were more affordable - just showing the number 666. This was understood to symbolize the same power of the original six by six grid; the same kind of "talismanic power"[310] Obama claimed his father had over people.

Obama has taken a lot of flak over fake birth certificates and social security numbers. We have all heard that his official Social Security number prefix is from Connecticut, not Hawaii. I for one conclude the evidence regarding the birth certificate we have been shown has almost certainly been faked. School records and medical records also appear to be unusually restricted – he seems to have an unusual seal over his records from Occidental College, Columbia University, and Harvard University; his Selective Service Registration, medical records, and Illinois State Senate records. Few have been satisfied with the certified copy of his original birth certificate, or the allegedly embossed and signed paper certification of live birth. Perhaps he generally wasn't really where he said he was. One biographer flat out says that his "account of his own experience was largely bogus... largely made up."[311] Why has so much effort and money been spent to hide Obama's past? Theories include:

He was really born in Kenya, therefore not eligible for the presidency
He was a citizen of Indonesia, therefore not eligible for the presidency
He is really a Muslim, hiding his past connections
He worked for the CIA, this is normal for an intelligence operative
His true birth date would reveal symbolic occult meaning
His real social security number would have 666 in it

His real name would have a gematria value of 666

We know that many world leaders have been considered as a potential fulfillment of the Antichrist throughout history, and many interpreters have applied gematria to famous names to come up with the number of their names, to see if it is 666. With Barack Obama, we are denied proper documentation. We are denied the possibility of seeing the name and number assigned to him at birth. Was he born in America? If so, did his original social security number – "the number of his name" contain the 666 we might expect? Was his birth name Barack Hussein Obama? Some documents have shown the last name Soetoro, even Soebarkah. As one analyst has commented on bogus documentation: there's nothing that unusual about these multiple names and social security numbers – that's what CIA agents do! The suggestion being that Barack Obama is "merely" a member of the intelligence community, groomed for the presidency for an agenda – but elected on the premise of a fake background.

The literal translations of our president's three official names are very interesting when English gematria values are attributed to the letters of the translations. Unlike the Hebrew and Greek alphabets, in which every letter has a clearly agreed upon numerical value, English gematria is controversial. There is no one agreed upon set of numerical values for English letters, nor is there agreement that ANY attribution of numerical values would be relevant. There is no scientific reason to assume that relationships between words with equal gematria values are relevant in any language – though many ancient Hebrews and Greeks believed it was meaningful.

With those uncertainties in mind, we need only concern ourselves with the opinion of John, who apparently believed that it is very important. He warned us that "the number of the beast" and "the number of his name" is "six hundred and sixty six." He said to "Let him who has understanding calculate the number of the beast." 1800 years ago, Irenaeus clarified: "reason also leads us to conclude that the number of the name of the beast, [if reckoned] according to the Greek mode of calculation by the [value of] the letters contained in it, will amount to six hundred and sixty-six."[312]

Here is one straightforward and reasonable way to calculate it, applying gematria to the English alphabet "according to the Greek mode of calculation" through decimal numerology, with the following values:

Ones: A=1 B=2 C=3 D=4 E=5 F=6 G=7 H=8 I=9

Tens: J=10 K=20 L=30 M=40 N=50 O=60 P=70 Q=80 R=90
Hundreds: S=100 T=200 U=300 V=400 W=500 X=600 Y=700 Z=800
In such a system:
Blessed is 2+30+5+100+100+5+4 = 246
Handsome is 8+1+50+4+100+60+40+5 = 268
Leaning is 30+5+1+50+9+50+7 = 152
246 + 268 + 152 = 666

It may help to know that "Barack" means "blessed," "Hussein" means "handsome" and "Obama" means "leaning."

Critics may suggest that the name itself should add to 666, or that it must do so in Hebrew or Greek to have any meaning, or that there are other possibilities for gematria values for English letters.... But this seems fairly straightforward without twisting anything to make it work. We reach the same 666 value with the phrases "Number of a man Barack Obama" and "Barack Obama as a President." Coincidence? It certainly could be. Many other unrelated names and phrases add to 666 the same way. Time will tell.

As the author of a very thorough study on the gematria of 666 suggests: "it is hard to see a definitive solution emerging, and we are left with the question that should, perhaps, have been asked at the outset: What serious purpose is likely to be served, anyway, in identifying an individual whose name bears this number?"[313] Since many names and titles are found to add up to 666, the gematria of a name proves nothing.

"A strictly literalistic approach to the riddle seemingly destined to fail, therefore…"[314] perhaps we should focus more on the mathematical properties of the number, and less on names. This too yields interesting results. In an earlier chapter we discussed the number 153, and its triangular nature – making a stack of dots with rows of 1 dot above 2 dots above 3 dots, etc… adding the 17th row gives a total of 153 dots in the triangle. 23 rows yield a triangle of 276, and 36 rows yield a triangle of 666 dots. I mention these because while nice round numbers and vague approximations fail to get my attention, (as in Matthew 14:21 "There were about five thousand men who ate") there are three very precise biblical numbers which stand out to me.

John 21:11 "Simon Peter went up and drew the net to land, full of large fish, a hundred and fifty-three; and although there were so many, the net was not torn."

Acts 27:37 "All of us in the ship were two hundred and seventy-six persons."

Revelation 13:1 has "a beast coming up out of the sea" and this is the same beast in Revelation 13:18 of which John says: "Here is wisdom. Let him who has understanding calculate the number of the beast, for the number is that of a man; and his number is six hundred and sixty-six."

Most numbers are not triangular, but all three of these are – and they are all linked to something coming out of the sea. I find it unlikely that these are coincidences; therefore I believe it has meaning. I am repeatedly drawn back to Revelation 13:18 "Here is wisdom. Let him who has understanding calculate the number of the beast." John clearly expects some of the wise to solve his riddle… but we are given the number 666! Since we are given the number of the beast we do not need to calculate it directly. Indirectly, what other calculations can we perform on this number? What can we learn from analyzing the number?

The number 666 has many interesting properties leading to patterns in 2 and 3 dimensional geometry which are beyond the scope of this book. But the very word "gematria" is derived from "geometry" and shapes ARE important to understanding it, so I will at least comment on one item which also involves the number 37. With 37 dots organized, not triangularly, but in rows of 1, 2, 7, 6, 5, 6, 7, 2, and 1, we can make a six-pointed Star of David. This Jewish symbol includes two overlapping triangles, one pointing up to God, and one pointing down to Earth (and man.) Combined, should they not be considered a geometric representation of the Messiah? This Jewish Star symbolizes man's attempt to search upwards for God, and also God's decision to send down a messiah.

Since 666 is shown to be a triangular number of 36 rows, does it not fall short of 37 – the number we used to make the Star of David? Reverse the numbers 3 and 7 to get 73 and we can make a larger Star of David out of 73 dots with rows of 1, 2, 3, 10, 9, 8, 7, 8, 9, 10, 3, 2, and 1. This time, if we remove the big triangle pointing up to God, we are left with three little triangles of six dots each – 6-6-6.

What I describe above is just a brief example of some of the 2D geometry of these numbers. There are also cubes and other 3D shapes relevant to 666. Unfortunately, (for the Bible tells us there is important wisdom in understanding this number) a thorough analysis is beyond the scope of this book, and quite possibly beyond my level of mathematical comprehension. I can only speculate that geometry involving three triangles, possibly three triangles like the pyramids at Giza, which point to the alignment of Venus behind the sun rising over Jerusalem on June 6 – are very relevant.

What other signs have we been given through this 666 number?

The winning "PICK 3" lottery number in Obama's home state of Illinois the day after he won the 2008 presidential election (11/5/2008) was 666. Everyone knows what 666 stands for. What are the odds? Only one in a thousand – not that impressive – it should happen every so many years. But the "PICK 4" lottery numbers in Illinois the same day were also symbolic – 7779.

The number 6 stands for humanity, imperfection, and incompletion. Multiplied, 666 symbolizes human failings at their most extreme. The number seven stands for the opposite: divinity, perfection, and completion. Multiplied for emphasis, the number 777 represents the completeness of God's perfect plans, such as when the world was completed within a seven day week, or the final seven years of Daniel's 70th week. The number "seven indicates the sense of a change after an accomplished cycle."[315]

Even the number 9, as the last of the single digits, represents the end, finality, a conclusion. The Temple was destroyed, first by Babylonians and again by Romans, on the 9th day of the Hebrew month of Av. In Jewish thinking, our sins for the year no longer matter after we atone for them on Yom Kippur (the Day of Atonement for sins) which starts at the end of the 9th day of the 7th month. "When other well-known numbers with combinations of digits that add to the number nine appear explicitly in the Bible, they often have even a more specific symbolism: the end of time."[316]

So while the PICK 3 lottery number (666) after Obama's election is the most impressive, perhaps the combination with the PICK 4 number (7779) is also meaningful – the final completion of God's plans through the Antichrist.

If I were personally hand-picking the lottery drawing numbers to comment on Obama's election, I could not come up with anything better. If I were making a sign with lottery numbers, I would do so right after the election results were in (11/05/2008) in the winner's home state (Illinois) with 666 as the PICK 3 number, and 7779 as the PICK 4 number. The odds of those two sets of numbers being drawn in the right state on the right date are 1 in

500,000,000. Despite such odds, it isn't necessarily a sign – it could just be a coincidence. You decide.

At least in my Bible (NASB) though not the same in some other versions like Catholic Bibles (Douay-Rheims, for example) the only description of what the Antichrist will appear as says "behold, a white horse, and he who sat on it had a bow; and a crown was given to him, and he went out conquering and to conquer." This phrase is at the beginning of Revelation chapter six – the 6th chapter of the 66th book in the Bible.

The first sin ever recorded was Eve disobeying God and eating the forbidden apple from the Tree of Knowledge in Genesis 3:6. Note the verse - 3:6 - or three sixes.

666 times 3 = 1998 + 6+6+6 = 2016   6 times 6 times 6 = 216

Barack Obama claims to have been born in Hawaii on August 4, 1961. August 4 is the 216th day of the year. If Barack Obama gets to be inaugurated for a third time by 20 January 2017, or simply doesn't leave office when a president normally would after eight years - it will be 666 months from the month that he says he was born. The combination of Obama's presidency being the 44th, along with his official birthday on 8/4, have led some people to John 8:44 "You are of your father the devil, and you want to do the desires of your father." If nothing else, that reminds me of the title: Dreams From My Father.

Obama himself described "my rejection of authority,"[317] which if taken to an extreme, could be compared to the very first rebel against authority. I mention this because one of Obama's early leftist mentors in Chicago, Mike Kruglik (and others) have commented on Obama's great skill at mastering the tactics in Saul Alinsky's book: Rules for Radicals – telling us Obama "was a natural, the undisputed master of agitation." Obama has used these tactics so well that many new books like Rules for Radicals Defeated: A Practical Guide for Defeating Obama/Alinsky Tactics and Barack Obama's Rules for Revolution: The Alinsky Model make extensive comparisons. But Obama's mastery of Alinsky's book is especially interesting if we read the dedication at the front of book: Alinsky's "Rules For Radicals is written for the Have-nots on how to take it away" and is dedicated to "the first radical known to man who rebelled against the establishment and did it so effectively that he at least won his own kingdom – Lucifer."[318] What kind of book gets dedicated to Lucifer? Apparently, the type of book that President

Obama studies. I see a clear parallel to the well-known student of this book, whom the book may as well have been dedicated to – and who has also won his own kingdom in America…

Is the number 666 a biblical clue pointing to America as well? Let's think about the gold King Solomon received every year – and where it came from. 1 Kings 10:14 tells us "Now the weight of gold which came in to Solomon in one year was 666 talents of gold." That number stands out. Are we meant to perceive an association between the source of this gold and the number of the beast? Where are these 666 talents coming in from?

1 Kings 10:11 mentions "the ships of Hiram, which brought gold from Ophir." King Hiram was the Phoenician king of Tyre, who helped build Solomon's Temple, and is known as Hiram Abiff to Freemasons – the great architect-king who was murdered for his great secret, which he did not reveal. Was the secret that Phoenicians had reached the Americas? No one knows for certain where "King Solomon's Mines" were located. But the Bible does give us clues.

1 Kings 9:26-28 tells us "King Solomon also built a fleet of ships in Ezion-geber, which is near Eloth on the shore of the Red Sea, in the land of Edom. And Hiram sent his servants with the fleet, sailors who knew the sea, along with the servants of Solomon. They went to Ophir…" So we can assume that Ophir was not anywhere between Israel and Spain within the Mediterranean Sea, because the Phoenician ships would have used Mediterranean ports in Israel or Phoenicia if that were the case. Wherever Ophir might be, it was easier to get there from a port on the Red Sea than from the sailors' homelands on the Mediterranean coast. (This also implies that the Phoenicians routinely circumnavigated the continent of Africa thousands of years before the Portuguese – which is backed up by ancient Phoenician descriptions no one believed at the time – that there were places where the sun could be directly overhead or even in the northern half of the sky.)

Their destination of Ophir must be very rich in gold, for many journeys there kept bringing back ample amounts of precious metals. 1 Kings 10:22 says "For the king had at sea the ships of Tarshish with the ships of Hiram; once every three years the ships of Tarshish came bringing gold and silver." Their destination must not have been mere days or weeks away – but at least an ocean away. David Hatcher Childress emphasizes: "it took three years (that's right, three years!) to go to Ophir and back."[319]

Interesting –

239 *But there are other possibilities - not just the Americas*

A story virtually identical to 1 Kings 10 is told in 2 Chronicles 9, except Ophir is not mentioned, only Tarshish – a land somewhere in the far west. The amount of gold is the same in 2 Chronicles 9:13 "Now the weight of gold which came to Solomon in one year was 666 talents of gold." This is a lot of gold, enough that it was obviously worth making the long journey repeatedly. 1 Chronicles 29:4 describes the use of "3,000 talents of gold, of the gold of Ophir" in the Temple. A talent of gold had approximately the same weight as a person. Even if we assume a weight much less than the typical American adult weighs today, and estimate a mere 120 pounds for a man of that place and time, times 16 ounces per pound, times about $1,300 per ounce at the time I'm writing this, we can assume just one talent of gold would be worth approximately 2.5 million dollars. Multiply by 3,000 and if the numbers are accurate then Solomon's Temple had billions of dollars' worth of gold in it.

The three year cycle of journeys to Ophir may have only required a fraction of the three years for sailing each half of the journey. The crews might have spent a year or two at Ophir to grow crops of food for the return journey while they mined gold, rather than taking three years of supplies with them. Few places outside the Americas were so rich in gold that, with ancient tools, a relatively small group of sailors could repeatedly mine and refine large quantities of gold ore in the space of perhaps one or two years.

"We know from Columbus' writings that he studied the Bible and other ancient sources like Josephus for clues about the location of Ophir and Tarshish, which he assumed were the same place.... Columbus realized he did not need to travel east to find it. Since by his day it was known that the world was round, he reasoned that it would take him much less time to reach Ophir and Tarshish if he traveled west—just a few weeks rather than the three-year round trip traveled by Solomon's ships."[320] Columbus believed Ophir and Tatshish were in Central America. The more modern consensus that Tarshish may have been in Spain would appear to be incorrect if Columbus was leaving Spain to look for it in the Americas. Tarshish was also referenced when Jonah tried to avoid having God send him to Nineveh and attempted to flee from God in Jonah 1:3 "But Jonah rose up to flee to Tarshish from the presence of the LORD." We should assume that Tarshish was chosen because it was extremely far away, the farthest place he could possibly sail to. If attempting to flee from God, you don't go next door. As history's greatest plunder of gold was the Spanish haul taken from Peru and Mexico, I am willing to assume that Ophir was in the Americas.

Revelation 13:18 "Here is wisdom. Let him who has understanding calculate the number of the beast, for the number is that of a man; and his number is six hundred and sixty-six." This verse is practically begging us to speculate and use our wisdom regarding this number. Wisdom is linked to Solomon, who received 666 talents of gold coming from Ophir, quite possibly Mexico. Is this convincing evidence linking 666 and the land of the Americas? Maybe not convincing, but certainly plausible. Before you dismiss the possibility, ask yourself the following: Would the Lord ask us to use wisdom and insight to identify the beast, (and his kingdom) then give us a virtually unsolvable puzzle with a number that could be manipulated with numerology or gematria to identify just about anyone as the antichrist? God is not the author of confusion. If we are to take Bible prophecy seriously, then we must be able to solve this.

Aside from the Antichrist and King Solomon, who else does the Bible associate with the Temple and the number 666? The only other Bible verse mentioning the number 666 is Ezra 2:13, which describes and counts some of the Jews returning to Jerusalem from Babylon, including "the sons of Adonikam, 666" of them. We see a theme shared with the Antichrist, as he comes from Mystery Babylon to Jerusalem – and many Jews are asked to return to Israel and flee Mystery Babylon before it is destroyed. I also notice the verses about the number 666 all contain the unlucky number 13... Revelation 13:18, 1 Kings 10:13, 2 Chronicles 9:13, and Ezra 2:13. This seems deliberate, and highly unlikely to be numbered this way by random chance all four times.

E.W. Bullinger noted in <u>The Companion Bible</u> that "Thirteen: Denotes rebellion, apostasy, defection, disintegration, revolution, etc."[321] from its very first biblical mention onwards. Genesis 14:4 "Twelve years they had served Chedorlaomer, but the thirteenth year they rebelled." We should not be surprised to see the number thirteen linked to 666 and the Antichrist.

One of the earliest historical figures compared to the Antichrist is Haman, an ancient Persian Prime Minister described in the Book of Esther. Esther 3:10 tells us who Haman is: "Then the king took his signet ring from his hand and gave it to Haman, the son of Hammedatha the Agagite, the enemy of the Jews." Hammedatha means "he who troubles the law" and reminds me of "The Lawless One" we know as the Antichrist. Agagite means "given by the moon" which makes me think of Islam's main symbol, the crescent moon that represented Arabia's Moon god, and Allah – in modern times. Using occult methods to pick a date on which it would be best to exterminate the

Jews in the Persian empire (after a prominent Jew named Mordecai refused to bow down to him) Haman drew lots and selected the thirteenth day of the thirteenth month after that moment – the thirteenth of the first month of the next year. Esther 3:6 (three sixes: 666?) describes his genocidal decision "But he disdained to lay hands on Mordecai alone, for they had told him who the people of Mordecai were; therefore Haman sought to destroy all the Jews, the people of Mordecai, who were throughout the whole kingdom of Ahasuerus." Esther, the king's beautiful new wife – was secretly Mordecai's cousin – herself a Jew. Since Mordecai had previously saved the king from a coup, and Queen Esther revealed her Jewish origins, the King did not allow Haman to kill the Jews. The failure of Haman's plans – the survival of the Jewish people after an attempt to exterminate them by an evil, Antichrist-like figure – is celebrated in the holiday of Purim – the day after the thirteenth day of that thirteenth month.

I don't know if it will prove to be significant or not, but I am reminded of Daniel's 1260, 1290, and 1335 day periods – with judgment and wrath for the 30 and 45 day differences. In 2016, as the thirteenth day of the month of Adar ends and the holiday of Purim begins at sunset – this is our March 23, exactly 75 days before June 6, when I expect the Antichrist to reveal himself. Could something important occur on March 23, 2016 – starting a chain of events that mirrors God's eventual judgment and wrath and culminates 75 days later?

One of the main Purim holiday traditions is to wear a mask, symbolic of hiding one's identity. Esther hid hers up until a decisive moment – and I expect the Antichrist will hide his true identity as well, until June 6, 2016. The story of Purim is riddled with details reminiscent of the Antichrist, and three sixes, and thirteens. We can rest assured that our King will save His bride and people in a similar turnaround of events in 2019.

One web site suggests: "Rev 13:18 starts with the phrase, ?Hode este sophia?, or ?here is wisdom? It is the colloquial way of saying, ?Here is a riddle?"[322]   Since the number we are asked to calculate is given, what else might the riddle mean? The same site suggests the answer: "?Here is a riddle. Let him that hath understanding determine the multitude of the beast; for it is a multitude of men, and [this] multitude is chi xi stigma.?" The anonymous author suggests that the symbols which John saw in his vision have meaning in two languages. In Greek, it looked like the letters chi xi stigma, and focus has been placed on the numerical value of those numbers, which happens to be 666. But in Arabic, the same symbols that look like the

Greek letters chi xi stigma look like the "Bismallah," the phrase that means "in the name of Allah." So the article concludes that we were not meant to take a number from the Greek letters – we were only meant to view the letters visually and recognize what is symbolized by those shapes. In Greek, they symbolize letters equaling 666. In Arabic, they symbolize submitting one's life to Islam. The article suggests that Revelation 13:18 should be read as: "?Here is a riddle. Let him that hath understanding determine the multitude of the beast: for it is a multitude of a men; and his multitude [is] in the name of Allah.?"[323] Going one step further: "determine the people of the beast to be the followers of the symbol of Islam."

Walid Shoebat, sometimes called a former PLO terrorist and convert to Christianity, says that when he first saw the Greek symbols for chi xi stigma, he immediately read it as the Bismallah in Arabic.[324] Now a Christian evangelist, Shoebat suggests that the "mark" of the beast (Greek: "chagarma") is not meant to be a number at all. We were meant to look only at the visual image of what John wrote as the Greek letters chi xi stigma – because one day, we would understand that in Arabic, it is the symbol for Islamic submission to Allah. He asks us to consider that (much like Luke may not have recognized "baraq 'o bamah" as a name) John could not read Arabic script and did not recognize the future Arabic words for "in the name of Allah" – but those visionary symbols looked very much like Greek letters John did know, so that is what he wrote down for posterity. "Is it possible that the Apostle John, while receiving his divine revelation, did not see Greek letters, but instead was supernaturally shown Arabic words and an Islamic symbol, which he then faithfully recorded?"[325] Is the number 666 just a misunderstanding?

Of course most people do pay attention to the number. And some Muslims believe there are two numbers central to Islam; 19 and 666. One web site calls "666 THE HOLY NUMBER OF ISLAM."[326] Another site (http://www.66619.org/thequran.htm) says "The truth is that This Quran is the 666, The Book from The Lord of the Universe." Rashad Khalifa, an Egyptian-born scientist with a PhD from the University of California, performed a numerical analysis of the Qu'ran and was especially impressed with the significance of the number 19 in the Qu'ran; slightly less so with the "mystery of 666" he felt he unraveled, and much less with the 29 times he was stabbed in a mosque in Arizona, possibly the first assassination of an American by Al-Queda. Someone did not appreciate his suggestion that 19 and 666 are central to the Qu'ran.

David Montaigne

In Surah 74 of the Qu'ran we can read a few verses apparently stating that "19" is central to the fires of hell:
74:27 "And do you know what is the scorching heat?
74:28 It does not spare nor leave anything.
74:29 Apparent to all humans.
74:30 Upon it is nineteen.
74:31 We have appointed only angels to be wardens of the Fire, and their number have We made to be a stumbling-block for those who disbelieve."

The number 19 appears frequently in the Qu'ran. There are apparently 19 "angels" who guard the fires of hell. Christians would generally view "angels" that live in hell as fallen angels or demons. The entire chapter (Surah 74) has the heading "The Cloaked One" which makes me think of either the Antichrist before he is revealed, or Satan himself. Though I may be a Bible scholar, I do not pretend to be an expert on the Qu'ran, so my insights here may be wild speculation. But when I read this chapter, several lines "add up" to me:

74:1 O thou enveloped in thy cloak,
74:6 And show not favour, seeking wordly gain!
74:7 For the sake of thy Lord, be patient!
74:11 Leave Me (to deal) with him whom I created lonely,
74:12 And then bestowed upon him ample means,
74:15 Yet he desireth that I should give more.
74:19 (Self-)destroyed is he, how he planned!
74:20 Again (self-)destroyed is he, how he planned! -
74:23 Then turned he away in pride
74:26 Him shall I fling unto the burning.
74:30 Above it are nineteen.

I may be reading into this verse, and I admit I am selecting some verses and leaving out others to emphasize my point. But to me this sounds like a story about the fall of Satan, whom God created for a high position – but of course, Satan was greedy and rebelled against God. In seeking to defeat and replace God, Satan destroys himself and was already cast out of heaven, before a final end in the lake of fire. I also find it interesting that the two lines in which he is destroyed are verses 20 and 19, as I believe the end comes in 2019. (The same two numbers show up for essentially the same event when the Antichrist and the False Prophet are "thrown alive into the lake of fire" in verse 20 of Revelation's chapter 19, and in Isaiah 19, verses 19 and 20, when the Pyramids in Egypt are finally recognized as an altar to the Lord.) The

244

Qu'ran's Surah 74 verse 19 has been noted for its gematria value, for when the number values of the letters in the words of that verse are added up, the total is 666.

There is a Muslim "End Times Research Center" online which suggests that the crucial window for the fulfillment of end times prophecy in the Qu'ran runs from 2014-2022. They expect their savior, the Imam Mahdi, to appear with the return of Jesus Son of Mary and defeat the false messiah, the Dajjal – who is what the Antichrist is for Christians – within this time frame. The writers at this site suggest "numerical analysis indicates that Barack Obama is likely to be the"[327] Antichrist (Dajjal.) They explain: "We perform numerical analysis of the Quran, Hadith, Arabic words, and Historical Events. Based on this analysis, we come to conclusions and make predictions regarding events in the End Times." Although I do not follow the logic of their numerical analysis, (I merely looked at their web site, and did not read the book of over 2800 pages which may have a full explanation) I do find some of their conclusions interesting. They also tell us "This may indicate that Obama is Gog and that he will attempt to revive Babylon."[328] Such views may not represent the majority of Muslims – but it still seems noteworthy.

Dreams

If someone were indwelt by Satan, or "possessed" by the Beast, how might they describe it to us? Mark 1:26 may describe the growling and screaming and shaking typical of demonic possession: "Throwing him into convulsions, the unclean spirit cried out with a loud voice." Urbandictionary.com gives one definition of "disturbia" as "a sign of possession or mind control where the individual shakes and moves so fast it's almost inhuman."[329] Perhaps the reader can visualize how "possession" like this has appeared in movies, such as when an agent transfers into a new body in "The Matrix," or how things shook like the bed in "The Exorcist" or "The Devil Inside." Of course, whether it's just "sleep paralysis" or "demonic possession" the victim often describes something like "I started to shake violently on my bed and the bed was shaking too." As one victim I met has described it "I could sense something pouring into me, dark and cold. It was as though a demon had entered my body and taken over."

Here is one very interesting dream a man had:

"I finally fell asleep, and dreamed I was walking along a village road. Children, dressed only in strings of beads, played in front of the round huts, and several old men waved to me as I passed. But as I went farther along, I began to notice that people were looking behind me fearfully, rushing into their huts as I passed. I heard the growl of a leopard and started to run into the forest, tripping over roots and stumps and vines, until at last I couldn't run any longer and fell to my knees in the middle of a bright clearing. Panting for breath, I turned around to see the day turned night, and a giant figure looming as tall as the trees, wearing only a loincloth and ghostly mask. The lifeless eyes bored into me, and I heard a thunderous voice saying only that it was time, and my entire body began to shake violently with the sound, as if I were breaking apart..." This was Barack Obama's own dream, as he wrote about it in <u>Dreams from My Father</u>, on page 372.

This dream sounds prophetic, especially with the "thunderous voice" Obama heard near the end announcing "that it was time." Time for what pre-destined event? And what about the leopard? Wearing leopard skins was a tradition of ancient kings and was strongly associated with Nimrod, the evil King of Babylon – even the root of his name "N-I-M-R" means leopard. Its spots are associated with camouflage and deception. Spots can also mean impurity. 1 Peter 1:19 describes Christ as "a lamb unblemished and spotless." Some translations of Daniel 12:10 (like the NIV) tell us "many will be purified, made spotless." The leopard appears as an example of a spotted, impure beast.

The growling leopard could also just be a reference to Obama's father – for our president also wrote that Barack Obama Sr.'s "favorite outfit [was] jeans and an old knit shirt with a leopard-print pattern."[330] But it could also be a reference to the Son of Perdition's father – Satan – at least, in the form of the Beast in Daniel 7:6 "like a leopard" or Revelation 13:2 "And the beast which I saw was like a leopard." In Obama's dream, the evil entity behind him that growled like a leopard and sent villagers into hiding apparently transforms into a giant, man-like figure (a world leader, perhaps?) which Obama describes as giant and ghostly, with lifeless eyes that bored into him... possessing him? The violent shaking he describes next may indicate a possession.

Obama describes "panting for breath." This reminds me of the story of Muhammad in the Cave of Hira, when "Gabriel" came to "inspire" Muhammad to write the Qu'ran and the "angel had enveloped him in a terrifying embrace so that it felt as though the breath was being forced from his body."[331]   Muhammad thought himself demon-possessed.[332]   What did Obama think after his dream?

If a candidate running for the presidency had spoken much about that dream, what would you have thought? Would you have voted for him?

On page 10 of <u>Dreams From My Father</u>, Obama made an interesting comment; a juxtaposition of two apparently unrelated questions on his mind: "Why did an omnipotent God let a snake cause such grief? Why didn't my father return?" It may mean nothing... but it gets my attention when I speculate that his "father" may be the biblical serpent. And Obama also repeatedly refers to his father as "The Old Man," which is strange because Barack Obama Sr. was not old. Born in 1936 and killed in a car crash in 1982, he was only 46 when he died, and only 35 when last seen by his son. Perhaps a different father, much, much older, is being described.

After the senior Obama died, Barack Obama Jr. wanted to visit his grave, and he eventually visited Kenya. He describes "the homecoming I had once imagined for myself: clouds lifting, old demons fleeing, the earth trembling as ancestors rose up in celebration."[333]   At best this is merely an example of very odd thinking; at worst we notice he refers to his first recorded trip to Kenya as "homecoming" (was he born there or something?) and that he imagined earthquakes, demons, and the dead rising at his presence. I am reminded of Isaiah 14:9 commenting on the death of the Antichrist: "Sheol from beneath is excited over you to meet you when you come; it arouses for you the spirits of the dead." <u>Dreams From My Father</u>. Who dreams like this? Aside from his own dreams, Barack Obama may also be mentioned in prophecies:

Luo Kenyan Prophecy

Barack Hussein Obama Sr. was a member of the Luo tribe in Kenya. The Nomiya Luo Church, which started in 1912, was the first independent Kenyan church. The founder of this church, Johanwa Owalo, is believed by many members to be a prophet similar to Jesus and Muhammad. Owalo had teamed up with a Catholic priest and began teaching a new theology that rejected the Pope and the doctrine of a trinity. Owalo also claimed he had a prophecy about the United States,[334] but that prophecy may mean more after reviewing the origins of the American president's names.

We know that Obama's first name is a biblical Hebrew name. Judges 4:6 starts off "Now she sent and summoned Barak the son of Abinoam...." This Barak was a commander who led his forces into the Valley of Har-Meggido (where we expect the battle of Armageddon, perhaps commanded by another of similar name?) The valley of this future battle is known and named for both the city of Jezreel (in the central valley) the city of Megiddo (in the southwest of the valley) and for Mount Tabor, always shown overlooking the valley in photographs. Judges 4:14-15 "So Barak went down from Mount Tabor with ten thousand men following him. The Lord routed Sisera and all his chariots and all his army with the edge of the sword before Barak."

The Hebrew meaning of the name Barak is "Lightning" or "Spark." His middle name, Hussein, means Handsome One in Arabic. His last name seems to mean "leaning" or "slightly bent" – this is a rare Luo Kenyan name, meaning a baby either born with a bent limb or perhaps a breech birth. While Obama is apparently a Luo Kenyan word, if it originally came from Hebrew like his first name did, it could have come from the word "bama." So we should also consider that in Hebrew the name Bama means "Son of prophecy."[335] So in combining the definitions above, the name Barack Hussein Obama could essentially mean the Handsome Lightning Son of Prophecy. Barack Obama may be at least a "son of prophecy."

Let us now return to the alleged 1912 prophecy by Johanwa Owalo, the founder of Kenya's Nomiya Luo Church, about the United States:

"So far have they [the United States] strayed into wickedness in those [future] times that their destruction has been sealed by my [father]. Their great cities will burn, their crops and cattle will suffer disease and death, their children will perish from diseases never seen upon this Earth, and I reveal to you the greatest [mystery] of all as I have been allowed to see that their [the United States] destruction will come about through the vengeful hands of one of our very own sons."[336]

Since Barack Obama's father is ethnically a Luo of Kenya, President Obama seems to meet the criteria above as being "one of our very sons." Perhaps, a "son of prophecy." The Luo in Kenya seem to have a prophecy about one of their sons destroying the United States. In Christian prophecy, we are concerned about the possibility that he is the Antichrist, who will go to Jerusalem to defile the Temple and proclaim his own religion with himself at the top. Which reminds me of another entity of the same name.

Barack is effectively "Buraq," which means lightning in Arabic and is the name of the magical white horse that, Muhammad said, in a single night in 621 A.D., carried him from Mecca to "the farthest Mosque" which Muslims have generally assumed to be the Temple in Jerusalem. At a minimum, the name means "lightning" and would be associated with bringing Muhammad and Islam to Jerusalem. Will another Barack do it again? Is it significant that the Antichrist rides a white horse?

Islamic prophecy:

There is an amazing Islamic prophecy that seems relevant here. It is a 17th century Shiite prophecy which may very well be describing Barack Obama. This is not in the Qu'ran, (which is a thousand years older) but it is still a centuries-old "Hadith" (tradition.) Shi'ite Mullah Majlisi wrote Bahar al-Anvar (Oceans of Light) – 132 volumes of religious commentary that (along with the Qu'ran on which it comments) is the foundation of modern Shi'ite Islam.

Mullah Majlisi wrote that, Imam Ali Ibn Abi-Talib (Mohammed's cousin and son-in-law) prophesied that just prior to the return of the Twelfth Imam – the Mahdi - the Ultimate end times Savior of Islam - a "tall black man will assume the reins of government in the West." Leading "the strongest army on earth," the new western ruler in the West will carry "a clear sign" from the third imam, (whose name was Hussein Ibn Ali.) Obama's middle name, Hussein, is believed to be that sign. The Hadith also says that "Shiites should have no doubt that he is with us." Although "Buraq" in Arabic means lightning, the slightly different name Barack, in both Arabic and Farsi (Persian) means blessing; Barack Hussein means "the blessing of Hussein" in both languages. Even the surname Obama, written in the Persian alphabet as O-Ba-Ma, means "he is with us," another key point of Majlisi's tradition.[337]

According to this Hadith, this tall, black, western leader is only a precursor to the Mahdi, the Islamic version of the Messiah who is expected to return to destroy Christianity and Judaism. If it refers to Obama (over six feet tall, generally considered black, and certainly leading the government in the West and probably still the strongest army) this prophecy merely portrays him as a pivotal figure accompanying the Mahdi in the end times – perhaps what Christians would call the False Prophet that accompanies the Antichrist, rather than the Antichrist himself.

If he survives an assassination attempt somewhere other than Jerusalem, and appears to be miraculously resurrected three days later and claims to be Jesus but does not desolate the Temple in Jerusalem with his claims... this would better fit the title of False Prophet. If the Mahdi were then to survive an assassination and claim divinity at the Temple in Jerusalem.... I would then agree that Obama merely accompanies the Antichrist. This Shiite prophecy still beckons us to keep a watchful eye on President Obama during the end times.

At first I hesitated to put faith in the legitimacy of this prophecy, despite its online origins on an Iranian pro-government web site. It sounded too good to be true (from the perspective of my research) and I could not find anything online about this prophecy prior to about a week before the presidential election in 2008. But apparently the "denunciations" of this prophecy from the Muslim world are not claiming that the prophecy cited is unreal or a hoax, rather they downplay the possibility that this very real prophecy's "tall black man" who takes power in the West is Obama.

Al Arabiya News wrote on November 4, 2008 (which happened to be election day in the US) "Prominent Shiite scholar Mohamed Hassan al-Amin, however, denied the rumors and said that not everything mentioned in the renowned book is necessarily true, particularly prophecies. 'All texts related to the future are sheer guess work. If God had wanted to reveal the future of the world, he would not have created human beings with the ability to make the future themselves,' Amin told AlArabiya.net."[338] That isn't saying the prophecy is a hoax. It is, perhaps, trying to calm down America's predominantly Christian voters on the eve of Obama's potential election and make them pay less attention to what Shi'ites suspect to be true – that Obama is an important MUSLIM leader during the end times.

Notice the question Forbes' writer Amir Taheri asked in his article titled: "Is Barack Obama the 'promised warrior' coming to help the Hidden Imam of Shiite Muslims conquer the world?" Watch how Obama handles foreign affairs. Commenting on how Obama treats various world leaders, one author noted: "Obama's cold shoulder towards the French prime minister, however, was nothing compared to his treatment of the British" yet he was "bowing from the waist to the king of Saudi Arabia."[339] Is this a sign of his dislike of the European powers that once held poor nations like Kenya as colonies? Is it a sign that he seeks approval from Mecca? We will find out soon enough.

Why have there been so many black presidents in apocalyptic movies in recent years?

Tommy Lister plays President Limberg in 1997's "The Fifth Element." "The story's premise is that every five thousand years, in conjunction with a planetary arrangement, a 'Great Evil' appears whose purpose is to destroy life."[340]

In 1998's "Deep Impact" Morgan Freeman plays President Tom Beck when the Earth is threatened with an ELE – an Extinction Level Event – from a comet hitting the Earth.

In 2005's "Left Behind III: World at War" Louis Gossett Jr. plays President Gerald Fitzhugh until he is killed during the Tribulation.

Danny Glover plays President Thomas Wilson in 2009's disaster epic "2012," in which solar flares lead to massive tsunamis and other earth changes that kill everyone without a billion dollar ticket on an ark.

This is a significant trend of black presidents in movies – when we consider there had never been a black president yet when any of these movies were filmed. Now, Hollywood is progressive and liberal - and these movies could merely have been developed as part of an effort to train more voters to mentally accept the idea of a black president before one had ever been elected. It doesn't require a giant conspiracy - just a few Hollywood directors and financiers who realize they share similar views and want to steer the public towards their way of thinking can easily do so.

But if so, why always associate such a presidency with impending doom and billions of deaths? Why not use a more positive, heroic movie idea like Air Force One? Why such a focus on apocalyptic movies? Could these have been the early stage of an agenda to mentally prepare us for having Obama as president during the end of the world?

Along the same line of thinking:

Newsweek Magazine covers have shown Obama as the "God of All Things" (November 22, 2010) and also used the phrase "Second Coming" over his photo for another cover. (January 18, 2013) Time Magazine's cover showed him with the caption "Obama's World." (January 30, 2012) New American Magazine's cover showed him with the caption: "Obama: Messiah?"

(10/13/2008) Have other presidents ever been portrayed this way? Is the media trying to prepare us for something?

Pergamum Altar / Satan's Throne

The Bible refers to this as the city Pergamum – NOT an altar named so – is Berlin

Obama gave his speech titled "The World that Stands as One" in Berlin, Germany, on July 24, 2008. When Obama ended his speech in front of the statue of the war goddess, he said, "With an eye toward the future, with resolve in our hearts, let us remember this history, and answer our destiny, and remake the world once again." This is what Hitler had promised to do and where he had planned to memorialize it. Those who know occult history took notice of the symbolism and location of the event near the Pergamum Altar, a great Temple of Zeus referred to in the Bible as Satan's throne.[341].

The altar is in Berlin – closed for 5 years to reappear in 2019 (as of 2014)

Revelation 2:13 "I know where you dwell, where Satan's throne is; and you hold fast My name, and did not deny My faith even in the days of Antipas, My witness, My faithful one, who was killed among you, where Satan dwells." Antipas, the first Christian bishop to be martyred, was roasted alive at the altar of Pergamum in Turkey. This altar was shipped to Berlin, temporarily taken by the Red Army to the Soviet Union, and returned to Berlin. Right by this altar, Obama made a speech about how great it would be if he gets to run the world, and was so convincing that one announcer over German radio said: "We have just heard the next president of the United States...and the future President of the World."[342]

The German audience by the Pergamum Altar were not the only foreigners swayed by candidate Obama. Britain's Economist Magazine conducted an international poll online, and over 80% of their 52,000 "voters" preferred Obama over McCain.[343] One blogger commented: "Barack Obama will not only be the President of the United States, but he will also be the President of the World if such an election were to take place" globally.[344]

Some people suggest that the acceptance speech Obama gave (for his party's nomination) at the Democratic Convention in Denver in August 2008 was staged to model the Pergamum Altar that Obama had seen the month before. There are striking similarities between the two structures.... Did Obama choose to accept leadership from a copy of Satan's throne? Was Obama mocking those who made this connection, when at another event in New York in October 2008 he joked: "Where are those Greek columns I ordered?"[345]

Signs in the Heavens

We have already reviewed the alignment of Venus, the Morningstar, opposite (or "anti-") the Sun (representing the Son of God) on June 6, 2016. My previous book, <u>End Times and 2019</u>, was largely devoted to astronomical signs of the entire 2012-2016-2019 timeline of events, especially the heavenly wedding at the end of the tribulation. But are any such signs in the heavens specifically pointing to Barack Obama?

Consider the Norway Spiral:

Do you remember the huge spiral of blue light that appeared over Norway on the night of December 9, 2009? Did you know it appeared right when Obama arrived in Norway, to accept his Nobel Peace Prize? Did you know the decision to grant him the Nobel Peace Prize was made two months earlier on the Jewish holiday of Sukkot? This is the Feast of Tabernacles, a day of intense celebration when Jews sing from Psalm 118: "Blessed is he who comes in the name of the Lord."

Obama' nomination for the Nobel Peace Prize came after just two weeks in office – so what had he done to earn it? When the news came out even he said: "I do not view it as a recognition of my own accomplishments." He later joked that he wasn't sure why he was receiving it. In his acceptance speech, he said: "...my accomplishments are slight.... But perhaps the most profound issue surrounding my receipt of this prize is the fact that I am the Commander-in-Chief of a nation in the midst of two wars."

Leaked rumors from the Nobel committee suggest three of the five panelists were against his nomination, and in some countries up to 70 per cent of those surveyed feel the award was a mistake. There is a petition to revoke it, which garnered almost 10,000 signatures the first day alone. Was Obama given a prize in advance of his terms in office, in the hope that the prize would influence him to become what they promoted him to be? Or is it part of a larger scheme to portray Obama as a messiah figure? Was the spiral just a failed Russian missile launch? This is the official explanation, but then why has the world never seen anything like it before? Could it be a heavenly sign of disapproval that the world was acknowledging Obama as some kind of Prince of Peace?

Alignments with Regulus

On August 11, 2015 – Jupiter – "the King of Planets" – will be within 0.4 degrees of Regulus, "the Heart of Leo" and "King of the Stars" just before sunset. There will be no other conjunctions of the two for over a decade. It occurs nine months and 26 days before the "birthing" or "revealing" of the Antichrist on June 6, 2016 – just possibly a date symbolic of conception. It could mean that an event that day will prove to be a relevant clue.

The last time ANY planet had a perfectly aligned conjunction and occulted (blocked our view of) ANY bright star was when Venus occulted Regulus on July 7, 1959. Is this the kind of sign that could clue us in to the Antichrist's identity from his birth? As astronomical conjunctions go, the Venus occultation of Regulus would be a significant astronomical sign or clue appropriate for the birth or conception of the Antichrist.

Obama claims to have been born on August 4, 1961, in Honolulu. Many internet "rumors" dispute this claim. Obama often fails to remember his official birthday, such as on July 15, 2011 – when Obama made headlines for stating "I'll be turning 50 in a week" – when his official birthday is August 4 – three weeks away. Is the stress of the office really so great that he can't keep track of when he was born? If this was the only occasion, perhaps we could ignore it. But there are others.

And there is no ignoring the birth certificate. A lot of people point out reasons why they think the online birth certificate appears to be a fake, with layers still visible, and all sorts of errors that indicate forgery. I'm not an expert on that. I am not aware of overwhelming evidence of an earlier birth. Let's just say his birth details are considered questionable.

British intelligence advisor Michael Shrimpton claims Obama was born in Mombasa, Kenya in 1960.[346] (Shrimpton is an Adjunct Professor of Intelligence Studies at American Military University, teaching masters degree level intelligence subjects to serving intelligence officers.) British authorities maintained colonial records in Kenya at the time, and Shrimpton says British records show President Obama was born in Kenya in 1960. Shrimpton also tells us that because of Barack Sr.'s involvement in Kenya's Mau-Mau uprising against British rule, the family was being watched and that Obama's mother Stanley Dunham was not even pregnant in July 1961.

In an affidavit from May 12, 2014, Shrimpton states: "It was my understanding then, and still is, that he was born in Mombasa in what was then the Kenyan Protectorate.... assuming the intelligence about the birth in Mombasa to be correct."[347]

If Stanley Ann Dunham did give birth to Barack Obama Jr. on August 4, 1961, she did not do so under the best of circumstances. Nine months earlier she was still 17 years old. Her signature on Obama's birth certificate uses her maiden name. And even our president has said: "how and when the marriage occurred remains a bit murky, a bill of particulars that I've never quite had the courage to explore. There's no record of a real wedding."[348] And while not physically impossible, the fact that Stanley Ann started college in Seattle two weeks after August 4, 1961 makes the story seem somewhat unlikely.

In May 2014, an online article: "Kenyan Authorities Release Obama Birth Records; Born 1960"[349] claimed Israeli and Kenyan sources say that "The Office of the Principal Register of the Nyanza Province, in Kenya, has finally released 11 exclusive documents concerning Barack Obama's alleged birth and early childhood in the country... These files, if they turn out to be verifiable, could mean that Mr. Obama had no legal right to become the American president under the country's law. The papers released today suggest that Barack Obama was actually born on March 7, 1960, in Lamu, Kenya."[350] Just a rumor, I suppose.

Obama's wife Michelle, at a speech on June 27, 2008 – said "Barack has led by example, when we took our trip to Africa and visited his home country in Kenya..." Could that just be a slip of the tongue? Maybe she just meant "ancestral home" or "family's motherland."

The literary agency Acton & Dystel wrote brief biographies of dozens of their new authors in a promotional booklet many years ago, including Barack Obama. It started his brief bio: "Barack Obama, the first African-American president of the Harvard Law Review, was born in Kenya and raised in Indonesia and Hawaii." Perhaps this was just an editorial error.

Another point of interest involves an article from the June 27, 2004 Kenya Sunday Standard newspaper. An article titled: "Kenyan-born Obama all set for U.S. Senate" can still be found, even at Snopes.com where internet rumors are torn apart.[351] Snopes says the Kenyan article was an altered version of the Associated Press version which, in the USA, does not claim

Obama was born in Kenya. Apparently, an editor in Kenya made the addition for their readers. Do Kenyans know something most Americans don't?

A Kenyan Security Intelligence Service memo from 2010[352] refers to the construction of a cultural site in Kogelo, Kenya "to honor the birthplace of President Barack Obama." Kenyan Parliament member James Orengo was quoted in 2010 discussing Obama's presidency as proof of the success of racial diversity in America: "If America was living in a situation where they feared ethnicity and did not see itself as a multiparty state or nation, how could a young man who is born here in Kenya, who is not even a native American, become the president of America?"[353]

We must assume one of two things. Either he was born in Kenya, and the Kenyans know it and are proud of the fact while groups in America are more concerned with eligibility issues and hiding the facts... or the Kenyans are wrong and making a false claim because they are proud of Obama's heritage and ancestry in Kenya. More interesting to me is the alleged birthdate one article suggested: March 7, 1960 – because if this were correct, Obama could have been conceived on July 7, 1959, when Venus occulted Regulus. Astronomically, that occultation when heavenly bodies representing kingship and the Dark Prince overlap would be exactly the kind of thing I would expect to see regarding the Antichrist. It is a very rare astronomical event – Venus will not pass directly in front of Regulus again until October 1, 2044. And if I were the Antichrist, I would want to hide any evidence of my birth (or conception) on that date. If I were an evil genius attempting to conceal evidence of WHEN I was born, I might brilliantly distract people with a question on WHERE I was born. If any stories come out claiming Obama's real birth date was July 7, 1959 or the early spring of 1960, we should pay attention.

But what is far more likely (than any particular date of birth) is his ineligibility to be president.

In addition to the possibility of Kenyan birth, there are the problems with Indonesian citizenship. Orly Taitz has investigated such claims. "A whistle-blower from Higher Education Services Corporation in Albany New York came forward and advised Attorney Orly Taitz that she personally reviewed Barack Obama's financial aid information, which stated that financial aid was given to Obama as foreign student and as a citizen of Indonesia."[354]

Daniel 11:21 warns: "a despicable person will arise, on whom the honor of kingship has not been conferred, but he will come in a time of tranquility and seize the kingdom by intrigue." This is generally believed to refer to the Antichrist. Could it refer to a peacefully elected president, who is not a king (as the Bible's ancient writers understood national leadership) and only came to power through a secret scheme of hiding evidence of ineligibility?

Could Obama's true birth details possibly reveal more Arab ancestry, associating him with Arab slave traders and "the people of the prince" from Daniel 9:26? A <u>London Telegraph</u> article in 2008 said: "Abdul Rahman Sheikh Abdullah, 53, says that he has evidence that as many as 8,000 Bedouin tribesmen from northern Israel are related to Mr. Obama.... We knew about it years ago but we were afraid to talk about it because we didn't want to influence the election."[355] The article explains that it was once common for wealthy Arabs to have African workers or slaves and that intermarriage was common.

We should also note that the Luo tribe in Kenya to which the Obama family belongs migrated south only a few centuries ago. Before arriving in Kenya, the Luo originated in Sudan, and many are still in Sudan. There would also have been intermixing with Arabs there, long before reaching Kenya, where the coastal regions saw frequent intermingling with Arab slave traders. One popular online rumor in 2008 stated that through his father, Barack Obama was as much as 7/16 Arab.[356] Another claims that his father "was officially referred to in Kenyan public records as an 'Arab African.'"[357] Others claim that "His father's Arab ancestry can be confirmed by the Kenyan government."[358]

This 7/16 proportion of Arab ancestry seems very unlikely to me. But I am not concerned with the percentages – only if he has some Arab ancestry. This seems very likely – for anyone with ancestors from Sudan and the coast of Kenya. "European and American historians assert that between the 8th and 19th century, 10 to 18 million people were bought by Arab slave traders and taken from Africa."[359] The duration and extent of the Arab slave trade alone, (not to mention other commerce) in East Africa almost ensures that significant intermixing occurred in Kenya between Arabs and native Africans.

I essentially agree with this online commentary from 2008: "Barack Obama Sr. might have been a little bit Arab, and it's certainly possible that some of Sen. Obama's ancestors sold their fellow black Africans to Arab slave

> To me, this means whichever people Titus descended from — not who he brought with him. Or the people that made up the entire Roman Empire.

traders. But this rumor that Barack Obama Sr. was 7/8th Arab is silly."[360]

Some people allege significant Arab ancestry for Barack Obama, and since Arabs made up the majority of "the people of the prince" Titus employed to sack Jerusalem in 70 A.D., some Arab ancestry would be essential for anyone we might consider as a candidate for the Antichrist. If Obama did know of such ancestry, he might have been motivated to hide such a link to Bible prophecy and to slave-owning ancestors. Keep in mind Obama's ancestors were not African Americans and the civil rights struggle applied to no one in his family. But he wanted African American voters to identify with him. A white mother might have been politically surmountable, maybe even an Islamic background – but slave-trading ancestors too? Better to hide that information about his ethnic background, assuming it may be correct.

What about his religious background? We know Obama's Indonesian stepfather Lolo was Muslim and that Obama went to school and religious services in Indonesia for years. Should we assume that he might have practiced Islam and prayed to Allah in his youth in Indonesia, but that he is now a Christian? Islam does not allow this. The majority of Muslim scholars hold the traditional view that apostasy (such as converting to Christianity) is punishable by death. So why would any Muslims view Obama as a potential savior of the Muslim world?

We already covered the example of the pro-Iranian web site promoting the Shi'ite prophecy about the tall black man coming to reign over the powerful government of the West and over the world's greatest army. Many of the world's Muslims hope Obama can fulfill this prophecy. President Obama tells Americans he is Christian. But consider the words of an Indonesian blogger who wrote: "Barack Hussein Obama might have convinced some Americans that he is no longer a Muslim, but so far he has not convinced many in the world's most populous Muslim country who still see him as a Muslim and a crusader for Islam."[361]

Many in the Islamic world consider Obama a Muslim and hope that he will lead Islam to victory: "A Pakistani newspaper is quoting one of the country's ministers as stating he wants President Obama to offer Muslim prayers at Ground Zero and become the 'Caliph,' or ruler, of the Islamic nation. 'The coming Eid [a fast at the end of the Muslim holiday of Ramadan] would expectedly be observed on 9/11; this is a golden opportunity for President Obama to offer Eid prayers at Ground Zero and become Amir-ul-Momineen or Caliph of Muslims. In this way, all the problems of Muslim World would be solved,' stated Minister of State for Industries and Productions Ayatullah Durrani, according to Pakistan's The Nation newspaper."[362]

Why would any Muslim devout enough to want a restored Islamic Caliphate want Barack Obama in charge? Consider the Islamic practice of Taqiyya - the idea that a Muslim may lie, deceive, conceal the truth, even blaspheme Allah and Mohammed, even deny his Muslim faith if he is at significant risk of persecution or if such actions benefit the greater good of the Islamic world overall. Even claiming to be a Christian, while not truly being one, is acceptable according to Taqiyya. "Mahdi-Antichrist starts off as a man of false peace, who may even play down or deny his Islamic faith to deceive Israel and the West."[363] In one hadith from Imam Jafar Sadiq (hadiths are commentaries on the Qu'ran, viewed like a book of Bible commentary would be viewed by a Christian) "You belong to a religion that whoever conceals it, Allah will honor him."[364]

Another similar term is Kithman. "Kithman is a command to deliberately conceal one's beliefs."[365] We can't know Obama's inner beliefs for certain. But we can assume that when a young Obama arrived in Indonesia in 1967, he learned the consequences of letting people know what you really think. In 1965 there was a coup in Indonesia, and the new dictator Suharto started a purge of communists and sympathizers that led to somewhere between 500,000 and 1,000,000 executions and perhaps 750,000 more jailed or exiled. Young Obama grew up during the purge, and I assume that he learned that talking openly about beliefs can get you killed, while hiding unpopular beliefs can get you by.

I wish I knew the truth about Obama for certain. Some Kenyans seem to think they know something most Americans don't know. So do certain Indonesians. And Iranians. And Pakistanis. And... Egyptians? Egyptian Foreign Minister Ahmed Aboul Gheit was on Nile TV in mid-January 2010 and said: "The American President told me in confidence that he is a Muslim," and that "Obama promised that once he overcame some domestic American problems (Healthcare), that he would show the Moslem [Muslim] world what he would do with Israel."[366] It didn't take long before "the Israeli ambassador to the United States, Michael Oren, stated that U.S. – Israel relations were at their worst point since the 1970s."[367]

There are many online articles and videos with "Obama's Betrayal of Israel" in the title. In one such article, the writer makes it clear that the Obama administration will not require the Palestinians to acknowledge Israel's right to exist as a first step in any negotiations. Of course, Israeli Prime Minister Netenyahu was smart enough to point out: "The central question at the end is of course 'Are you willing to recognize that the state of Israel is the nation state of the Jewish nation?' ...They say that they will not recognize a Jewish state.... So then what are we even talking about here? That a Palestinian state will be established but it will continue its conflict against the state of Israel with more preferential borders? We are a lot of things, but we are definitely not fools."[368] Trading land for peace didn't work well for Native Americans and few Israelis believe it will work for them either. And the Bible suggests that God does not look favorably on dividing the land of Israel.

If Saudi Arabian radio represents that nation's thinking on the subject, then Saudis also think Obama is Muslim who will work against Israel. "In one broadcast prior to the 2008 elections, the Saudis claimed that 'we will have a Muslim in the White House.' Another Saudi broadcast said: 'Obama's job is to terminate the Shiite threat [Iran] and the Jewish threat [Israel].'"[369] Obama did bow down and kiss the ring of the Saudi king (a traditional sign of loyalty) while he did not show similar respect for the Queen of England. Are the Saudis correct in thinking Obama is on their side?

One could argue that no matter what evidence there may be from the past, no matter what Indonesians, Iranians, Pakistanis, Egyptians, Saudi Arabians, and his own pastor may think – we should believe President Obama when he says he is a Christian. Perhaps. You decide.

The issue of religion becomes very important when we consider that Obama could be Muslim and may be the Antichrist. There is much evidence for "the Islamic Antichrist theory," which points out that at the time of the end, the Bible warns us there is a false religion headed by the Antichrist and the False prophet which has many similarities to Islam and its end times leadership.

Daniel 9:27 tells us there will be a seven year covenant: "he will make a firm covenant with the many for one week, but in the middle of the week he will put a stop to sacrifice." This is believed to mean that the Antichrist will break whatever covenant he initiates, renews, or strengthens halfway through the final seven years. My timeline of events starts 12/21/2012 and raises the question: where's the peace covenant for Israel? You know, the peace treaty mentioned in Daniel 9:27 where the Antichrist renews or strengthens a seven year covenant with Israel - which he breaks halfway through after 42 months. Wouldn't that peace-renewal covenant have to have started on 12/21/2012, if it ends seven years later on December 21, 2019?

There is already a peace covenant for Israel - and the "Covenant of Peoples" began on 12/21/2012 when "messianic" John Kerry was nominated as Secretary of State to handle the peace process and the plans for Obama's "Covenant of Peoples" tour began. Some point out that Obama did not visit Israel until March 2013, when he completely fulfilled Daniel 11:16-17 "he will also stay for a time in the Beautiful Land, with destruction in his hand. He will set his face to come with the power of his whole kingdom, bringing with him a proposal of peace which he will put into effect."

I believe the plans for the tour were set in December, but it was important to go to Israel in March. Obama entered Jerusalem six days before Passover, perhaps in a subtle effort to mimic Jesus Christ. Jesus rode into Jerusalem six days before Passover, riding on a donkey. Obama literally rode in on the presidential limo, which the Secret Service calls "the Beast" (instead of Cadillac One or Limousine One as they did for other presidents.) Their code name for Obama is "Renegade" which is also appropriate for rebellion. When I do a Google search of the words "renegade definition" I get "a person who deserts and betrays an organization, country, or set of principles. synonyms: traitor, defector, deserter, turncoat, rebel, mutineer."[370]   What does the Secret Service expect him to betray?

And figuratively, Obama "rode in" (to power at least) through the Democratic Party, symbolized by the donkey. During the "Covenant of Peoples" tour, America has again pressured Israel to accept a bad deal regarding it's Muslim neighbors – starting with territorial concessions and allowing Iran to have nukes - under the premise that the United States will always protect Israel, that we have an "unbreakable alliance" and a "covenant of peoples." Daniel 11:16-17 hints at international pressure on Israel through "the power of his whole kingdom" when "he will also stay for a time in the Beautiful Land, with destruction in his hand. He will set his face to come with the power of his whole kingdom, bringing with him a proposal of peace which he will put into effect." This implies it was created (December 2012) earlier, but put into effect later (March 2013.)

In Daniel 9:27 the Antichrist breaks the seven year covenant after 42 months and defiles the Temple with abominations "on the wing." "Wing" is an unfortunate translation into English because it distracts readers from the obvious meaning of this phrase. In the Greek word "pterugion," English readers may recognize the root for "wing" in the first four letters "pter" and think, perhaps, of the prehistoric winged reptile, the pterodactyl. But although "wing" and "pinnacle" are both a form of extensions - "pterugion" means "pinnacle," as it was used in Matthew 4:5 "Then the devil took Him into the holy city and had Him stand on the pinnacle of the temple."

We should also understand that the pinnacle, or high point, of the Temple may very well have also been on a wing, or extension of the main building, at the front entrance. Especially in Greek, and in reference to the Temple, the two words are closely related. Sometimes translations made out of context, without the benefit of seeing the actual building being described, and influenced by buildings contemporary with the translator – can cause minor problems.

Let us assume the abomination Daniel speaks of is important. Let us assume it is not placed off to the side on some secondary "wing" of the Temple. Let us assume the abomination is placed "front and center" on the Temple, just as Satan placed Jesus, on the pterugion, the pinnacle. On every Islamic Mosque there is a spire holding up a golden crescent moon, the symbol of Islam, at this very point. This is the same crescent moon symbol Arabs have venerated for thousands of years; the same one Gideon removed from his enemies in Judges 8:21. When the Jews do rebuild a Temple in Jerusalem, and the Muslims wish to reestablish a Caliphate with Jerusalem as its capital, I would be astounded if victorious (temporarily victorious) Muslims did not place a crescent moon upon the pinnacle of the Temple and rededicate it to Allah. The symbol of Islam will prove to be the abomination of desolation, along with the Antichrist who fights for Islam. As Obama wrote in The Audacity of Hope: "I will stand with the Muslims should the political winds shift in an ugly direction,"[371] When the Apocalypse comes, I suspect that the Antichrist may be Muslim, and that it may be Barack Obama.

THE ISLAMIC CALIPHATE

Outside the Muslim world, Muhammad is viewed as the founding prophet of the Islamic religion. Muhammad's father died while his mother was pregnant with him, and his mother died when he was only six years old. Despite having been born into a wealthy clan of Arab merchants, custom prevented young children from inheriting anything and Muhammad was somewhat impoverished until approximately age 25, when he married Khadija, a wealthy merchant who was fifteen years older.

His home city of Mecca dominated the caravan trade routes of the coast of western Arabia, where goods (and ideas) from East Africa, the Byzantine Empire, the Persian Empire, and India flowed freely. The Arabs in Mecca had worshipped hundreds of pagan gods for centuries, but wealth from trade was bringing increased opportunities for leisure time, and education, and the reevaluation of old ideas. As many Arabs travelled to new lands and interacted with foreigners they learned new foreign traditions, and this may have made conditions ripe for new religious ideas to spread through Arabia after Muhammad started preaching the message of Islam.

Muslims, however, do not view Islam as "new" to the 7th century Meccans. Muslims view their religion as the original monotheistic religion known by Adam, Abraham, Moses, and Jesus – and they view Muhammad as the last and final prophet to whom the original and unaltered faith was restored. This occurred late in 610 A.D. in the Cave of Hira, in Saudi Arabia. Muhammad made a habit of going to this cave a few miles northeast of Mecca in order to meditate and pray without interruptions. One night, now known as "the Night of Power" or "the Blessed Night," Muhammad was visited by the Archangel Gabriel and given divine revelation. Muhammad was a very capable man and his revelation spread quickly.

After Muhammad's death, Islam was divided into two main factions. Shia or Shiite Islam is the minority faction, most prevalent in Iran, with significant populations in Iraq and Lebanon as well. Adherents believe that the leadership of the Islamic world should remain in the family of Muhammad's direct descendants. They believe that after Muhammad, succession for leadership of the Islamic world should have immediately gone to Muhammad's son-in-law and cousin, Ali bin Abu Talib. The word "Shiite" or "Shia" in Arabic basically translates as "a supportive group of people." The term is shortened from "Shia-t-Ali" or "the Party of Ali." They follow spiritual leaders known as Imams, whom they believe are infallible as they are acting under divine authority. One could argue this faction is more dangerous because they tend to follow the commands of their Imams no matter how extreme the request.

Sunni Islam represents the overwhelming majority of the Muslim population; they believe that leadership should be elected from any of the capable and faithful followers. The word "Sunni" is derived from an Arabic word meaning "one who follows the traditions of the Prophet." Sunnis prevailed when Muhammad died; they elected Abu Bakr to be the first "rightly guided Caliph." Abu Bakr was one of Muhammad's first followers, closest friends, and eventually his father in law, after Muhammad married his daughter Aisha. Sunnis represent about 85 per cent of the Muslim population. Sunnis recognize a legitimate succession of Muslim leadership from the death of Muhammad in 632 A.D. until the last Ottoman Caliph was removed after WWI. This was a devastating loss of legitimate Muslim leadership for Sunnis.

Sunnis and Shiites fought bitterly over succession after Muhammad's death in 632 A.D. In 656 A.D., supporters of Ali killed the third caliph. In retaliation, the Sunnis soon killed Ali's son Husain, but not Ali himself, who ruled as the fourth Caliph from 656 to 661 A.D. Shiites believe that the first three caliphs were not legitimate, and that legitimate leadership only existed from Ali until the disappearance of the Twelfth Imam in 931 A.D. This Twelfth Imam, Shiites believe, went into hiding as a young boy, disappearing from the funeral of the eleventh Imam (his father) in 874. Some non-Shiite commentators suggest that as the last descendant of Muhammad through the line of Ali, it was completely unacceptable within their religious beliefs for that bloodline to end; therefore when the child disappeared, many stories of his survival emerged. He was believed to survive for many decades in hiding, and to have been reachable through intermediaries until 931. This is when Shiite Islam felt their devastating loss of divinely appointed leadership.

This Twelfth Imam is a very important figure in Muslim end times prophecy, as many Shiites believe he has been kept supernaturally hidden in a well by Allah, and will reemerge to lead them during the final seven years. Sunnis do not attribute any importance to genetic descent from Muhammad through Ali, and do not believe the Mahdi was already alive in the form of the Twelfth Imam. I am reminded of the main difference between Jewish and

Christian views on the coming Messiah: Christians believe Jesus was the Messiah and will be returning, while Jews do not think Jesus was the Messiah and that when the Messiah does come, it will be for the first time.

Sunni and Shiites also disagree on exactly what happened to Muhammad in the Cave of Hira. Shiites believe that Muhammad was expecting Gabriel, who merely officially ordained and encouraged Muhammad on a spiritual mission which he already had thoughts of pursuing. Sunnis believe Muhammad was surprised and terrified by Gabriel, who pressured him (literally repeatedly "squeezing" or "choking" the breath out of him) into memorizing the revelations which became the Qu'ran. In the Sunni tradition, Muhammad returned home to his wife cold and in shock, upset that he had been touched by a jinn – an evil spirit or demon. (Keep in mind, Muslims consider Satan a jinn.) Many Sunnis believe he even considered taking his own life rather than be polluted by evil.[372] I can't help but think of Galatians 1:8 "But even if we, or an angel from heaven, should preach to you a gospel contrary to what we have preached to you, he is to be accursed!"

The revelation from Gabriel is believed to have occurred in late in the Islamic holy month of Ramadan, on one of the odd-numbered nights in the last ten days of the month. Many scholars prefer to assume the 27th night of Ramadan is Laylat Al-Qadr. This is in the range of what is now known as the middle of August in our Gregorian calendar, and several sources use the date of August 10, 610 A.D. The cave of Hira is described as a tiny cave, even an alcove, just large enough for one person. One description of Jabal al-Nour (the Mountain of Enlightenment) says "The cave is quite small, four arm's length long by 1.75 arm's length wide."[373] Some commentators feel it is unlikely that Gabriel stood **inside** the cave with Muhammad, and suggest that perhaps Muhammad received his revelation inside the cave but looked **outside** the cave entrance to see Gabriel: "When he stepped outside the cave he saw an angel on the horizon."[374]

Further research shows this is probably taken from the words of Bilal, a slave bought and freed by Abu Bakr. Bilal's duties included waking Muhammad in the morning, and Bilal was also the first muezzin – the title given to those who officially call Muslims to prayer. Bilal was quoted saying "What I relate now, I have by authority. I was told it by Abu Bakr, who heard it from Saeed, who heard it from Ali, who knew it from Khadija, who received it from the lips of Muhammad, who experienced it. Moreover it is confirmed, in the second part, by God in eighteen verses of the Surah of Najm (meaning the Star). Therefore, it is a fact irrefutable and an evidence of religion.... he

saw Gabriel clearly in the figure of a man standing on the horizon."[375]   The
Surah of Najm - Surah 53 describes Gabriel as giving Muhammad divine
revelation and in verse seven places Gabriel on the horizon.

The Cave of Hira is northeast of Mecca and faces Mecca, which means it
faces southwest. I cannot find clear written confirmation that the cave
entrance faces southwest, (only that Mecca is in the field of view) but based
on many photos of the cave entrance with the sun at the same angle off to the
side, and assuming one would try to visit (and photograph) anything in the
Arabian desert in the early morning, before the heat is too intense – photos
seem to confirm this south to southwestern view. What would Mohammad
have seen, if he looked south or southwest from the Cave of Hira around
August 10? That depends on the time. One source tells us: "he was asleep
when the angel Gabriel appeared and demanded that he read. Since
Mohammed was illiterate, he protested that he could not read. Then the angel
pressed down on him to the point that he thought he was going to smother to
death. When the angel released him, Mohammed sat up and read. On
awakening, Mohammed felt that words were engraved on his heart. He fled
out of the cave, into the early morning sunlight, and beheld a vision of the
angel Gabriel."[376]   If this is correct, Muhammad would have been visited by
Gabriel at night, and would have looked out of the cave just before sunrise.

Due south, the sky would have been dominated by the constellation Orion at
sunrise on that date, and we have already established that the prophet Daniel
indicates an association between Gabriel and Orion.   An interesting
conjunction to the southwest, however, would also have gotten anyone's
attention that morning – Jupiter was within two degrees of the full moon,
with Saturn slightly below it less than 3 degrees from the moon. It may have
seemed like the moon god, so central to the religious beliefs of the pre-
Islamic Arabs, had two witnesses that night – the same two planets I suspect
are relevant as Christian end-times witnesses. But any early focus on the
astronomy of that night – on the moon and its witnesses, on Orion, or the
possibility of an evil demon constricting Muhammad until he conceded to
memorize the first five verses of the Qu'ran - was soon glossed over as focus
shifted to more urgent matters like spreading Islam throughout the world.

Muslim control quickly spread outwards from its base around the cities of
Medina and Mecca in the Hejaz portion of western Arabia. The first
successor, or Caliph, after Muhammad's death in 632 A.D. was his close
friend and father in law, Abu Bakr. Though he only lived two more years as
Caliph, by the end of his reign, Islam had conquered the entire Arabian

peninsula, and spread into Iraq and Syria. The Middle East was ripe for the taking, as the population was exhausted by constant fighting between the Byzantine and Persian Empires (and the heavy taxes both empires forced on the people to pay for constant warfare.)

Just one generation after Muhammad, Islam ruled more of the world than the Roman Empire had ever controlled. By the year 750 the Islamic Caliphate was a theocratic empire – a type of religious empire that had never arisen before – spreading Islamic sharia law from Spain to India. It already matched important descriptions given in Daniel 7:7 "and behold, a fourth beast, dreadful and terrifying and extremely strong; and it had large iron teeth. It devoured and crushed and trampled down the remainder with its feet; and it was different from all the beasts that were before it."

But just like the Roman Empire, which eventually broke into a western half ruled from Rome and an eastern half ruled from Constantinople - the Islamic conquests proved too large a domain to control from one location, and various Caliphates ruled from Mecca, Damascus, Baghdad, Cordoba, and Cairo – sometimes with more than one caliphate at the same time – for the next 700 years. In 1453, a Turkish dynasty we know as the Ottomans conquered Constantinople, snuffing out the last official rule by a Roman Empire. The Turks made the city their own new capital and renamed it Istanbul. They declared a Caliphate, and within a few centuries this empire became one of history's largest. The Ottoman Caliphate ruled all of North Africa except for Morocco, through Egypt down the Red Sea coasts of northeast Africa and Arabia, through all of Turkey and the Middle East into western Iran, the entire coast of the Black Sea into southern Russia and Ukraine, and southeast Europe up to Vienna in Austria, which they besieged repeatedly from 1529 to the peak of the Ottoman Empire's power in 1683, when the last siege of Vienna began on September 11.

When most Americans think of a Caliphate, they think of the Ottoman Caliphate ruling from Istanbul – the only Caliphate in existence since America was discovered by Columbus. (Up until I was putting the finishing touches on this book, when a new Caliphate was declared in the summer of 2014.) The Ottomans never did subdue the entire Persian Empire. But other Islamic Caliphates did, and extended much further east into India. Considering all of the Islamic Caliphates, the Islamic Empire is the only contender for Daniel's Fourth Kingdom, which defeats and absorbs the lands of the Babylonian, Persian, and Greek Empires in their entirety. The Roman Empire only briefly held Babylonia for a few months around 116-117 A.D., and they never defeated Persia or annexed any of its land. Sir Robert Anderson, author of <u>The Prince to Come</u>, also noted that "Ancient Rome was precisely the one power which added government to conquest, and instead of treading down and breaking in pieces the nations it subdued, sought rather to mould them to its own civilization." Anderson concluded that "that the entire vision of the seventh chapter may have a future reference"[377] which is east of Rome and largely east of Jerusalem....

Several authors on our topics conclude that the final end times empire Daniel describes is a revived Islamic Caliphate, and that the Antichrist will be a Muslim. They explain that the Bible's description of the Antichrist is mirrored in Islam's savior, the Imam Mahdi – and that the False Prophet corresponds to the person Muslims expect when Jesus returns – as they are expecting a Muslim Jesus who denounces and persecutes Christians and Jews and denies having been crucified or being the son of God. Both religions expect a savior who will ride in on a white horse and endure a seven year period of trouble. Both expect their savior to triumph over their enemies and rule the entire world from Jerusalem. I agree with Joel Richardson and other authors who explain the Islamic Antichrist theory so well. I assume a restored Islamic Caliphate will emerge [has emerged] that will unify the Islamic world and march against Jerusalem. And as of July 2014, a new Islamic Caliphate was recently declared in Syria and Iraq. I predict it will expand. I assume the "Muslim Savior," the Imam Mahdi, will soon arise and try to take over the world for Islam.

This may seem to be at odds with my suggestion that U.S. President Barack Obama seems to be the most likely candidate for the title of Antichrist. Could the leader of the United States, who says he is Christian, become the leader of the Islamic world, as one Pakistani Minister hoped?

Many people believe that Obama is a "closet" Muslim, pretending to be Christian but secretly holding Muslim beliefs. A Pew poll in 2010 said that "Only 34 percent of Pew's respondents identified Obama as Christian — down 14 percentage points since last year. And 43 percent said they don't know what Obama's religion is."[378] They were less clear on the overall percentage who think he is Muslim, but since they said 31% of Republicans, 18% of independents, and 10% of Democrats think he is Muslim – perhaps we can assume about 20% of Americans believed he was Muslim as of 2010. "The same question presented to 686 likely Mississippi Republican primary voters found just 12 percent believe Obama to be Christian. But 52 percent say he is Muslim."[379] I suspect those numbers are rising.

Many people believe Obama is some kind of "Manchurian Candidate" who wants to destroy America from within.

Many people believe Obama is the Antichrist.

Right wing end times radio host Rick Wiles has made perhaps the most extreme statement of all, calling Obama a "traitor in the White House who is openly helping jihadis."[380]

Political analyst Dinesh D'Souza makes none of those claims; but he does suggest that "the president is driven by a Third-World, anti-American ideology."[381]   He notes that "his behavior on behalf of the Muslim jihadis seems so inexplicable that some people conclude that Obama must be a closet Muslim."[382]   D'Souza also notes that when an uprising in a Muslim country is by religious fundamentalists against a moderate and pro-American government, (as in Egypt) Obama supports the fundamentalists and helps depose the ally.   When the uprising is by moderates seeking democracy, attempting to overthrow religious fundamentalists (as in Iran) Obama acts to help keep the existing anti-American regimes in power.   D'Souza would argue that this is done to reduce and minimize America's unfair geopolitical advantages, and level the global playing field.[383]

"Rush Limbaugh on Wednesday [9/10/14] said former Vice President Dick Cheney is 'exactly right' when he says President Barack Obama's policies only empowered the Muslim Brotherhood, giving radical Islamist groups an opportunity to gain power in the Middle East."[384]   Speaking about the Islamic State on September 10, 2014 "Obama said flatly that this group, which is trying to install a caliphate in the Middle East, 'is not Islamic.'   He didn't say they are perverting their religion; he said they're not even part of that religion."[385]   Just what is Obama trying to do?   Will Americans fall for it?

Some Americans may hate Obama for working to destroy the American Dream in exchange for more global equality.   But for billions of non-Americans living a relatively meager existence in the Third World, chafing under the economic, military, and cultural influence of America – Barack Obama is a savior.   He is like the messiah Jews were expecting two thousand years ago, a political leader who would free them from foreign oppression, righting the wrongs they perceived in their homeland.   I agree with D'Souza that Obama "harbors grand visions of himself as the savior"[386] and that he would be all too happy to give America's (and Europe's) "unfair" advantages, power and wealth away to the Africans, Asians, and Arabs that deserve a bigger slice of the global pie. If he someday offers the world's poor nations a "fair" redistribution I assume they will support him.

Let us consider – as the premise of a fictional story loosely based on current events and prophecies – (for I certainly don't mean to accuse President Obama of anything) What if all of these views are right?

What if a president came to power with the goals of bringing America down and helping Islam conquer the world? What if he did everything he could to put America's military resources to good use – for the Islamic world? What if he had the supernatural power of Satan backing him up? If I was in such a position, and I wanted to conquer the world for Islam, some of my ideas would include:

Policies designed to fail and weaken America economically, such as adding more massive debts faster than ever before

Policies designed to aggravate allies and leave America diplomatically isolated

Firing patriotic military leadership, replacing countless high ranking officers with those who will follow my orders no matter what

Overthrowing Arab dictatorships, supporting rebellions, encouraging civil disorder, and supporting pan-Islamic political/religious groups like the Muslim Brotherhood, with covert operations to ensure regime change in in the Arab world as a grand policy aiming at establishing a revived Islamic Caliphate (Saudi Arabia would be next on my hit list – especially if they stop trading oil exclusively in US dollars and start using rubles or yuan.)

Releasing major terrorists to get back to work (some reports say that ISIS leader "Caliph" al-Baghdadi was released from Camp Bucca in Iraq in 2009.)

Transferring nuclear weapons into the hands of Islamic groups or nations who would use them wherever I wanted them to

A false flag event like the staged nuclear destruction of New York City, which would collapse the stock markets and the economy as a whole, paving the way for martial law, suspension of elections, special presidential powers, and dictatorship. I would probably blame it on a group of U.S. military veterans with Christian religious fervor, and claim that such people are America's worst enemies. I would suggest that we need to confiscate guns and suppress Christianity. There would be a few thousand arrests of people I considered potential adversaries. I might also blame Israel for supplying the Christian veterans with the nuclear weapon.

I would start wars in the Middle East, and encourage millions of Middle Easterners to apply for American citizenship as refugees. I would convince Americans that we should allow millions of new Muslim immigrants.

If I did not feel America could realistically be converted easily to become the new center of Islamic power, I would concentrate America's military forces for two possible objectives in the Middle East. One plan would be to stage a false flag event in which Israel is blamed for attacking America. It could involve pinning blame on them for an old event like 9/11, or staging a new attack. This could lead to American retaliation against Israel. If I were the Islamic Antichrist President, I would be thrilled to attack the "little Satan" (as some Muslims view Israel) with the forces of the "great Satan" (as some Muslims view America.)

If this were not possible, I could at least put the bulk of America's forces in harm's way, purposefully making "bad" strategic decisions about the spread of the American military around the world – allowing so much destruction of American personnel and hardware that America might either stay out of WWIII, or require years to rebuild before making an effective entry.

Daniel 11:11 warns "The king of the South will be enraged and go forth and fight with the king of the North. Then the latter will raise a great multitude, but that multitude will be given into the hand of the former. When the multitude is carried away, his heart will be lifted up, and he will cause tens of thousands to fall; yet he will not prevail."

What if while in the Middle East, visiting the U.S. armies I command, I simply announce I have been Muslim all along? What if I claim to be the Mahdi, that I am about to betray and destroy Israel, and that the Islamic world should follow me into Jerusalem? If I said that side by side with even one major Islamic leader – if the leader of Iran, or Turkey, or Egypt, or Saudi Arabia stood at my side and agreed, what would happen? What if three or four of them stood by me? If a false flag event had already been blamed on Israel, what would American troops do? If New York had already been nuked and martial law had already been declared, the internet and news media could be severely compromised. Would Americans even necessarily know what was happening in the Middle East? Do many Americans even know the truth now?

If my policies worked, America could be defeated, or at least greatly weakened and neutralized – while a new Islamic Empire could arise, potentially conquering Israel and substantial parts of Europe and Africa. The Islamic world could position itself to be ready for global domination, if additional plans could manipulate China and Russia to fight each other – or if I knew that China and Russia were about to be decimated by a pole shift which will make their homelands largely uninhabitable.

Consider this possible timeline of events in June 2016:

June 3, exactly 1260 days into the final seven years, the extremely popular, savior-like politician who will soon be revealed as the Antichrist is in Jerusalem when there is an assassination attempt and he is shot in the head. This act may be blamed on the Jews.

June 4, forty days after Easter, is Ascension Day, when Jesus rose to heaven. Some will make an analogy to our apparently dying leader.

June 5, when according to Andrew Simmons, Mystery Babylon/New York is destroyed. This could also be blamed on the Jews.

June 6, the savior-like politician is miraculously revived, and from the Temple in Jerusalem he makes many bold and allegedly holy claims regarding who he is and what his new mission is.

Of course this is just an outrageous and fictional speculation.

I certainly hope I never see America destroyed from within by a president who is secretly Muslim and uses his office to help Islam dominate the world. It's not like Obama says anything like "my Muslim faith" that should make us wonder…. No statements like "America is not – and will never be – at war with Islam" or the Islamic State/Caliphate "is not Islamic." It would be wrong to take his words out of context and wonder what he thinks when he brings up "partnership between America and Islam." Even if just fighting negative stereotypes, I find it interesting that he describes the conditions under which "I will stand with the Muslims."[387]

Getting back to the reality of what the Bible tells us – the prophet Daniel describes three historical empires that dominated the Middle East: The Babylonian, Persian, and Greek Empires. Daniel 2:40 warns: "Then there will be a fourth kingdom as strong as iron; inasmuch as iron crushes and shatters all things, so, like iron that breaks in pieces, it will crush and break all these in pieces." "All these." The fourth empire crushes all three of the previous empires. Rome cannot be Daniel's fourth empire. But "the historical Islamic Caliphate fully, absolutely, completely conquered all the lands of the others."[388] "The Roman Empire does not sufficiently meet the criteria of the fourth-kingdom text, whereas the Islamic Caliphate fulfills all of the criteria perfectly."[389] A revived Islamic Caliphate is the most likely fulfillment of Daniel's prophecies – no matter who helps lead it.

The second chapter of Daniel focuses on Daniel's interpretation of a dream that had confused Babylon's King Nebuchadnezzar. The dream involved a statue with a gold head, silver abdomen, bronze legs, and feet of iron mixed with clay. Daniel interpreted these as a succession of empires, the last of which would be internally divided, as described in Daniel 2:43 "And in that you saw the iron mixed with common clay, they will combine with one another in the seed of men; but they will not adhere to one another, even as iron does not combine with pottery." I would not be the first to point out that the Islamic world is divided between hard-line Shiites and more moderate Sunnis; or that the Hebrew word for "mixed" is "עֲרָב" (ar-ab')[390] and this may very well refer to Arabs and the revived Islamic Caliphate.

Daniel 7:24 says "The fourth beast will be a fourth kingdom on the earth, which will be different from all the other kingdoms and will devour the whole earth and tread it down and crush it." This fourth empire not only dominates the world much more completely, but it will be inherently different from the other kingdoms before it. I suggest the difference is that it is a religious empire. Daniel 7:25 "As for the ten horns, out of this kingdom ten kings will arise; and another will arise after them, and he will be different from the previous ones and will subdue three kings." I have previously suggested the possibility that Obama may fulfill this description as the eleventh and very different leader of Postwar America... and he has already overthrown the "kings" of Egypt and Libya as of 2014.

E.W. Bullinger tells us "If ten is the number which marks the perfection of Divine order, then eleven is an addition to it, subversive of and undoing that order. If twelve is the number which marks the perfection of Divine government, then eleven falls short of it. So that whether we regard it as being 10 + 1, or 12 - 1, it is the number which marks disorder, disorganization, imperfection, and disintegration."[391]   I certainly would not rule Obama out, as this is not a bad description of his presidency and he is the 11th leader of Postwar America. But it is also possible that America and its leader are not the eleventh kingdom and king; or that like so many other verses, this prophecy has multiple fulfillments – and that the ten kings within the kingdom of the fourth empire represent many Islamic nations within a new Islamic Caliphate.

Revelation 17:10-11 also describes several empires, but this time there are eight of them, and the eighth appears to be described as a revived form of one of the seven: "they are seven kings; five have fallen, one is, the other has not yet come; and when he comes, he must remain a little while. The beast which was and is not, is himself also an eighth and is one of the seven, and he goes to destruction." These first five of these eight empires had already fallen by the time this was written in the first century: the Egyptian, Assyrian, Babylonian, Persian, and Greek Empires were already gone. "One is" – meaning that empire was in existence when John had his revelation – this of course would be the Roman Empire. "The other has not yet come" because Muhammad had not yet established the Islamic religion. The Islamic Caliphate remained a while, and could be interpreted to be revived and reestablished in the end times as the kingdom of the beast that is "also an eighth and is one of the seven." It is no coincidence that a new Islamic Caliphate was just recreated in 2014.

Some people describe a Roman interpretation of these passages. They ignore Rome's failure to conquer Babylon and Persia and focus on the idea that some kind of European Union will be a revived form of the Roman Empire. They also point to Daniel 9:26, which tells us that "the people of the prince who is to come will destroy the city and the sanctuary." This passage makes many think the people who eventually come to destroy Jerusalem and the Temple in the end times are Romans, because the prince who came in 70 A.D. was Roman.

But what they don't recognize is that the men serving under Titus – "the people" – included very few men who were Italian or even European. Roman army soldiers were largely provincial, especially in the eastern half of the empire. The Roman historian Tacitus said Judea was attacked by Rome's 5th, 10th, and 15th divisions. Titus recruited most of them near Judea. The 12th division also came from Syria, along with some from the 18th and 3rd divisions in Egypt, and we are also told that Titus "was accompanied... by a strong contingent of Arabs, who hated the Jews with the usual hatred of neighbors."[392]   According to the Jewish historian Josephus, Titus came through Syria "with a considerable number of auxiliaries from the kings in that neighborhood" and his three main legions were gathered from Syria. Josephus also wrote that 6,000 men were from Malchus, king of Arabia, which made 60,000 men all together – mostly from Syria and Arabia.[393]

Much like in America, where blacks and Hispanics were rare amongst the mostly white soldiers of WWII, but had become the majority two generations later – the Roman army also experienced a huge demographic shift in the first century. To quote a few historians familiar with the Roman army: we are told that by 68 A.D. Roman troops in the east were "almost exclusively of provincials"[394] and that by the year 70 A.D., only about twenty per cent of the entire empire's army was Italian. "Legions of the East consisted largely of 'orientals'" and "legions long stationed in the East contained a very high proportion of men born in the eastern provinces."[395]   "Legions based in Cappadocia, Syria, and Egypt were made up almost entirely of recruits from Asia Minor, Syria, and Egypt."[396]   Only about one man out of twelve in the eastern legions that sacked Jerusalem under Titus were from the western part of the Roman Empire such as Italia, Gaul, or Spain.[397]   It seems clear that "the people" of the prince mentioned in Daniel 9:26 were mostly of Arabs.

Many believe "the lineage of Antichrist is hidden – or rather revealed – through 'the people of the prince.'"[398]   It could be argued that both through some Arab ancestors and through support of the religion of the Arab people, an American president could be "the prince" in question. The analogy to Titus may be even stronger if the prince himself is not from the Middle East.

Daniel 9:26-27 seems to indicate that a prince of these people will come again in the end times to make and break a seven year covenant with the Jews: "the people of the prince who is to come will destroy the city and the sanctuary. And its end will come with a flood; even to the end there will be war; desolations are determined. And he will make a firm covenant with the many for one week, but in the middle of the week he will put a stop to sacrifice and grain offering; and on the wing of abominations will come one who makes desolate, even until a complete destruction." This prince who is to come is apparently the Antichrist, leading the Arab or Muslim world.

As for breaking the covenant: Muslims have a tradition called "Hudna" which dates back to Muhammad. In a commentary on the Qu'ran Surah 9:5 on this subject, Ad-Dahhak bin Muzahim said, "It abrogated every agreement of peace between the Prophet and any idolator, EVERY TREATY, AND EVERY TERM."[399] Hudna is the concept that a treaty with infidels does not have to be honored – meaning that when Muslims make a legal agreement with Jews, Hindus, Christians, etc. – they are not obliged to honor it.

But Ibn Kathir suggests to fellow Muslims in his book, Tafsir: "Take not the Jews and Christians as friends... We smile in the face of some people although our hearts curse them...."[400] Which itself is based on the Qu'ran, Surah 3:28 "Let not the Believers take the Unbelievers as friends."

Muslim philosopher Ibn Taymiyah, in his book: The Sword on the Neck of the Accuser of Muhammad, tells Muslims: "Believers should lie to the People of the Book to protect their lives and their religion."[401] Under Islamic Sharia Law, it is an acceptable tactic to make peace agreements with such enemies from a position of weakness, use the time of peace to prepare for war, and break the agreement when convenient. The first example may be the ten year peace agreement Muhammad made with the citizens of Medina. Within a few years he gained more followers and took Medina by force. This tradition of breaking agreements will be completely acceptable to the Muslim followers of the Antichrist when he breaks the seven year covenant with Israel halfway through. A false flag event blaming Israel for attacking America could even justify it to the American people – if they are made to think Israel violated the covenant of peace first.

But how does the Antichrist convince people to offer worship when he enters the Temple in Jerusalem, sitting in place of God? Many Christians have assumed there must be a new religion centered on worship of the Antichrist. But what if the religion already exists, and the Antichrist is merely claiming to be Allah's representative on earth? Catholics kiss the pope's ring and kneel before him for approval, treating the pope as God's representative on earth. The Muslims' duties to obey their Caliph will just be more extreme.

Joel Richardson writes: "The coming of Jesus the Jewish Messiah bears many striking resemblances to the coming Antichrist of Islam... the Bible's Antichrist bears numerous striking commonalities with the primary messiah figure of Islam, who Muslims call the Mahdi. In other words, our Messiah is their antichrist and our Antichrist is their messiah.... Islam teaches that when Jesus returns, He will come back as a Muslim prophet whose primary mission will be to abolish Christianity."[402] Perry Stone agrees that "The Antichrist will claim the Islamic religion as his religion and will proclaim himself – and be received as – Islam's final awaited 'messiah.'"[403] Tim

LaHaye describes "Satan's persecution of the Church [and] his propagation of Islam."[404]   John Preacher suggests that "Christianity and Islam are diametrically opposed to each other.   All the claims made by one are completely denied and contradicted by the other which means one of them is not just 'misguided' but WRONG. One is of God and the other the Devil."[405]

Daniel 11:37 says of the Antichrist: "He will show no regard for the gods of his fathers or for the desire of women." One way to view not regarding the desires of women is to note the subservient role of women under Islamic Sharia Law and assume the Antichrist follows Sharia Law regarding the role of women. Winston Churchill said in his book The River War in 1899: "The fact that in Mohammedan law every woman must belong to some man as his absolute property, either as a child, a wife, or a concubine, must delay the final extinction of slavery until the faith of Islam has ceased to be a great power among men."[406]   One might hope this has changed since 1899, but I see many signs that it has not. The evidence shows that in many Muslim nations women still have few rights by western standards.

In the Islamic Republic of Iran, a fundamentalist theocracy was established through a revolution in 1979. "Ayatollah Khomeini severely curtailed rights that women had become accustomed to under the shah.... women were barred from becoming judges... the legal age of marriage for girls was reduced to 9... women were barred from attending regular schools... The Islamic revolution is ideologically committed to inequality for women."[407] In Afghanistan, "Immediately after coming into power, the Taliban declared that women were forbidden to go to work and they were not to leave their homes unless accompanied by a male family member. When they did go out it was required that they had to wear an all-covering burqa. Under these restrictions, women were denied formal education... During the Taliban's five-year rule, women in Afghanistan were essentially put under house arrest. Some women who once held respectable positions were forced to wander the streets in their burqas selling everything they owned or begging in order to survive... for several reasons, it was difficult for women to seek medical attention. It was extremely frowned upon for women to need to go to a hospital, and those who did try to go to a hospital were usually beaten."[408]

Those examples seem tame when we consider "Female genital mutilation (FGM), also known as female genital cutting and female circumcision," is the practice (prevalent in the Islamic world) of complete or partial circumcision of female genetalia including the clitoris. It is perhaps the most extreme method of sexually controlling women – by denying the possibility of sexual pleasure…. It is typically carried out, with or without anaesthesia, by a traditional circumciser using a knife or razor. The age of the girls varies from weeks after birth to puberty."[409]   This practice isn't going away in the 21st century – it's spreading with Muslim immigration into Europe and America. "School health services in the small Swedish city of Norrköping have found 60 cases of female genital mutilation (FGM) among schoolgirls since March, [2014] with evidence of mutilation found in all 30 girls in one class, 28 of the most severe form."[410]   The "desire of women" has been eliminated in this way for an estimated 125 million Muslim women today.

But the inferior role of women under Islamic Law is not the only possible interpretation of Daniel's comment on not regarding "the desire of women:" this was a common Jewish phrase of the era Daniel wrote in, and would have once been understood to mean the desire to be the mother of the Messiah. Not having regard for this desire could mean the Antichrist rejects the concept of the Father and the Son – or Christianity. Qu'ran Surah 3:151 says "We cast terror into the hearts of the Unbelievers, for that they joined companions with Allah, for which He had sent no authority." John 16:2-3 warns "an hour is coming for everyone who kills you to think that he is offering service to God. These things they will do because they have not known the Father or Me."

Denying that Jesus is God's Son is a central tenet of Islam. Islam emphasizes that Jesus was merely one of the prophets, that His teachings have been warped and misunderstood, and that Muhammad was greater. Qu'ran Surah 2:191 commands – regarding unbelievers like Jews and Christians – "kill them wherever you find them." Surah 5:33 says "The punishment of those who wage war against Allah and His messenger and strive to make mischief in the land is only this, that they should be murdered or crucified or their hands and their feet should be cut off on opposite sides." Surah 8:12 "I will cast terror into the hearts of those who disbelieve. Therefore strike off their heads and strike off every fingertip of them." Surah 9:5 "slay the idolaters wherever you find them." Surah 9:29 "Fight those who believe not in Allah." Surah 9:30 "the Christians say: The Messiah is the son of Allah; these are the words of their mouths; they imitate the saying of those who disbelieved before; may Allah destroy them." These are just some of the many violent quotes from the first ten chapters of the Qu'ran (which has 114 chapters.)

Should anyone assume this is ancient history and that Muslims would not act this way today, I would suggest that they talk to the Kurdish Yazidi people of northern Iraq. Because their religious beliefs have unusual elements which most Muslims misunderstand and view as non-Islamic or even devil-worship, the Yazidi people have repeatedly been persecuted and are suffering again as I write. In August 2014 there are reports of the Islamic State rounding up hundreds of Yazidi women and selling them as slaves. "The militants are keeping hundreds of Yazidi, Christian, and Turkoman women in Mosul's Badush prison, gang-raping some and selling others as brides for as low as $25."[411] Tunisia's main newspaper has also reported on the enslavement of women and also the forced mass circumcision of hundreds of Yazidi and Christian men with crude knives and no anesthesia.[412] I assume these must be effective ways to convince unwanted portions of the local population to leave. Even worse are the mass executions, often by burying people alive. The Yazidi leader has asked for Western help to defend themselves against this "purification" or what we would call genocide.

This is no surprise, if we go back to the Book of Genesis and understand how God described the Arab descendants of Ishmael, the son Abraham had with Hagar. Genesis 16:11-12 "you will bear a son; and you shall call his name Ishmael, because the Lord has given heed to your affliction. He will be a wild donkey of a man, his hand will be against everyone, and everyone's hand will be against him." I would guess that most Arabs would prefer not to dwell on that description, and instead focus on the promise in Genesis 16:10 "I will greatly multiply your descendants so that they will be too many to count." Most Arabs probably also disagree with the biblical premise that the Jews, the descendants of Isaac, have the rights to the land of Canaan (modern Israel) and that Genesis 16:12 suggests the Arab descendants of Ishmael will only have rights outside of Israel "to the east of all his brothers." Especially in the minds of many of the descendants of Ishmael, there is some unfinished business with the descendants of Isaac over the land of Israel.

As I am finishing this book in 2014, Palestinian rockets are being launched into Israel from Gaza, and the Israelis are retaliating against Gaza. Israel's Iron Dome, and the Israeli Defense Forces in general, seem to be doing a good job defending Israelis from Hamas' rocket attacks. But an alleged CNN interview with a representative of Hamas suggests God is intervening on Israel's behalf. The "Hamas representative allegedly claimed that Hamas rockets are extremely accurate and that "80%" of the rockets Hamas fires are diverted to uninhabited areas by the god of Jews."[413] Despite thousands of rockets being launched into Israel, casualties are almost non-existent. I can't help but think of Ezekiel 39:3-6 when God says to those attacking Israel: "I will strike your bow from your left hand and dash down your arrows from your right hand.... And I will send fire upon Magog and those who inhabit the coastlands in safety; and they will know that I am the Lord."

"Their God changes the path of our rockets in mid-air, said a terrorist," was the headline in the July 18 edition of the <u>Jewish Telegraph</u>. A more credible article has a far better story: "More claims of divine intervention are being reported in the ongoing conflict between Israel and Hamas, with an operator of Israel's Iron Dome missile-defense system saying he personally witnessed "the hand of God" diverting an incoming rocket out of harm's way.... The commander recalled: 'A missile was fired from Gaza. Iron Dome precisely calculated [its trajectory]. We know where these missiles are going to land down to a radius of 200 meters. This particular missile was going to hit either the Azrieli Towers, the Kirya (Israel's equivalent of the Pentagon) or [a central Tel Aviv railway station]. Hundreds could have died. We fired the first [interceptor]. It missed. Second [interceptor]. It missed. This is very rare. I was in shock. At this point we had just four seconds until the missile lands. We had already notified emergency services to converge on the target location and had warned of a mass-casualty incident. Suddenly, Iron Dome (which calculates wind speeds, among other things) shows a major wind coming from the east, a strong wind that ... sends the missile into the sea. We were all stunned. I stood up and shouted, 'There is a God!' I witnessed this miracle with my own eyes. It was not told or reported to me. I saw the hand of God send that missile into the sea."[414]

President Obama, of course, would not have us focus on Islamic terrorism. He does not describe Islamic views on war or subduing enemies. Obama tells us a different story, that Islam is "a religion of peace." On June 4, 2009 he said "Islam is not part of the problem in combating violent extremism; it is an important part of promoting peace." He has also said "Islam has a proud tradition of tolerance" and that "throughout history, Islam has demonstrated through words and deeds the possibilities of religious tolerance."[415]

Ayatollah Ibrahim Amini says "The Mahdi will offer the religion of Islam to the Jews and Christians, if they accept it they will be spared, otherwise they will be killed."[416] Revelation 12:17 warns us "the dragon was enraged with the woman, and went off to make war with the rest of her children, who keep the commandments of God and hold to the testimony of Jesus." There will be little sympathy for the Jews in the Muslim world. Hatred may be blamed on recent grievances or some future Israeli activity against Iranians or Palestinians but the animosity already has a long heritage.

Even before the 1967 war in which Israel captured the lands now claimed by Palestinians, Syria's "Voice of the Arabs" radio station called for "the extermination of Zionist existence." (5/18/67) Egypt's Presdent Nasser said "We will not accept any... coexistence with Israel." (5/27/67) Iraqi President Abdur Rahman Aref said "The existence of Israel is an error which must be rectified... Our goal is clear – to wipe Israel off the map." (5/30/67)[417] We still see the same type of comments today. In a video which was translated into English in January 2013, the internet was full of comments after we learned that Egyptian President Morsi referred to "Zionists" as "bloodsuckers who attack Palestinians" as well as calling Jews "the descendants of apes and pigs." Of course he is just quoting the Qu'ran, which calls the Jews "apes and pigs" in Surah 5:60. (They are just "apes" in Surah 2:65 and Surah 7:166.)

Egypt's "Sheikh Mohammed Badie, chairman of the MB, [Muslim Brotherhood] signaled his movement's intentions, calling for a 'jihad for the recovery of Jerusalem,' and described religious warfare against Israel as a 'duty for all Muslims.' Badie's comments underscored the disappointing fact that, unlike the old Mubarak regime that was a cornerstone of regional stability, the new Islamist-governed Egypt opposes peace with Israel and is joining the rejectionist camp of the region's fundamentalist forces, promoting unending hostilities, and seemingly seeking to lead the radical bloc. By issuing calls for jihad, Badie has taken Egypt a step closer toward adopting, as Egypt's foreign policy, Hamas and its ideology."[418] This should not surprise anyone who is awake: Hamas is basically the Palestinian branch of the Egyptian Muslim Brotherhood, as stated in the Hamas charter.

"At a Muslim Brotherhood election rally held earlier this year, an event attended by Mohammed Morsi shortly before he became president, a cleric hailed the Brotherhood's candidate as a leader who would work to ensure that 'our capital shall not be Cairo, Mecca, or Medina. It shall, Allah willing, be Jerusalem. Our cry shall be: Millions of martyrs march toward Jerusalem.' As Morsi looked on smilingly, the cleric told the crowds that, 'We can see how the dream of the Islamic Caliphate is being realized, Allah willing, by Dr. Muhammad Morsi and his brothers, his supporters, and his political party. We can see how the great dream, shared by us all -- that of the United States of Arabs ...shall, Allah willing, be restored.'"[419]

The United States of Arabs may be coming in the form of the new Islamic Caliphate. Lest anyone assume someone else is putting words in Morsi's mouth, and that he is not an extremist, here are some of Morsi's own words from a speech on May 13, 2012: "'The Koran [Qu'ran] is our constitution, the Prophet is our leader, jihad is our path and death in the name of Allah is our goal... Today Egypt is close as never before to the triumph of Islam at all the state levels,' he said. 'Today we can establish Sharia law because our nation will acquire well-being only with Islam and Sharia.'"[420] This from a "moderate" leader the Americans groomed for power during (and after) his education at USC. Many other "reasonable" and "moderate" leaders have been swept into power since the "Arab Spring" was orchestrated by American intelligence agencies... Israel is under constant threat by next door neighbors that hope to conquer it and wipe it off the map.

But God will deal with the enemies of Israel. "The most emphasized basis for the judgment of God's people" is hating Israel.[421] In Genesis 12:3 God told the Jewish people: "I will bless those who bless you, and the one who curses you I will curse." Ezekiel 35:5-6 says "'Because you have had everlasting enmity and have delivered the sons of Israel to the power of the sword at the time of their calamity, at the time of the punishment of the end, therefore as I live,' declares the Lord God, 'I will give you over to bloodshed, and bloodshed will pursue you; since you have not hated bloodshed, therefore bloodshed will pursue you.'" Which nations are specifically mentioned in the Bible? "The nations that the Scriptures identify as marked for judgment are Islamic."[422] Egypt, Sudan, Libya, Turkey, Arabia, Syria, Iraq, Lebanon, Iran (Persia), and Sudan (though the Greeks called it Ethiopia) are all mentioned in verses like Ezekiel 30:1-5, Zephaniah 2:3-13, and Ezekiel 38:5. I have also read a few articles claiming that Obama "hates Israel."[423]

Gog and Magog, along with Meschech and Tubal, were sometimes mistakenly attributed to Russia by well-meaning anti-communists... But Gog is from the Lydian Gyges in western Turkey, and generally refers to invaders from the north (from Turkey.)[424] Every Bible Atlas puts Meschech and Tubal in Turkey. Pliny the Elder said the city of Hieropolis on the modern border of Turkey and Syria is Magog, though Maimonides placed it slightly further into Syria.[425] Turkey had been an ally of Israel, largely because the Turks were scared of the Russians and allied with America – and its allies like Israel. But Turkey – the most moderate and non-religious Muslim nation – has changed tremendously in the last ten to twenty years. The Turks tried to join the European Union; and when the Europeans didn't want them, Turkey shifted its search for friends to the Islamic world. There has been a huge Islamic revival in once secular Turkey. As one modern Turkish poem says: "Mosques are our barracks, domes our helmets, minarets our bayonets, believers our soldiers. This holy army guards my religion. Almighty, our journey is our destiny, the end is martyrdom."

This sounds like something Osama bin Laden might have said. But the poem was written by Turkey's President Erdogan, who also said: "Democracy is like a streetcar. You ride it until you arrive at your destination and then you get off."[426] I worry that for Turkey – the former home of the Caliphate, and Gog, and Satan's throne – the destination is fundamentalist Islam and a revived Islamic Caliphate.

Ammon, Edom, and Moab all refer to the nation of Jordan, which also suffers wrath in end times prophecies such as Jeremiah 49:1-33, Psalm 83:6, or especially Isaiah 63:1-4 "Who is this who comes from Edom, with garments of glowing colors from Bozrah, [Petra] this One who is majestic in His apparel, marching in the greatness of His strength? 'It is I who speak in righteousness, mighty to save.' 'Why is Your apparel red, and Your garments like the one who treads in the wine press?' 'I have trodden the wine trough alone, and from the peoples there was no man with Me. I also trod them in My anger and trampled them in My wrath; and their lifeblood is sprinkled on My garments, and I stained all My raiment. For the day of vengeance was in My heart, and My year of redemption has come.'" When Jesus returns to Jerusalem, he will already be stained with blood from slaying enemies in Jordan.

Ezekiel 28:24 "And there will be no more for the house of Israel a prickling brier or a painful thorn from any round about them who scorned them; then they will know that I am the Lord God." Eventually, none of the Islamic nations surrounding Israel will pester her anymore.

Islamic fundamentalists have been known to kill Jews and Christians in the name of Allah. Muslims, of course, believe Allah is God and Islam is the true religion. Others have suggested that the same Draco constellation that symbolizes Satan also is represented by "laam" (the Arabic letter "L") and the name "Allah." They suggest that it was not the Archangel Gabriel who intimidated Muhammad into writing the Qu'ran, but an evil spirit – just as Sunni Muslims claim Muhammad assumed at the time. Daniel 11:38 says the Antichrist "will honor a god of fortresses, a god whom his fathers did not know." Allah is a god of war, a god of fortresses, promoting "Jihad" or holy war against the non-Muslim world. As John Preacher puts it: "Antichrist-Mahdi will also be possessed by Satan-Allah."[427]

There is still the problem of the Antichrist demanding our worship from the Temple in Jerusalem. Muslims would not worship a man as if he were God – they are even less likely to do so than Christians are. But the Greek word "proskyneo" may not mean worship, so much as submission, respect, reverence, and acknowledgement. We may once again have been slightly misled by focusing our attention on the only translation we know – in English. If "proskyneo" is properly translated, Richardson argues, such "worship" could be like the "bay'ah" – the Muslim pledge of allegiance to any Caliph, punishable by death if refused. Taking an oath of loyalty to the Islamic Caliph/Mahdi/Antichrist while worshipping Allah or Satan would be fully in line with the Bible on this issue.[428]

Since the Antichrist appears to honor this god of fortresses, (Allah) he might not quite be proclaiming to be God, when he desecrates the Temple, which is God's seat. He may merely be suggesting that he does not think the God worshipped by Jews, known as Yahweh, even exists. He certainly will not acknowledge Jesus Christ as the Son of God.

In fact, Muslims expect Jesus to return in the end times and help lead the battle for the Islamic world against the followers of Christianity. Muslims expect Jesus to descend into Damascus, proclaim the glory of Islam, and explain how the teachings from his time on earth when he visited as a prophet (not God's Son) two thousand years earlier have been warped and misunderstood by Christians. Isa, (Muslim Jesus) will denounce Christianity and call all the people of the world to submit to Allah under the banner of Islam. In the Qu'ran, Surah 4:159 says "on the day of Resurrection he will be a witness against them."

In fact, Isa must be in Jerusalem several years before the day of Resurrection. "Part of Satan's strategy is that when the real Jesus returns there will already be a worldwide religious leader claiming to be Jesus."[429] I expect that in 2019, Muslims will accuse the real Jesus of being the Dajjal – the Muslim Antichrist – especially if Jews accept Him as their Messiah. They expect the Dajjal to be Jewish. (Some Muslims also expect him to have the word "infidel" on his forehead, but this word will be seen only by Muslims and will be invisible to infidels like Christians.) Muslims believe when Isa (Muslim Jesus) returns (in 2016?) he will proclaim Christianity has been perverted, that Islam is the true religion, that He was never crucified, that He was not the Son of God, that He will kill swine (Jews) and break crosses (dismantle Christianity), eliminate the jizyah tax on non-Muslims (because no non-Muslims will be allowed to live) and kill the Dajjal (the Muslim's

Antichrist, quite possibly the Christian and Jewish Messiah) and his followers. I can't emphasize enough that while Muslims do acknowledge Jesus, they believe in a different kind of Jesus – a genocidal killer of billions who will be an Islamic evangelist and establish Sharia Law over the earth. As Abdulaziz Abdulhussein Sachedina says in <u>Islamic Messianism,</u> "He [Jesus] will kill the swine, break the cross, and kill all the Christians."[430]

Muslims believe Jesus will, 21 years after descending to earth, marry and have children, live 19 more years, then be buried next to Muhammad. If Muslims believe Allah wants Jesus (and all other Muslims) to kill Jews and Christians in the end times, then John 16:2 makes sense: "an hour is coming for everyone who kills you to think that he is offering service to God." How are they likely to be killed? Beheadings are mentioned specifically in Revelation 20:4 "I saw the souls of those who had been beheaded because of their testimony of Jesus and because of the word of God, and those who had not worshipped the beast or his image, and had not received the mark on their forehead and on their hand."

Beheadings have been a common form of punishment in Arabia even before Muhammad. Islam adopted the practice and spread it through the Muslim world. After an early battle near Mecca, when the city sent an army against Muhammad to stop his caravan raids, Muhammad defeated the forces from Mecca. After the battle, his lieutenant Abdullah hacked off the head of the still living enemy Abba Hakam "the father of wisdom" and took Hakam's head to cast at Muhammad 's feet. "'It is more acceptable to me,' cried Muhammad, hardly able to contain his joy, 'than the choicest camel in all Arabia.'"[431]   In 627 A.D., Muhammad oversaw approximately 600-900 beheadings after the Jewish village of Qurayzah had surrendered.

Muhammad's successor, Abu Bakr, was the first "rightly Guided Caliph." He sent a message to every foreign leader he could, from nearby tribal chiefs to the Pope in Rome and perhaps even to the Emperor of China, "inviting" them to join Islam and threatening them with the wrath of "a people who love death just as you love drinking wine" if they fail to submit to Islam. Persians and Christians in the nearby village of Ullays were among the first to refuse this offer, which leads to the story of "The Blood Canal" where captives were beheaded non-stop for several days until the desert sand held so much human blood that it could not absorb any more.[432]

There are still beheadings in the Islamic world in modern times. Afghani warriors beheaded thousands of British soldiers in the 1800s, and an estimated 3,000 Soviet troops in the 1980s;[433] the United States simply chooses to hide the beheadings of American troops in Afghanistan by not reporting them. (Some have been reported by private contractors.) There are other recent examples of beheadings in Pakistan, Algeria, Iran, and Borneo. Saudi Arabia has beheaded 19 people just in August 2014, about half of them for non-violent crimes and some with "confessions" obtained by torture.[434] American journalist James Foley had his beheading filmed by the new Caliphate/the Islamic State on August 19, 2014. (Many Muslims believe 19 is a number with special significance to Islam and demons.) As the Qu'ran's Surah 47:4 says: "When ye encounter the infidels, strike off their heads." Such executioners may rightly be described as beasts.

The Antichrist, the first and main "beast," (coming before a second and lesser beast – the False Prophet) is described in Revelation 13:1 as "a beast coming up out of the sea." Some interpret this to mean he is from the "sea" of non-Jewish, gentile people of the world. But if this is the correct interpretation, then the second beast, the False Prophet, would apparently be Jewish, for in Revelation 13:11 there is "another beast coming up out of the earth." I have a different interpretation. I suspect the Antichrist comes from a land far away from Israel, from a land across the sea, like the Americas or Australia. The False Prophet is much more local, from the Middle East. But there is yet another way to interpret this: that people think he literally comes up out of the earth.

Muslim tradition tells us that the Mahdi is the 12th descendant of Muhammad (leading to the alternate name – the Twelfth Imam) and some believe that he fell into a well at the age of five and has been supernaturally held by Allah in this well deep in the earth, from which he will ascend (or by now, has ascended) for the final seven years. This is reminiscent of Revelation 17:8 "The beast that you saw was, and is not, and is about to come up out of the abyss and go to destruction. And those who dwell on the earth, whose name has not been written in the book of life from the foundation of the world, will wonder when they see the beast, that he was and is not and will come."

There are interesting references to something similar in the Book of Enoch. Enoch did not make the final version of the Bible we know, but should we care to listen, 1 Enoch 10:4 tells us that the fallen angel Azazel is imprisoned in a well in the desert. 1 Enoch 8:1-3 also says: "Bind Azazel by his hands and his feet, and throw him into the darkness. And split open the desert which is in Dudael, and throw him there. And throw on him jagged and sharp stones, and cover him with darkness; and let him stay there forever." This seems to have occurred at the last pole shift, so the fallen angel Azazel may simply be a man-like constellation which "fell out of heaven" into the skies of the southern hemisphere. 1 Enoch 10:7-8 says "And restore the earth which the angels have ruined, and announce the restoration of the earth, for I shall restore the earth, so that not all the sons of men shall be destroyed through the mystery of everything which the Watchers made known and taught to their sons. And the whole earth has been ruined by the teaching of the works of Azazel, and against him write down all sin." "Several additional references to Azazel also appear in 1 Enoch. However, they all describe him as fulfilling the role of a fallen archangel, intent on deceiving the human race. Thus 1 Enoch confirms the fact that 'Azazel' was understood in demonic terms by a segment of Jewish apocalypticists."[435]

In summary, Azazel is associated with being a demon or fallen angel, and a kind of scapegoat for sins, who was cast down into an abyss or cave or well in the desert just after a destruction and restoration of the earth, which has end times connotations.[436] If the Madhi has been has been supernaturally held in a well in the desert, Christian traditions do not offer much hope about his true nature. Even Islamic commentary on this is scary. In the Qu'ran, Surah 27:82 says "And when the word is fulfilled concerning them, we shall bring forth a beast of the earth to speak unto them because mankind had not faith in Our revelations."

Christians will undoubtedly view such men as the Antichrist or the False Prophet. When the man Muslims recognize as Jesus/Isa arrives, he will say he is Jesus, but he will not be the Jesus Christians know. Muslims have been told that Isa will have the power to make fire come down (nuclear war?) from the sky and Christians know the False Prophet will perform such miracles. Revelation 13:11-14 warns us that after the Antichrist comes "Then I saw another beast coming up out of the earth; and he had two horns like a lamb and he spoke as a dragon. He exercises all the authority of the first beast in his presence. And he makes the earth and those who dwell in it to worship the first beast, whose fatal wound was healed. He performs great signs, so that he even makes fire come down out of heaven to the earth in the presence of men. And he deceives those who dwell on the earth because of the signs which it was given him to perform in the presence of the beast, telling those who dwell on the earth to make an image to the beast who had the wound of the sword and has come to life."

Revelation 13:11 tells us that the False Prophet was "like a lamb" which

probably indicates an imitation of Jesus – but "he spoke as a dragon" –
perhaps meaning that he supports Islam and denounces Christianity. Isa/The
False Prophet will probably stand in the Temple denouncing Christianity,
right next to the Antichrist as he mocks the God of the religions he does not
take seriously. The Antichrist may not claim to be God, but may merely
assert that as Allah's representative he is superior, or more powerful, than the
apparently non-existent god who didn't defend the Temple Jews had briefly
worshipped at.

Abduallrahman Kelani, author of <u>The Last Apocalypse</u>, tells us that the
"Mahdi will receive a pledge of allegiance as a caliph for Muslims. He will
lead Muslims into many battles of jihad. His reign will be a caliphate that
follows the guidance of the Prophet. Many battles will ensue between
Muslims and the disbelievers."[437] It is foretold that the Mahdi will ride a
white horse, be a religious and political and military leader, rule for seven
years, rule from Jerusalem, be granted supernatural powers from Allah over
wind and rain, and be involved with a seven year peace agreement with the
progeny of Aaron – probably indicating the Jewish priesthood and a deal
involving the Third Temple.[438] This sounds very similar to the Christian
Antichrist. The Mahdi is preceded by an army from the East carrying black
flags or banners of war from the region of Khurasan in Iran. The Mahdi will
take over this army and use it to conquer Israel. We know from Bible
prophecy there must be an upcoming war between Israel and her neighbors,
as described in Ezekiel 38-39, Psalm 83, Revelation, Daniel, and very
specifically in Isaiah 17:1-4:

"'Behold, Damascus is about to be removed from being a city and will
become a fallen ruin…. The fortified city will disappear from Ephraim, and
sovereignty from Damascus and the remnant of Aram; they will be like the
glory of the sons of Israel,' declares the Lord of hosts. Now in that day the
glory of Jacob will fade, and the fatness of his flesh will become lean." This
seems to indicate that Israel wins a pyrrhic victory over Syria, destroying its
capital (Damascus) but not without some devastation in Israel – as "the glory
of Jacob will fade." Israel either suffers destruction from bombs, or perhaps
this merely refers to suffering under the rule of the Antichrist.

All of Daniel 11 talks about war in the Middle East, but whether or not the
events take place in the distant past or the future – is hard to say for certain.
Daniel 11:1 starts off talking about "the first year of Darius the Mede" as
King of Persia, fighting the Greeks. This is obviously about events over
2500 years ago. But by Daniel 11:21 we read about someone fitting the

description of a future Antichrist, "a despicable person will arise… the prince of the covenant." Daniel 11:40 starts off "At the end time" before continuing to describe events with the same key players as earlier verses. It seems like there are wars with some evil leader against the King of the North, King of the South, the Ships of Kittim, (the West) Egypt, and several other enemies, also "rumors from the East" that upset him. He enters the beautiful land, (Israel) and many nations fall. Daniel 11 ends with "He will pitch the tents of his royal pavilion between the seas and the beautiful Holy Mountain; yet he will come to his end, and no one will help him." It sounds like he is encamped with his forces between Jerusalem and the sea, perhaps near Har Meggido (Armageddon.) Zechariah 14:2 also warns us "For I will gather all the nations against Jerusalem to battle, and the city will be captured, the houses plundered, the women ravished and half of the city exiled." The entire Middle East will be at war – maybe the entire world. A war with most or all Islamic nations on one side, and most or all Christian nations on the other side – will probably draw in almost every nation in the Americas and Europe (including Russia) and probably China and most of Asia as well. Will history call it World War III, or Armageddon, or the Apocalypse?

Daniel 12:1-4 continues where Daniel 11 ends – and is clearly describing the last of the end times: "Now at that time Michael, the great prince who stands guard over the sons of your people, will arise. And there will be a time of distress such as never occurred since there was a nation until that time; and at that time your people, everyone who is found written in the book, will be rescued. Many of those who sleep in the dust of the ground will awake, these to everlasting life, but the others to disgrace and everlasting contempt. Those who have insight will shine brightly like the brightness of the expanse of heaven, and those who lead the many to righteousness, like the stars forever and ever. But as for you, Daniel, conceal these words and seal up the book until the end of time."

Many will not be faithful to God, they will succumb to the threats of the Antichrist, and their names are not written in the book of everlasting life. A small number will remain faithful, as described by those who would pray in Psalm 5:2 "Heed the sound of my cry for help, my King and my God, for to You I pray." Most will yield to the pressure of the Antichrist to take his mark to buy and sell, and to worship him. Michael will help the faithful few. Billions of others will be killed. The faithful of Israel will finally resist the Antichrist, but it will be Jesus Christ who defeats him. Ezekiel 21:25 says: "Wicked one, the prince of Israel, whose day has come, in the time of the punishment of the end,' thus says the Lord God, 'Remove the turban and take off the crown.'" The Antichrist will be removed from his position of religious and political authority over many nations. In the King James Bible, Ezekiel 21:27 continues "I will overturn, overturn, overturn, it: and it shall be no more, until he come whose right it is; and I will give it him." I believe that in 2019 the earth is overturned figuratively with Christ taking the throne, and literally overturned in a pole shift.

In conclusion – it's tough to write a conclusion on topics often described as wild speculation. Although I have tried to take a scientific approach, this is in the end a religious interpretation of events. In some countries, more than half the population describe themselves as agnostic or atheist. We can't even agree on the existence of God, let alone which religion, if any, is correct. If we can't all agree on when Jesus was born, or if He even existed, we are unlikely to agree on who the Antichrist will be, or if there will ever be one, or when....

Over a billion Christians believe Jesus is the Son of God and that He will return to rule the world. Over a billion Muslims believe Jesus was just a prophet and that He will help destroy Judaism and Christianity in the name of Islam. At least a billion people must be wrong. Despite all the evidence supporting my interpretations, I realize my ideas sound extreme and that I could be wrong on several points. But Islam's savior does appear to be Christianity's Antichrist. Many believe they are both coming soon.

I believe that astronomical cycles are central to understanding Christianity, and that we should be paying attention to heavenly signs. I believe we can calculate the dates of end times prophecies. I believe that New York and America represent Mystery Babylon. I suspect we already know the role of Islam, and America, and Barack Obama in end times events. And I believe we will know these roles with absolute certainty after reaching the critical date for the mid-point of the final seven years, as established by so many specific clues.

I realize there are a few major developments that would have to take place in the Middle East, and in America, for my scenario to play out as described. If I am wrong, America will continue on about the same as it is today, and President Obama will leave office uneventfully in January 2017. But as he said at the White House Correspondents' Dinner in May 2014: "Everywhere I look there are reminders that I only hold this job temporarily. [Laughter] But, it is a long time between now and 2016. And anything can happen."[439]

Selected Bibliography:

Scripture taken from the <u>NEW AMERICAN STANDARD BIBLE</u>®, Copyright © 1960,1962,1963,1968,1971,1972,1973,1975,1977,1995 by The Lockman Foundation. Used by permission.

Asimov, Isaac. <u>Asimov's Guide to the Bible: The New Testament</u>. NY: Avon Books, 1969

Asimov, Isaac. <u>Asimov's Guide to the Bible: The Old Testament</u>. NY: Avon Books, 1968

Biltz, Mark. <u>Blood Moons: Decoding the Imminent Heavenly Signs</u>. Washington, DC: WND Books, 2014

Cahn, Jonathan. <u>The Harbinger</u>. Mary, FL: Frontline Publishing – Charisma House, 2012

Chafer, Lewis and John Walvoord. <u>Major Bible Themes</u>. Grand Rapids, MI: Zondervan, 1974

Coughlin, Charles. <u>Antichrist</u>. Bloomfield Hills, MI: Charles Coughlin, 1972

D'Souza, Dinesh. <u>Obama's America: Unmaking the American Dream</u>. NY: Threshold Editions, 2012

D'Souza, Dinesh. <u>The Roots of Obama's Rage</u>. Washington, D.C.: Regnery Publishing, 2011

Harper, Larry. <u>The Antichrist</u>. Mesquite, TX: The Elijah Project, 1992

Krieger, Douglas. <u>Signs in the Heavens and</u> on the Earth. 2014

Krieger, Douglas, and Dene McGriff and S. Douglas Woodward. <u>The Final Babylon: America and the Coming of the Antichrist</u>. Oklahoma City, OK: Faith Happens, 2013

Kurschner, Alan. <u>Antichrist: Before the Day of the Lord</u>. Pompton Lakes, NJ:

Eschatos Publishing, 2013

LaHaye, Tim. <u>Revelation Unveiled</u>. Grand Rapids, MI: Zondervan, 1999

Lemesurier, Peter. <u>The Great Pyramid Decoded</u>. Element Books, Rockport, MA: 1996

Leoni, Edgar. <u>Nostradamus and His Prophecies</u>. NY: Bell Publishing, 1982

Montaigne, David. <u>End Times and 2019</u>. Kempton, IL: Adventures Unlimited Press, 2013

Nietzsche, Frederick. <u>The Antichrist</u>. Amherst, NY: Prometheus Books, 2000

Obama, Barack. <u>Dreams from My Father</u>. NY: Broadway Paperbacks, 1995

Obama, Barack. <u>The Audacity of Hope</u>. NY: Vintage Books, 2008

Pink, Arthur. <u>The Antichrist</u>. Swengel, PA: Bible Truth Depot, 1923

Preacher, John. <u>The Islamic Antichrist</u>. Kingdom Publishers, 2013

Richardson, Joel. <u>The Islamic Antichrist</u>. Los Angeles: WND Books, 2009

Richardson, Joel. <u>Mideast Beast: The Scriptural Case for an Islamic Antichrist</u>. Washington D.C.: WND Books, 2012

Rood, Michael. <u>The Mystery of Iniquity: The Legal Prerequisites to the Return of the Messiah</u>. Alachua, FL: Bridge-Logos, 2009

Ryrie, Charles C. <u>Revelation</u>. Chicago: Moody Press, 1968

Ryrie, Charles. <u>The Ryrie Study Bible</u>. Chicago: Moody Press, 1976

Shorey, John. <u>The Window of the Lord's Return: 2012-2020</u>. Oviedo, FL: Higher Life Publishing, 2013

Thiel, Bob. <u>Barack Obama, Prophecy, and the Destruction of the United States</u>. Arroyo Grande, CA: Nazarene Books, 2012

END NOTES:

[1] Miller, Stephen. <u>The Complete Guide to Bible Prophecy</u>. Ulrichsville, OH: Barbour Publishing, 2010, p. 5

[2] Simmons, Andrew. "When is Babylon Destroyed?" October 7, 2010. http://wakeupbabylon.blogspot.com/2010/10/when-is-babylon-destroyed.html

[3] Krieger, Douglas. <u>Signs in the Heavens and on the Earth</u>. 2014, p. xxiii

[4] Chafer, Lewis and John Walvoord. <u>Major Bible Themes</u>. Grand Rapids, MI: Zondervan, 1974, p. 128

[5] "Jesus the Stonemason." National Geographic video. http://channel.nationalgeographic.com/videos/jesus-the-stone-mason/ also see http://jamestabor.com/2012/07/17/did-you-know-that/

[6] Cohen, Gary. <u>Understanding Revelation</u>. Collingwood, NJ: Christian Beacon Press, 1968, p. 8

[7] Shorey, John. <u>The Window of the Lord's Return: 2012-2020</u>. Oviedo, FL: Higher Life Publishing, 2013, p. 20

[8] Biltz, Mark. <u>Blood Moons: Decoding the Imminent Heavenly Signs</u>. Washington, DC: WND Books, 2014, p. 85

[9] Krieger, Douglas. <u>Signs in the Heavens and on the Earth</u>. 2014, p. 5

[10] Seiss, Joseph. <u>The Gospel in the Stars</u>. Claxton: Philadelphia, 1882, p. 5

[11] Missler, Chuck. "Signs in the Heavens." http://khouse.org/articles/2014/1193

[12] Gordon, Dane. <u>Old Testament in its Cultural, Historical, and Religious Context</u>. Englewood Cliffs, NJ: Prentice Hall, 1985, p. 291

[13] http://www.zmescience.com/tag/forensic-science/

[14] Sky & Telescope Magazine, December 16, 2013 http://www.skyandtelescope.com/sky-and-telescope-magazine/beyond-the-printed-page/dating-an-impressionists-sunset/ and also the Feb/2014 issue

[15] Sky & Telescope Magazine, July 23, 2003. http://www.skyandtelescope.com/press-releases/celestial-sleuths-reveal-exact-date-van-gogh-painted-moonrise/

[16] http://www.cliveruggles.net/

[17] Montaigne, David. <u>End Times and 2019</u>. Kempton, IL: Adventures Unlimited Press. 2013, p. 285

[18] Nabaeteuo, Carlos Montana. "The Biblical King of Babylon (aka Lucifer) on the Day of America's Destruction . . . Could this Man be Obama?: A Look at Numerical Clues from Key Verse Isaiah 14:12." August 17, 2012. http://nabiy4america.wordpress.com/2012/08/10/the-biblical-king-of-babylon-aka-lucifer-on-the-day-of-americas-destruction-could-this-man-be-obama-a-look-at-numerical-clues-from-key-verse-isaiah-1412/

[19] Clarke, Adam. <u>Adam Clarke's Commentary on the Bible</u>. Nashville, TN: Thomas Nelson, 1997.

[20] Ryrie, Charles. <u>The Ryrie Study Bible</u>. Chicago: Moody Press, 1978, p. 1285

[21] Richardson, Joel. <u>Mideast Beast: The Scriptural Case for an Islamic Antichrist</u>. Washington, D.C.: WND Books, 2012, p. 68

[22] Collard, Rebecca. "The Iraqi Government Seems Helpless to Stop ISIS's New Caliphate." <u>Time Magazine</u>. June 30, 2014 http://time.com/2941128/isis-declares-caliphate-in-iraq/

[23] Pink, Arthur. <u>The Antichrist</u>. Swengel, PA: Bible Truth Depot, 1923, p. 47

[24] Ryrie, Charles. <u>Revelation</u>. Chicago: Moody Press, 1971, p. 101

[25] Pink, Arthur. The Antichrist. Swengel, PA: Bible Truth Depot, 1923, p. 50

[26] Ryrie, Charles. The Ryrie Study Bible. Chicago: Moody Press, 1978, p. 1201

[27] Weidner, Jay and Vincent Bridges. The Mysteries of the Great Cross of Hendaye: Alchemy and the End of Time. Rochester, VT: Destiny Books, 2003, pp. 103-104

[28] Jenkins, John Major. Maya Cosmosgenesis 2012. Santa Fe, NM: Bear & Company, 1998, p. 60

[29] Montaigne, David. End Times and 2019. Kempton, IL: Adventures Unlimited Press, 2013, pp. 189-190

[30] Pink, Arthur. The Antichrist. Swengel, PA: Bible Truth Depot, 1923, p. 53

[31] http://www.yourdictionary.com/antichrist

[32] Clinton, Mike. "The Riddle Of The Jews; The Most Profound Mystery In The World." April 17, 2013 http://beforeitsnews.com/prophecy/2013/04/the-riddle-of-the-jews-the-most-profound-mystery-in-the-world-2446568.html?utm_term=http%3A%2F%2Fb4in.info%2Fp8zH&utm_content=awesm-fbshare-small&utm_medium=facebook-post&utm_campaign=&utm_source=https%3A%2F%2Fwww.facebook.com%2F

[33] Nietzsche, Frederick. The Antichrist. Amherst, NY: Prometheus Books, 2000. p. 1

[34] Nietzsche, Frederick. The Antichrist. Amherst, NY: Prometheus Books, 2000. pp. 110

[35] Nietzsche, Frederick. The Antichrist. Amherst, NY: Prometheus Books, 2000. pp. 1-111

[36] Hippolytus's Treatise on Christ and Antichrist, part 2

[37] Walid, "Islam and the Final Beast." http://www.answering-islam.org/Walid/gog.htm

[38] Pink, Arthur. Antichrist. Swengel, PA: Bible Truth Depot, 1923. p. 125

[39] Preacher, John. The Islamic Antichrist, Kingdom Publishers, 2012. p. 56

[40] Kurschner, Alan. Antichrist: Before the Day of the Lord. Pompton Lakes, NJ: Eschatos Publishing, 2013, pp.41-42, but originally from George Ladd, The Blessed Hope: A Biblical Study of the Second Advent and the Rapture. Grand Rapids, MI: Eerdmans, 1956, pp. 6-7

[41] Mcclain, Ernest. The Myth of Invariance: The Origin of the Gods, Mathematics and Music from the Rg Veda to Plato. York Beach, ME: Nicolas-Hays, 1984, p. 122

[42] Pink, Arthur. The Antichrist. Swengel, PA: Bible Truth Depot, 1923. p. 65

[43] LaHaye, Tim. Revelation Unveiled. Grand Rapids, MI: Zondervan, 1999, p. 218

[44] The Qu'ran, Surah 2, especially 2:223

[45] Obama, Barack. Dreams from My Father. NY: Broadway Paperbacks, 1995. p.407

[46] Asimov, Isaac. Asimov's Guide to the Bible: The Old Testament. NY: Avon Books, 1968. p. 537

[47] Pink, Arthur. The Antichrist. Swengel, PA: Bible Truth Depot, 1923. p.5

[48] Pink, Arthur. The Antichrist. Swengel, PA: Bible Truth Depot, 1923. p. 102

[49] Ryrie, Charles. The Ryrie Study Bible. Chicago: Moody Press, 1976. p. 1285

[50] Richardson, Joel. Mideast Beast: The Scriptural Case for an Islamic Antichrist. Washington D.C.: WND Books, 2012, pp. 7 and 9

[51] Harper, Larry. The Antichrist. Mesquite, TX: The Elijah Project, 1992. P. 25

[52] Harper, Larry. The Antichrist. Mesquite, TX: The Elijah Project, 1992. P. 35

[53] Groschel, Craig. The Christian Atheist: Believing in God but Living As If He Doesn't Exist. Grand Rapids, MI: Zondervan, 2011, p. 14

[54] Suetonius, as quoted in Life of Claudius, cited by Josh McDowell in The New Evidence that Demands a Verdict. Colorado Springs, CO: Here's Life Publishers, 2004, p. 121

[55] Coughlin, Charles. Antichrist. Bloomfield Hills, MI: Charles Coughlin, 1972, p. 12

[56] Voltaire, in a letter in 1768, addressed to an anonymous author of "The Three Impostors"

[57] Voltaire, Questions sur les Miracles à M. Claparede, Professeur de Théologie à Genève, par un Proposant: Ou Extrait de Diverses Lettres de M. de Voltaire

[58] Lewis, C.S. Surprised by Joy. San Diego, CA: Harcourt, Brace, Jovanovich, 1966, p. 35

[59] Lewis, C.S. Surprised by Joy. San Diego, CA: Harcourt, Brace, Jovanovich, 1966, p. 124

[60] Missler, Chuck. "A Hidden Message: The Gospel in Genesis." http://www.khouse.org/articles/1996/44/

[61] Thorndike, E.L. and Clarence L. Barnhart. Thorndike Barnhart Advanced Dictionary, Second Edition, 1974. Glenview, IL: Scott, Foresman and Company, pp. 917 and 685

[62] Cahn, Jonathan. The Harbinger. Mary, FL: Frontline Publishing, 2012, p. 11

[63] Krieger, Douglas, and Dene McGriff and S. Douglas Woodward. The Final Babylon: America and the Coming of the Antichrist. Oklahoma City, OK: Faith Happens, 2013, p. xiii

[64] Krieger, Douglas, and Dene McGriff and S. Douglas Woodward. The Final Babylon: America and the Coming of the Antichrist. Oklahoma City, OK: Faith Happens, 2013, p. 57

[65] Leoni, Edgar. Nostradamus and His Prophecies. NY: Bell Publishing, 1982, p. 439

[66] Pink, Arthur. The Antichrist. Swengel, PA: Bible Truth Depot, 1923, p. 172

[67] Pink, Arthur. The Antichrist. Swengel, PA: Bible Truth Depot, 1923, p. 177

[68] Pink, Arthur. The Antichrist. Swengel, PA: Bible Truth Depot, 1923, p. 178

[69] Ryrie, Charles C. Revelation. Chicago: Moody Press, 1968, p. 101

[70] Rood, Michael. The Mystery of Iniquity: The Legal Prerequisites to the Return of the Messiah. Alachua, FL: Bridge-Logos, 2009, p. 75

[71] Nabaeteuo, Carlos Montana. "The Mayan Calendar End Date, Obama, America, and 2016." December 5, 2012. http://nabiy4america.wordpress.com/2012/12/05/the-mayan-calendar-end-date-america-obama-and-2016/

[72] McTernan, John. As America has done to Israel. New Kensington, PA: Whitaker House, 2008, p. 73

[73] Leahz, Lyn. "End Times Jewish Holocaust Begins! Barack Obama Stopping Jews From Returning To Israel, and Jews Being Forced Out of France Right Now!" July 22, 2014 http://beforeitsnews.com/prophecy/2014/07/end-times-jewish-holocaust-begins-barack-obama-stopping-jews-from-returning-to-israel-and-jews-being-forced-out-of-france-right-now-shocking-video-2463016.html

[74] Rood, Michael. The Mystery of Iniquity: The Legal Prerequisites to the Return of the Messiah. Alachua, FL: Bridge-Logos, 2009, p.4

[75] Carter, Mary. Edgar Cayce on Prophecy. NY: Paperback Library, 1968, p. 100

[76] Harding, Luke. The Snowden Files. NY: Vintage Books, 2014, p. 255

[77] Harding, Luke. The Snowden Files. NY: Vintage Books, 2014, p. 263

[78] Harding, Luke. The Snowden Files. NY: Vintage Books, 2014, p. 271

[79] "Wilhem II of Germany" entry at http://www.answers.com/topic/wilhelm-ii-of-germany

[80] Snyder, Michael. "Does 'Putin's Brain' Believe That The United States Is The Kingdom Of Antichrist?" June 12, 2014, http://endoftheamericandream.com/archives/does-putins-brain-believe-that-the-united-states-is-the-kingdom-of-antichrist

[81] Simmons, Andrew. "My June 5, 2016 Theory." December 1, 2010.

[82] Coughlin, Charles. Antichrist. Bloomfield Hills, MI: Charles Coughlin, 1972, p. 82

[83] Miller, Dan. "President Obama still considers Islam the beautiful religion of peace." May 7, 2014 http://www.freerepublic.com/focus/bloggers/3153280/posts

[84] Krieger, Douglas, and Dene McGriff and S. Douglas Woodward. The Final Babylon: America and the Coming of the Antichrist. Oklahoma City, OK: Faith Happens, 2013, p. 41
[85] Preacher, John. The Islamic Antichrist. Kingdom Publishers, 2013, p. 123
[86] D'Souza, Dinesh. Obama's America: Unmaking the American Dream. NY: Threshold Editions, 2012, p. 29
[87] Krieger, Douglas, and Dene McGriff and S. Douglas Woodward. The Final Babylon: America and the Coming of the Antichrist. Oklahoma City, OK: Faith Happens, 2013, p. 9
[88] D'Souza, Dinesh. Obama's America: Unmaking the American Dream. NY: Threshold Editions, 2012, p. 1
[89] Simmons, Andrew. "70 Years are Determined." March 22, 2011.
http://wakeupbabylon.blogspot.com/2011/03/70-years-are-determined-part-4.html
[90] Simmons, Andrew. "Wake Up, Babylon!" March 22, 2011.
http://wakeupbabylon.blogspot.com/2011/03/70-years-are-determined-part-3.html
[91] Montaigne, David. Nostradamus, World War III. Mumbai, India: BPI, 2002, p. 11
[92] Amazon.com's book description for Will Clark's King Obama: America's Greatest Danger. Motivation Basics, 2013 http://www.amazon.com/King-Obama-Americas-Greatest-Danger-ebook/dp/B00E8KBI68/ref=sr_1_1?s=books&ie=UTF8&qid=1406643188&sr=1-1&keywords=king+obama
[93] Buckley, F.H. "King Obama our latest Monarch." USA Today, April 27, 2014.
http://www.usatoday.com/story/opinion/2014/04/27/king-obama-monarch-constitution-column/8312137/
[94] USA Today, July 3, 2014. "Poll: Obama 'worst president' since World War II."
http://www.usatoday.com/story/theoval/2014/07/02/obama-george-w-bush-quinnipiac-poll-reagan-clinton/11985837/
[95] Anderson, Sir Robert. "A PERSONAL ANTI-CHRIST" from "Things to Come," 1897
http://www.newble.co.uk/anderson/antichrist.html
[96] Walid, "Islam and the Final Beast." http://www.answering-islam.org/Walid/gog.htm
[97] Leoni, Edgar. Nostradamus and His Prophecies. NY: Bell Publishing, 1982, p. 337
[98] Leoni, Edgar. Nostradamus and His Prophecies. NY: Bell Publishing, 1982, p. 337
[99] Kurschner, Alan. Antichrist: Before the Day of the Lord. Pompton Lakes, NJ: Eschatos Publishing, 2013, p. 20
[100] Coughlin, Charles. Antichrist. Bloomfield Hills, MI: Charles Coughlin, 1972, p. 73
[101] Shorey, John. The Window of the Lord's Return: 2012-2020. Oviedo, FL: Higher Life Publishing, 2013, p. 37
[102] Janvier, Thomas. The Dutch Founding of New York. NY: Harper Brothers, 1903, p. 24
[103] Church of the Holy Trinity vs. United States, 143 US 457, 36 L ed 226, Justice Brewer
[104] Ferdinand C. Iglehart, Theodore Roosevelt – The Man As I knew Him. NY: A.L. Burt, 1919
[105] Coughlin, Charles. Antichrist. Bloomfield Hills, MI: Charles Coughlin, 1972, pp. 1-2
[106] Geller, Pamela. The Post-American Presidency: The Obama Administration's War on America. NY: Threshold Editions, 2010. pp. 329-330
[107] D'Souza, Dinesh. The Roots of Obama's Rage. Washington, D.C.: Regnery Publishing, 2011, p. 200
[108] Smith, Jack. Islam: The Cloak of Antichrist. Enumclaw, WA: WinePress publishing, 2012, p. 7
[109] Graham, Billy. "My Heart Aches for America." July 19, 2012
http://billygraham.org/story/billy-graham-my-heart-aches-for-america/

[110] Cahn, Jonathan. The Harbinger. Mary, FL: Frontline Publishing, 2012 p. 31

[111] Cahn, Jonathan. The Harbinger. Mary, FL: Frontline Publishing, 2012 p. 49

[112] "40 Shocking Quotes from Barack Obama on Islam and Christianity." April 15, 2014 http://conservativetribune.com/obama-islam-and-christianity/

[113] Krieger, Douglas, and Dene McGriff and S. Douglas Woodward. The Final Babylon: America and the Coming of the Antichrist. Oklahoma City, OK: Faith Happens, 2013, p. xviii

[114] Wiker, Benjamin. "Benedict vs. the Dictatorship of Relativism." February 25, 2013. National Catholic Register. http://www.ncregister.com/blog/benjamin-wiker/benedict-vs.-the-dictatorship-of-relativism/

[115] McTernan, John. As America has done to Israel. New Kensington, PA: Whitaker House, 2008, many pages

[116] Shorey, John. The Window of the Lord's Return: 2012-2020. Oviedo, FL: Higher Life Publishing, 2013, p. 29

[117] Coughlin, Charles. Antichrist. Bloomfield Hills, MI: Charles Coughlin, 1972, p. 77

[118] http://custance.org/Library/Volume6/Part_III/Chapter2.html

[119] http://custance.org/Library/Volume6/Part_III/Chapter2.html

[120] http://biblepoleshifts.webs.com/

[121] Krieger, Douglas. Signs in the Heavens and on the Earth. 2014, pp. xviii-xix

[122] Singer, Isidore. (Editor) A Descriptive Record of the History, Religion, Literature, and Customs of the Jewish People from the Earliest Times to the Present Day, Volume 5. New York: Funk and Wagnalls, 1906, p. 211

[123] Hall, Manly. Freemasonry of the Ancient Egyptians. Los Angeles: Philosophical Research Society, 1937, p. 48

[124] "Newton the Man" in The Royal Society, Newton Tercentenary Celebrations, 1947, p. 29

[125] Montaigne, David. End Times and 2019. Kempton, IL: Adventures Unlimited Press, 2013, p. 23

[126] White, Michael. Isaac Newton: The Last Sorcerer. Cambridge MA: Da Capo Press, 1999, p. 158

[127] Lemesurier, Peter. The Great Pyramid Decoded. Rockport, MA: Element Books, 1996, p. 228

[128] "The Ancient Jewish Wedding Ceremony." http://www.laydownlife.net/yedidah/AncientJewishWeddingCeremony.htm

[129] "The Messiah and the Jewish Wedding." http://www.yeshuatyisrael.com/messiah_wedding%201.htm

[130] Plato, The Republic. p. 546b

[131] Adam, James. The Nuptial Number of Plato. London: C.J. Clay and Sons, 1891, p. 69

[132] Aristotle, Politics, Book V, 12, p. 8

[133] Lemesurier, Peter. The Great Pyramid Decoded. Rockport, MA: Element Books, 1996,, p. 320

[134] Phaure, Jean. Le Cycle de L'Humanite Adamique, Dervy, Paris, 1983, p. 614

[135] Montaigne, David. End Times and 2019. Kempton, IL: Adventures Unlimited Press, 2013, p. 74

[136] Jenkins, John Major. The 2012 Story. NY: Penguin, 2009, p. 91

[137] Godwin, Jocelyn. Atlantis and the Cycles of Time. Rochester VT: Inner Traditions, 2011, p. 353

[138] http://www.fromthestars.com/page171.html

[139] "Dalai Lama says no need for successor." September 7, 2014
http://news.yahoo.com/dalai-lama-says-no-successor-215550161.html

[140] http://www.bibliotecapleyades.net/profecias/esp_profecia01f1.htm

[141] Mcclain, Ernest G. The Myth of Invariance: The Origin of the Gods, Mathematics and Music from the Rg Veda to Plato. York Beach, ME: Nicolas-Hays, 1984, p. 122

[142] Such as http://www.mayabaktun.com/prophecies_eng.html

[143] http://2012forum.com/forum/viewtopic.php?f=6&t=12389

[144] Biltz, Mark. Blood Moons: Decoding the Imminent Heavenly Signs. Washington, D.C.: WND Books, 2014, p. 43

[145] Jenkins, John Major. Maya Cosmogenesis 2012. Santa Fe, NM: Bear & Company, 1998, p. 95

[146] Rg Veda 10.129.6

[147] http://www.fivedoves.com/letters/sep2012/David_Flynn.1173922.pdf

[148] http://biblepoleshifts.webs.com/

[149] Kurschner, Alan. Antichrist: Before the Day of the Lord. Pompton Lakes, NJ: Eschatos Publishing, 2013, p. 59

[150] Ryrie, Charles C. Revelation, Chicago: Moody Press, 1968, p. 119

[151] Shorey, John. Window of the Lord's Return: 2012-2020. Oviedo, FL: Higher Life Publishing, 2013, p. 151

[152] http://www.scripturescholar.com/JoshuasLongDay.htm

[153] Kak, Subhash. "Birth and Early Development of Indian Astronomy" in H. Selin (Ed.) "Astronomy Across Cultures: The History of Non-Western Astronomy" Dordrecht, Netherlands, Kluwer, 2000, p. 311

[154] Mcclain, Ernest G. The Myth of Invariance: The Origin of the Gods, Mathematics and Music from the Rg Veda to Plato. Nicolas-Hays, York Beach, Maine, 1984. P. X

[155] Plato, Critias and also in Timaeus http://classics.mit.edu/Plato/timaeus.html

[156] http://www.jayweidner.com/AlchemyAndTime.html

[157] Leoni, Edgar. Nostradamus and His Prophecies. NY: Bell Publishing, 1982, p. 333

[158] Coe, R.S. "New evidence for extraordinarily rapid change of the geomagnetic field during a reversal." Nature Magazine, April 20, 1994
http://www.nature.com/nature/journal/v374/n6524/abs/374687a0.html

[159] Bogue, S. W et al., "Very rapid geomagnetic field change recorded by the partial remagnetization of a lava flow," Geophysical Research Letters, November 10, 2010
http://onlinelibrary.wiley.com/doi/10.1029/2010GL044286/abstract;jsessionid=6E01485F01
2E8D10C26D96B494C4F63A.f04t02

[160] 12,410 years B.P. (Before Present = 1950 A.D. means 10,460 B.C.)
http://en.wikipedia.org/wiki/Dendrochronology

[161] Hancock, Graham, and Robert Bauval. The Message of the Sphinx. NY: Three Rivers Press, 1996, p. 249

[162] LaViolette, Paul. Radio Interview: "Dr Paul Laviolette On Superwaves..." December 18, 2013 https://www.youtube.com/watch?v=X241Q3YkjSs

[163] LaViolette, Paul. Earth Under Fire. Rochester, VT: Bear & Company, 2005, p. 306 also http://www.netplaces.com/guide-to-2012/surfing-the-galactic-superwave/galactic-superwave-theory.htm

[164] LaViolette, Paul. "Possible Arrival of a Galactic Superwave…" November 29, 2012. http://starburstfound.org/superwaveblog/?p=267#comment-293

[165] LaViolette, Paul. "Possible Arrival of a Galactic Superwave…" November 29, 2012. http://starburstfound.org/superwaveblog/?p=267#comment-293

[166] http://www.endtimes2014.com/end_of_time.htm

[167] Qu'ran, Surah 14:48

[168] Biltz, Mark. Blood Moons: Decoding the Imminent Heavenly Signs. Washington D.C.: WND Books, 2014, p. 33

[169] Biltz, Mark. Blood Moons: Decoding the Imminent Heavenly Signs. Washington D.C.: WND Books, 2014, p. 35

[170] Kurschner, Alan. Antichrist Before the Day of the Lord. Pompton Lakes, NJ: Eschatos Publishing, 2013, p. 62

[171] Aveni, Anthony. Skywatchers of Ancient Mexico. Austin, TX: University of Texas Press, 2001. Table 3 on p. 67

[172] Houck, C.M. The Celestial Scriptures: Keys to the Suppressed Wisdom of the Ancients. Lincoln, NE: Writer's Club Press, 2002, p. 147

[173] Preacher, John. The Islamic Antichrist. Kingdom Publishers, 2013, p. 188

[174] Montaigne, David. End Times and 2019. Kempton, IL: Adventures Unlimited Press, 2013 p. 284

[175] Kurschner, Alan. Antichrist Before the Day of the Lord. Pompton Lakes, NJ: Eschatos Publishing, 2013, p. 14

[176] LaHaye, Tim and Jerry Jenkins. Are We Living in the End Times? Wheaton, IL: Tyndale House, 1999, p. 127

[177] Kurschner, Alan. Antichrist Before the Day of the Lord. Pompton Lakes, NJ: Eschatos Publishing, 2013, pp. 14-15

[178] LaHaye, Tim and Jerry Jenkins. Are We Living in the End Times? Wheaton, IL: Tyndale House, 1999, p. 159 – but quoting from Tribulation Force, pp. 373-374

[179] Ronen, Gil. "Defense Minister: Kerry is 'Obsessive and Messianic.'" January 14, 2014 http://www.israelnationalnews.com/News/News.aspx/176269#.VB7lwxaqaM8

[180] Krieger, Douglas, and Dene McGriff and S. Douglas Woodward. The Final Babylon: America and the Coming of the Antichrist. Oklahoma City, OK: Faith Happens, 2013, p. 145

[181] Watch after the 40 second mark: https://www.youtube.com/watch?v=JQoyFcaZOC8

[182] Shorey, John. Window of the Lord's Return: 2012-2020. Oviedo, FL: Higher Life Publishing, 2013, pp. 172-173

[183] Frere Michel de la Sainte Trinite. The Whole Truth About Fatima, Volume III. Buffalo, NY: 1990. pp. 578–579

[184] "13 April 2017: the forthcoming Miracle at San Sebastián de Garabandal in Northern Spain" Posted by "Tribunus" on April 13, 2013 at http://www.bibliotecapleyades.net/profecias/esp_profecia05.htm

[185] "13 April 2017: the forthcoming Miracle at San Sebastián de Garabandal in Northern Spain" Posted by "Tribunus" on April 13, 2013 at http://romanchristendom.blogspot.com/2013/04/13-april-2017-forthcoming-miracle-at.html

[186] Conte, Ronald. "Fatima and the Start of the Tribulation." May 28, 2013, http://ronconte.wordpress.com/2013/05/28/fatima-and-the-start-of-the-tribulation/

[187] originally from the October 1981 issue of Stimme des Glaubens.

[188] http://romanchristendom.blogspot.com/2013/04/13-april-2017-forthcoming-miracle-at.html

[189] http://www.tldm.org/News10/MalachiMartinBelievedInBayside.htm

[190] http://garabandalnews.overblog.com/2014/01/fatima-3rd-secret-and-facts.html

[191] http://garabandalnews.overblog.com/the-years-of-truth

[192] Martin, Malachi. The Keys of This Blood. NY: Simon & Schuster, 1991 p. 633

[193] Biltz, Mark. Blood Moons: Decoding the Imminent Heavenly Signs. Washington D.C.: WND Books, 2014, p. xviii, also see p. 38

[194] Hagee, John. Four Blood Moons: Something is About to Change. Brentwood, TN: Worthy Publishing, 2013, p. 221

[195] Harper, Larry. The Antichrist. Mesquite, TX: The Elijah Project. 1992, p. 22

[196] Harper, Larry. The Antichrist. Mesquite, TX: The Elijah Project. 1992, p. 23

[197] Harper, Larry. The Antichrist. Mesquite, TX: The Elijah Project. 1992, p. 24

[198] LaHaye, Tim. Revelation Unveiled. Grand Rapids, MI: Zondervan, 1999, p. 164

[199] Montaigne, David. End Times and 2019. Kempton, IL: Adventures Unlimited Press, 2013, p. 285

[200] http://www.merriam-webster.com/dictionary/lucifer

[201] Rood, Michael. The Mystery of Iniquity: The Legal Prerequisites to the Return of the Messiah. Alachua, FL: Bridge-Logos, 2009, p. 34

[202] Montaigne, David. End Times and 2019. Kempton, IL: Adventures Unlimited Press, 2013, p. 285

[203] Leoni, Edgar. Nostradamus and His Prophecies. NY: Bell Publishing, 1982, p. 201

[204] "Bible Prophecy Numbers" at http://www.1260-1290-days-bible-prophecy.org/1260_days-bible-prophecy-numbers-ch-2d.htm

[205] Talmud, Sanhedrin 97b

[206] Talmud, Sanhedrin 97b

[207] http://endtimesforecaster.blogspot.com/2013/04/the-second-coming-and-2016.html

[208] http://www.finaltimeprophecy.com/dark-sentences.html

[209] Pink, Arthur. The Antichrist. Swengel, PA: Bible Truth Depot, 1923. p. 48

[210] Thomas, Oliver. "Newton's Interpretation of Daniel 9:25." January 7, 2011 http://www.fivedoves.com/letters/jan2011/olivert17.htm

[211] Bullinger, E.W. Number in Scripture. Whitefish, MT: Kessinger Publishing, 2003, p. 283

[212] Harper, Larry. The Antichrist. Mesquite, TX: The Elijah Project. 1992, p. 32

[213] Rood, Michael. The Mystery of Iniquity: The Legal Prerequisites to the Return of the Messiah. Alachua, FL: Bridge-Logos, 2009, p. 34

[214] http://biblehub.com/hebrew/1966.htm

[215] Rood, Michael. The Mystery of Iniquity: The Legal Prerequisites to the Return of the Messiah. Alachua, FL: Bridge-Logos, 2009, p. 68

[216] Stone, Perry. VIDEO: "The Bloodline of the Antichrist." February 13, 2014. https://www.youtube.com/watch?v=s5kxBm5zw3A

[217] Simmons, Andrew. "Wake Up, Babylon!" March 20, 2011 http://wakeupbabylon.blogspot.com/2011/03/70-years-are-determined-part-1.html

[218] De Fuga in Persecutione, I - as cited in Harper, Larry. 7 Simple Steps to Salvation, The Elijah Project, Mesquite, TX: 2012, p. 20

[219] Richardson, Joel. The Islamic Antichrist. Los Angeles: WND Books, 2009, pp. 164-166

[220] Richardson, Joel. The Islamic Antichrist. Los Angeles: WND Books, 2009, pp. 164-194

[221] Shorey, John. Window of the Lord's Return: 2012-2020. Oviedo, FL: Higher Life Publishing, 2013, p. 139

[222] http://beforeitsnews.com/prophecy/2014/05/pastors-tell-their-congregations-you-can-take-the-mark-of-the-beast-and-still-be-saved-outrage-2461144.html

[223] Lewis, C.S. Mere Christianity. NY: Harper One, 1980, p. 154

[224] Gordon, Dane. Old Testament in its Cultural, Historical, and Religious Context. Englewood Cliffs, NJ: Prentice Hall, 1985, p. 224

[225] from David Flynn, http://www.fivedoves.com/letters/sep2012/David_Flynn.1173922.pdf

[226] Michell, John. The Dimensions of Paradise. Rochester, VT: Inner Traditions, 2008, p. 124

[227] http://www.fivedoves.com/letters/sep2012/David_Flynn.1173922.pdf

[228] LaHaye, Tim and Jerry Jenkins. Are We Living in the End Times? Wheaton, IL: Tyndale House, 1999, p. 123

[229] Jeffrey, Grant. Armageddon: Appointment with Destiny. Toronto: Frontier Research Publications, 1988, p. 110

[230] Jeffrey, Grant. Armageddon: Appointment with Destiny. Toronto: Frontier Research Publications, 1988, p. 113

[231] http://www.thechristiansolution.com/doc2012/528_ObamaJewish.html

[232] Krieger, Douglas. Signs in the Heavens and on the Earth. 2014, p. xxix

[233] Ryrie, Charles. Revelation. Chicago, Moody Press, 1968, p. 71

[234] Chafer, Lewis Sperry, and John Walvoord, Major Bible Themes. Grand Rapids, MI: Dallas Theological Seminary, 1974, p.372

[235] Preacher, John. The Islamic Antichrist. Kingdom Publishers, 2013, p. 113

[236] Pike, Albert. Morals and Dogma. Charleston, SC: The Supreme Council of the Thirty Third Degree for the Southern Jurisdiction of the United States, 1871, p. 819

[237] Krieger, Douglas, and Dene McGriff and S. Douglas Woodward. The Final Babylon: America and the Coming of the Antichrist. Oklahoma City, OK: Faith Happens, 2013, p. 127

[238] Krieger, Douglas, and Dene McGriff and S. Douglas Woodward. The Final Babylon: America and the Coming of the Antichrist. Oklahoma City, OK: Faith Happens, 2013, pp. 130-131

[239] http://www.newswithviews.com/Horn/thomas127.htm

[240] Carter, Mary Ellen. Edgar Cayce on Prophecy. NY: Paperback Library, 1968, pp. 107-8

[241] Hancock, Graham, and Robert Bauval. The Message of the Sphinx. NY: Three Rivers Press, 1996, p. 249

[242] Lemesurier, Peter. The Great Pyramid Decoded. Rockport, MA: Element, 1996, p. 146

[243] Lemesurier, Peter. The Great Pyramid Decoded. Rockport, MA: Element, 1996, p. 24

[244] Lemesurier, Peter. The Great Pyramid Decoded. Rockport, MA: Element, 1996, p. 193

[245] Lemesurier, Peter. The Great Pyramid Decoded. Rockport, MA: Element, 1996, pp. 15-16

[246] Lemesurier, Peter. The Great Pyramid Decoded. Rockport, MA: Element, 1996, p. 222

[247] Lemesurier, Peter. The Great Pyramid Decoded. Rockport, MA: Element, 1996, p. 176

[248] READING 5748-5. This psychic reading was given by Edgar Cayce at his home in Virginia Beach on June 30, 1932

[249] Lemesurier, Peter. The Great Pyramid Decoded. Rockport, MA: Element, 1996, p. 30

[250] Lemesurier, Peter. The Great Pyramid Decoded. Rockport, MA: Element, 1996, p. 154

[251] Lemesurier, Peter. The Great Pyramid Decoded. Rockport, MA: Element, 1996, p. 155

[252] Lemesurier, Peter. The Great Pyramid Decoded. Rockport, MA: Element, 1996, p. 154

[253] Lemesurier, Peter. The Great Pyramid Decoded. Rockport, MA: Element, 1996, p. 22

[254] Krieger, Douglas. Signs in the Heavens and on the Earth. 2014, p. 65

[255] Lemesurier, Peter. The Great Pyramid Decoded. Rockport, MA: Element, 1996, p. 261

[256] Lemesurier, Peter. The Great Pyramid Decoded. Rockport, MA: Element, 1996, p. 176

[257] Lemesurier, Peter. The Great Pyramid Decoded. Rockport, MA: Element, 1996, pp. 19-21

[258] Lemesurier, Peter. The Great Pyramid Decoded. Rockport, MA: Element, 1996, p. 108

[259] Lemesurier, Peter. The Great Pyramid Decoded. Rockport, MA: Element, 1996, pp. 19-21

[260] http://www.pierpaoloricci.it/dati/occsolepia_eng.htm

[261] Simmons, Andrew. "2016: Converging Clues and Timelines." July 19, 2012.
http://wakeupbabylon.blogspot.com/2011/03/2016-converging-clues-and-timelines.html

[262] Knoller, Mark. "Obama checks out Sphinx and Pyramids." June 4, 2009.
http://www.cbsnews.com/news/obama-checks-out-sphinx-and-pyramids/

[263] Falaq, Amin. "The Ramadan Impact on Khalifa." July 15, 2014.
http://patch.com/illinois/joliet/the-ramadan-impact-on-khalifa-part-three-of-three#.VAk0EWO0qM8

[264] Coughlin, Charles. Antichrist. Bloomfield Hills, MI: Charles Coughlin, 1972, p. 74

[265] Asimov, Isaac. Asimov's Guide to the Bible: The New Testament. NY: Avon Books, 1969, p. 176

[266] Leoni, Edgar. Nostradamus and His Prophecies. NY: Bell Publishing, 1982, p. 253

[267] Leoni, Edgar. Nostradamus and His Prophecies. NY: Bell Publishing, 1982, p. 341

[268] Leoni, Edgar. Nostradamus and His Prophecies. NY: Bell Publishing, 1982, p. 173

[269] Nabaeteuo, Carlos Montana. "The Mayan Calendar End Date, Obama, America, and 2016." December 5, 2012. http://nabiy4america.wordpress.com/2012/12/05/the-mayan-calendar-end-date-america-obama-and-2016/

[270] LaHaye, Tim. Revelation Unveiled. Grand Rapids, MI: Zondervan, 1999, p. 356

[271] Stott, John. Basic Christianity. Grand Rapids, MI: Eerdmans Publishing, 2008, p.14

[272] Miller, Zeke. "OBAMA SLAMS PERRY: 'Don't Compare Me To The Almighty, Compare Me To The Alternative.'" Business Insider Magazine, September 25, 2011
http://www.businessinsider.com/obama-calls-out-perry-gop-debate-audiences-2011-9

[273] Men's Vogue Magazine, April 2007
http://www.mensvogue.com/business/politics/feature/articles/2007/04/status_report_obama?currentPage=1

[274] Gallups, Carl. The Rabbi Who Found Messiah. Washington, DC: WND Books, 2013, p. 23

[275] CNN Staff. "Obama lampoons Trump, releases 'birth video' at annual dinner." May 2, 2011. http://www.cnn.com/2011/POLITICS/05/01/white.house.correspondents.dinner/

[276] "US elections: Barack Obama jokes he is Superman." October 17, 2008.
http://www.telegraph.co.uk/news/worldnews/barackobama/3213768/US-elections-Barack-Obama-jokes-he-is-Superman.html

[277] Reeaalist. "Did President Obama 'Declare The Coming New World Order'?" July 26, 2014
http://www.dailypaul.com/323154/did-president-obama-declare-the-coming-new-world-order

[278] Kreiger, Douglas, and Dene McGriff and S. Douglass Woodward. The Final Babylon:America and the Coming of the Antichrist. Oklahoma City: Faith Happens Books, 2013. p. 240

[279] Harris, Paul. "One in four Americans think Obama may be the antichrist, survey says" April 2, 2013 in The Guardian. http://www.theguardian.com/world/2013/apr/02/americans-obama-anti-christ-conspiracy-theories

[280] Krieger, Douglas, and Dene McGriff and S. Douglas Woodward. <u>The Final Babylon: America and the Coming of the Antichrist</u>. Oklahoma City, OK: Faith Happens, 2013, p. xix

[281] Thiel, Bob. <u>Barack Obama, Prophecy, and the Destruction of the United States</u>. Arroyo Grande, CA: Nazarene Books, 2012, pp.13-14, and p. 44

[282] Shorey, John. <u>The Window of the Lord's Return: 2012-2020</u>. Oviedo, FL: Higher Life Publishing, 2013, p. 74

[283] Harper, Larry. <u>The Antichrist</u>. Mesquite, Texas. The Elijah Project. 1992. P. 26

[284] Chafer, Lewis Sperry, and John Walvoord. <u>Major Bible Themes</u>. Grand Rapids, MI: Dallas Theological Seminary, 1974, p.128

[285] http://biblehub.com/hebrew/1300.htm

[286] Kenaston, Walter. "Upharsin and Peres." http://home.earthlink.net/~walterk12/HIB/Words/vprsin.html

[287] Pollak, Joel. "Obama Praises Communist Dictator & American Enemy Ho Chi Minh." July 25, 2013. http://www.breitbart.com/InstaBlog/2013/07/25/Obama-Praises-Communist-Dictator-American-Enemy-Ho-Chi-Minh

[288] D'Souza, Dinesh. <u>The Roots of Obama's Rage</u>. Washington, D.C.: Regnery Publishing, 2011, pp. 175 and 185

[289] D'Souza, Dinesh. <u>The Roots of Obama's Rage</u>. Washington, D.C.: Regnery Publishing, 2011, p. 218

[290] Nabaeteuo, Carlos Montana. "The Biblical King of Babylon (aka Lucifer) on the Day of America's Destruction . . . Could this Man be Obama?: A Look at Numerical Clues from Key Verse Isaiah 14:12." August 17, 2012. http://nabiy4america.wordpress.com/2012/08/10/the-biblical-king-of-babylon-aka-lucifer-on-the-day-of-americas-destruction-could-this-man-be-obama-a-look-at-numerical-clues-from-key-verse-isaiah-1412/

[291] D'Souza, Dinesh. <u>Obama's America: Unmaking the American Dream</u>. NY: Threshold Editions, 2012, p. 175

[292] D'Souza, Dinesh. <u>Obama's America: Unmaking the American Dream</u>. NY: Threshold Editions, 2012, p. 26 probably citing Stephens, Brett. "Is Obama Smart?" Wall Street Journal, August 9, 2011

[293] Hassett, Kevin. "Manchurian Candidate Starts a War n Business." Bloomberg.com, March 9, 2009

[294] D'Souza, Dinesh. <u>Obama's America: Unmaking the American Dream</u>. NY: Threshold Editions, 2012, p. 7

[295] Anburajan, Aswini. "Obama Asked About Connection to Islam." December 24, 2007, MSNBC https://web.archive.org/web/20080306042204/http://firstread.msnbc.msn.com/archive/2007/12/22/531492.aspx also Saul, Michael. "I'm no Muslim, says Barack Obama." December 22, 2007, <u>New York Daily News</u>.

[296] Obama, Barack. <u>The Audacity of Hope</u>. NY: Vintage Books, 2008, p. 203

[297] Tapper, Jake. ABC News: "President Obama: 'I am a Christian By Choice...'" September 29, 2010. http://abcnews.go.com/blogs/politics/2010/09/president-obama-i-am-a-christian-by-choicethe-precepts-of-jesus-spoke-to-me/

[298] Obama, Barack. <u>The Audacity of Hope</u>. NY: Vintage Books, 2008, p. 206

[299] Thiel, Bob. <u>Barack Obama, Prophecy, and the Destruction of the United States</u>. Arroyo Grande, CA: Nazarene Books, 2012, p. 34

[300] "Obama: 'Young Muslim Socialist that I used to be' by Allen Z. Hertz February 26, 2014 The Times of Israel http://blogs.timesofisrael.com/obama-young-muslim-socialist-that-i-used-to-be/#ixzz2zzlYjQrj

[301] https://www.youtube.com/watch?v=f36ZbzL-9Yo "Glenn Beck Exposes Obama's Fraudulent History and Radicalized Beliefs" 2/16/14

[302] Staff writer, Huffington Post. "Madonna: Obama Is 'A Black Muslim In The White House.'" September 25, 2012 http://www.huffingtonpost.com/2012/09/25/madonna-obama-black-muslim_n_1912400.html

[303] "40 Shocking Quotes from Barack Obama on Islam and Christianity." April 15, 2014 http://conservativetribune.com/obama-islam-and-christianity/

[304] https://www.youtube.com/watch?v=JQoyFcaZOC8 watch after the 40 second mark

[305] Zahn, Drew. "I Pledge Allegiance to Obama," World News Daily, 1/20/2009 http://www.wnd.com/2009/01/86695/

[306] McShea, Thomas. The Antichrist is Here. Xulonpress.com 2007. p. 55

[307] McShea, Thomas. The Antichrist is Here. Xulonpress.com 2007. p. 54

[308] Obama, Barack. Dreams from My Father. NY: Broadway Paperbacks, 1995, p. 86

[309] Asimov, Isaac. Asimov's Guide to the Bible: The New Testament. NY: Avon Books, 1969 p. 552

[310] D'Souza, Dinesh. The Roots of Obama's Rage. Washington, D.C.: Regnery Publishing, 2011, pp. 67-68

[311] D'Souza, Dinesh. The Roots of Obama's Rage. Washington, D.C.: Regnery Publishing, 2011, p. X

[312] Harper, Larry. The Antichrist. Mesquite, Texas. The Elijah Project. 1992. P. 23

[313] Jenkins, Vernon. http://homepage.virgin.net/vernon.jenkins/sixes.htm from The Ultimate Assertion: Evidence of Supernatural Design in the Divine Prologue, CEN Tech.J., vol.7(2), 1993, pp.184-196

[314] Jenkins, Vernon. http://homepage.virgin.net/vernon.jenkins/sixes.htm from The Ultimate Assertion: Evidence of Supernatural Design in the Divine Prologue, CEN Tech.J., vol.7(2), 1993, pp.184-196

[315] "Properties of the Number 7" at http://www.ridingthebeast.com/numbers/nu7.php

[316] Street, Matthew. "What Does The Number Nine Mean In The Bible?" 01/11/12 http://www.bible-reflections.net/resource/what-does-the-number-nine-mean-in-the-bible/2882/ a brief article summarizing Randall Gannaway's Cracking the Bible's Numeric Code: How to Interpret the Numbers of the Bible

[317] Obama, Barack. The Audacity of Hope. NY: Vintage Books, 2008, p. 30

[318] Alinsky, Saul. Rules for Radicals. NY: Vintage Books, 1972, dedication page

[319] Childress, David Hatcher. Lost Cities & Ancient Mysteries of Africa and Arabia. Kempton, IL: Adventures Unlimited Press, 1989, p. 77

[320] Weitzman, Steven. Solomon, The Lure of Wisdom. New Haven, CT: Yale University Press, 2011. Also "The Fool's Gold of Ophir." http://www.bibleinterp.com/articles/wei358002.shtml

[321] Bullinger, E.W. "THE SPIRITUAL SIGNIFICANCE OF NUMBERS." http://www.lighthouselibrary.com/pdf/BULLINGER,%20E.%20W/SPIRITUAL%20SIGNIFICANCE%20OF%20NUMBERS%20%5BE.%20W.%20Bullinger%5D.pdf based on Appendix 10 of Bullinger's The Companion Bible.

[322] "666 is not a Number!" May 9, 2007 http://www.ridingthebeast.com/comments/666-is-not-a-number-171.html

[323] "666 is not a Number!" May 9, 2007 http://www.ridingthebeast.com/comments/666-is-not-a-number-171.html

[324] "Satanic Origins: 666" as posted by "Amos 3:7" at http://amos37.com/2008/10/12/satanic-origins-666/

[325] Shoebat, Walid. God's War on Terror: Islam, Prophecy and the Bible. Newtown, PA: Tope Executive Media, 2008, p. 371

[326] "666 THE HOLY NUMBER OF ISLAM." http://www.666soon.com/666_the_holy_number_of_islam.htm

[327] http://www.endtimes2014.com/

[328] http://www.endtimes2014.com/

[329] http://www.urbandictionary.com/define.php?term=Disturbia

[330] Obama, Barack. Dreams from My Father. NY: Broadway Paperbacks, 1995, p. 8

[331] Richardson, Joel. The Islamic Antichrist. Los Angeles, CA: WND Books, 2009 p. 98

[332] Richardson, Joel. The Islamic Antichrist. Los Angeles, CA: WND Books, 2009 p. 98, quoting Armstrong's Muhammad (p.46)

[333] Obama, Barack. Dreams from My Father. NY: Broadway Paperbacks, 1995, p. 305

[334] http://www.cogwriter.com/barack-obama-prophecy-antichrist.htm

[335] http://babynames.allparenting.com/list/Hebrew_Baby_Names/Bama/details/

[336] Thiel, Bob. Barack Obama, Prophecy, and the Destruction of the United States. Arroyo Grande, CA: Nazarene Books, 2012, p. 43

[337] Taheri, Amir. "Obama and Ahmadinejad." Forbes Magazine, 10/26/2008 http://www.forbes.com/2008/10/26/obama-iran-ahmadinejad-oped-cx_at_1026taheri.html

[338] Nayouf, Hayyan. "Shiite scholar denies Obama link to Muslim savior." November 4, 2008 http://www.alarabiya.net/articles/2008/11/04/59490.html

[339] D'Souza, Dinesh. The Roots of Obama's Rage. Washington, D.C.: Regnery Publishing, 2011, p. 41

[340] http://fifth-element.wikia.com/wiki/The_Fifth_Element

[341] http://www.newswithviews.com/Horn/thomas205.htm

[342] http://www.raidersnewsupdate.com/petrus-seventeen.htm

[343] "Obama sweeps the board," The Economist, London, October 28, 2008.

[344] Arkwriter. "Is Barack Hussein Obama the Antichrist of the End Time?" http://arkwriter.hubpages.com/hub/antichristourtime

[345] https://www.youtube.com/watch?v=1cen37qxA7E

[346] http://www.birtherreport.com/2014/03/stunning-birther-report-interviews.html

[347] http://www.orlytaitzesq.com/wp-content/uploads/2014/05/Shrimpton-affidavit.pdf

[348] Obama, Barack. Dreams from My Father. NY: Broadway Paperbacks, 1995, p. 22

[349] http://beforeitsnews.com/obama-birthplace-controversy/2014/05/breaking-report-kenyan-authorities-allegedly-released-docs-stating-that-obama-was-born-march-7-1960-in-laimu-kenya-more-than-a-year-before-his-2478272.html

[350] http://www.birtherreport.com/2014/05/israeli-newspaper-claim-kenyan.html

[351] http://www.snopes.com/politics/obama/birthers/ap.asp

[352] NSIS Bulletin #9056/2009/05

[353] Zahn, Drew. "Kenyan Official: Obama Born Here." Worldnetdaily.com April 11, 2010

[354] http://freedomoutpost.com/2013/08/whistleblower-obama-was-indonesian-citizen-given-financial-aid-as-foreign-student-at-occidental-college/#qzrBGvjexpRfs1lx.99

[355] Bailey, Charlotte. "Bedouin tribe claims blood link to Barack Obama." London Telegraph, November 13, 2008
http://www.telegraph.co.uk/news/worldnews/barackobama/3450138/Bedouin-tribe-claims-blood-link-to-Barack-Obama.html

[356] http://john-gaultier.blogspot.com/2013/05/obama-is-43-arab-and-rabs-were-biggest.html

[357] http://www.examiner.com/article/obama-s-arab-heritage-if-known-would-it-have-made-a-difference

[358] http://www.sodahead.com/united-states/obama-is-not-a-bronot-afro-americanbut-an-arab/question-2833259/?link=ibaf&q=&esrc=s

[359] http://en.wikipedia.org/wiki/Arab_slave_trade

[360] Sailer, Steve. "Obama is not 7/16 Arab." June 11, 2008.
http://isteve.blogspot.com/2008/06/obama-is-not-716th-arab.html

[361] Quoted by Perry Stone in Nightmare Along Pennsylvania Avenue. Lake Mary, FL: Frontline Publishing, 2010, p. 26

[362] Klein, Aaron. "Pakistani plea: Make Obama supreme leader of Muslims." Worldnetdaily, 9/9/2010

[363] Preacher, John. The Islamic Antichrist. Kingdom Publishers, 2013, p. 28

[364] Richardson, Joel. Mideast Beast: The Scriptural Case for an Islamic Antichrist. Washington D.C.: WND Books, 2012, p. 153

[365] Richardson, Joel. Mideast Beast: The Scriptural Case for an Islamic Antichrist. Washington D.C.: WND Books, 2012, p. 152

[366] http://pamelageller.com/2010/06/-obama-tells-egyptian-foreign-minister-i-am-a-muslim-stealth-coup-on-the-white-house.html/#sthash.DYKBzRY4.dpuf, also see "Obama, a 'Strategic Catastrophe'" by Aviel Schneider, Israel Today Magazine, May 2010, p. 3

[367] D'Souza, Dinesh. Obama's America: Unmaking the American Dream. NY: Threshold Editions, 2012, p. 169

[368] Klein, Joseph. "Obama's Betrayal of Israel as a Jewish State." March 10, 2014.
http://www.frontpagemag.com/2014/joseph-klein/obama-sides-with-palestinian-rejection-of-the-jewish-state/

[369] Mordechai, Victor. "Obama's Plans to Islamicize America." Israel Today, June 28, 2011.
http://www.israeltoday.co.il/tabid/178/nid/22844
/language/en-US/Default.aspx

370 https://www.google.com/search?sclient=psy-ab&q=renegade+definition&btnG=

[371] Obama, Barack. The Audacity of Hope. NY: Vintage Books, 2008, p. 261

[372] http://www.al-islam.org/restatement-history-islam-and-muslims-sayyid-ali-ashgar-razwy/birth-islam-and-proclamation-muhammad

[373] http://en.wikipedia.org/wiki/Jabal_al-Nour

[374] "Revelation of Gabriel."
http://www.brogilbert.org/islam_christianity/2islam_revelation.HTM

[375] Taken from "Bilal" by H.A.L. Craig. http://www.ummah.com/forum/archive/index.php/t-106658.html

[376] http://www.sangraal.com/library/gsa9.html

[377] Walid, "Islam and the Final Beast." Quoting Anderson, source not given at http://www.answering-islam.org/Walid/gog.htm

[378] Grieve, Tim. "31% of Republicans believe Barack Obama is Muslim." http://www.politico.com/news/stories/0810/41248.html

[379] Public Policy Polling March 12, 2012 http://www.publicpolicypolling.com/pdf/2011/PPP_Release_SouthernSwing_312.pdf

[380] Patton, Joshua. "End Times Broadcaster Ending Show…." August 28, 2014 http://issuehawk.com/patton/2014/08/28/end-times-broadcaster-ending-show-because-america-is-doomed-echoes-deeper-conservative-rhetorical-trend.html

[381] D'Souza, Dinesh. Obama's America: Unmaking the American Dream. NY: Threshold Editions, 2012, p. 10

[382] D'Souza, Dinesh. Obama's America: Unmaking the American Dream. NY: Threshold Editions, 2012, p. 59

[383] D'Souza, Dinesh. Obama's America: Unmaking the American Dream. NY: Threshold Editions, 2012, pp. 30, 175-176

[384] Howerton, Jason. "Rush Limbaugh Says Dick Cheney's Reported Claim About Obama and the Muslim Brotherhood Is 'Exactly Right.'" September 10, 2014 http://www.theblaze.com/stories/2014/09/10/rush-limbaugh-says-dick-cheneys-reported-claim-about-obama-and-the-muslim-brotherhood-is-exactly-right/

[385] Blake, Aaron. "Obama says the Islamic State 'is not Islamic.' Americans are inclined to disagree." The Washington Post. September 11, 2014. http://www.washingtonpost.com/blogs/the-fix/wp/2014/09/11/obama-says-the-islamic-state-is-not-islamic-americans-are-inclined-to-disagree/

[386] D'Souza, Dinesh. Obama's America: Unmaking the American Dream. NY: Threshold Editions, 2012, p. 214

[387] Obama Speech in Cairo, June 4, 2009 http://www.whitehouse.gov/the_press_office/Remarks-by-the-President-at-Cairo-University-6-04-09

[388] Richardson, Joel. Mideast Beast: The Scriptural Case for an Islamic Antichrist. Washington D.C.: WND Books, 2012, p. 59

[389] Richardson, Joel. Mideast Beast: The Scriptural Case for an Islamic Antichrist. Washington D.C.: WND Books, 2012, p. 59

[390] http://biblehub.com/hebrew/6151.htm See also Preacher, John. The Islamic Antichrist. Kingdom Publishers, 2013, p. 57

[391] Bullinger, E.W. "Eleven: Its Spiritual Significance." As taken from Number in Scripture. http://philologos.org/__eb-nis/eleven.htm

[392] Richardson, Joel. Mideast Beast: The Scriptural Case for an Islamic Antichrist. Washington D.C.: WND Books, 2012, p. 92

[393] Richardson, Joel. Mideast Beast: The Scriptural Case for an Islamic Antichrist. Washington D.C.: WND Books, 2012, pp. 92-93

[394] Keppie, Lawrence. Legions and Veterans. Verlag: Franz Steiner, 2000, p. 116

[395] Phang, Sara. Roman Military Service. Cambridge: Cambridge University Press, 2008, pp. 58 and 44

[396] Pollard, Nigel. Soldiers, Cities, and Civilians in Roman Syria. Ann Arbor, MI: University of Michigan Press, 2000, p. 114

[397] Richardson, Joel. <u>Mideast Beast: The Scriptural Case for an Islamic Antichrist</u>. Washington D.C.: WND Books, 2012, p. 96

[398] Preacher, John. <u>The Islamic Antichrist</u>. Kingdom Publishers, 2013, p. 24

[399] From <u>Tafsir Ibn Kathir</u> (Abridged) Volume 4. Riyadh, Saudi Arabia: Darussalam Publishers, 2000, pp. 375 as cited at http://www.answering-islam.org/Shamoun/badawi_tolerance.htm

[400] From <u>Tafsir Ibn Kathir</u> as cited at http://www.altafsir.com/Tafasir.asp?tMadhNo=4&tTafsirNo=109&tSoraNo=5&tAyahNo=51&tDisplay=yes&UserProfile=0&LanguageId=2

[401] Taymiyah, Ibn. <u>The Sword on the Neck of the Accuser of Muhammad</u>, p. 221, as quoted by Richardson, in <u>Mideast Beast</u>, p. 156

[402] Richardson, Joel. <u>Mideast Beast: The Scriptural Case for an Islamic Antichrist</u>. Washington D.C.: WND Books, 2012, p. IV

[403] Stone, Perry. <u>Unleashing the Beast</u>. Lake Mary, FL: Frontline Publishing, 2009, p. 37

[404] LaHaye, Tim. <u>Revelation Unveiled</u>. Grand Rapids, MI: Zondervan, 1999, p. 200

[405] Preacher, John. <u>The Islamic Antichrist</u>. Kingdom Publishers, 2013, pp. 15-16

[406] Churchill, Winston. <u>The River War</u>. 1899

[407] - http://en.wikipedia.org/wiki/Women%27s_rights_in_Iran#Women_and_the_Iranian_Revolution

[408] http://en.wikipedia.org/wiki/Women%27s_rights_in_Afghanistan

[409] http://en.wikipedia.org/wiki/Female_genital_mutilation

[410] Synon, M.E. "Rise in Female Genital Mutilation, Inspectors Find Entire School Classes Victims" June 20, 2014 http://www.breitbart.com/Breitbart-London/2014/06/20/Female-genital-mutilation-in-Sweden-all-30-girls-in-one-class-cut

[411] Kuruvilla, Carol. "Islamic State militants are gang-raping, selling hundreds of Yazidi women inside Iraqi prison: report." <u>New York Daily News</u>, August 29, 2014. http://www.nydailynews.com/news/world/islamic-state-militants-gang-raping-selling-hundreds-women-report-article-1.1921553

[412] Raad, Nadine. "Irak: circoncisions de chrétiens et 700 femmes yazidies vendues à 150 dollars pièce !" <u>Tunisia Daily</u>. August 16, 2014. http://www.tunisiadaily.com/2014/08/16/irak-circoncisions-de-chretiens-et-700-femmes-yazidies-vendues-a-150-dollars-piece/#

[413] Bluke, Marty. "God, Not The IDF, Not The Iron Dome, Is Saving Israel From Hamas Rockets Haredi Columnist Says." July 21, 2014 http://failedmessiah.typepad.com/failed_messiahcom/2014/07/god-not-the-idf-not-the-iron-dome-is-saving-israel-from-hamas-rockets-haredi-columnist-says-234.html Commenting on Chain Cohen's article at http://www.kikarhashabat.co.il

[414] Kovacs, Joe. "Hand of God Sent Missile Into the Sea." August 7, 2014 http://www.wnd.com/2014/08/hand-of-god-sent-missile-into-sea/#31flBDFJOuS70TjX.99

[415] Obama Speech in Cairo, June 4, 2009 http://www.whitehouse.gov/the_press_office/Remarks-by-the-President-at-Cairo-University-6-04-09

[416] Richardson, Joel. <u>The Islamic Antichrist</u>. Los Angeles: WND Books, 2009, p. 42

[417] Hagee, John. <u>Four Blood Moons: Something is About to Change</u>. Brentwood, TN: Worthy Publishing, 2013, pp. 212-213

[418] Lappin, Yaakov. "Egypt's 'United States of Arabs' Muslim Brotherhood Plan Belligerent Pan-Islamic Super-State." October 30, 2012
http://www.gatestoneinstitute.org/3422/united-states-of-arabs

[419] Lappin, Yaakov. "Egypt's 'United States of Arabs' Muslim Brotherhood Plan Belligerent Pan-Islamic Super-State." October 30, 2012
http://www.gatestoneinstitute.org/3422/united-states-of-arabs

[420] Morsi's pre-election speech made in Cairo on May 13, 2012

[421] Richardson, Joel. Mideast Beast: The Scriptural Case for an Islamic Antichrist. Washington D.C.: WND Books, 2012, p. 51

[422] Richardson, Joel. Mideast Beast: The Scriptural Case for an Islamic Antichrist. Washington D.C.: WND Books, 2012, p. 25

[423] Pletka, Danielle. "Does Obama 'hate Israel?'" September 25, 2012 http://www.aei-ideas.org/2012/09/does-obama-hate-israel/

[424] Asimov, Isaac. Asimov's Guide to the Bible: The Old Testament. NY: Avon Books, 1968, p. 594

[425] Richardson, Joel. The Islamic Antichrist. Los Angeles: WND Books, 2009, p. 206

[426] "Turkey as the Antichrist Nation..." August 3, 2012
http://www.vriendenvanisrael.nl/?p=2155

[427] Preacher, John. The Islamic Antichrist. Kingdom Publishers, 2013, p. 26

[428] Richardson, Joel. Mideast Beast: The Scriptural Case for an Islamic Antichrist. Washington D.C.: WND Books, 2012, pp. 134-136

[429] Richardson, Joel. The Islamic Antichrist. Los Angeles: WND Books, 2009, p. 77

[430] Sachedina, Abdulaziz Abdulhussein. Islamic Messianism, The Idea Of The Mahdi in Twelver Shi-ism, pp. 171-172, as cited by Jack Smith in Islam, the Cloak of the Antichrist, Enumclaw, WA: WinePress Publishing, 2012 p. 206

[431] Preacher, John. The Islamic Antichrist. Kingdom Publishers, 2013, pp. 143-144 (Preacher was quoting from Ali Sina, "The Examples of Muhammad")

[432] Preacher, John. The Islamic Antichrist. Kingdom Publishers, 2013, p. 146

[433] Richardson, Joel. The Islamic Antichrist. Los Angeles: WND Books, 2009, p. 129

[434] "Saudi Arabia Remains on U.N. Human Rights Council despite 19 Beheadings, including One for 'Sorcery'" August 26, 2014 http://www.allgov.com/news/us-and-the-world/saudi-arabia-remains-on-un-human-rights-council-despite-19-beheadings-including-one-for-sorcery-140826?news=854071

[435] Helm, Robert. Azazel in Early Jewish Tradition. Berrien Springs, MI: Andrews University Press. 1994, pp. 217-226 http://faculty.gordon.edu/hu/bi/ted_hildebrandt/otesources/03-leviticus/text/articles/helm-azazel-lev1-auss.pdf

[436] Preacher, John. The Islamic Antichrist. Kingdom Publishers, 2013, p. 22

[437] Richardson, Joel. The Islamic Antichrist. Los Angeles: WND Books, 2009, p. 25

[438] Richardson, Joel. The Islamic Antichrist. Los Angeles: WND Books, 2009, pp. 29-32

[439] "TRANSCRIPT: President Obama speaks at the White House Correspondents' Association Dinner." The Washington Post. May 4, 2014
http://www.washingtonpost.com/lifestyle/style/transcript-president-obama-speaks-at-the-white-house-correspondents-association-dinner/2014/05/04/2dd52518-d32f-11e3-95d3-3bcd77cd4e11_story.html

David Montaigne

ABOUT THE AUTHOR

David Montaigne combines intensive research and logical analysis with a passion for history and prophecy, especially when his research leads him to clues that can help solve great mysteries. Years ago you may have passed him near the archives in Washington D.C., London, or the Vatican – or shared a bus ride to a pyramid or temple in places like Israel, Egypt, Turkey, Greece, Mexico or Guatemala… but it is now more likely he is searching for answers online – at home in Lancaster County, Pennsylvania – where he celebrates every possible moment with his three inquisitive children, who remind him that we should never stop asking questions.

Nostradamus, World War III, 2002 – reviews Nostradamus' prophecies about a long, worldwide conflict between Islamic and Christian nations, which Montaigne concluded would begin no later than early 2002.

End Times and 2019 – compares Bible prophecies about the end of the present world with myths, monuments, and scientific facts to conclude that the Bible and other sources repeatedly point to an end in December 2019.

Antichrist 2016-2019 – establishes the location of "Mystery Babylon," the "King of Babylon," and the evidence that he will be revealed to the world as the Antichrist at the mid-point of the world's final seven years in June 2016.

Made in the USA
Middletown, DE
04 August 2016